D1211998

AN ELEMENTARY CHRISTIAN METAPHYSICS

. . . being that is in created things cannot be understood except as derived from divine being, just as a proper effect cannot be understood except as derived from its proper cause.

— St Thomas Aquinas, *De Pot.*, III, 5, ad 1m.

CHRISTIAN CULTURE AND PHILOSOPHY SERIES

GENERAL EDITOR
DONALD A. GALLAGHER, PH.D.
PROFESSOR OF PHILOSOPHY
BOSTON COLLEGE

The colophon for the CHRISTIAN CULTURE AND PHILOSOPHY SERIES consists of the Greek letters X and P, symbolizing Christianity, embraced by C, a variant of Σ, representing the Greek word *sophia*.

AN ELEMENTARY CHRISTIAN

METAPHYSICS

JOSEPH OWENS, C.Ss.R.

Pontifical Institute of Mediaeval Studies, Toronto

THE BRUCE PUBLISHING COMPANY

MILWAUKEE

IMPRIMI POTEST:

George T. O'Reilly, C.Ss.R.
Provincial Superior

NIHIL OBSTAT:

Armand A. Maurer, C.S.B.
Censor librorum

IMPRIMATUR:

✠ Francis V. Allen
Auxiliary Bishop of Toronto
June 15, 1962

Library of Congress Catalog Card Number: 63–11878

MADE IN THE UNITED STATES OF AMERICA

Foreword

The following text is called an elementary metaphysics. Its aim is confined to arousing and developing in rudimentary form a habit of mind that will equip the undergraduate student to approach metaphysical subjects. The treatment accordingly is general in scope. It leaves further investigation for specialized study, listing regularly bibliographical data sufficient to open the field of source material for term papers and seminar work. In the same spirit it avoids in the text detailed discussions of the traditional controversies, mentioning them rather in footnotes along with the bibliographical items required for their study. In so relegating them to a secondary position, it does not at all impugn the value of the controversies for awakening interest and sharpening intellectual penetration. Rather, it considers out of place in an elementary coverage the complicated and exact historical knowledge without which even a preliminary or practical understanding of the disputed topics is impossible. Likewise it consigns to the footnotes the pseudo problems that clog the history of metaphysics, limiting the text itself to themes of genuinely constructive nature.

The work is also called a Christian metaphysics. The coupling of the notion "Christian" with any branch of philosophy is still highly controversial, and has been understood in surprisingly various senses.[1] In the present context the title indicates merely the application of metaphysical principles to issues that arise in a specifically Christian environment. It implies a metaphysical investigation of the integral world in which a Christian lives.

Can this be done without stepping over into the paths of sacred

[1] For a discussion of the controversy during the past few decades on the notion of a "Christian philosophy," see Maurice Nédoncelle, *Is There a Christian Philosophy?* tr. Illtyd Trethowan (New York, 1960), pp. 85–114. In the present context, "Christian metaphysics" is not understood in any of the senses discussed by Fr. Nédoncelle. It denotes rather a metaphysical treatment of the actual world, a unified world that is known basically through the senses but in a further way through Christian faith. See Etienne Gilson, *The Philosopher and Theology* (New York, 1962), pp. 175–199.

theology? Apriori, no reason to the contrary is apparent. Some things known through revelation, for instance the angels, may be investigated also in the light of principles obtained through metaphysical analysis of sensible things. Metaphysics need not have any means of demonstrating that angels really exist. Proof of their real existence, one can argue, may well pertain only to the sphere of revealed faith and sacred theology. But even if metaphysics accepts the existence of angels as proven only in sacred theology, it has certain things to say about their nature. Traditionally in Aristotelian metaphysics, and certainly in the Averroistic interpretation, the existence of immaterial substances was accepted from another science, natural philosophy. The nature of the separate intelligences was then made the subject of metaphysical study. Accordingly, nothing prevents metaphysics from receiving for its own investigation things whose existence is established by other sciences. There should consequently be no objection to its investigating, always from the viewpoint of its own principles, something whose existence is accepted on faith or is demonstrated by sacred theology. Without in any way using principles taken from revelation, metaphysics may have much to demonstrate about the nature of immaterial substances. Moreover, the possibility of demonstrating the existence of one immaterial substance, God, is accorded by Christian tradition to unaided human reason. With regard to another spiritual substance, the human soul, may not both its existence and nature fall within the scope of metaphysical inquiry? Does the fact that metaphysically demonstrable truths are first accepted on faith render them in any way less demonstrable? Are not atoms and electrons, for instance, firmly believed in by the student before he commences his course in physics? Correspondingly, metaphysically demonstrable truths are not withdrawn from the domain of metaphysics because they happen to have been divinely revealed.

That, however, is but one type of revealed doctrines. The great majority of dogmatic truths believed in through Christian faith allow, on the other hand, neither their nature nor their existence to be probed by metaphysics. Yet even in some Scholastic circles where the notion of a specifically Christian philosophy is rejected, does not one find quite often that treatises on metaphysics and other philosophical sciences do not hesitate to apply their principles to themes occasioned by transubstantiation, grace, beatific vision, person and nature in the Trinity or Incarnation? Metaphysics, of course, cannot undertake to show that there are no contradictions in revealed truths of this further type. That would be to establish the intrinsic possibility of the truths and so would be above the powers of human reason. But does not belief in these mysteries raise certain questions regarding some genuinely metaphysical notions that are used by a Christian philosopher? Do they not bring to the fore specific problems concerning substance and accident, nature and person, and the like? The Christian metaphysician is prompted by his religious belief to scrutinize these notions more closely from definite angles. He is not thereby at all trying to prove that revealed truths of this other type contain no contradiction. He is not, in fact, making his inquiry bear upon either the existence or the essence of these revealed truths in any way whatsoever. Rather, he is dealing with bona fide metaphysical notions only. Nor does he in any way base his demonstrations on revealed premises. On the strength of his own principles, obtained from knowledge of sensible things, he is examining metaphysical notions in a special way because of certain problems in them that have been suggested by his Christian beliefs. He is thereby directed toward a specific set of problems somewhat as physical and chemical research during a cold war is directed to definite areas by military concerns. Because of belief in this second type of revealed truths a choice of problems may characterize a metaphysics as Christian.

In a word, the present text envisages a metaphysical study not of any abstract order but rather of the complicated universe in which a Christian actually and existentially lives. By the same token it might be called also an existential metaphysics, with the reservation that the starting point of its investigation is dominantly the existence of external, sensible, nonhuman things. Though it derives its inspiration and its guidance overwhelmingly from the reading of St Thomas Aquinas, it is nevertheless quite hesitant in making claim to the title of a Thomistic metaphysics. In metaphysical contexts the term "Thomistic," particularly in regard to the all-pervasive theme of essence and existence, and consequent explanation of the divine concurrence, has come to denote a type of thinking that has arisen in later Scholastic controversy and that is at variance with the metaphysics developed in the present book. The interpretations of St Thomas' metaphysical principles are in fact so widely divergent today that any dogmatic claim to present faithfully the original Thomistic doctrine must be regarded as presumptuous, or at least premature. The treatment in the present book, however, would direct the student to approach reality under the guidance of original Thomistic texts. Perhaps the best explanation ever given of the role of a philosophy manual is vigorously sketched by Etienne Gilson in his Marquette Aquinas Lecture.[2] There the function of a manual is shown to consist in leading beginners to some great philosopher. It then allows the illuminating genius of the philosopher himself to give guidance to the first principles and causes of

[2] *History of Philosophy and Philosophical Education* (Milwaukee, 1948).

things. The present treatment claims to be Thomistic just in the sense that it uses the texts of St Thomas as its guide in the study of things. But the things themselves, directly known, are the source for the principles of the science.

The scope of metaphysics, as understood in the following pages, through the exigencies of its principles includes not only a general investigation of beings but also the study of knowledge and of the divine nature and attributes in the light of natural reason.[3] The two latter topics are often dealt with in separate courses entitled respectively "epistemology" and "natural theology" or "theodicy." The reasons for including their subject matter under the one science of metaphysics will become apparent from the ensuing "Historical Introduction" to the main treatment in this book. Presupposed for the study is an acquaintance with the standard notions of Aristotelian logic, such as categories, substance, the different accidents, genus and species, predicables, propositions, and demonstration. The notions of form and matter, act and potency, and principle and cause, are also presupposed, preferably from natural philosophy; yet a technical knowledge of these notions should be familiar enough to anyone who has had Aristotelian logic — e.g., genus is matter and potency to species as form and act, science is knowledge through causes, and the premises are the cause of the conclusion.

The teaching of metaphysics is meant first and foremost to develop in the student's mind a living habit of thinking (in the Aristotelian sense of *habitus,* the first subdivision of the category of quality). The presentation of its subject matter in a text for college use should therefore keep that purpose unswervingly in view. Metaphysics is *primarily* a vital quality and activity of the intellect, and not a collection or systematic organization of data either in print or in the memory. In its own nature metaphysics exists solely in intellects, and not in books or writings,[4] though

[3] The coverage of the undergraduate course in which the present metaphysics was originally given had been outlined in *General Announcement, Assumption University of Windsor, 1960–1961,* in these terms: "Metaphysics. The philosophy of being. The concept and intuition of being; essence and existence; substance and accident; the transcendental attributes of being. The metaphysics of knowledge, epistemology. The existence of God, the divine attributes" (p. 140). With this general conception of what an elementary course in metaphysics should cover, the author found himself in entire agreement. The existence of God, however, has to enter the treatment in two different moments, as noted by George P. Klubertanz, "A Comment on 'The Intelligibility of Being,'" *Gregorianum,* XXXVI (1955), 195. In the first moment, it emerges solely from the study of being and appears as the nature in the light of which the being of sensible things can be understood. In the second moment, the study of intellection and volition has opened the way for the more explicit study of the divine nature and attributes.

[4] On this topic, see Gerald B. Phelan, "Being and the Metaphysicians," in the collec-

the name may be used, in a secondary sense, to denote a body of truths known through the metaphysical *habitus*, and to designate a treatise or a course in which metaphysical thinking is communicated.[5] In this latter sense, natural language words like being, truth, goodness, form, or actuality can readily become technical metaphysical terms. They are in themselves susceptible of the analogous and other partially equivocal uses required to express metaphysical thought. Mathematical symbols, on the other hand, are univocal. They are incapable of the extension that would be necessary for them to function in the metaphysical order. Even in regard to diagrams and schemata, considerable vigilance has to be exercised. They are visual aids for the learner in organizing his metaphysical knowledge taken as a body of truths. There is ample authority and solid justification for their inclusion in books on metaphysics. They are truly helpful for the moment in giving a view of a metaphysical notion from one particular angle. In that way they contribute to the formation of a metaphysical *habitus*. But if relied upon in permanent or stereotyped fashion, they tend to fossilize the multiple vibrant and highly nuanced metaphysical conceptions. Left to the improvisation of the oral instructor, however, they can be controlled and kept changing in focus as much as their themes demand.

For the same reason formal and fixed definitions are given little emphasis in the following text. They encounter difficulties in expressing multivalent metaphysical notions, and their deceptive simplicity and rigidity can sap the lifeblood of metaphysical thinking. Instead, properly metaphysical terms are printed in boldface type the first time they occur in their technical sense. The meaning or meanings shown for them on that occasion become the basis for their subsequent use throughout the book. In keeping things themselves steadily in mind rather than jejune formulae and definitions constructed in the human intellect's abstraction, the pursuit of metaphysical wisdom throughout a college course will stand the best chance of developing its *habitus* in the individual student and of playing its role in restoring metaphysics to her traditional place among the commonly accepted sciences.

My deep debt to the interpretation of St Thomas given in Gilson's writings will be easily recognized in the pages that follow. Less obvious perhaps, except to those who know him personally, is the influence of Msgr. Gerald B. Phelan, whose unfailing patience I have often put to severe tests with my problems. Neither of these trustworthy guides to

---

tion *From an Abundant Spring*, ed. staff of *The Thomist* (New York, 1952), pp. 427, 440–441.

[5] See Chapter 1, n. 9.

the understanding of St Thomas' thought, however, is at all to blame wherever I have failed to reach the genuine meaning of the Angelic Doctor. I express my thanks also to my colleagues in the Pontifical Institute of Mediaeval Studies and in the department of philosophy in the University of St Michael's College for help and counsel on a number of different questions. Finally, may I express my gratitude to Dr. Donald Gallagher for the invitation to contribute to the CHRISTIAN CULTURE AND PHILOSOPHY SERIES, of which he is the general editor, and to Mr. William E. May for many helpful suggestions and improvements in his editing of the manuscript. Translations, except where otherwise noted, are my own.

J. O.

Abbreviations

A-T — René Descartes, *Oeuvres*, ed. Charles Adam and Paul Tannery, 12 v. (Paris: L. Cerf, 1897–1910).

DK — Hermann Diels, *Die Fragmente der Vorsokratiker*, ed. Walther Kranz, 3 v. (Berlin: Weidmann, 1934–1937).

D.L. — Diogenes Laertius, *Lives and Opinions of Eminent Philosophers.*

K R V — Immanuel Kant, *Critique of Pure Reason.*

P L — *Patrologia Latina*, ed. Jacques-Paul Migne, 221 v. (Paris: Garnier, 1878–1890).

Greek philosophers are cited by the abbreviated titles in Henry George Liddel and Robert Scott, *A Greek-English Lexicon* (Oxford: University Press, 1940), I, xvi–xxxviii. The major works of St Thomas Aquinas are referred to in the manner described by Vernon J. Bourke, *Thomistic Bibliography* (St Louis: The Modern Schoolman, 1945), pp. 5–6.

Contents

PART THREE . . . KNOWLEDGE

PART FOUR . . . SPIRIT

AN ELEMENTARY CHRISTIAN METAPHYSICS

Historical Introduction

The term "metaphysics" is of Greek origin. It appears first among the Peripatetics, members of a philosophical school inaugurated in the last half of the fourth century B.C. by Aristotle of Stagira. Etymologically the word is derived from a Greek title *ta meta ta physica.* With both components in the neuter plural, the title means "what come after the physical." It is certainly a vague enough expression when taken just in itself. In the course of its long history it has been given various interpretations. How is its proper meaning to be reached? Surely the first step is to determine the original use for which the expression was coined. Did the neuter plural "physical" refer to physical things, or to writings and discussions on physical topics? Correspondingly, did the first *ta* in the Greek title, a neuter plural article, mean things or treatises, or perhaps both? In the translation just given, the vagueness of the Greek article is preserved in the English indefinite "what." For a more literary rendition, a noun has to be added to the article. Should it be the "things that come after the physical," or the "studies (treatises, discussions) that come after the physical"? According to the usage of the times, either signification was possible. Could both perhaps have been meant? In any event, the immediate meaning of *meta* is "after."

Actually, the term "metaphysics" is not found in Aristotle's own writings. It seems to have been coined, however, among his immediate disciples.[1] It dates accordingly from an epoch when Greek philosophical thinking had for some time reached its brilliant maturity and was still able to probe its own structure with warm and sensitive fingers. As a title,

[1] See H. Reiner, "Die Entstehung und Ursprüngliche Bedeutung des Namens Metaphysik," *Zeitschrift für Philosophische Forschung,* VIII (1954), 210–237. Werner W. Jaeger, *Studien zur Entstehungsgeschichte der Metaphysik des Aristoteles* (Berlin, 1912), p. 180, placed it as far back as at least the second century B. C. See also Jaeger's *Aristotle,* tr. R. Robinson (Oxford, 1934), pp. 378–379. Paul Moraux, *Les Listes Anciennes des Ouvrages d'Aristote* (Louvain, 1951), p. 314, traced it to within about a century after Aristotle's death. Reiner, p. 235, going still farther back to the immediate followers of Aristotle, suggests Eudemus of Rhodes as the pupil who coined the term.

ta meta ta physica was used by the Peripatetics to denote a particular group of Aristotelian treatises. They were treatises that outlined a science called by Aristotle himself "primary philosophy" or "theology," or simply "wisdom," in the sense of wisdom in its highest instance. The science treated of things that were separate from matter. These beings were in consequence immaterial or supersensible. They were regarded by Aristotle as divine and as the primary causes of the sensible universe. They were not, of course, immediately observable. Because supersensible, they could not be seen or heard or felt. Only as the result of a long reasoning process could they be known by men. The reasoning process presupposed conclusions established in the Aristotelian natural philosophy. This natural philosophy was a study of the sensible or physical universe, and was developed in writings that Aristotle himself referred to as "the physical treatises." As a scientific pursuit, then, the Aristotelian primary philosophy had to come after the physical investigations of the universe in order to reach its own subject, the supersensible beings.

"Metaphysics," accordingly, meant in this setting a study of the supersensible. It denoted a scientific investigation that in doctrinal order came *after* the study of sensible — or, in the Aristotelian sense, physical — things. These two aspects of the science, viewed against their historical background, were but the obverse and converse sides of the same notion. In Neoplatonic times the implication of going *beyond* the physical was emphasized in the use of the title. In the middle ages, the notion of somehow transcending the physical order was uppermost in the understanding of the term as "*trans*physical," though the aspect that the study comes in doctrinal sequence *after* the physical was not forgotten in the title.[2] Down to the late eighteenth century the term "metaphysics" was invariably given the doctrinal meaning of a science that transcended the study of the sensible universe, or that followed in objective order upon the physical inquiries, or that exhibited both phases of the notion.

[2] "Therefore this science is called *transphysical:* for since a certain nature determined by quantity or contrariety does exist, it is grounded on the principles of absolute being, which transcend the being thus called physical." Albertus Magnus, *Metaphysicorum Lib. XIII,* I, 1, 1; ed. A. Borgnet, v. VI (Paris, 1890), p. 3b. "For these are found to be transphysical in the procedure of resolution, as the more common after the less common." St Thomas Aquinas, *In Metaphysicam Aristotelis,* Proem, c. fin.; cf. *In Boeth. de Trin.,* V, 1c (ed. P. Wyser, Fribourg and Louvain, 1948), p. 26.31–39. See Reiner, "Die Entstehung der Lehre vom Bibliothekarischen Ursprung des Namens Metaphysik," *Zeitschrift für Philosophische Forschung,* IX (1955), 78–79. Cf.: "In Greek, 'beyond something' is expressed by the word *meta.* Philosophical inquiry into the realm of being as such is *meta ta physika;* this inquiry goes beyond the essent, it is metaphysics." Martin Heidegger, *An Introduction to Metaphysics,* tr. Ralph Manheim (New Haven, 1959), p. 17. Aristotle (*Metaph.,* Z 4, 1029b12) understood in this sense of *trans* the *meta* in *metabainein,* "to pass over."

Toward the end of the eighteenth century, however, a German philologist and historian of philosophy, Johann Gottlieb Buhle (1763–1821), published at the early age of twenty-five a forty-two page discussion on the authenticity of the Aristotelian *Metaphysics*.[3] In the course of that examination Buhle eliminated from the unity of the *Metaphysics*, mostly on grounds of obvious failure to satisfy internal coherence, seven of its fourteen books. In his final paragraph (pp. 41–42), as though by way of afterthought, he asked how such alien documents found their way into the group of Aristotelian treatises on first philosophy, and replied that this became clear from the history of their transmission. Repeating the traditional account he went on without any change in style to narrate, as though part of the tradition, some further details that purported to round off the story: Andronicus of Rhodes, the first century B.C. editor of the Aristotelian treatises, arranged the *Physics* as the last in order according to his own systematic plan; but Andronicus still had a number of treatises left over that he did not know how to classify, and hence he appended them to the collection under the general title of *ta meta ta physica*, understood in the editorial sense of treatises placed after the physical ones!

Buhle offered no evidence or reasons or arguments for this assertion. Actually, there were none to offer.[4] But his fantastic statement was taken up by encyclopedias and textbooks as it stood, and was universally accepted almost without question until the middle of the present century. Today it continues to be repeated, even though it is rejected unhesitatingly on historical grounds by scholars who have carefully considered the evidence.[5] It is an explanation that would render the term "metaphysics" as doctrinally meaningless as the heading "appendices" over a nondescript group of documents unable to be absorbed into the regular sequence of a book.

That, however, is quite the way many philosophers today would like to regard the subjects that have been treated through the centuries under the title "metaphysics." In fact, the vicissitudes undergone by the term are but a faint indication of those experienced by its subject matter. If you

---

[3] "Über die Aechtheit der Metaphysik des Aristoteles," in *Bibliothek der Alten Litteratur und Kunst* (Göttingen), IV (1788).

[4] See Reiner, *art. cit.* (1955), p. 85. Reiner takes into account the fact that in 1571 Francesco Patrizi, the Italian Renaissance Platonist, had already named Andronicus of Rhodes as the one who coined the title "metaphysics"; but he shows that Patrizi meant it as a doctrinal and not as an editorial designation.

[5] See above, n. 1. On the history of the practically universal acceptance of Buhle's notion, see Reiner, *art. cit.* (1955), pp. 85–99, and the instances cited in his preceding article (1954), pp. 211–213.

look at any book on astronomy from the time of the ancient Greeks right down to the present day, you will invariably find that it deals with the heavenly bodies. The agreement on positive subject matter is definite and continuous through the centuries. But will you find anything comparable to such unanimity in regard to metaphysics? As coined by the Peripatetics the term "metaphysics" referred to the Aristotelian science of beings as beings,[6] that is, the study of things from the viewpoint of their being. An explanation of the cosmos from the standpoint of its being had already been undertaken by Parmenides of Elea early in the fifth century B.C. For that reason the great Eleatic thinker may be regarded as the actual founder of Western metaphysics long before the term itself had appeared.

In the wake of Parmenides' reasoning, being came to mean what is permanent and unchanging, directly in contrast to the ever changing sensible world. Being was opposed to becoming. Against this background, Plato in the first half of the fourth century B.C. strove to ground on eternal and unchangeable Ideas the being that is reflected in sensible things. In the Ideas alone was found true being. Sensible things were but shadowy and fleeting images of that reality. The study of the Ideas, called by Plato dialectic, was accordingly the highest type of science, ranked by him above even the mathematical sciences.[7] Following in this tradition, Aristotle endeavored to show that the being of sensible things was derived from immobile separate substances. Being wholly separate from matter, the supersensible entities were completely devoid of any principle of becoming or of change. As entirely immaterial they were entirely being, in the Parmenidean contrast of being with becoming. In understanding being, in this view, one explained whatever was definite and stable in things.

In studying the supersensible substances, consequently, one was studying being simply as being. To that same study belonged therefore the investigation of all that was permanent and unchanging, for instance the treatment of axioms such as the fundamental principle that a thing cannot

[6] "It is clear then that it is the work of one science also to study the things that are, *qua* being." Aristotle, *Metaph.*, Γ 2, 1003b15–16; Oxford tr. The term "being" that follows the *qua* in this sentence translates a plural participle. When the whole formula is given in the singular as "being *qua* being," the first "being" has to be understood in its Aristotelian setting quite concretely as "that which is" (*to on*). In the course of its history, as will be seen, the formula has lent itself to a wide variety of interpretations.

[7] See Plato, *Republic* VI, 509D–511E, where dialectic is placed in the top section of the divided line, with mathematics immediately below it. With Aristotle (*Metaph.*, E 1 and K 7), metaphysics is likewise placed above mathematics. It was listed after the mathematical treatises; see Moraux, *op. cit.*, p. 315.

be and not be at the same time in the same respects. Features such as unity, sameness, equality, similarity, and their opposites, and all such aspects that exhibit definiteness and stability, came for the same reason under its scope. Likewise it dealt with substance and the various kinds of accidents, for these are definite forms.[8] All things, in fact, have stable forms, and in this regard come under the aspect of being. The study of being as such, then, is the study of all things universally from the viewpoint of their being. In accordance with this doctrine Aristotle was able to state decisively that the study of separate substance was the primary science and that it was universal in its scope because it was primary.[9] For him the one science that had as its subject matter the supersensible *thereby* treated of all things universally from the standpoint of their being. It had as its object a particular type of being, the supersensible, yet for that very reason it dealt with the general aspects of all things. On both counts it was supreme among the sciences.[10] It was indeed a science, for it was knowledge of things through causes. It was the highest science, because it explained things in the light of their highest causes.

The troublesome tensions latent in this conception of the subject matter of metaphysics made themselves felt in the course of subsequent history. That being as such was a plurality of objects led the Neoplatonists to locate the supreme principle of things in a unity that ranked above the whole order of being. Confrontation with the ineffable God of scriptural revelation posed difficulties for the view that the first cause of the universe was the subject of a merely human science. Avicenna, the eleventh-century Arabian theologian, maintained accordingly that the most high God could not be the subject of this science.[11] The subject of metaphysics, rather, was being insofar as it is being, understood in the sense of being in general, namely the aspect of being that is in some way common to all things whatsoever and not proper to the supersensible substances. In this Avicennian acceptation, being as being was sharply distinguished from the ultimate causes.[12] Averroës, on the other hand,

---

[8] *Metaph.*, Γ 2–3, 1003a33–1005b1.

[9] *Ibid.*, E 1, 1026a10–32; K 7, 1064a33–b14.

[10] *Ibid.*, A 2, 982a4–b10.

[11] "Therefore let us inquire what the subject of this science is, and consider whether the subject of this science is the most high God Himself. . . . I say therefore that it is impossible that God Himself be the subject of this science, for the subject of any science is a thing whose existence is conceded, and the science itself inquires only about the dispositions of that subject. . . ." Avicenna, *Metaph.*, I, 1BC; in *Opera* (Venice, 1508), fol. 70r1–2.

[12] "It will be necessary then that being in so far as it is being should be the subject. . . . Therefore the destruction of that opinion according to which the ultimate causes are the subject of this science has been made manifest. But you

continued in the twelfth century to maintain the original Aristotelian notion that the supersensible substances were the subject of metaphysics.[13] These two Arabians were regarded in the mediaeval Christian world as the representatives of the rival views on the question.[14] Christian thinkers, however, even Siger of Brabant, could not regard God as properly the subject of this science. Instead, they considered common being, understood in radically divergent ways but always in contrast to divine being, as the subject of metaphysics.[15] But in one way or another they kept under metaphysics whatever knowledge unaided human reason could obtain about God. They remained free from the tendency to set up a special philosophical science of God in the guise of a natural theology.

A further tension was that the scriptural teaching on creation jarred with the Aristotelian doctrine of being. Belief in creation meant holding that all things other than God receive their existence from Him. Of themselves creatures are not being. At least they do not provide their own existence. Some operative distinction between a thing and its being was imperative.[16] Being had to receive explanation not merely in the Greek sense of the definite and stable, but also in the signification of existence, whether necessary or contingent. In meeting this issue the many and fundamental disagreements in mediaeval metaphysics became devastating. They rendered impossible any hope of unity among the metaphysicians, and precluded the development of a standard metaphysics in the universities. Instead, metaphysics took on the appearance of an arena of endless controversy. The dead Aristotelian formulae remained in current use, but the blood that now coursed through them was of many and often reciprocally destructive types. The Aristotelian framework of the sciences was still respected. In it metaphysics continued (in the latter part of the middle ages) to be regarded as the highest of the merely human sciences, even though as late as the mid-thirteenth century the ancient Stoic division had been maintained by St Bonaventure with the newly recovered metaphysics reduced to a subdivision of natural philosophy.[17] But

should know nevertheless that they are its completion and goal of inquiry." *Ibid.*, fol. 70v1.

[13] See Averroës, *Physica*, I, 83FG; ed. Venice (1562), fol. 47r2–vl.

[14] See the long debate in Duns Scotus, *Quaest. Metaph.*, I, 1; in *Opera Omnia*, ed. Vives (Paris, 1891–1895), VII, 11–37.

[15] I have listed a few representative instances of this in *The Doctrine of Being in the Aristotelian* Metaphysics (Toronto, 1951), p. 5.

[16] For Aristotle, "being" did not add anything new in a thing: ". . . for 'one man' and 'man' are the same thing, and so are 'existent man' and 'man,' and the doubling of the words in 'one man and one *existent* man' does not express anything different. . . ." *Metaph.*, Γ 2, 1003b26–29; Oxford tr.

[17] St Bonaventure, *De Reductione Artium ad Theologiam*, 4; ed. Quaracchi (1882–1902), V, 321a.

throughout the middle ages metaphysics remained the science of being, in spite of the widely differing ways in which being was understood.

At Francis Bacon's clarion call for a reform of the sciences, the sorely tried and artificially sustained structure of traditional metaphysics became badly splintered. Bacon himself retained the name "metaphysics" for a branch of natural philosophy that investigated formal and final causes. "First (Primitive, Summary) Philosophy" he made a different science, laying down as its object the common axioms and the transcendental conditions of essences. The study of God, angels, and spirits was given to still another science called "Natural Theology."[18] In this way the subject matter of traditional metaphysics was divided among three different sciences. On the continent, Descartes retained under the one title "First Philosophy" the treatment of the human mind, of God, and of the general axioms, though his starting point of the *cogito*, or human thinking, separated his philosophy at its very root from the traditional Aristotelian procedure of commencing with sensible things. Pascal found metaphysical reasoning so distant from the ordinary way of men's thinking that its help was problematical and at best of momentary effect.[19] Spinoza dealt with the traditional subject matter of metaphysics under the general heading of ethics. In the nominalism of Locke, metaphysics is quietly left out of the sciences, and whatever knowledge man may have of spirits, including God, is placed under natural philosophy.[20] With Leibniz the general defense of the Christian notion of God was built up with arguments from reason and revelation alike under the title "theodicy."[21]

The eighteenth century, then, found the traditional subject matter of metaphysics dismembered in openly chaotic fashion. Against this background Christian Wolff sought to restore the science to organic unity. Metaphysics was "the science of being, of the world in general, and of spirits."[22] It was divided into four branches. One, called ontology,[23] or first philosophy, was the study of the most abstract predicates, namely being in general and the common affections of being. It was a study of

---

[18] *On the Dignity and Advancement of Learning*, III, 2–4.

[19] "The metaphysical proofs of God are so remote from the reasoning of men, and so involved, that they have but little force; and should this be helpful to some persons, it would be so only during the moment that they are seeing the demonstration. . . ." *Pensées*, 543.

[20] See *An Essay concerning Human Understanding*, IV, 21, 2; cf. IV, 8, 9.

[21] See Leibniz, *Essais de Théodicée*, I, 1.

[22] *Logica, Discursus Praeliminaris*, III, 79.

[23] The term "ontology" had already been coined shortly before Wolff made use of it. See Etienne Gilson, *Being and Some Philosophers* (Toronto, 1949), pp. 112–113.

"notions and the principles that depend on those notions,"[24] and not directly a study of things. The second branch was the investigation of the sensible universe, named general cosmology. The third was the study of the human soul, called psychology. The fourth was the philosophical inquiry about God, and as with Bacon it was called natural theology.[25]

This Wolffian conception of metaphysics furnished a background against which the nineteenth-century revival of Scholastic philosophy took shape. Without much pertinent change in titles, ontology was regarded as general metaphysics; and special metaphysics was divided into cosmology, rational psychology, and natural theology.[26] Today Neoscholasticism has succeeded fairly well in ridding its metaphysics of cosmology, relegating that science to its ancient level of natural philosophy.[27] In retaining the conception of rational psychology as a unitary science, however, it experiences a tendency to reduce likewise the study of the spiritual soul to the natural philosophy plane. Some efforts have been made to restore general metaphysics and natural theology to the ancient unity of a single science, but so far the results have been rather desultory. A very recent development of the ontological trend, in the wake of linguistic analysis, conceives Aristotelian and Thomistic metaphysics in their negative and larger aspect as a therapy of human concepts, and on the positive side as "epiphanic," in the sense of elucidating concepts.[28] The viewpoint of an ontology, that is, of a general metaphysics distinct from a philosophical theology, persists however in most Neoscholastic circles. The study of intentional or cognitional being, moreover, which does not fit very well under the Wolffian divisions, is sometimes found removed at least partly from metaphysics proper and placed in a separate investigation of knowledge called epistemology.[29]

---

[24] ". . . notionibus ac pendentibus inde principiis." Wolff, *Disc. Prael.*, III, 73.

[25] *Disc. Prael.*, III, 57–73. Cf. *Cosmologia Generalis*, Prol. 1–3.

[26] I have listed some typical instances in "Theodicy, Natural Theology, and Metaphysics," *The Modern Schoolman, XXVIII* (1957), 127, nn. 3–5. A defense of the term "ontology" in Neoscholastic usage may be found in Fernand Van Steenberghen, *Ontologie* (Louvain, 1946), pp. 9–10. "Theodicy," because of its apologetic origins, is unsuitable as a philosophical term.

[27] Some Louvain writers still regard natural philosophy as a subdivision of metaphysics, e.g., "cosmology or the metaphysics of nature," Van Steenberghen, *Epistemology*, tr. M. J. Flynn (New York, 1949), p. 290. Cf. *ibid.*, table opposite p. 294, and *Ontologie*, p. 10.

[28] See Maxwell John Charlesworth, *Philosophy and Linguistic Analysis* (Pittsburgh and Louvain, 1959), pp. 213–215.

[29] Many Thomistic writers, however, while using the name "epistemology," regard it as part of metaphysics; e.g., "Epistemology is a department of metaphysics rather than an introduction to metaphysics. . . ." Peter Coffey, *Epistemology* (London, 1917), I, 24. So Yves Simon, *Introduction à l'Ontologie du Connaître* (Paris, 1934), 1–20, treats of cognitional being under the caption of ontology. On the history of

Outside Scholastic circles, the unstable metaphysical structure erected by Wolff was almost immediately shattered by the powerful critique of Kant. The latter did not think for a moment of denying the Cartesian revolutionary starting point. What the mind knows directly is it own internal product.[30] What the mind synthesizes, though, is only sensible experience. Human concepts are not meant for use outside this sphere. When used outside possible sense experience they are without objects (in ontology), or lead necessarily to antinomies (in cosmology) or to paralogisms (in psychology), or function merely as an ideal (in natural theology). In this way things in themselves and the whole supersensible realm are excluded from scientific treatment in the speculative order, though the human mind retains a natural disposition to inquire about such things. Kant, however, allowed the term "metaphysics" to be used in another sense of all pure philosophy, including his own critique. He extended its coverage even to the practical order under the title "metaphysics of morals,"[31] an impossible combination in the original Aristotelian classification of the sciences.

To fill the void caused by the Kantian destruction of metaphysics proper, a void that seemed like "the removal of all object of cult from an otherwise splendidly decorated temple,"[32] Hegel developed metaphysics anew as a logic of the internal necessities of ideas. This set afoot many grandiose systems of idealistic metaphysics in the nineteenth century. Their goal of reaching the absolute by transcending all inconsistencies in ideas eventually came to be recognized as impossible of attainment.[33] But re-

---

this topic, see Georges Van Riet, *L'Epistémologie Thomiste* (Louvain, 1946), and the remarks of Louis-Marie Régis, *Epistemology* (New York, 1959), pp. viii, 105.

[30] "For I can only know what is contained in the object in itself when it is present and given to me. It is indeed even then incomprehensible how the intuition of a present thing should make me know this thing as it is in itself, as its properties cannot migrate into my faculty of representation. . . ." *Prolegomena to any Future Metaphysic*, 9 (43); tr. J. P. Mahaffy (London, 1889), p. 34.

[31] *Critique of Pure Reason*, B 869. Against this background has arisen the fairly current use of "metaphysics" as a synonym for philosophy in general, as opposed to positive science; e.g., "The terms *philosophy* and *metaphysic* are therefore co-incident in point of applicability; properly applied they are two names for the same pursuit." Shadworth H. Hodgson, *The Metaphysic of Experience* (London, 1898), I, 10. For Wolff (*Disc. Prael.*, III, 92–93) practical philosophy received its principles from metaphysics and so followed upon metaphysics.

[32] See Hegel's *Logik*, Preface to the first edition (1812).

[33] ". . . for we have found that mere thought could never, as such, be completed; and it therefore remains internally inconsistent and defective. And we have perceived, on the other side, that thought, completed, is forced to transcend itself. It has then to become one thing with sense and feeling. And since these conditions of its perfection are partly alien to itself, we cannot say either that, by itself, it can arrive at completion, or that, when perfected, it, as such, any longer exists." Francis Herbert Bradley, *Appearance and Reality*, 2nd ed. (Oxford, 1897), p. 339.

actions against the Hegelian-inspired type of metaphysics were violent, and made themselves felt in two opposite trends.

On the one hand, there arose a persistent movement deliberately to do away with metaphysics altogether. Nineteenth-century positivists dismissed it as a youthful phase in the march toward positive science, and so as a pursuit to be abandoned without regret now that maturity had been reached.[34] Pragmatism watered it down to a clarifying but fictionlike procedure for the tender-minded.[35] Logical positivism branded it as nonsense because its sentences "fail to conform to the conditions under which alone a sentence can be literally significant,"[36] namely sensible verification. Its statements belonged to the category neither of the true nor of the false, but of the meaningless. Linguistic analysis distinguished it sharply from science, regarding it either as a diseased intellectual condition to be cured by the therapy of the linguistic analyst,[37] or as a group of problems that inevitably arise from the use of natural language and that are to be solved by linguistic elucidation.[38] Mathematical logic showed that metaphysics could not conform to the new quantitative rules of thought, since it had to use cross-type arguments that mixed the necessary and the contingent,[39] and so was a logically impossible procedure. It was branded an emotional outpouring that should use poetry as its medium, but instead used didactic language in an effort to represent itself as objective truth.

---

[34] See Auguste Comte, *Discours sur l'Esprit Positif* (Paris, 1909), pp. 5–6.

[35] See William James, *Pragmatism* (New York, etc., 1907), pp. 52–53, 69–75, 85–89. Cf. *Some Problems of Philosophy* (New York, 1916), p. 27.

[36] Alfred Jules Ayer, *Language, Truth, and Logic*, 2nd ed. (London, 1946), p. 35. Accordingly, a metaphysical statement "is neither true nor false but literally senseless." *Ibid.*, p. 31. Cf.: ". . . to say that there is or that there is not a transcendent reality is to utter a pseudo-proposition, a word-series empty of logical content. . . ." Ayer, "Demonstration of the Impossibility of Metaphysics," *Mind*, N.S. XLIII (1934), 336. "Metaphysics results when men attempt to extrapolate their emotions: they wish to present them not as feelings of their own, but somehow objectively as facts. . . ." *Ibid.*, p. 342.

[37] For a survey of this Cambridge school of therapeutic analysis, see M. J. Charlesworth, *Philosophy and Linguistic Analysis*, pp. 150–167.

[38] ". . . philosophical problems can be solved by understanding how language is ordinarily used, how certain uses of it have provoked these problems and how it has been misused in many alleged solutions." Margaret Macdonald, "The Philosopher's Use of Analogy," in *Essays on Logic and Language*, ed. A. Flew (Oxford, 1951), p. 100.

[39] Being, with which metaphysics traditionally deals, is as a matter of fact both necessary and contingent to sensible things. Every sensible thing has to be a being at least as necessarily as it has to be a body, yet its being is always contingent. For a study of the texts of St Thomas on this topic, see J. Owens, "The Accidental and Essential Character of Being in the Doctrine of St. Thomas Aquinas," *Mediaeval Studies*, XX (1958), 1–40. On the stand that metaphysical arguments are "trans-type," see N. R. Hanson, "On the Impossibility of Any Future Metaphysics," *Philosophical Studies*, XI, no. 6 (1960), 86–96.

On the other hand, various attempts were made to develop types of metaphysics that would be proof alike against Hegelian rationalism and the positivistic onslaught. Bergson envisaged the function of metaphysical science[40] as consisting in an intuition of ever mobile duration or "perpetual becoming,"[41] an "intellectual sympathy"[42] that was deeper than any rational grasp of the stable and definite and permanent. Existentialists sought to vitalize metaphysics in the more profound subjectivity of human existence, as opposed to the comparatively superficial objectivity of essence and science,[43] finally offering it as a practical help in therapy for the deepest personality ills.[44] In a different direction Collingwood, against the Kantian and Hegelian background that being as such has no content, conceived metaphysics as not at all a doctrinal science of being but as a positive science that consisted in an historical cataloguing of the absolute presuppositions of persons or groups of persons,[45] a science without any "doctrines" whatsoever.[46] Others tried to safeguard metaphysics by locat-

---

[40] Henri Bergson, *An Introduction to Metaphysics*, tr. T. E. Hulme (London, 1913), p. 8.

[41] *Ibid.*, p. 39.

[42] *Ibid.*, p. 6. On the well-known Bergsonian simile of the intellect's cinematographical activity in making immobile pictures of the ever mobile duration, see the fourth chapter of Bergson's *Creative Evolution*, tr. A. Mitchell (London, 1911), pp. 287–333.

[43] E.g., ". . . existence precedes essence, or, if you prefer, that subjectivity must be the starting point." Jean-Paul Sartre, *Existentialism*, tr. Bernard Frechtman (New York, 1947), p. 15. See also John Daniel Wild, *Human Freedom and Social Order* (Durham, N. C., 1959), pp. 18–20, 135–137, 148, 232–233.

[44] "The distinctive character of existential analysis is, thus, that it is concerned with *ontology*, the science of being, and with *Dasein*, the existence of this particular being sitting opposite the psychotherapist." Rollo May, in *Existence, A New Dimension in Psychiatry and Psychology*, ed. R. May, E. Angel, H. F. Ellenberger (New York, 1958), p. 37. The therapeutic activity, however, should not be viewed as metaphysics itself, but rather as a practical use of metaphysical notions: "The existentialist analyst is not so much a licensed metaphysician as a practitioner of applied metaphysics." G. A. Schrader, "Existential Psychoanalysis and Metaphysics," *The Review of Metaphysics*, XIII (1959), 155. Aristotle, *E N*, I, 13, 1102a5 ff., had practical science use notions taken from the speculative science of the soul, and he himself makes important use in his ethics of metaphysical contemplation as the ultimate goal for human activity. But just as the practical science of medicine makes use of knowledge taken from the speculative science of biology, without thereby becoming a type of biology, so therapy may make use of metaphysical notions, if it finds them helpful, without thereby becoming itself a metaphysics.

[45] "Metaphysics is the attempt to find out what absolute presuppositions have been made by this or that person or group of persons, on this or that occasion or group of occasions, in the course of this or that piece of thinking." Robin George Collingwood, *An Essay on Metaphysics* (Oxford, 1940), p. 47. "Metaphysics has always been an historical science. . . ." *Ibid.*, p. 58. On the Kantian and Hegelian background, see *ibid.*, pp. 14–15.

[46] Collingwood, *op. cit.*, p. 68. Metaphysics, accordingly, has "the form of a *catalogue raisonné*" (*ibid.*).

ing it in the currently respectable domains of logic and epistemology,[47] while still others replaced it with phenomenology through bracketing all existence. Others again have very prudently left it to feel its way forward under the vague caption of the study of reality.[48]

The foregoing historical survey, sketchy but hardly oversimplified in presenting the general lines of the picture, should indicate that today metaphysics is not to be approached as though it had a generally accepted field and method, like arithmetic, for instance, or botany. If someone should define ichthyology as the philosophy of law, who would take time out to tell him that he was getting his fishes mixed up with court decisions? Yet one writer can state that metaphysics is a doctrinal study treating of supersensible being. Another can say that metaphysics is not a doctrinal study and has nothing to do with objective being whatsoever but is an historical cataloguing of human presuppositions. One can say that metaphysics is the most profound of the sciences and the most desirable of human intellectual pursuits. Another can say that it is literally nonsense. All are assured of a respectable hearing.[49] Neither the subject matter nor the formal procedure of metaphysics, then, can be pointed to with the finger in approaching the study, in the way one isolates

---

[47] E.g., ". . . we shall use 'metaphysics' from time to time to denote the combination of ontology and epistemology." James K. Feibleman, *Ontology* (Baltimore, 1951), pp. 4–5. "The largest logical system is the system of ontology." *Ibid.*, p. 124.

[48] So Alfred E. Taylor, *Elements of Metaphysics*, 13th ed. (London, 1952), p. 5, calls it "an inquiry into the meaning of reality." Cf. *ibid.*, p. 4. The Metaphysical Society of America, in the first article of its constitution, defines its purpose as "the study of reality."

Still more vaguely, Whitehead states: "Metaphysics is nothing but the description of the generalities which apply to all the details of practice." Alfred North Whitehead, *Process and Reality* (New York, 1929), p. 19. Cf. *Religion in the Making* (New York, 1926), p. 84, n. 1.

[49] Collingwood interprets the situation quite drastically: "The history of metaphysics since Aristotle shows that at no point have people become quite clear in their minds as to what metaphysics was about." *An Essay on Metaphysics*, p. 61. Yet the wide variety in metaphysical views need not be any greater deterrent to the pursuit of metaphysics than the widely divergent theories that have made their appearance throughout the history of physics. Most of the latter have been gradually eliminated through the process of verification. Faulty metaphysical views, on the other hand, can be set aside only by painstakingly developing them to open contradictions in their own internal consequences, or by the still more difficult way of showing that the starting points from which they follow are unacceptable. A global awareness of the complexity of the subject matter seems necessary in the approach to metaphysics, in order to avoid a too simplified view of its demonstrations. Henri Renard, however, claims that ". . . over-insistence on the historical aspect of philosophical thought, as well as a thorough presentation of the different doctrines of dissenting philosophies, would only confuse beginners." *The Philosophy of Being* (2nd ed., Milwaukee, 1957), p. 3. Rather, the historical acquaintance seems necessary to alert the beginner to the tremendous complications in the apparently simple notions with which he is dealing.

ancient scripts as the subject of paleography, or mathematical symbolism as the method of modern logic.

In Scholastic terminology, this means that metaphysics cannot be assigned beforehand a material object or any formal object *quod* or *quo*. Even among Neoscholastics disagreement is so radical that any dogmatic attempt to state in advance its scope and procedure would bear today the taint of arbitrariness, and would encourage a superficiality crippling to serious intellectual penetration. What is recognizable and admitted on all sides, however, is a persistent disposition — whether grounded in human nature itself or in the exigencies of natural language — toward the way of thinking that historically has been called metaphysical. That disposition is continually present, and is so observable and positive a fact that Etienne Gilson has been able to show on demonstrable historical grounds that metaphysics invariably buries its undertakers.[50] The disposition, there is good reason to believe, is found in every thinking man or woman.[51] The soundest method in approaching metaphysics today, accordingly, is to arouse that disposition, set it in motion, and observe where it leads. In particular, one may watch whether or not it succeeds in formulating meaningful statements, whether it develops a properly scientific procedure in the traditional sense of knowledge through causes, and finally whether the knowledge it provides is really worthwhile for the enrichment of human living and able to repay the tremendous and concentrated efforts demanded for its pursuit.

SUGGESTED READINGS AND REFERENCES

Etienne Gilson, *Being and Some Philosophers*, first ed. (Toronto: Pontifical Institute of Mediaeval Studies, 1949).

---

[50] Etienne Gilson, *The Unity of Philosophical Experience* (New York, 1937), pp. 306–308. Gilson meant this as a factual conclusion from the history of Western philosophy. It is also true, however, in the sense that anyone who seriously undertakes a refutation of metaphysics soon finds himself buried under metaphysical principles of his own, principles that he has to adopt in order to come to grips with his subject. Cf.: "The theory of meaning which denies meaning to metaphysical propositions is itself a metaphysics, as has been repeatedly shown." Wilbur Marshall Urban, *Language and Reality* (London, 1939), p. 630.

[51] See Urban, *op. cit.*, pp. 631–632, 685–686. On the objections, see G. J. Warnock, "Criticisms of Metaphysics," in *The Nature of Metaphysics*, ed. D. F. Pears (London: Macmillan, 1957), pp. 124–141, and Bela von Brandenstein, "A Note on the Method of Metaphysics," *International Philosophical Quarterly*, I (1961), 264–272. On the natural disposition in terms of an incurable desire for knowledge, see G. B. Phelan, "Being and the Metaphysicians," in *From an Abundant Spring*, ed. staff of *The Thomist* (New York, 1952), pp. 423–429.

Gerald B. Phelan, "Being and the Metaphysicians," in *From an Abundant Spring*, ed. the staff of *The Thomist* (New York: P. J. Kenedy & Sons, 1952), pp. 423–447.

Richard J. Blackwell, "The Structure of Wolffian Philosophy," *The Modern Schoolman*, XXXVIII (1961), 203–218.

Anton-Hermann Chroust, "The Origin of 'Metaphysics,'" *The Review of Metaphysics*, XIV (1961), 601–616.

PART ONE . . . BEING

CHAPTER 1

The Science of Beings as Beings

Science. Have you ever tried to realize how much it means to *know* things? Twenty-three centuries ago the Greek philosopher Aristotle (384–322 B.C.) began the first book of the *Metaphysics* with the observation that by their very nature all men desire to know. In the profoundly innate yearning for knowledge Aristotle located the need of a yet undeveloped science that later was to be called metaphysics. Is the natural desire for knowledge, one may ask, still as active as it was in the fourth-century Greek culture? And does it continue to point as clearly in the direction emphasized by Aristotle?

The answer to the first of these two questions should be obvious. Has the deeply rooted urge for knowledge ever been more strikingly apparent than today, stimulated as it is by radio, television, press, libraries, and popular education? In consequence, today perhaps more than ever before, does not any normal person like to be aware of what is taking place around him, of what other people are thinking and saying, of what is happening in the world at large? Does he not want to understand the objects with which he comes in contact in his daily life, the things he uses in his work and in his recreation? And is he content to leave these bits of knowledge in a haphazard, disjointed state? Rather, does he not try to group them in organized fashion? Does he not strive to interrelate them, to grade them, and especially to explain them in function of what he finds to be their causes?[1] In so doing he is on the track of what may be called scientific

[1] In this fashion the natural disposition toward metaphysical thinking was located by Aristotle (*Metaph.*, A 1–2, 980a22 ff.) within the general desire of men for knowledge. Wonder, especially at things that happen in an unusual way, such as the movements of marionettes, prompts the inquiry into the cause. Accordingly wonder, as Plato (*Tht.*, 155D) had noted, was the beginning of philosophy. For Plato (*Men.*, 97B–98A) knowledge through cause had meant knowledge according to a common Idea that manifested the nature of the individual. Against that background, universal knowledge of the particulars, and knowledge of a particular in the light of its cause, were equated by Aristotle in these opening chapters of the *Metaphysics*. The natural desire, in this setting, tended toward not just a description of the

knowledge. Thereby he is but following the profoundly human desire that through centuries of progressive endeavor has resulted in the intellectual achievements of today's civilization.

This knowledge through causes, in fact, has enabled man to probe the material world from the inner recesses of the atom to the staggering expanse of the outer galaxies. It has made possible superb technical progress in engineering, electronics, space travel and exploration, as well as in medicine, economics, sociology, and numerous other spheres. The dread of war, moreover, is occasioning frantic efforts to bring scientific understanding into the world's political order. In regard to the more spiritual phases of man's life, the need for truly scientific knowledge has made itself felt, keenly though gropingly, in confrontation with the awesome questions of human destiny, in spite of a contemporary reluctance here to use the term "science." On every plane, one may say without exaggeration, the natural yearning for knowledge makes itself more apparent today than ever before.

Qualitative Procedure. Through the stimulus of this natural desire, the various arts and sciences have been gradually built up in Western culture. The development, far from steady in its history, has taken place on noticeably different levels. On the first level the phenomena of the heavens, and of the mineral, plant, and animal kingdoms, have been classified in detail and probed in depth by multiple sciences of nature. The sensibly observable features and activities special to each of the realms or their many subdivisions have provided standpoints from which the whole world of nature has been painstakingly investigated. Natural sciences like botany and zoology have conducted their research in this fashion. They have accumulated and systematized massive stores of data. The classification and study from a viewpoint of sensibly observable characteristics in things may be called **qualitative** procedure. In it scientific investigation is carried on from the standpoint of colors, sounds, odors, tastes, temperature, hardness, and similar features, known in a general way as qualities. It is through these qualities that sensible things are primarily[2]

"how," but toward a penetration into the "why." Cf. Aristotle, *Ph.*, II 7, 198a14–21. Even today, according to the ordinary use of language, scientific inquiry is regarded as causal at least in the sense of asking the "why": "But in the way in which the term 'why' is most commonly used, science *does* explain why. . . ." J. Hospers, "What is Explanation?" in *Essays in Conceptual Analysis*, ed. Anthony Flew (London, 1956), p. 117.

[2] In Scholastic terminology, qualities like color, sound, taste, were regarded as properly and primarily (*per se primo*) sensible, in contradistinction to extension and number and motion, and to qualities like shape and figure. See Joseph Gredt, *Elementa Philosophiae Aristotelico-Thomisticae,* 7th ed. (Freiburg i. Breisgau, 1937),

observable to human cognition. By procedure according to qualities the descriptive sciences of nature first took their rise among the Greeks.

Quantitative Procedure. Sensible qualities, however, are always found extended through measurable distance, and are perceived in measurable degrees of intensity. As a result, things endowed with sensible qualities can be treated mathematically. It was not long before this deeper and general aspect of sensible things opened the way to a more profound scientific investigation. This more incisive treatment is called **quantitative,** in contrast to the merely qualitative type considered in the preceding paragraph. It proceeds according to exact measurement and count, which are based on what is technically known as the quantity of things. Quantitative procedure was applied to sensible things by the Greeks as they developed the sciences of astronomy, harmonics, optics, and mechanics. In modern times it has culminated in astounding achievements throughout the varied branches of what is known as Science with a capital S. Not only in the world of nature, but also in the fields of psychic phenomena, of speech, of reasoning, of artistic activity and of moral and political conduct, have its techniques made possible the progress of which the twentieth century is justifiably proud.

Knowledge of the Supersensible. The sciences so far mentioned are concerned with things perceptible through external senses such as sight and touch or through internal senses such as the imagination, or at least with things that can be represented with exactitude by visible (mathematical) symbols and figures. The objects of these sciences, when they are objects found in the real or external world, may be grouped under the designation **sensible things** or **extended things.** In contrast, if something exists without any sensibly perceptible qualities, primary or secondary, and without any feature that can be measured quantitatively, it may be called **supersensible** or **spiritual.** The Christian tradition that forms the background of present-day Western civilization asserts the existence of such spiritual beings — God, angels, and human souls. Can these be brought under any form of scientific

---

II, 379 (no. 487). Locke's (*An Essay concerning Human Understanding*, II, 8, 23; ed. Fraser, I, 178–179) terminology is quite different, and is usual today. For Locke "bulk, figure, number, situation, and motion or rest" are called primary qualities, while colors, sounds, and the like, are named secondary qualities. Locke's viewpoint was the dependence of his secondary qualities upon the primary, for they consisted in powers of the primary qualities to operate upon the senses. The Scholastic viewpoint was the proper correspondence of the *per se primo sensibile* to the specific sense. No matter what status is assigned to them in themselves, though, the sensible qualities provide a means for scientific investigation of the activities and functions of sensible things.

inquiry? Certainly they cannot be studied or investigated from the viewpoint of qualities observable through the senses. Insofar as they are supersensible they lack all such qualities. Just as little can they be approached from a quantitative standpoint. Being spiritual they lack extension, and so are not capable of measurement. They cannot, accordingly, be attained by any sciences that proceed in quantitative fashion, such as chemistry or physics. Yet the profoundly human desire for knowledge reaches out also in their direction, once their existence is accepted on Christian faith. The human mind wishes to know what it can about them, just as it does about anything else.

Indeed, against the background of Christian culture, the mind wishes to know *especially* about these supersensible things, even though they are subject to neither qualitative nor quantitative treatment. In its scientific quest the mind seeks to explain things in general by their causes. Can it then remain indifferent to what Christian faith presents as the supreme cause of all things, God? In endeavoring to guide human conduct and to work out human destiny, can the mind of a Christian honestly sidestep the telling considerations that arise from the immortal nature and the dignity and responsibility of a spiritual soul, as revealed by faith? The Christian mind, rather, craves for whatever knowledge it may be able to acquire about God and the spirituality of the soul, and about the supersensible world in general. Is it possible, then, to have any kind of scientific knowledge about these spiritual things? Is there any knowable feature besides quality and quantity that might provide the viewpoint for a properly scientific investigation of the supersensible order?

Viewpoint of Being. First, how may supersensible entities be approached? They do not present themselves directly to human cognition. All objects directly known through the human faculties are sensible things.[3] These are endowed with visible or tangible qualities.

[3] This has been the unswerving stand of the Aristotelian tradition in all its various forms. Another tradition that goes back to Plato and that influenced Christian thought especially through St Augustine and other Church fathers gave the spiritual soul a direct knowledge of itself. Descartes (*Discourse on Method*, p. IV; A-T, VI, 37.13–14) maintained that the ideas of God and the soul could never have been first involved in sensible cognition, against the commonly accepted Scholastic position that whatever is in the intellect has first been in the senses in some way. Accordingly the Cartesian starting point for philosophical thinking is not the sensible world but thought itself and the mind. Even against the Cartesian background, however, Locke in the first book of his *Essay concerning Human Understanding* showed through a detailed and painstaking investigation that the human mind had no innate ideas or innate principles; it attained all its knowledge from experience, whatever may be the origin of experience.

All one can do in this regard is to examine one's own concepts and see if any has a content that cannot be reduced to what is known through sensation. If no ele-

They are extended in length, breadth, and thickness, and so are measurable. Such characteristics are not to be found in supersensible things, and accordingly do not as such offer any viewpoint from which spiritual beings may be reached. The physical sciences,[4] bound to qualitative and quantitative procedures, are therefore totally unable to reach the properly supersensible plane. Yet no other starting point than sensible things is vouchsafed to human cognition. Sensible things themselves will have to provide the standpoint for any scientific investigation even of the supersensible. Is there then any other characteristic left in them when all quantitative and qualitative features are removed from consideration? Does there still remain any aspect that might be common both to the immediately known sensible things and to the traditionally accepted supersensible entities?

At the very least, the aspect of being is attributed to both types of things. Both are said to be, in some way. If they were not in some way beings, they would not be anything at all. There would be nothing whatever to talk about in their regard. Even things that exist only in the imagination or the mind, like a daydream or a poem, to that extent have being, and can be understood and talked about. They may lack existence outside thought, but they certainly have being in one's mind as they are

ments of non-sensible origin appear, the presumption is that one's knowledge has no other origin than the sensible. On the mode of human cognition, compared with the angelic and divine, see St Thomas, *CG*, I, 3.

[4] Besides the qualitative and quantitative investigations of nature, there is also the Aristotelian inquiry called natural philosophy, or, in the Scholastic vocabulary, *physica*. This philosophical science undertakes to explain sensible things in the light of their substantial principles, matter and form. Further treatment and references on the topic may be found in my paper "Our Knowledge of Nature," *Proceedings of the American Catholic Philosophical Association*, XXIX, (1955), 63–86. For Averroës, *Physica*, I, 83FG (Venice, 1562), fol. 47r2–vl, only natural philosophy could establish the existence of the supersensible entities that constitute the subject of metaphysics. Suarez, *Disputationes Metaphysicae*, XXIX, 1, 7, in *Opera Omnia*, ed. Vives (Paris, 1856–1877), XXVI, 23a–27a, showed that the Aristotelian physical procedure cannot reach the immaterial, let alone the uncreated. Some Neoscholastic thinkers, however, in reaction against the Wolffian conception of metaphysics, still require the proof from natural philosophy to give content to the subject of metaphysics; e.g., V. E. Smith, "The Prime Mover: Physical and Metaphysical Considerations," *Proc. Am. Cath. Philos. Assn.*, XXVIII (1954), 78–94. But the stand that qualitative or quantitative principles or the principles used in natural philosophy do not provide a means of reaching the supersensible in no way implies that the supersensible cannot be known from what is found in sensible experience. That possibility is still left open for a further science that proceeds in the light of the sensible thing's being. There is no apriori ground at all for the bald statement: "Surely from empirical premises nothing whatsoever concerning the properties, or even the existence, of anything super-empirical can be legitimately inferred." Alfred Jules Ayer, *Language, Truth, and Logic*, 2nd ed. (London, 1946), p. 33. Cf. St Thomas, *De Ver.*, X, 6, ad 2m.

considered or discussed. An intramercurial planet may be conjectured and so receive being in the mind of an astronomer. The question of its real existence may then be asked. Similarly the mind can think of supersensible beings and propose the question of their real existence. In point of fact, sensible things are perceived as they are in the real world. God, angels, and the spiritual soul are believed by the Christian to exist as real beings. Being, then, may in one way or another be attributed to all things without exception, both sensible and supersensible. As found in sensible things, might not being offer a viewpoint from which the supersensible may be approached?

But what is being? A tentative and to a considerable extent tautological answer might describe it as the characteristic that makes anything be or that makes anything a being, just as whiteness makes something white. It is at least the characteristic that makes a **thing**[5] differ from nothing. Without possessing it a thing could not be thought of or spoken of. To describe it negatively through contrast with nothing is in fact to describe it in terms of a thing, as the word formation "no-thing" shows. Even when one thinks of and speaks of nothingness itself, for the moment one has to endow the object "nothingness" with being, by giving it existence in one's thought. It exists in the mind while it is being considered and discussed. While it is an object of actual consideration it enjoys cognitional being or existence. Being, therefore, is what actually makes any object a thing, whether in the sensible or supersensible, the real or cognitional orders. It is an aspect that is common to all things.

There may be other aspects that are likewise common to all things, for instance unity, in the sense that everything is some way in itself one thing; or intelligibility, insofar as something true can be said about everything; or possibly goodness, to the extent that everything is good in some respect or other. But of all these aspects, being seems *prima facie* the characteristic most obviously present throughout all orders of things. It is worthwhile, then, to inquire first if being provides a viewpoint from which supersensible things may be investigated scientifically. If so, it will give rise to what may properly be called a science of beings, for it will be

[5] The term "thing" is used here for the vaguest of all objects presented to human cognition and the most widely extensive. In this sense it applies even to God and soul and angels, in spite of personalist or existentialist reluctance to extend the term outside the material order. The same observation holds, correspondingly, for the term "being." At least as able to be discussed or honored or adored, God is something spiritual and has being or is being, in the sense in which these terms are here used. "Thing," then, is meant as the most general term for anything that can be in the real order, such as water, stones, plants, animals, men, angels, God, or that can be imagined, such as a mountain of gold, or that can be constructed by human reason, such as the square root of two.

investigating them under the aspect that makes them beings. It will be a science of beings insofar as they are beings, a science of beings as beings.

Scientific Viewpoint. The viewpoint of being that is required for a study of the supersensible will of course have to appear in sensible things. No other kind of being is directly known to human cognition. But is the being that is present in sensible things able to lead the human intellect into the supersensible order? No answer to this question is immediately apparent. The only satisfactory way of finding out is to make the attempt. Just as scientific study of chemical changes, undertaken from the viewpoint of their quantity, leads to acquaintance with the atomic constitution of bodies, and as a corresponding study of the observable phenomena leads in physics to knowledge of the nucleus and electrons, so a study of sensible things from the viewpoint of their being may be projected as an avenue to knowledge of the supersensible. But just as in chemistry and physics, so in the present case the only way of finding out is to apply an appropriate scientific method and see to what it will lead.

There may be a preliminary hesitation arising from the use of the term "science" in popular literature and in the division of the high school courses. In these circles the term is restricted to qualitative and quantitative procedures like those of the physical sciences. Obviously there can be no question at all that "science" understood in this manner would ever reach the supersensible. By definition it would be constituted incapable of going beyond the boundaries of the sensible order.[6] The notion "scientific" would accordingly be restricted to qualitative and quantitative procedures.

There are, however, no etymological nor even valid historical reasons for so arbitrary a restriction of a long-established term. The word "science" (Latin *scientia,* used to translate the Greek *epistêmê*) meant knowledge. In Greek and Latin philosophical usage it was given the technical sense of "knowledge through causes." It has remained fixed in that meaning through centuries of university tradition from the middle ages down to the present time. Natural philosophers, logicians in the Aristotelian tradition, metaphysicians, moralists, still refer unhesitatingly to their subjects as sciences and to their procedures as scientific. As long as there is seriously a procedure of investigating things in the light of their causes,

[6] Words are of arbitrary imposition, and have to be accepted according to general use. The term "scientist," for instance, appears around the year 1840, and was used to denote the type of thinker who works in a laboratory or who gathers and classifies specimens, the man whose procedure is qualitative and quantitative. No metaphysician, accordingly, would class himself as a scientist. Yet he may call his pursuit a science and his procedure scientific, for these are words established by centuries of use to denote knowledge through causes.

the method and the work is properly scientific, according to the centuries-old and traditionally established meaning of the term.

Does procedure from the standpoint of being, though, conform with the notion of investigation through causes? A thing can be understood and spoken about *because* it has being. In this way being emerges as the cause that makes a thing more than mere nothing. It is the cause that makes a thing something. At the deepest of levels it answers a question why. It would appear therefore to be the first and most profound of all causes in the thing. A study of something in the light of its being should accordingly be the most profoundly scientific investigation possible to unaided human reason. There may be difficulties in isolating the aspect of being that is present in sensible things, in order that it be used as the viewpoint for subsequent investigation. Once it shows itself, however, as truly a cause of things, there need not be the least hesitation in terming scientific in the fullest sense of the word the metaphysical procedure that treats of things in the light of their being.

Order of Things and of Sciences. If being can in fact be isolated as a viewpoint from which all things (including the supersensible) may be treated of scientifically, it will thereby ground a science that deals universally with things from the aspect that is most profound and all-embracing in every one of them. It will accordingly provide a standpoint from which the order and interrelations of things to one another may be investigated with the deepest penetration possible to the unaided human mind. It will allow the general order of things to be understood, insofar as all things constitute the one universe. Moreover, the order of the sciences may be expected to follow the order of the things that form their objects. The problem of examining the respective rank, interrelations, and essential coordination of the various sciences will accordingly pertain to the science of being.[7] This role of the science was

[7] This function belongs to metaphysics rather than logic, for logic does not proceed in terms of being as being, but on the level of a particular way of being, and more noticeably when the logic is mathematical. Modern logicians would like their logic to be the arbiter of the worth of metaphysical reasoning. The notion of "multiple norms of logical validity, with philosophy as arbiter" is termed "a curious inversion" by W. V. Quine in his preface to Joseph T. Clark's *Conventional Logic and Modern Logic* (Woodstock, Md., 1952), p. v. In that setting, mathematics becomes the seal of reality and of science. Whatever it cannot measure is denied recognition. The case of metaphysics is submitted to the adverse judgment of ". . . a body of knowledge which, to those who accept it, appears to invalidate much traditional philosophy, and even a good deal of what is current in the present day. In this way, as well as by its bearing on still unsolved problems, mathematical logic is relevant to philosophy." Bertrand Russell, *Introduction to Mathematical Philosophy*, reprint, 2nd ed. (London & New York, 1930), p. vi. Mathematics is in fact represented as the mature form of logic: ". . . logic is the youth of mathematics and

expressed in the ancient adage "To the wise man belongs the setting up of order."[8]

Besides giving knowledge of supersensible things, then, a science that proceeds from the viewpoint of being will investigate the general order of things among themselves. It will also have the office of determining its own place and the respective places of all the other sciences in the general framework of human knowledge. It will provide an extremely desirable view of knowledge as somehow integrated in its multiply varied totality, the view of human knowledge as an organized whole. Such, then, are the purposes of a metaphysical investigation of things.

Role of Metaphysical Knowledge. But of what use will such knowledge be? Aristotle was quite outspoken in maintaining that metaphysical knowledge was pursued for no use at all.[9] In so speaking, he meant that it was above all use. It could not be subordinated to anything else, for it was the highest goal that man could achieve. It was an end in itself, and was not meant for anything outside itself. It was not like medical science, for instance, which is meant for health, nor like meteorological knowledge, which is helpful for sailing and agri-

---

mathematics is the manhood of logic." *Ibid.*, p. 194. As a result, only the measurable is admitted as meaningful, in accordance with "our fundamental dictum that things which cannot in principle be measured have no meaning." Percy Williams Bridgman, *Reflections of a Physicist* (New York, 1950), p. 97. So: "The odd belief prevails in our culture that a thing or experience is not real if we cannot make it mathematical, and somehow it must be real if we can reduce it to numbers." Rollo May, *Existence* (New York, 1958), p. 39.

For St Thomas Aquinas, metaphysics is expressly the science that is "regulative of the others" (*In Metaph.*, Proem). Logic, it is true, is also a general science. But it deals with things only as they exist in human reason. Accordingly, "such, namely being of reason, is properly the subject of logic" (*In IV Metaph.*, lect. 4, no. 574), and not being without restriction. Metaphysics is the only science that deals with being simply as such, and with particular beings from the viewpoint simply of being: "For none of them judges about being absolutely, that is, about being in common, nor even about any particular being insofar as it is a being." *In VI Metaph.*, lect. 1, no. 1147. Cf. no. 1151.

[8] St Thomas Aquinas, *In I Eth.*, lect. 1 (ed. Pirotta), no. 1. Cf. *In I Metaph.*, lect. 2 (ed. Cathala), no. 42.

[9] *Metaph.*, A 2, 982b20–28. According to this passage, metaphysical wisdom is "the only free science, for it alone exists for its own sake" (b27–28; Oxford tr.). In contrasting it with the useful, then, Aristotle did not at all mean that it was a luxury, but rather the supreme goal of human life. In its nature it is primarily an activity of the intellect, and secondarily the habitual and possessive inclination (*habitus*) to that activity. But as in the case of any cognitive *habitus*, the name may denote also the objective body of knowledge by which it is specified. In this regard St Thomas states: "In another way that which is held through the *habitus* may be called a *habitus*; just as what is held through faith is called the faith . . . as also the indemonstrable principles in speculative sciences are not the *habitus* of the principles itself, but are the principles of which it is the *habitus*." *ST*, I–II, 94, lc.

culture. Rather, metaphysical thought was meant entirely for itself. To its attainment all other human activities had to be subordinated. All else was useful for its acquirement, while it itself had a far higher value than the useful. Yet even for Aristotle these considerations made his metaphysics play an extremely important role in human conduct. Metaphysical contemplation was established as the supreme purpose of human activity and so as the ultimate end to which all human life, public as well as private, had to be directed.

To a Christian thinker, such a view is of course incompatible with revealed truth. Metaphysical knowledge is not at all the ultimate goal of human striving. It does not provide salvation. God alone, as attained in the Beatific Vision of the divine essence, is the final end of man. Metaphysical knowledge, like all other human knowledge during the present life, can have only an ancillary function in this regard. Its purpose and its utility will lie in the way it helps a man attain his true ultimate end. Revealed faith and the elucidation of that faith through sacred theology are the ordinary guides of a Christian life. But in providing the necessary teaching about God and the soul and the supersensible world in general, faith and theology do not explain their subjects from many angles that the inquiring human mind seeks to probe on the strength of its own natural abilities. Perhaps the great majority of Christians feel very little or no inquietude from this source. Others, however, are not sufficiently at ease in their spiritual life until they have made the journey over the trails that human reason blazes into the supersensible. For such persons metaphysical thinking will form an integral part of a Christian life.

The general view of all reality and of all the sciences that is provided by metaphysical knowledge has likewise its important role in intellectual life. It shows how the various orders of things fit together into one complete universe, and how the individual sciences are to be integrated in their functions of explaining such a world. It makes apparent, for instance, the limits of physical science, showing why no knowledge of the supersensible can be obtained by nuclear physics and why no trace of the human soul can be discovered by organic chemistry. It shows why an authority on astrophysics remains entirely a layman when making pronouncements on human destiny or on the existence of God. By the same token it will make clear the reasons why it itself does not furnish any of the knowledge pertaining to the particular sciences, and why it does not at all substitute for such knowledge. It provides, accordingly, a balanced view of the various types of human science.

Résumé. The foregoing considerations may be summed up very briefly. Knowledge of things from the standpoint of their being has as its purpose the scientific understanding of supersensible things, a grasp of the all-pervading order that unites everything into a single universe, and the general integration of the sciences by which both intellectual and practical life is guided. To these goals the natural human desire for knowledge tends strongly, if it is not inhibited by positivistic prejudice or stifled by absorption in sensible pleasures or routine occupations of greed and gain. In the Aristotelian tradition especially is the natural disposition to metaphysics — a disposition admitted by all as a positive fact — given intelligible explanation. It is shown to be the culmination of man's deepest innate tendency as an intellectual being, the tendency to a comprehensive rounding off of human knowledge and to its uttermost penetration into things in the strictly human order. Today, as in fourth-century Greek civilization, the natural desire to know still points to metaphysics as its ultimate requirement on the properly human level.

SUGGESTED READINGS AND REFERENCES

Aristotle, *Metaphysics*, A I–II, 980a21–982a3 (i.e., Chapters 1 and 2 of the first book).

St Thomas Aquinas, *In Librum Boethii de Trinitate*, V, 1 and 4; English tr., Armand Maurer, *The Division and Methods of the Sciences*, 2nd ed. (Toronto: Pontifical Institute of Mediaeval Studies, 1958), pp. 3–17, 36–45.

——— *In Metaphysicam Aristotelis Commentaria*, Prooemium; English tr., in A. Maurer, *The Division and Methods of the Sciences*, pp. 80–83 (Appendix II).

Martin Heidegger, "What is Metaphysics?" in *Existence and Being*, tr. R. F. C. Hull and Alan Crick (Chicago: H. Regnery, 1949), pp. 355–392.

Jacques Maritain, *The Degrees of Knowledge*, Chapters 1 and 2; ed. Gerald B. Phelan (New York: Charles Scribner's Sons; 1959), pp. 1–67.

Alfred Jules Ayer, "Demonstration of the Impossibility of Metaphysics," *Mind*, N.S. XLIII (1934), 335–345. Or:

——— "The Elimination of Metaphysics," Chapter 1 in *Language, Truth and Logic*, second ed. (New York: Dover, 1946), pp. 33–45.

Robin George Collingwood, *An Essay on Metaphysics*, Chapters I–III (Oxford: Clarendon Press, 1940), pp. 3–20.

Robert John Henle, *Method in Metaphysics* (Milwaukee: Marquette University Press, 1951).

Etienne Gilson, *Wisdom and Love in Saint Thomas Aquinas* (Milwaukee: Marquette University Press, 1951).

Joseph Owens, *St. Thomas and the Future of Metaphysics* (Milwaukee: Marquette University Press, 1957).

William Oliver Martin, *Metaphysics and Ideology* (Milwaukee: Marquette University Press, 1959).
——— "Communism, Religion, and Co-Existence," *Religious Education*, LVI (July–August, 1961), 288–296.
Norwood Russell Hanson, "On the Impossibility of Any Future Metaphysics," *Philosophical Studies*, XI (1960), 86–96.

CHAPTER 2

Being and Things

Isolation of Being. If metaphysical inquiry is to proceed in the light of the being that is found in sensible things, it will try first to isolate that being and examine it as far as possible just in itself. In this manner it may well make evident a viewpoint from which all things whatsoever can be investigated, including the supersensible. As was noted in the preceding chapter, being is the cause that makes a thing differ from nothing. So distinguished, being is in some way set apart from the thing itself. It appears as something the thing has. The thing is itself, but has its being. What type of distinction is indicated in this way between a thing and its being? If a meaningful distinction can be established here and properly elucidated, it should provide a lead toward isolating the aspect of being and setting it up as a viewpoint according to which a scientific inquiry may proceed.

Real Being. What, then, is meant by the aspect of being that is present in things? It is an aspect too primal to describe. Yet it cannot escape recognition. The houses sold for demolition to make a downtown parking lot have real being today. A few months from now they will no longer be anywhere outside the memories of those who knew them. Their existence in reality makes them be in a palpably different way from the being they will have when they exist merely in human recollection. There could hardly be a more primitive observation. The antithesis of "to be or not to be," in the sense of the difference between real existence and lack of real existence, is too obvious to call for or even allow any further delineation. The music of a symphony has its being while played, the colors of a rainbow enjoy their shortlived existence after the rain, pleasant sensations of taste arise and pass away during the brief contact of the food with the tongue. The clearcut distinction between being and not-being in such instances is continually experienced in daily life.

In more pronounced contrast, one may note the difference in status between things that exist in the present, and their counterparts of ages long past. American culture, for instance, still flourishes; the ancient Egyptian and Chaldean civilizations have perished. The armies of Napoleon are gone, the Red army still marches. What is now, and what is no longer though it once was, are set apart sharply enough in too many instances to require any laboring of the distinction.

The above examples are concerned with being in the real world, in the world that exists whether or not any man is thinking about it at the moment. Technically, such being may be called **real being**, or **being in reality**.[1] These phrases, perhaps, are none too satisfactory,[2] but they are traditional, and they seem the best available. Taken globally, the notion they express is readily grasped. It may be illustrated, for instance, by the difference between a fifty thousand dollar home already constructed, and that same house when it was once just a pipe dream. It means being in the world that exists outside mere thought or imagination. In this perspective, things that exist in the real world may be said to have being **in themselves**,[3] in contrast to being in someone's cognition.

Cognitional Being. However, the things so far mentioned can as a matter of fact exist also in human thought. They can come to be or cease to be in the cognition of different people while still having real being in themselves. They can likewise continue to exist in human thought long after they have ceased to be in reality. Many of them may exist in thought or in imagination before they acquire real being. A house

ESSE IN RE

ESSE IN INTELLECTU

---

[1] In Scholastic Latin, this way of being is termed esse *reale*, esse *in re*, esse *in rerum natura*, *esse naturae*, *esse naturale* or esse *physicum*, and, negatively, esse *extra animam* or esse *extra intellectum*. The real world or world of nature, that is, the world experienced through such external senses as sight, touch, and hearing, is contrasted in these expressions with things as they exist in human thought and imagination.

[2] The main difficulty with the expression "real being" is that "real" comes from the Latin word *res*, "thing." It should mean being that belongs to a thing. But cognitional being as well as real being is possessed by things. *Esse in re*, understood as "being in a thing," is meant in direct contrast to being in cognition; see below, n. 3. Understood, however, as "being in reality" in the general sense of "real being," it throws the problem back to the meaning of "real." A quite legitimate use of "real" allows a poem or a doubt or a fear to be called "real": "For we encounter persons and poems, tables and chairs, hopes and fears. All are real. . . ." John E. Smith, "John Dewey: Philosopher of Experience," *Review of Metaphysics*, XIII (1959), 78. In Scholastic terminology, though, *esse reale* and *esse naturae* are conventionally restricted to the being that is found outside and independent of human cognition. This occasions a difficulty in regard to the term *ens reale*; see below, n. 18.

[3] The Scholastic Latin term is esse *in se*, as opposed to esse *in anima* or esse *in intellectu*. "In," of course, is not necessarily confined to spatial signification: "The locution, 'idea in my mind,' has in its own right at least as good sanction as any other use of 'in' . . ." D. Williams, "Mind as a Matter of Fact," *Review of Metaphysics*, XIII (1959), 213.

exists in the architect's mind previous to its construction in reality. On the other hand, buildings already demolished may be recalled, and so brought again into being in human memories. For a moment they exist again, not in reality, but only in thought. The symphony, the rainbow, the pleasant tastes, all may be dwelt upon later and so given fresh being in one's cognition.

Moreover, a thing that in the real world is in one place only, may come to exist simultaneously in thousands of different minds. The presidential candidate is in just one city in reality as he makes his final campaign speech, yet he is present simultaneously in the cognition of millions of televiewers located all over the country. No matter how distant a thing is in the real order, it may be actually present in anyone's mind. This consideration led Parmenides of Elea (fl. ca. 485 B.C.), the Greek thinker who inaugurated Western metaphysics, to write:

> "See, though, how things in their absence are present to mind with all sureness;
> Never indeed will the mind sever being from union with being,
> Neither as scattered afar through the myriad ways of a cosmos
> Nor as right closely conjoined" (*Fr.* 4; DK, 28B).

In accord with this observation, Parmenides drew the conclusion that all things coalesce in being. They all come together, as anybody can testify, in the mind. This simply expresses their cohesion in reality, he urged. They are all a single continuous whole. So, Parmenides reasoned, all things whatsoever are united in real being.

Spontaneously one is repelled by such a conclusion. Being in reality and being in thought are only too obviously different ways of being. They are subject to conditions so divergent that one does not at all feel justified in arguing from status in thought to status in reality, and especially to an exactly corresponding status in the real order. One can make a fifty thousand dollar house exist in one's own mind at will. To make it exist in reality is a more complicated matter. One may imagine at will how the next football game is going to be played, without having to believe at all that it will follow such a pattern in reality. But need one thereby hesitate to agree wholeheartedly with the Parmenidean observation that things absent in the real order are present in the mind? The same things, quite apparently, can exist in two different ways. They can exist in reality, they can also exist in cognition; or they may have for the moment the one way of existing, while lacking the other.

In contrast to the being that is conferred upon things by real existence, existence in the mind or imagination or sensation may be called **cogni-**

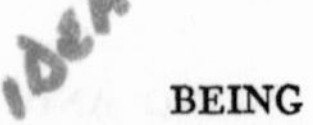

tional being. Still more technically, it is termed intentional being. "Intention" in this sense seems to have meant originally an idea, or representation in thought.[4] Later the etymology of the word was used to bring out the notion that cognition "tends" toward or into its object.[5] But in whatever way "intentional" may be understood, the distinction between real existence and cognitional existence is too clear for the ordinary normal person to question it in any serious way.

Philosophical Objections. There are, however, some well-known objections that arise from certain philosophical approaches. A skeptical argument often brought against the clearcut distinction between real and cognitional being goes back as far as the ancient Greeks.[6] Madmen, or people when dreaming or in states of hallucination, cannot distinguish between real and cognitional existence. Such persons think that their phantasies are really existent. Therefore the distinction between the two ways of being is entirely missed in these cases, and so is not at all immediately evident in itself. — For the student of metaphysics can this type of objection carry any appreciable weight? A science of being is not developed in a dream, nor during hallucinations, nor by madmen. If a person is in a state in which he can pursue a problem from the viewpoint of being, he is able at the same time to see clearly enough the difference between real and cognitional existence. It is indeed only while he is in the state in which such a difference is definitely experienced that he is capable of thinking in a metaphysical way. Qua

[4] The Latin *intentio* was used by mediaeval translators to render the Arabic *ma'nä*, a word that meant "idea" or "notion" in general; see Amélie-Marie Goichon, *Lexique de la Langue Philosophique d'Ibn Sīnā* (Paris, 1938), pp. 253–255 (no. 469); cf. pp. 172–173 (no. 353); André Hayen, *L'Intentionnel dans la Philosophie de Saint Thomas* (Paris, 1942), pp. 47–53. St Thomas, *De Ver.*, XXI, 3, ad 5m, clearly distinguished the meaning of the term in its cognitional sense from the meaning implied by its etymology.

[5] ". . . on account of the intervention of the will, the intelligence is capable of an *activity tending* toward a real object, under the attraction of that object." Hayen, *op. cit.*, p. 248. On the two different traditions, Augustinian and Arabian, back of this notion of intentionality, see *ibid.*, pp. 222–223, and Peter Nash, "Intention in Knowledge according to Giles of Rome," in *L'Homme et son Destin, Actes du Premier Congrès International de Philosophie Médiévale* (Louvain & Paris, 1960), pp. 653–661.

[6] See Sextus Empiricus, *Adv. Math.*, VII, 402–413. The argument was exploited by Descartes in the first of the *Meditations on First Philosophy* (A–T, VIII, 19.1–23). As far as present purposes are concerned, the question is not exactly which state is absolutely the normal one, but which state makes possible the pursuit of metaphysics. Hobbes stated the situation bluntly: ". . . I am well satisfied, that being awake, I dream not; though when I dream, I think myself awake." *Leviathan*, I, 2, 6. On the general problem, see Norman Malcolm, "Dreaming and Skepticism," *Philosophical Review*, LXV (1956), 14–37.

student of metaphysics, then, he is not hindered by the age-old skeptical objections on this score. He is moving on another level. He is content to leave to the psychologist the explanation of what happens in states different from the normal one in which metaphysical thinking takes place. During the time he engages in metaphysics he himself can distinguish without difficulty between the existence accorded the roc in imagination, and the existence enjoyed by the canary that is singing in the cage on the opposite wall of his room.

A more recent tendency allows both ways in which things may be, namely in the real world and in human cognition, but denies that the real existence of things is an evident datum of experience. Real existence is accepted on animal faith (Santayana) or on belief,[7] or in some other way that lacks the status of strict evidence. Cognitional being is accepted without question, against a background that is ultimately Cartesian.[8] — These views admit both ways of being, but deny the character of immediate evidence in one's grasp of real being. This is a most serious objection against the capacity of real being to serve as a viewpoint for scientific investigation. It will call for careful scrutiny in the inquiry about the way in which real being is known by the human intellect.[9] But in regard to the immediate point under consideration, it does not exert any of its destructive force. It admits in effect the two different ways of existing — real and cognitional — that one identical thing may enjoy.

Another type of objection would restrict genuine existence to the real order.[10] It would deny that cognitional existence is an authentic way of

[7] E.g.: "The conclusion, then, is in fact a well-known one, that while every perceptual act when lived in believes in the reality of its object, reflection upon perception discloses that the real existence of the intended object is not *given* at all, is not an object for intuition, but is the correlate of another mode of consciousness, *belief*. . . . while every perceptual act believes in the reality of its object, the real existence of the object and its implicated world can never form the *datum* for any intuitive, perceptual consciousness." W. Earle, "The Life of the Transcendental Ego," *The Review of Metaphysics*, XIII (1959), 12–13.

[8] On the Cartesian revolution in starting philosophy from human thought instead of from external things, see E. Gilson, *The Unity of Philosophical Experience* (New York, 1947), pp. 176–197. Cf. Locke, *Essay concerning Human Understanding*, IV, 2, 14; ed. Fraser, II, 185–188.

[9] See Chapter 3. If being is to serve as the viewpoint for a properly theoretical science, it will have to be an intelligible aspect, and it will have to be grasped by the intellect in the cognition of sensible things. Accordingly it will have to be part of the *datum*, it will have to be *given* in experience. In Scholastic Latin, it will have to be an *intelligibile*. It cannot, as in Husserl's phenomenology, be bracketed as irrelevant.

[10] E.g.: "Affirmative existential propositions are true if, and only if, the descriptive phrase applies to an individual existing in the actual world. There is no other mode of existence. . . . This is plain common sense." L. Susan Stebbing, *A Modern Introduction to Logic*, 6th ed. (London, 1948), p. 56. Cf.: ". . . it is maintained that

being. It implies that intentional existence is extrinsic to the thing while real existence is intrinsic to it,[11] even going so far, perhaps, as to reduce intentional being to a mere extrinsic denomination[12] of the thing known.

Zeus, Utopia, the *King of Utopia,* have being or *exist* in their respective non-actual universes. This assumption is absurd and unnecessary." *Ibid.,* p. 55. Accordingly, unicorns and centaurs belong to "the class of nothing existent." Clarence Irving Lewis and Cooper Harold Langford, *Symbolic Logic,* 2nd ed. (New York, 1959), p. 28.

Existence, whether real or cognitional, has to be actual. If the existence were not actual, it would not be there at all; for the thing concerned, even though able to exist, would not yet exist. There would be just possibility, and not existence. In the phrase "the potential existence of a thing," it is rather the thing itself that is potential, or able to exist. The existence is had either actually or not at all. When a thing acquires cognitional existence, it is actually existing in the knower. Yet a Scholastic etiquette that goes back to the earliest disputes on essence and existence, between Giles of Rome and Henry of Ghent, refers regularly to real existence as *esse actualis existentiae.* This etiquette presumes a kind of being that is non-existential and that coincides with what is expressed in the definition of the thing. Such being could be regarded as *existing* only in the mind, but as potential in respect to real existence. That potentiality became *actual* when real existence was acquired, and in this setting real existence was viewed as actual existence: "Et est illud esse rei definitivum quod de ipsa ante esse actuale solum habet existere in mentis conceptu de quo dicitur quod definitio est oratio indicans quid est esse." Henry of Ghent, *Quodl.,* I, 9; (Paris, 1518) fol. 7r. Hence arose the expressions *esse potentiale* and *esse possibile* (Suarez, *Disputationes Metaphysicae,* XXXI, 2, 7–11; ed. Vivès, XXVI, 231a–232b) in the meaning of essential being that could be given real existential being by its causes. Where "being" (esse) is understood to coincide with the existence, on the other hand, no place is left for any *esse possibile.*

This cognitional existence, which has to be actual, sounds to some modern ears like a contradiction in terms. To say a thing is imaginary seems the equivalent of saying that it does not exist: "Philosophers . . . wish to assert that imaginary and illusory objects have some sort of being. It seems a self-contradiction to say that they exist." A. J. Ayer, "Demonstration of the Impossibility of Metaphysics," *Mind,* N.S. XLIII (1934), 341. Cf.: ". . . many terms which do not exist, for example, the points in a non-Euclidean space and the pseudo-existents of a novel." Bertrand Russell, *The Principles of Mathematics,* 2nd ed. (London, 1937), p. 45 (no. 48). On the other hand, the opposite view is found stated just as strongly, though perhaps more circumspectly: "Thus we usually think that it is an error to say that a hippogriff exists, even though it may exist in idea." Paul Weiss, *Modes of Being* (Carbondale, 1958), p. 202. Existence, accordingly, "is a predicable of every idea," because every idea "occurs at some time, in some one's mind or language." *Ibid.* Against a strong Avicennian background, *esse in re* and *esse in anima* were accepted unhesitatingly in mediaeval times as the two ways in which a thing could exist.

[11] Suarez, for instance, continually insists on the *intrinsic* character of real existence to the thing, as though intentional existence were extrinsic to it; e.g., *Disp. Metaph.,* XXXI, 1, 1–13 (ed. Vivès, XXVI, 224b–228b). Modern writers have stated it explicitly. E.g.: "incipiunt esse *extrinsece* et *objective,* nimirum cognoscuntur. . . . cum illorum esse sit *cognosci.*" Joannes J. Urráburu, *Ontologia,* 2nd ed. (Paris and Rome, 1891), p. 97. ". . . extrinsic ideal being, or esse *intentionale* . . ." Peter Coffey, *Ontology* (London, 1918), p. 87. In this tradition, intentional being is called also esse *logicum* and esse *objectivum,* and contrasted with esse *physicum,* an expression meant here to characterize all real being, including the supersensible.

[12] "Extrinsic denomination" is given a thing when no change internal to it takes place, though it is brought into a new external relation with something else. For

Just as being labeled or being named or being catalogued does not make any change in the object itself, so being known or imagined or seen does not at all, this view urges, intrinsically affect the thing. — It is true that the thing remains the same thing while being known. Insofar as it is perceptible or conceivable, a thing is not changed in any way by being known. If it were changed in the activity of cognition, a different thing would be known. Even the possibility of undergoing change in the cognitional process would render all knowledge dubious.[13] The thing has to remain the same if there is to be knowledge of it. But it does come to *be* in a new way every time it is known, even though it is not affected at all in itself or in its real existence. It comes to be in someone's cognition, and acquires there an existence that it did not have before.

The label and name and catalog, on the other hand, do not make the thing exist in any new way. They are merely symbols that will cause a person familiar with them to recall the object signified. Only when the person actually recalls the object does it begin to exist anew, this time in his cognition. "Being known" denotes, therefore, something far more profound than "being named" or "being listed." It does not in any way, it is true, make the thing a different kind of thing. From that point of view it may be an extrinsic denomination. Yet it involves considerably more than just the extrinsic denomination. It gives the thing a new existence, existence in the cognition of the person who is perceiving or knowing. Because of the new existence, the thing is then able to be denominated "perceived" or "known." But the new existence itself is much more than that extrinsic denomination. It is genuinely an existence. In a way it can be regarded as extrinsic to the thing itself, in the same manner as real existence is extrinsic to what the thing is. The thing can lose its real existence and still remain the same thing as it is remembered

instance, a column is said to be now at the right, now at the left, according as you change your position, even though no change occurs in the column itself; see Suarez, *Disp. Metaph.*, LIV, 2, 9 (ed. Vivès, XXVI, 1020a).

[13] "The qualities, as distinct, are always made so by an action which is admitted to imply relation. They are made so, and what is more, they are emphatically kept so. And you cannot ever get your product standing apart from its process." Francis H. Bradley, *Appearance and Reality*, 9th impr. (Oxford, 1930), p. 23. In reaction to this view, cf.: "I could no longer believe that knowing makes any difference to what is known." Bertrand Russell, in *Contemporary British Philosophy*, ed. J. H. Muirhead, vol. I (London & New York, 1924), p. 360. The question here is not at all the same as the problem in physics concerning the interaction, on an atomic level, of experimental apparatus with the thing observed. Rather, the indivisibility of the physical experiment, that is, of process of observation and thing observed, still belongs to the domain of real existence. It is what is known. The question of cognition regards the new intentional existence given that indivisible experiment. In acquiring this new existence, the nature of the completed and epistemologically indivisible physical phenomenon remains entirely unchanged.

through cognitional existence. Real existence may be exercised in the thing itself, and cognitional existence in the knower. Yet both ways of existing remain decidedly extrinsic to what the thing is, even though both are more than extrinsic denominations.

Finally, in quite opposite fashion a view that may be termed "Idealistic" maintains that things are known only in their cognitional existence. Any existence outside thought remains inevitably, according to this approach, outside thought, that is, it is unthinkable.[14] Yet ordinary experience indicates quite the reverse. Only in terms of things outside it can thought itself be known and understood by men in their present life. Thought and cognition are indeed known immediately, but indirectly. The Greek philosopher Aristotle long ago made the observation that "evidently knowledge and perception and opinion and understanding have always something else as their object, and themselves only by the way."[15] You know directly sensible things, each grasped as having a real existence of its own. By reflexion, you are conscious of giving those things new existence in your cognition, and are thereby conscious of your own activities and your own self. But if you had never known sensible things in their extramental existence, you would not be able to know any cognitional existence or cognitional subject at all.[16] Human thought, accordingly,

[14] This attitude, in spite of its Idealistic intentions, seems unwittingly to represent cognition after the model of merely material or non-cognitional reality. A material thing is confined spatially to its own dimensions, and any other material thing is outside those dimensions. With cognition, on the other hand, something other than itself may be more directly present to it than is its own self. Cf.: "Thought, far from being a relation with itself, is on the contrary essentially a self-transcendence." Gabriel Marcel, *Being and Having*, tr. Katharine Farrer (Westminster, 1949), p. 30.

[15] *Metaph.*, Λ 9, 1074b35–36. Cf.: "The principle that I am adopting is that consciousness presupposes experience, and not experience consciousness." Alfred North Whitehead, *Process and Reality* (New York, 1929), p. 83.

[16] Gilson, after a detailed study of a number of attempts to establish a starting point outside sensible reality, expresses the resulting conclusion as follows: "Indeed one starts from being in a realism, and one already has knowledge of it, whereas one begins from knowledge in critical idealism, and one never rejoins this knowledge to being." *Réalisme Thomiste et Critique de la Connaissance* (Paris, 1939), p. 156. For anyone who insists on starting from thought in Idealistic fashion "a 'beyond thought' is unthinkable," Gilson, *Le Réalisme Méthodique* (Paris, 1936), p. 87; cf. pp. 89–90. Changing the terms from "thought" to "knowledge," Gilson emphasizes that knowledge always implies something other than itself: ". . . it is certain that all *knowledge* implies a 'beyond thought,'" *Ibid.*, p. 89. As another French writer expresses it, our mind "cannot think itself except in and through the thought of that which is other than itself." Aimé Forest, *La Structure Métaphysique du Concret selon Saint Thomas d'Aquin* (Paris, 1931), p. 275. The point is not just that "anything beyond thought is unthinkable because the object of thought is *everything which exists*," Fernand Van Steenberghen, *Epistemology*, tr. Martin J. Flynn (New York, 1949), p. 187. Rather, human thought itself cannot be known except in terms of what is beyond it.

requires as its condition an *au delà de la pensée,* something on the other side of thought itself. Only through knowing extramental reality can it know itself and its activities and its products. It must know what is outside thought, in order to know thought itself. Cognitional existence in general, then, presupposes real existence, even though a particular thing like a house may exist cognitionally in the mind of its producer before it exists in reality.

Distinction of Thing and Being. The conclusion emerging from these considerations is that a sensible thing and its being are not entirely the same. The thing may have real being, lose that way of being, and still retain or acquire cognitional being. The thing, then, is not exactly the same as either its real being or its cognitional being. It remains the same thing as it loses one way of being and acquires the other way of being. Sensible things, accordingly, are in some way other than their being.

What type of distinction, though, falls between such things and their being? Is it a distinction that is present in the things as they exist in reality, regardless of any work of the human mind? A distinction of that type is found, for instance, between an apple and its red color. The apple was an apple before acquiring the ripe color, and so is different from the color prior to any consideration by a human intellect. This kind of distinction is called a **real distinction.** On the other hand, what is extracted from iron ore may be conceived as either iron or metal. In the reality that is conceptualized through these two notions there is no distinction between the metal and the iron. Both concepts denote the one reality. The concepts are distinct; for the one, metal, is generic, while the other, iron, is specific. But prior to the work of the human intellect in forming those concepts, there is no distinction between the iron and the metal. Here you have not a real, but a **conceptual distinction,** for the distinction lies only between different concepts of the same thing. Finally, concept as well as reality may remain the same while designated by different words, as when the two names Tully and Cicero are used to denote the famous Roman orator. The distinction between Tully and Cicero is merely one of words, and so may be called a **verbal distinction.**[17]

[17] In Scholastic Latin a verbal or a conceptual distinction is called a *distinctio rationis.* The genitive *rationis* indicates human reason as the origin or cause of the distinction. If there is no intrinsic basis in the thing itself, the distinction is called *rationis ratiocinantis.* In this distinction human reason appears as active in collating different things or making different constructions. Accordingly the distinction is designated by the participle in the active form *ratiocinantis.* If there is a real extrinsic basis in other things, the distinction may be called an extrinsic virtual distinction, as in the distinction between essence and existence in God. If on the other hand the basis is intrinsic to the thing, it gives rise not to a *distinctio rationis ratiocinantis,*

Which of these distinctions is found between a thing and its being? Is it merely a question of using two words, thing and being, to denote the same reality? Or do the words represent two different concepts that the human intellect makes of the one identical reality? Or is a sensible thing distinct from its own being, prior to any work of the human mind? This problem will require long and careful investigation. Upon the way in which things are distinguished from their being will depend the way in which being is isolated as a viewpoint that could make possible a science of metaphysics. The preliminary and basic importance of correctly establishing the distinction becomes in this way apparent. From the considerations so far undertaken, however, one can say merely that some kind of a distinction is indicated between sensible things and their being.

Constitution of Beings. Either of the two ways of existing, these considerations show, makes a thing be. Either existence, real or cognitional, renders it a being. If the thing has real existence, it is called a **real being.** Even if it is merely capable of having real existence, though at the moment when one speaks it has only cognitional existence, it may nevertheless, according to traditional terminology, be likewise called a real being. The real existence it is able to acquire is regarded as sufficient to denominate it real.[18] Stones, trees, animals, and

---

but to a *distinctio rationis ratiocinatae*. The participle is in the passive, indicating that human reason is induced by the thing itself to make the distinction. Since its basis is intrinsic to the thing, this distinction may be called an intrinsic virtual distinction. It is known as a major virtual distinction if one of the distinguished aspects may be found in real things apart from the other. Animality and rationality, for instance, are so distinguished. Animality is found in the brute world, and so apart from the rationality with which it is joined in man. But if the two aspects could never be found in reality apart from each other, because in a real thing each inevitably involves the other, they are distinguished only by a minor virtual distinction. Such is the distinction between being and unity, or between the divine attributes. In the minor virtual distinction one concept does not prescind from the other, while in the major distinction there either may or may not be precision of one concept from the other.

Another noted Scholastic distinction was the formal distinction of Duns Scotus, present wherever distinct formalities were found in a thing. These formalities could be entities distinct in reality, like individuality and common nature for Scotus, or could be without real distinction, like the divine attributes. See *Opus Oxoniense*, II, d. 3, qq. 5 and 6, nos. 9–15; ed. M. F. Garcia (Quaracchi, 1912–1914), II, 264–270 (nos. 285–289); and I, d. 8, q. 4, a. 3, nos. 17–18; I, 633–634 (no. 669). Still another was the "intentional distinction" used by Henry of Ghent (*Quodl.*, I, 9; ed. cit., fol. 7v). It was not a distinction between realities, yet it was more than a conceptual distinction, for it implied real dependence upon an efficient cause.

For the purposes of the present investigation, the threefold classification of distinctions as real, conceptual, and verbal, will prove amply sufficient.

[18] A possible, that is, something that could exist but does not yet exist in reality, for instance a tunnel under the English Channel, is accordingly considered a real being

everything else that exists or could exist in the real world, are accordingly termed real beings. If on the other hand something may exist in thought but is incapable of existing as such in the real order, it is called technically a **being of reason.** The terminology is clumsy, but it denotes with sufficient clarity that this type of thing is produced only in human reason. Human reason is able to combine notions each taken separately from reality, even though their combination in a real thing is impossible. A square circle, for example, cannot exist in reality. It is a combination of two notions, each taken from the shapes of real sensible things, but each of which negates the other. If a thing is circular, it is not square, and vice versa. The combination can exist only when human reason joins the two concepts in a way that is extrinsic to and contrary to their own natures. A centaur, likewise, is half man and half horse. It implies a nature that is simultaneously rational and non-rational. Either feature negates the other. Similarly, express **negations** like nothingness have no being in reality, yet they are given being in human thought when they are considered and discussed. **Privations** also, like blindness, when taken in themselves, and certain relations like identity, can have being only in human reason. They are not things that can exist as such in the real world. They are beings, but only beings of reason. In that sense they may legitimately be called things, even though they cannot exist in reality. Accordingly, nothingness, or a square circle, *is something* that can be reasoned about and discussed.[19]

Either way of existence, then, confers being upon things. Sharply different as they are in the manner in which they make a thing be, they are both authentic ways of being. Both the one and the other are sufficient to constitute something a being, either a real being or a being of reason.

Ambiguity of Being. These considerations show, further, that being has more than just one meaning. It can mean existence

---

even though it has no real existence. It is impossible to systematize the terminology in any better way. If the actual possession of real being were required to denominate a thing "real," a house that is about to be constructed would have to be called something unreal. For philosophical purposes it is much more convenient always to call things like stones, trees, and houses, "real things," even though they do not as a present fact exist in the real world. The technical term "possible," therefore, refers to the thing itself rather than to any existence that the thing may acquire. On the problems involved in this topic, see W. Norris Clarke, "What is Really Real?" in *Progress in Philosophy*, ed. J. A. McWilliams (Milwaukee, 1955), pp. 61–90; "The Possibles Revisited: A Reply," *The New Scholasticism*, XXXIV (1960), 79–102. In ordinary English use, however, "real" has regularly the sense of existent — a house becomes real when it actually exists.

[19] On the various kinds of *entia rationis*, see Urráburu, *Ontologia*, pp. 98–108.

in reality, it can mean existence in cognition. In either way a thing may be, different though the meaning is in each of the two cases. From one point of view there is an order of priority in these two ways of being. Cognitional being presupposes the real being of the knower, for cognition has to take place in a really existent subject. But the cognitional being of the object known does not necessarily presuppose the object's real being. The intramercurial planet in the mind of the astronomers did not require the real existence of Vulcan. Conversely, a thing's real existence does not involve its existence in any human cognition. Neptune existed in reality long before it came to exist in the knowledge of the astronomers. Accordingly, the real existence of a sensible thing cannot be deduced from its cognitional existence, nor does the fact that a thing exists in reality offer ground for saying that it exists also in some human mind. Each existence, real or cognitional, in the case of a sensible thing, has to be known through an original and irreducible experience.

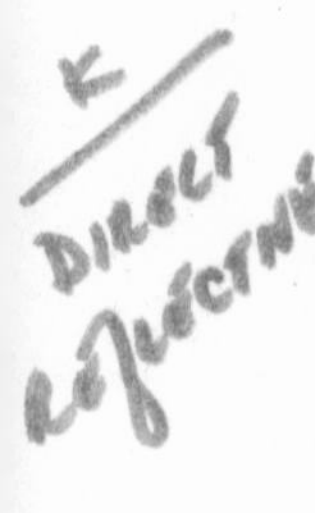

Both these ways of being, then, are immediately observable to human cognition. The real being of sensible things is experienced directly. The cognitional being is experienced indirectly or reflexively, though nonetheless immediately. Both ways of being are existential. One is existence in reality, the other is existence in cognition. These two seem to cover the ways in which a thing may exist. But is there any other way besides existence in which a thing may be? Is there any way of being that is non-existential? Might not a rose be a flower even though it existed neither in reality nor in any cognition? In fact, is it not eternally a flower whether it exists anywhere or not?[20] Or is this situation only an illusion? If the rose existed neither in cognition nor in reality, how would it be in any way at all? Rather, would you not have absolutely nothing? At least, no such non-existential being is immediately experienced. It will not enter, therefore, into the data from which a metaphysical inquiry commences. It can safely be shelved for subsequent treatment.[21]

For the moment, then, the ambiguity of being may be restricted to the two kinds immediately experienced, namely real existence and cognitional existence. What is rendered existent in either of these two ways is a being or a thing. The immediate question of a distinction between thing and being is concerned accordingly with the thing on the one hand and on

---

[20] The rose was a standard Scholastic example for this kind of being (*esse essentiae*) that abstracted from existence. See: Godfrey of Fontaines, *Quodl.*, II, 2; ed. De Wulf-Pelzer (Louvain, 1940), p. 64. Capreolus, *Defensiones Theologiae D. Thomae Aquinatis*, In *I Sent.*, 8, 1, 1, la concl.: ed. Paban-Pègues (Turin, 1900), I, 303a. Cajetan, *In De Ente et Essentia*, *Quaest.* XII, ed. M.-H. Laurent (Turin, 1934), p. 157 (no. 100).

[21] See below, Chapter 9, nn. 8 and 9.

the other with its real existence and its cognitional existences. The question bears on the kind of distinction, whether verbal, conceptual, or real, that falls between thing and either way of existing. The suggestion of a non-existential type of being, however, leaves the question deepened for subsequent consideration. Is it just a distinction between a thing and its existence? Or is it a distinction between a thing and all its being whatsoever? Or do these two questions wholly coincide?

Résumé. In any case, the framework in which the distinction of being from thing has to be approached emerges clearly enough from the foregoing considerations. An identical thing can have being in reality and being in cognition. It remains itself while having diverse existences. In saying that a thing is itself but has its being, are you merely expressing *one* and the same *notion* in different words? If so, there will be merely a verbal distinction between a thing and its being.[22] Or are you expressing *two* different *notions* of the same reality? In that case, a conceptual distinction falls between being and thing. Or is a thing itself, regardless of human notions, distinct from any being it may possess? If so, the distinction will be more than conceptual. Indeed, in the case of a thing's real existence, will it not be a real distinction?

To learn whether or not the distinction here is set up by the human mind, an investigation will first have to be made of the way in which the mind knows and names being. This will at least be a step toward learning whether or not the distinction between being and thing antecedes the human intellect's activity. The occurrence of a verbal distinction between them is of course evident in the use of the two different names, "thing" and "being." Furthermore, the different form of expression in the statements that a thing "is itself," but "has its being," seems to indicate a distinction of concepts. Something had or possessed is at least conceived as different from the possessor. What a thing is, on the other hand, is conceived as identical with it. If the conceptual distinction can be established, the still further problem remains about its basis. Is it based upon a real otherness of being and thing, an otherness that is there whether or not any human mind is considering the thing? Or is it merely a case of two distinct concepts formed by the human mind of one identical reality?

A real distinction, accordingly, gives rise to distinction in concepts. A conceptual distinction, on the other hand, does not necessarily indicate a real distinction. One may therefore quite legitimately establish first a

[22] Cf.: "The verbal difference between 'one man' and 'a man is' does not imply that each refers to a different being; for both expressions apply to only a single man that comes into being and passes away." Aristotle, *Metaph.*, Γ 2, 1003b27–30; tr. Richard Hope.

conceptual distinction, and then examine whether or not the distinction of concepts leads to a more fundamental distinction in reality itself. The exact nature of the distinction, once it is made clear, should in turn show how being may be isolated as a viewpoint for the metaphysical investigation of things.

SUGGESTED READINGS AND REFERENCES

Francis Suarez, *On the Various Kinds of Distinctions*, tr. Cyril Vollert (Milwaukee: Marquette University Press, 1947).

Denis John Bernard Hawkins, *Being and Becoming* (London and New York: Sheed and Ward, 1954), pp. 33–65 (Chapters II–IV, 2).

Joseph Owens, "A Note on the Approach to Thomistic Metaphysics," *The New Scholasticism*, XXVIII (1954), 454–476.

Leonard J. Eslick, "What is the Starting Point of Metaphysics?", *The Modern Schoolman*, XXXIV (1957), 247–263.

Robert G. Miller, "Realistic and Unrealistic Empiricisms," *The New Scholasticism*, XXXV (1961), 311–337.

CHAPTER 3

Apprehension of Being

Conceptual Content. From one point of view, being does not involve any addition to thing. Kant (1724–1804), the German critical philosopher, insisted that one hundred actual dollars do not contain anything more than one hundred possible ones. Being, therefore, he urged, is not a real predicate. It is not the concept of something that could be added to the concept of a thing. It is merely the placing of the thing in itself.[1]

Every dollar, whether existent in reality or merely in one's mind, is expressed by the same concept, namely a monetary value of one hundred cents. The real being of the dollar adds nothing to that content. The dollar still remains one hundred cents.[2] Real being, from that viewpoint, merely places the dollars in themselves instead of just in the mind. As far as conceptual content is concerned, one hundred really existent dollars have exactly the same meaning as one hundred dollars that exist solely in human cognition. What is conceptualized under each of the two existences is entirely the same. A thing that really exists, as has been emphasized in the preceding chapter, remains wholly the same thing when it is known. Existence does not add anything to the conceptual content of a thing.

[1] " '*Being*' is obviously not a real predicate; that is, it is not a concept of something which could be added to the concept of a thing. It is merely the positing of a thing, or of certain determinations, as existing in themselves. Logically, it is merely the copula of a judgment. . . . Otherwise stated, the real contains no more than the merely possible. A hundred real thalers do not contain the least coin more than a hundred possible thalers." Kant, *Critique of Pure Reason*, B 626–627; tr. Norman Kemp Smith. Cf.: "For the being of a thing, although other than its essence, nevertheless is not to be understood as something superadded in the fashion of an accident, but is as it were constituted by the principles of the essence." St Thomas Aquinas, *In IV Metaph.*, lect. 2, no. 558.

[2] The obviousness as well as the irrelevance of Kant's observation is noted by Paul Weiss: ". . . it is hard to understand why Kant thought this a remark worth making." *Modes of Being* (Carbondale, 1958), p. 200. Cf.: ". . . *the grasping of the being of the other person occurs on a quite different level from our knowledge of specific things about him.*" Rollo May, in *Existence*, ed. R. May, etc. (New York, 1958), p. 38.

Being, whether real or cognitional, does not make any difference in regard to *what* a thing is.

Meaning of Existence. But does conceptualization exhaust the activity by which human cognition attains its object? Has the mind no other way of grasping the meaningful? Surely one hundred dollars really existing in one's pocket have much more meaning than one hundred dollars that exist merely in imagination. In fact, the real existence of the dollars would seem to be the most meaningful of all in their regard. Might not one even say that the deepest meaning for anything is to exist? If a person had no existence, what could anything else mean for him? His nature, his definition, would be the same, namely man or rational animal, even though he were never brought into real existence. But what would all the gifts of statesmanship and artistry and literary skill have meant, say to Winston Churchill, if he never had real being?

This consideration applies to anything whatsoever. It holds in a corresponding way for things that have only cognitional being. What would all the grandeurs of the *Iliad* or the *Paradiso* mean if those poems had never come to exist in the minds of their authors and their readers? Without existence, either real or cognitional, nothing else matters for a thing. Being, rather, is the primary consideration in meaning.[3] Without

[3] "Meaning" in the present context is understood as the intelligibility manifested in any way by a thing itself. It is not restricted to the function of standing as a sign for something else, just in the way a word has meaning. Rather, it extends to whatever is intelligible in a thing. In this way existence is "significantly apprehended" — Paul Weiss, *Modes of Being*, p. 185; cf. p. 23 (1.03). It is quite obviously grasped by the intelligence: "Were Existence not intelligible, we would not know what it was for something to exist rather than not to exist. But this we know." *Ibid.*, p. 198. Even from the "sign" viewpoint, however, one may say: "The question of the nature of existence or reality is one of the most meaningful of all questions, for until its meanings are determined we cannot speak intelligibly." William M. Urban, *Language and Reality* (London, 1939), pp. 710–711. Cf.: "In other words, metaphysical language is the language of maximum context. The meaningfulness of the other languages always depends upon the meaningfulness of metaphysical language." *Ibid.*, p. 630.

The meaning of "meaning" has given rise to extensive discussions during the past few decades. In the "sign" conception, of course, "only words or symbols have *meaning*." L. Susan Stebbing, *A Modern Introduction to Logic*, 6th ed. (London, 1948), p. 499. But there are many different notions of meaning. Charles K. Ogden and I. A. Richards, *The Meaning of Meaning*, 10th ed. (London, 1949), pp. 186–187, give sixteen as a "representative list of the main definitions." They consider that the philosophers "are not to be trusted in their dealings with Meaning" (p. 185), and strive to develop a new science of "Symbolism" (pp. 242, 249), with a basically psychological procedure. L. Abraham, "What is the Theory of Meaning About?" in *The Monist*, XLIV (1936), 231–238, lists fifty-one accepted senses of meaning, and with "no pretensions to completeness." On the motives and results of recent preoccupations with the topic, see Gilbert Ryle, "The Theory of Meaning," in *British*

it, a thing cannot have any meaning at all. Being is what is most striking, what is deepest, in everything. It has, moreover, a very pronounced meaning of its own. The meaningful difference between cognitional being and real being in the case of one hundred dollars illustrates this clearly enough.

Judgment. The existence of things with its own proper meaning is accordingly grasped in human cognition. But how? Certainly not through conceptualization. Through conceptualization the mind knows *what* the thing is. But full knowledge of *what* a thing is does not include knowledge of the thing's existence, as has been seen in case of the one hundred dollars. Knowledge of the thing's being, then, will take place through a mental act that is other than conceptualization. What is the nature of that act? Is it merely an acceptance of the thing's existence through some kind of belief without full evidence? Or is it truly an act of knowledge that is based upon evidence in the strictest sense?

"Belief" in the present context does not mean the acceptance of something upon the word of another. It means rather a relatively firm acceptance of something to which sense knowledge inclines, though without intellectually grasped evidence. In the Platonic tradition, for instance, the intellectual object is different from the sensible object. The sensible object cannot be the ground for knowledge, but only for belief.[4] No matter how sure you are of some occurrence in the sensible world, you do not properly know it but merely believe it, for Plato, as long as your cognition of it is based only on sensible things.[5] In some later philosophies all acceptance of real existence in the sensible world has been explained through belief.[6]

Philosophy in the Mid-Century, ed. Cecil Alec Mace (London, 1957), pp. 239–264. On "ontological meaning," see H.-E. Hengstenberg, "The Phenomenology of Meaning as Approach to Metaphysics," *International Philosophical Quarterly*, I (1961), pp. 110–112.

[4] For Plato true opinion could be changed into knowledge by recollection of the thing's Idea, because the Idea had been known before birth (*Men.*, 97D–98A). In this case, however, the cognition is no longer based properly on the sensible thing, but rather upon the supersensible Idea.

[5] The levels of human cognition and their corresponding objects are illustrated by Plato in the simile of the divided line, *Rep.*, VI, 509D–511E. Cf. Hume's rating of belief as sensation: ". . . *belief is more properly an act of the sensitive than of the cogitative part of our natures.*" *A Treatise of Human Nature*, I, 4, 1; ed. Selby-Bigge (Oxford, 1896), p. 183.

[6] See above, Chapter 2, n. 7. For Locke it was a perception of the mind, carrying a lesser degree of certainty than the perception of an *idea's* existence, yet higher than mere probability and beyond real doubt: "There is, indeed, another perception of the mind, employed about *the particular existence of finite beings without us*, which, going beyond bare probability, and yet not reaching perfectly to either of the fore-

In ordinary speech, "belief" is in fact used to designate the firm acceptance of something without strictly necessitating evidence on the intellectual plane. It may be an acceptance sufficient to decide the gravest issues in life. A witness at a bank robbery trial, when asked to swear to the identity of the accused, may well say: "I saw him only once before, for just two minutes, when he was dressed in different clothes, and had a different expression on his face; yet I believe it is the same man." Assent based upon this type of belief is regularly made the guide of human conduct, and as a rule in practical matters it is sufficient to do away with all real doubt. Similarly in matters of supernatural faith there may be no real doubt whatsoever. Here the absolutely firm adhesion is caused not by any evidence of credibility that conditions the act of faith, but by a supernatural gift in the intellect itself.

When you know that a man is actually standing before you in the real world and talking to you, however, you know this in a different way from your belief that angels exist or from the belief of the witness that the accused is the same man he saw for a couple of minutes three months before. Degree of adhesion is not concerned. There is firm conviction in all three cases. The question is rather about the way in which one's cognition attains the existence of the angels, the identity of the accused, and the existence of something directly present in the sensible world. You do not perceive the angels themselves. Your cognition does not attain them directly. Demonstratively it grasps only the evidence that their existence is credible. The witness does not see the identity of the accused, directly, with the criminal of three months ago. He compares the defendant with an image in his memory. Through trust in memory and confidence that sufficiently observed characteristics identify persons, he is convinced beyond real doubt. But you directly perceive[7] that in the

---

going degrees of certainty, passes under the name of *knowledge*. There can be nothing more certain than that the idea we receive from an external object is in our minds: this is intuitive knowledge. But whether there be anything more than barely that idea in our minds . . . here I think we are provided with an evidence that puts us past doubting. For I ask anyone, whether he be not invincibly conscious to himself of a different perception, when he looks on the sun by day, and thinks on it by night . . .?" Locke, *An Essay concerning Human Understanding*, IV, 2, 14; ed. Fraser (Oxford, 1894), II, 185–186. On the expression "*real* doubt," see above, Chapter 2, n. 2.

[7] "To perceive is to experience existence, and to say through judgment that such an experience is true is to know existence." E. Gilson, *Being and Some Philosophers* (Toronto, 1949), p. 207. Cf.: "It is a radical error to restrict the object of the intellect to the object of the first operation of the mind." J. Maritain, *A Preface to Metaphysics* (New York, 1939), p. 20.

In every case an existent sensible thing is seen, heard, felt, or perceived through some other sense, when perception takes place through the external senses. In no

man talking to you something exists. You know it by direct intellectual cognition. Through physics and experimental psychology you learn that your perception of him as distant from you and as different from the surrounding objects is mediate. But your perception that something exists in front of you in reality is immediate. You see it intellectually. You do not just believe it.

The real existence of things in the sensible world, then, is directly attained by human intellectual cognition. The sensible things are immediately perceived to exist. But what act of intellection is the means of perceiving that they exist? It cannot be conceptualization, for, as has been seen, conceptualization of the thing misses both real and cognitional existence. It has to be a different act from conceptualization. It can be described and defined only in terms of its object, existence. Things are known to exist. The intellectual act by which existence is directly known is the proper way to define this cognition. Technically it may be called **judgment**, in accord with a traditional division of the acts of human intellection.[8] In this technical sense, however, it does not imply any preceding deliberative process. In moral matters a deliberative, and in speculative matters an investigative, process leads up to a *conclusion* in which something is judged to be or not to be, to be or not to be so, to be or not to be done. But judgment as it immediately attains the existence of things does not require or allow any *preceding* intellectual process. It is the im-

instance, properly, is the color seen, or the sound heard, or the hardness felt. Rather, it is the thing that is seen, heard, or felt. It is seen according to its color, heard according to its sound, felt according to its hardness. What is seen or felt is always a thing and an existent. It is known according to *what* it is, that is, according to its nature, through the intellect in simple apprehension. It is known according to its being, likewise through the intellect, but in the act of judgment. In all this cognition there is no question of temporally successive stages or of any mediation. There is only the one knower and the one thing known, the knowledge or cognition taking place simultaneously through the different means of knowing — sensation, conceptualization, and judgment. Accordingly the being of things is experienced and is observable, in contradiction to Ayer's sweeping assertion that the metaphysician's "statements do not describe anything that is capable, even in principle, of being observed . . ." *Language, Truth, and Logic*, 2nd ed. (London, 1946), p. 14. On the unity of the knowing subject, see texts below, Chapter 15, n. 5.

[8] "Judgment" is the regular Scholastic term for the second of the three acts of the mind listed in traditional logic. The other two acts are "simple apprehension" and "reasoning." The Oxford translation of Aristotle does not hesitate to use the term "judgement" in this sense, *Int.*, 14, 23a32 ff. The word comes from court procedure, where it refers to the conclusion of a process and not to something immediately known. In denoting an immediate grasp of being, the term is transferred to the cognitive order and undergoes a quite radical change in meaning. The transfer is awkward, as is so often the case with metaphysical terms in their technical use. But the awkwardness need not at all stand as an argument against the Scholastic tradition of naming the second operation of the intellect a "judgment," nor against the use of the term to designate in the full sense an *apprehension* of being. See below, n. 21.

mediate perception that a thing exists, an immediate apprehension of being.

Nature and Being. The human intellect, of course, cannot judge that something exists without at the same time conceptualizing the object that exists. It conceptualizes it as a stone, a tree, a horse, an animal, a body, or at least as a thing or a being. In this way the intellect may be said to grasp the thing according to the thing's **nature.** "Nature" is here used technically to mean whatever is intelligible in the thing regardless of any particular existence the thing may have.[9] A phoenix, for instance, may be conceptualized as a bird that burns itself to death every five hundred years or so, and rises rejuvenated from its own ashes. Vulcan may be understood as an intramercurial planet even though present-day astronomical knowledge does not show that such a planet really exists. A man like Plato's Timaeus may be conceptualized as a rational animal without knowing thereby anything concerning his real historical existence. In this way the nature of any sensible thing is known in **abstraction** from its real being.[10] The intellectual act by which anything is so known according to its nature is technically called **simple apprehension,** in contrast to the complexity of judgment.

Human cognition, however, can never attain anything through simple apprehension without simultaneously knowing it as existent either in reality or in the mind. In perceiving a really existent tree, it thereby both apprehends the tree according to the tree's general nature, and judges that the tree really exists. It does both at once. It cannot apprehend a tree that is actually before its eyes without simultaneously knowing that the tree really exists. When on the other hand it imagines the spreading chestnut tree of Longfellow's poem "The Village Blacksmith," it both conceives the tree in simple apprehension and knows that the tree exists in its own cognitive activity. One can never know a thing according to its nature without simultaneously knowing the being that it presents to the mind, whether that being is real or cognitional.[11] The activity by

[9] See St Thomas Aquinas, *De Ente et Essentia*, c. I; ed. Roland-Gosselin, reprint (Paris, 1948), p. 4.3–7. This sense of "nature," as defined by Boethius, *Liber de Persona et Duabus Naturis*, c. I (*PL*, LXIV, 1341B), extended to both substance and accidents. It is therefore a much wider sense than the special meaning of the term "nature" in Aristotelian natural philosophy. However, it shows no concern with existence.

[10] St Thomas, *De Ente*, c. III (ed. cit., p. 25.9–26.9); c. IV (p. 34.10–14).

[11] "Abstraction and judgment are never separated in the mind, because essence and existence are never separated in reality." E. Gilson, *Being and Some Philosophers*, pp. 203–204. ". . . it apprehends and judges in the same instant. It . . . utters its first judgment while forming its first idea." J. Maritain, *Existence and the Existent* (New York, 1948), p. 23. Cf. *ibid.*, pp. 22–37, especially n. 13. For the grasp of

which the human mind grasps anything, then, is always complex. Through simple apprehension it knows the thing according to the thing's nature, and at the same time through judgment it knows the thing according to the thing's being. The one activity cannot be had without the other. Timaeus, Vulcan, and the phoenix cannot be conceptualized apart from the simultaneous knowledge that they exist in one's own cognition, even though that apprehension of their being does not arise from what is conceptualized in them. The tree in the real world cannot be directly perceived by a man without causing the judgment that it really exists, though such knowledge is not at all given in the concept of the tree, when "concept" is taken to mean what is attained through simple apprehension.

Complexity of Being. The being of a thing, accordingly, is always attained by the human mind in a complex manner. Something like a tree or a stone or Socrates is conceptualized and judged either to exist or not to exist. If judged to exist, the thing is represented as having being, as entering into composition with its existence. Socrates, for instance, is conceived as a fifth century B.C. teacher of Athenian youth, and is judged to have existed in the minds of Aristophanes and the other Socratic writers. By nearly all historians he is judged to have existed also in reality. He is perceived by you to exist in your own mind at the present moment while you think of him. The one object, Socrates, is seen in composition with these various existences, real or cognitional. "Being," however, does not appear as an object in itself, like a tree or stone or anything else that can be directly attained through simple apprehension. It is always grasped as belonging to something else, and so in composition with the thing that is conceptualized. The being of a thing, therefore, is expressed in the complex form of a proposition, as "Planets exist."

There is more to the complexity of being, however, than just its composition with the thing. In sensible things it itself arises from composition within the thing, and consists in that composition.[12] It is

---

the first principle of being, Maritain uses the expression "judicative intuition," *The Degrees of Knowledge*, tr. Gerald B. Phelan (New York, 1959), p. 134. For Joseph Maréchal, *Le Point de Départ de la Métaphysique*, 2nd ed. (Brussels and Paris, 1949), V, 304, judgment is an inferior substitute for intellectual intuition.

[12] "But the being of composites arises from the components . . ." St Thomas, *In IX Metaph.*, lect. 11, (ed. Cathala), no. 1903; cf. nos. 1896–1902. "The second operation regards the thing's very being, which in composites springs from the union of the principles of the thing . . ." *In Boeth. de Trin.*, V, 3c; ed. Wyser (Fribourg and Louvain, 1948), p. 38.10–12. ". . . being follows upon the composing of matter and form. . . ." *In I Sent.*, d. 23, q. 1, a. 1, Solut.; ed. Mandonnet (Paris, 1929), I, 555. ". . . the being of a thing composed of matter and form . . . consists in a certain composing of the form with the matter, or of the accident with its subject." *In I Sent.*, d. 38, q. 1, a. 3, Solut.; I, 903. The judgment may have the form not

not a further nature like whiteness or hardness superadded to the thing and knowable through simple apprehension. As is apparent in Kant's example of the one hundred dollars, being does not add any new conceptual content to the thing. Rather, it may from this standpoint be regarded as constituted by the very elements that compose the thing,[13] as it places the thing in reality or in cognition. Every sensible thing, as is shown in Aristotelian natural philosophy,[14] is composed of two substantial principles, matter and form. Of its own nature the matter is not united to any particular form, since in the process of substantial change it passes from one form to another. Correspondingly, the form is not of its nature united to any particular matter; thus in the phenomenon of nutrition the same form can acquire different matter. The composition of the matter and the form takes place only in being. This can be seen much more readily in the case of accidental qualities. A man, for instance, may be pale. But there is nothing in the nature of man that requires him to be pale. He could be ruddy, or dark, and still be a man. The composition of man and paleness does not emerge just from human nature. It occurs rather in accidental existence.

Quite similarly, though on a different plane, human nature enters into composition with the various individual men, like Julius Caesar or Napoleon Bonaparte. There is nothing in human nature itself that requires it to be found in Caesar. It could have existed in thousands of other men if Caesar had never lived nor been thought of. Its composition with Caesar is expressed in the proposition "Caesar is a man." Generic natures, likewise, are not of themselves bound to be any particular species. An animal, for instance, may be either a man or a brute beast. The composition take place in being: "A horse is an animal." In the very composing of horse with animal, of Caesar with man, of matter with form, of subject with quality, is the being of the thing found. Since it is a composing, the being of a sensible thing may be regarded as dynamic. In comparison, what is attained through simple apprehension, such as man, pale, stout, appears as still life. Each of these notions, obtained in simple apprehension, is expressed by a single word. But the being of a thing, as apprehended through judgment, can be expressed only through the complexity of a proposition. Judgment, accordingly, is not a simple apprehension, but a complex one. It is a dynamic grasp of the existential composing that is being.

---

only of "It exists," but also of "It is a tree," or "It is brown." In all three the being consists in a composition.

[13] See above, n. 1.

[14] Aristotle, *Ph.*, II 1, 192b8 ff.

Being is dynamic
Apprehension of being appears as still life.

Composition in Time. The existential composing in sensible things, moreover, is always occurring in time. The being that you had a year ago has perished, the being that you will have an hour from now has not yet arrived. You exist only in the present moment, yet you had being in the past and will have more being in the future. You remain the same person, the same individual, yet your being is continually changing. You are self-contained, but your being is not. Much of it, namely all the past and all the future, is outside its actual self.[15] Only the present is in being. So it is with all sensible things. The car that you start this morning may be the same car that you put in the garage last night, but the being that it had last evening is irretrievably gone in the past. The house that you leave at present will be the same house to which you will return tonight, but its existence of this evening is not yet existence. The existence of sensible things is confined to the present time, as far as its actuality is concerned. They may have the potentiality of existing in the future, and they did have existence in the past, but the only time they do exist is at the present; and the present is continually changing as it perishes into the past and goes on into the future.[16] The very nature of sensible things calls for being that is spread out in time. They all have matter as one of their substantial principles; and, as the Aristotelian natural philosophy shows, matter is the principle of mobility and time follows upon motion.[17]

Since the being of sensible things is inexorably conditioned by time, it is expressed in a proposition in which the verb shows this condition. Where the being is directly apprehended in the judgment, it is expressed by the present tense; for instance, "I am typing." Being in the past, which now exists only in memory, is denoted by the past tense; as, "I was reading an hour ago." Future being may be known in its causes, and is expressed by the future tense; as "I will fly to New York tomorrow" is known through my intentions, means, and the services available for air travel to New York. In every instance there is a composition between subject and

[15] "But our being has something of itself outside itself: for it lacks something that has already gone by of itself, and that which is to be." St Thomas, *In I Sent.*, d. 8, q. 1, a. 1, Solut.; I, 195.

[16] "Hence, just as the mobile thing is the same in substance during the whole movement, it changes in being, as it is said that Socrates in the market place is other than he himself at home, so . . ." *In I Sent.*, d. 19, q. 2, a. 2, Solut.; I, 470.

[17] Aristotle, *Ph.*, IV 11, 218b21–220a26. Cf.: ". . . everything that has matter is mobile. . . ." St Thomas, *In I Phys.*, lect. 1 (ed. Leonine), no. 3. An approach from a viewpoint of logic makes time more basic than existence: "It is merely the fact that different terms are related to different times that makes the difference between what exists at one time and what exists at another." Bertrand Russell, *The Principles of Mathematics* (Cambridge, Eng., 1903), I, 471 (no. 443).

predicate in their being, and that composition takes place in a definite time, whether past, present, or future.[18] The dynamic composition of the judgment mirrors that composition of its object, and is expressed in the complex form of the proposition.

Diversity of Being. The actual composing in which being is seen to consist is obviously particularized in each instance. In every occurrence in the real world it is a composing of this particular matter with this particular form, or of this particular subject with this particular quality or other characteristic, or of this particular individual with this specific or generic nature. It is a new composing in every case, a composing, moreover, that never remains the same for any two successive instants of time. It is a continual, one-directional flux toward the future. This means that the being of sensible things is not just different in every case and at every moment, but is **diverse** in the fullest sense of the term. Things are said technically to be different if they coincide in a specific or generic trait while they are distinct through some further characteristic. "Diverse" is a wider term, and applies also to things that do not coincide in any specific or generic feature.[19] All men coincide in their human nature, though they differ as individuals; but in their being they are diverse. Their being is not a common nature present in all, a nature that could be perceived in a simple apprehension. Their being, rather, is a new composing in every individual case, a composing that does not present itself in the manner of a common feature or trait that could be grasped immediately in universal fashion. It has to be judged separately in every instance and according to each successive part of time. As attained by the judgment, then, being is simply diverse in its every occurrence, while the things that exist coincide in their various specific and generic traits.

Activity of Judgment. Simply speaking, you would say that every act of knowing is an activity performed by the knower. Yet from one point of view, simple apprehension may be regarded as the passive viewing of a fixed and abiding nature. Like the plate of a camera, it catches what is stable and permanent in the thing. In this sense it

[18] "For 'being' that signifies the composition of a proposition is an accidental predicate, because the composition is made by the intellect according to a determined time. Now to be in this time or in that, is an accidental predicate." St Thomas, *In X Metaph.*, lect. 3, no. 1982. Cf. *In I Periherm.*, lect. 3 (ed. Leonine), no. 13; lect. 5, no. 22; lect. 14, no. 19.

[19] ". . . things that 'differ' have to be in some way composite, since they differ in one feature and agree in another. But according to this, although everything that is 'different' is 'diverse,' not everything that is 'diverse' is 'different.'" St Thomas, *ST*, I, 90, 1, ad 3m. This distinction between "difference" and "diversity," however, is a nicety that is often not observed in practice.

gives a flat picture, a still-life photo. Accordingly it may be called incomplex knowledge, even though it may gather many different features of the thing for consideration by the mind. In contrast, judgment is essentially active.[20] There is no abiding nature in the thing for *it* to photograph. It apprehends the thing's being, which is a composing in time. It can apprehend it only through an active composing of subject with form or predicate, as expressed in a proposition. The being of sensible things consists in a composition, and can be apprehended solely through an active composing in the mind. It cannot be photographed. There is nothing about it that can pose long enough for even the quickest camera shot in simple apprehension.

Because judgment grasps the thing's being through an active composing instead of a passive viewing, it has been mistakenly regarded as merely a subsequent uniting of what has already been apprehended, without being in any way itself an act of apprehension. Yet it is the only way in which the being of a thing can be immediately and evidently grasped. When you know that a man is standing in front of you as you see him and talk to him, when you know that you are alive and thinking and speaking as you reflect upon yourself, you are apprehending the existence of yourself and your companion with immediate evidence. You perceive that both exist. You have not the least real doubt about the existence of either. You know that both you and he are there. Such being, as is clear from the preceding investigation, entirely eludes simple apprehension. Yet it is directly perceived, it is known, it is apprehended. The grasping of it immediately in judgment is therefore an act of apprehension, not of simple apprehension but of apprehension through a complexity.[21]

---

[20] ". . . in so far as it judges of things, the mind is not passive in regard to things, but rather is in a certain way active." St Thomas, *De Ver.*, I, 10c; ed. Spiazzi (Turin and Rome, 1949), I, 20a. There is, of course, a sense in which every cognitive act, simple apprehension as well as judgment, is active; for every cognitive act is an operation performed by the knower. Likewise, there is a sense in which every cognitive act is passive; for it is a reception and not a production of something else. The immediate grasp of being in the synthesis of judgment is accordingly an attaining of the being that is there in the thing, and not a Kantian synthesis that fails to make manifest the being of the thing in itself. Correspondingly, the permanent thing that exists is not in Bergsonian fashion just a cinematographical stabilization snapped by the intellect, but is an abiding reality that is passively known as such by the intellect. The cinematographical simile is used by Bergson to explain human cognition in *Creative Evolution*, tr. A. Mitchell (London, 1911), p. 287 ff.

[21] For the opposite view, and a discussion of the Scholastic controversy whether the perception of the union of subject and predicate is distinct from the assent, see Francis Martin Tyrrell, *The Role of Assent in Judgment* (Washington, D. C., 1948). This thesis defends the view that the *perspicientia nexus* is an act of simple apprehension, really distinct from the judgment, in the sense that apprehension and assent are "irreducibly distinct" (p. 148). Similarly Louis-Marie Régis, *Epistemology* (New

Judgment, however, is not restricted to immediate apprehension. The conclusion of a reasoning process, as is shown in logic, is a mediate judgment. In it the intellect judges about being that it does not immediately apprehend. The active character of the judgment lends itself naturally to this type of knowing. On the strength of legitimate reasons it can pronounce that subject and predicate are joined together in being, even though it does not directly perceive that being. Hence mediate judgment allows the possibility of error, a possibility that is excluded where the judgment is the immediate apprehension of a thing's being. But the facts that in the conclusion of a reasoning process the judgment affirms being that it does not immediately apprehend, and that in the case of error it affirms being that just is not there, do not at all militate against the nature of the judgment as basically an act of apprehension, the apprehension of being. Rather, they testify to the active character of judgment. In its composing it is not limited to what it immediately apprehends as composed, but can go on to make other compositions of its own. If such affirmations

York, 1959), p. 321, characterizes judgment as "an act in no way resembling apprehension." F. A. Cunningham, "Judgment in St. Thomas," *The Modern Schoolman*, XXXI (1954), 207, with the courtroom connotations of "judgment" in mind, questions the use of the term in St Thomas to describe the second operation of the intellect (but see St Thomas, *In I Periherm.*, lect. 3, Leonine nos. 9–13). In "The Second Operation and the Assent vs. the Judgment in St. Thomas," *The New Scholasticism*, XXXI (1957), p. 5, Fr. Cunningham, against a logical background, also distinguishes judgment from assent, and sees assent without judgment in the second operation of the intellect regarding the first principles. He brands as a "strange innovation" (*ibid.*, p. 23) the listing in the *Oxford Dictionary* for "judge" as meaning "to apprehend mentally."

The philosophic difficulties involved seem to lie in a failure to understand that existence, as more basic than nature, is known originally through a deeper act of cognition. Judgment is "an operation which answers an act of existing," and an "epistemology in which judgment, not abstraction, reigns supreme, is necessarily required by a metaphysics in which 'to be' reigns supreme in the order of actuality." E. Gilson, *Being and Some Philosophers*, pp. 207–208. Often enough St Thomas contrasts composition in the second with apprehension in the first operation, but nowhere does he deny that the second operation itself is an apprehension. Rather, he terms it explicitly so on occasion: "It pertains to the intellect to judge, and this is called 'to know' and 'to apprehend' . . ." *In III De An.*, lect. 4 (ed. Pirotta), no. 629. ". . . composition when the intellect compares one concept with another, as it were apprehending the conjunction or identity of the things of which they are conceptions; division when it so compares one concept with another as to apprehend that the things are diverse." *In I Periherm.*, lect. 3, no. 4. ". . . the apprehension of the cognitive power that is proportioned to the thing's being." *In I Sent.*, d. 19, q. 5, a. 2, Solut.; I, 491. "But our intellect, whose cognition takes its rise from things that have composite being, apprehends that being only by composing and dividing. . . ." *In I Sent.*, d. 38, q. 1, a. 3, ad 2m; I, 904. ". . . a false apprehension of itself. . . ." *De Ver.*, I, 10c; ed. Spiazzi, I, 20a. St Thomas also refers to the act of judgment as "knowing" (*cognoscere* — *In I Peripherm.*, lect. 3, no. 9) and as "understanding" (*intelligere* — *In IV Metaph.*, lect. 6, no. 605).

are not made on legitimate grounds, they will be unjustified and may easily be false. They are always modeled, however, on what was originally attained through the judgment's immediate apprehension.

Distinct Apprehensions. What was called by Kant the positing of a thing in itself turns out, from the above considerations, to be the deepest of all meanings for the thing. True, that meaning escapes conceptualization or simple apprehension, but it is apprehended nonetheless firmly and evidently in the complex activity of judgment. It is the being of the thing. If the term "evident" is artificially restricted to what appears through a concept in simple apprehension,[22] it would not be applicable to the thing's existence. Being is not contained in the simple apprehension of any sensible subject. But such a restriction of the word "evident" is entirely unjustified.[23] In ordinary language and in court procedure, no one hesitates to affirm as evident the existence as well as the nature of what he perceives. Both things and their being are immediately apprehended, though in two different ways. The one apprehension is simple, the other is by way of a complex uniting or composing. The two apprehensions are undoubtedly distinct. Is this enough to show that you have one concept for a thing, and another concept for its being? Is it sufficient to establish a conceptual distinction as well as a verbal distinction between thing and being?

If apprehension through judgment may be termed a concept, it would at once allow its object to be regarded as conceptually distinct from the object of simple apprehension. If however, as is usual today, "concept" is restricted to the realm of simple apprehension, the problem is not entirely solved. In this sense we do have a concept of being, for we speak of the being of a thing just as we speak of the whiteness of a wall. In so speaking we are not affirming or denying that anything exists. It is not a question of judgment, but of conceptualization. What is the origin of this concept of being? Is it distinct or is it not distinct from the concept of a thing?

---

[22] On the question of applying the term "concept" to the activity of the judgment, see Etienne Gilson, *Being and Some Philosophers*, Appendix, 2nd ed. (Toronto, 1952), pp. 216–227.

[23] Immediately apprehended existence may accordingly be called "self-evident," e.g., "the self-evidence ascribed to the existence of sensible things" — R. W. Schmidt, "The Evidence Grounding Judgments of Existence," in *An Etienne Gilson Tribute*, ed. Charles J. O'Neil (Milwaukee, 1959), p. 230. There is no need to restrict the notion of "self-evident" to what is contained in the definition of a thing. The being of sensible things, though not contained in their definition, is evident to the mind's judgment not through any demonstration in Cartesian fashion, but immediately by itself. Allowing "self-evident" the full sense of whatever immediately and clearly manifests itself to a knower, one may affirm as "self-evident" that things exist in the real world and that they exist in one's thought.

Résumé. Sensible things, in which human cognition originates, are known by two simultaneously elicited acts of intellection. In their nature, which is common to all instances of their species and which forms as it were a flat object of inspection, sensible things are known through simple apprehension. In their being, which is diverse in every instance and which is a dynamic composing that never remains still, they are known through judgment. Simple apprehension, accordingly, may be compared to still-life photography. Judgment, on the other hand, though an apprehension of being, is not a simple apprehension but rather the complexity of an active composing. Without the simultaneous occurrence of these two acts no sensible thing can be known by the human intellect.

SUGGESTED READINGS AND REFERENCES

Henri Bergson, *Introduction to Metaphysics*, tr. T. E. Hulme, ed. T. A. Goudge (New York: Liberal Arts Press, 1949). Originally appeared in French in *Revue de Métaphysique et de Morale*, XI (1903), 1–36.

John A. Oesterle, *Two Essays on the Problem of Meaning* (Baltimore, Md.: n.p., 1945). Reprinted from *The Thomist*, VI (1943), 180–229; VII (1944), 233–263.

Gerald B. Phelan, "The Existentialism of St. Thomas," *Proceedings of the American Catholic Philosophical Association*, XXI (1946), 25–40.

Francis C. Wade, "The Judgment of Existence," *Proceedings of the American Catholic Philosophical Association*, XXI (1946), 102–106.

Etienne Gilson, "Knowledge and Existence," Chapter VI, pp. 190–215, and "Appendix," pp. 216–232, in *Being and Some Philosophers*, 2nd ed. (Toronto: Pontifical Institute of Mediaeval Studies, 1952).

Joseph Owens, "Diversity and Community of Being in St Thomas Aquinas," *Mediaeval Studies*, XXII (1960), 257–302.

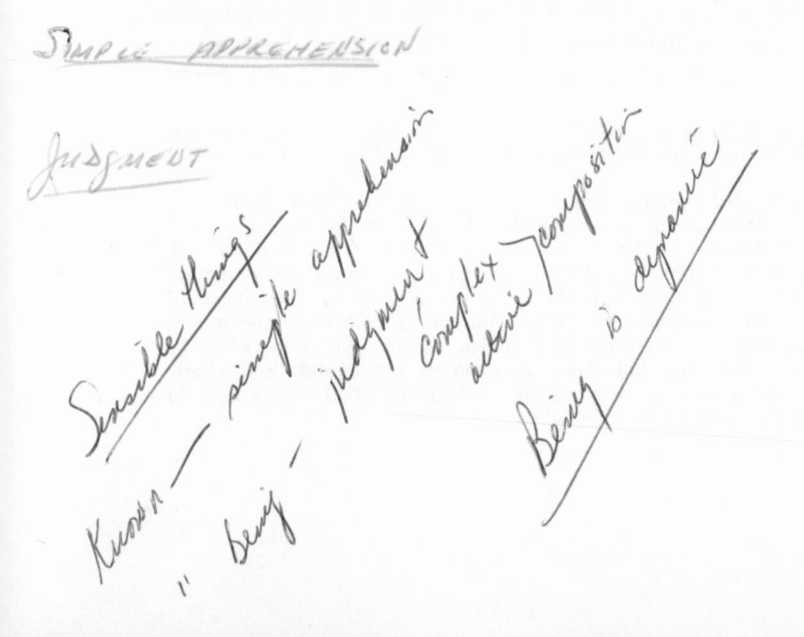

CHAPTER 4

Conceptualization of Being

Being and Universality. If there is to be a science of beings insofar as they are beings, it will have to regard them under an aspect that is in some way universal. Science is of the universal, logic shows,[1] and not of the individual as such. The aspect according to which metaphysics deals with things is being. If metaphysics is truly a science, being is in some manner a universal notion. Yet being, as originally apprehended through judgment in sensible things, is a highly individual composing that is new and diverse in every individual instance and occurs in an ever fleeting moment of time. It offers nothing of the permanence and stability and community required in a universal notion. Yet it is in fact used like a universal predicate. One says that a tree exists, a stone exists, Mars exists, and thousands upon thousands of other things exist. They all have being, just as all men have animality. How can existence be shared by many subjects, if it is diverse in every case? How can it have the universality requisite for science?

Act, Perfection. As "whiteness" is represented as something that makes a surface white, so what the mind apprehends in judgment is represented as making a thing be, and is called the thing's "being" or "existence." In reality, whiteness does not exist in itself. There are only white bodies. The bodies exist in themselves and are white, insofar as they have white surfaces. That is the way the mind perceives them. Yet for purposes of its thinking the mind is able to conceptualize whiteness as though it were something in itself and so is able to use it as a subject of predication, for instance in the sentence: "Whiteness is a color." In this way it is able to think about and speak about whiteness.

[1] ". . . any deductive or inductive inference, no matter how much it may be dignified by the prominent place it occupies in the context of genuinely scientific knowledge, is nevertheless wholly dependent upon the factor of universality." Francis H. Parker and Henry B. Veatch, *Logic as a Human Instrument* (New York, 1959), p. 251.

Similarly it conceptualizes what it apprehends through judgment, and so is able to think and speak of the being of a thing even though it has not perceived that being as something existent in itself any more than it perceived whiteness as something existent in itself. In so conceptualizing being it universalizes it. Just as whiteness applies to any instance of a white body, so does being, when thus conceptualized, apply to anything whatever that exists. In conceptualizing anything the mind knows it under a universal aspect. That way of knowing pertains to the nature of the mind's conceptualizing act, as is observable through reflexion.

There is, of course, a profound difference between the conceptualization of whiteness and the conceptualization of being. The notion "white" was originally obtained through the simple apprehension of a white body. The knowledge of being, on the other hand, was not originally attained through any simple apprehension at all. It was attained through a composing, and in the conceptualization of being that actual composing is lost. The result is that while whiteness retains the full conceptual content that was originally attained in simple apprehension, the concept of being does not show that anything exists. What is most important and meaningful in the original knowledge of being escapes it. Even when it is conceived as infinite it does not provide any grounds for arguing that it really exists.[2] Of itself it does not make manifest even its own being, which is other than itself and can be grasped only through an act of judgment. It depends upon the activity of the mind for its own existence. Yet it represents, as far as conceptualization may do so, the characteristic that makes a thing be. It represents it in the fashion in which whiteness makes a thing white. The fashion is that of subject and characteristic possessed by the subject. The thing is conceived as a subject, and being is conceived vaguely as that which makes such a subject be, just as whiteness makes a body white.

There are technical terms at hand from the Aristotelian natural philosophy to designate this relation of subject and characteristic. The basic subject of change in the sensible world is matter, and what characterizes matter is called form. Since form is perceptible through simple apprehension, and is regularly understood to remain in the order of what is attained by simple apprehension, it keeps overtones that interfere with its application to being. But the form, in Aristotelian terminology, was also known as the **act** (*energeia*) and the **perfection** (*entelecheia*) of the subject. As "act" it implied that its subject was a **potency** in regard to it, just as the activity of mining requires a mine that is able to be operated.

[2] See St Thomas' critique of the Anselmian argument for God's existence, *ST*, I, 2, 1, ad 2m, and *CG*, I, 11.

MATTER FORM ACT PERFECTION

As "perfection" it implied that its subject, as subject, lacked what it conferred, just as a pupil lacks the knowledge that is about to be imparted by the teacher. These two technical terms lend themselves readily to extension beyond the strict order of form and matter. They may be used to designate the function of the being that is apprehended through judgment. Without its being, the thing would not exist, would be nothing. Being, therefore, may be regarded as a perfection that makes the thing exist and as an act that the thing is able to enjoy. In this way, being is conceptualized technically as an act or perfection of a subject. Accordingly it is universalized in the concept of act or perfection without adding any *special* conceptual content of its own. It is distinguished only by the reference it bears to what was attained in judgment. It expresses the act or perfection that makes a thing be. Yet just in itself, without the reference to judgment, the concept does not express anything *proper* to being. No proper concept of being is naturally available to the human mind.

Common Being. But if an act or perfection is diverse in every instance, as is the case with being, how can it be at all represented by a common concept? Is it like the concept of individuality? The concept "individual" applies to any individual whatsoever. It is a universal concept, even though what it designates is different in every instance. Yet the parallel is not entirely exact. "Individual" pertains to what is called the second intention. The first intention in this case is "Socrates," or "Plato," or "Charlemagne," or "Genghis Khan."[3] The concept "individual" arises only from the considering of Plato, Charlemagne, and so on, in relation to the specific humanity they share in common. But being is directly apprehended in the thing through judgment. However, the *concept* of being does constitute a second look at it, and in that sense it may be called a second intention,[4] even though what it represents is immediately apprehended. What it denotes is there in the thing itself, and does not arise from the mind's cognition of the thing. Accordingly, the designation "second intention" is better avoided here, though it does

[3] "But the individual can be signified in two ways: either by a word of the second intention, like this word 'individual' or 'singular,' which does not signify a singular thing, but the intention of singularity; or by a word of the first intention, which signifies the thing to which the intention of particularity belongs; . . ." St Thomas, *In I Sent.*, d. 23, q. 1, a. 3, Solut.; ed. Mandonnet, I, 563.

[4] ". . . the abstract notion of being we form in our mind when we conceive it in its universality. Understood in this latter way, being is the most general of our concepts. It is a universal; that is to say, a being of second intention with no other reality of its own than that of a known object in our intellect." E. Gilson, *Elements of Christian Philosophy* (New York, 1960), p. 135. On second intentions, cf. St Thomas, *De Pot.*, VII, 9c.

bring out the all-important consideration that being is not originally attained through conceptualization. Like the concept of individuality, the concept of being can represent universally what was attained as strictly individual in preceding acts of cognition.

Being, then, is universally what makes a thing different from nothing. It may therefore be called the act of all acts and the perfection of all perfections.[5] In this way it is conceptualized as common to all, even though the act that does make a thing different from nothing is diverse in every single case. Conceived as common, it can be applied to any act of existing. But when it is predicated of something whose existence is not known through judgment, it does not carry along with it any knowledge that this second thing exists. That knowledge can come only through a new judgment. The concept of humanity cannot be applied to a person without thereby representing him as human. Yet you can conceive a mountain of gold as really existing in the Himalayas without thereby meaning that it does so exist. Your concept of being remains indeed open to such knowledge. But it can be given that meaning only on the basis of a new judgment. The real being that is conceived for the mountain of gold in the Himalayas could take on the sense that the mountain really existed, if it were actually seen there. The real being of the mountain would then be directly apprehended through judgment. That knowledge, however, cannot be found in the concept itself of real being, when the concept is applied to the mountain in detachment from the perception that it exists. The concept of a really existent mountain of gold does not at all guarantee that there is such a mountain in the real world. The same holds for cognitional being. When you are thinking of a mountain of gold, you know that it is existing in your mind at the time. But that knowledge of existence comes from the accompanying judgment, and not from anything in the conceptualization of the mountain. To apply to it the notion of existence in someone else's mind gives no assurance that it exists there. Just in itself, the notion "existence" remains a question mark.

Unlike other common concepts, then, the concept of being does not of itself apply to its subject the most pertinent meaning of what it conceptualizes. Common being conceptualizes the being that is grasped through the act of judgment when the intellect knows that something exists. When applied just on its own strength to something else, however, the common concept does not carry along with it the knowledge that

[5] St Thomas, *De Pot.*, VII, 2, ad 9m. Cf. *ST*, I, 3, 4c. The Scholastic formula that existence places a thing outside nothing and outside causes may or may not be understood against a background that preserves the doctrine of St Thomas; see Cornelio Fabro, "L'Obscurcissement de l' 'Esse' dans l'École Thomiste," *Revue Thomiste*, LVIII (1958), 446–447.

this second thing exists. But it can always be used to represent any other act of being that is known through a new judgment. It can be kept focused on that act and like a spotlight follow it through in its consequences. In this way it can be used in reasoning processes and so permit the development of a science of being. Common being, accordingly, constitutes the subject of metaphysics.[6] Yet extreme caution has to be exercised not to regard common being in the fashion of other common concepts. It represents a perfection that was not originally attained through conceptualization, a perfection that exhibits no special conceptual content. From the viewpoint of original conceptual content it is the equivalent of nothing,[7] it is empty. To be used in metaphysics it has to be kept trained upon being that is judged. Used in this way it retains existential content, a content that is the richest and most meaningful of all.

The Concrete and the Abstract. Since being is conceived as an act or perfection that makes a thing differ from nothing, it can be understood either in the abstract or in the concrete. "Abstract" means "taken away from," and "concrete" signifies literally "grown together." So "white" in the notion "a white body" is expressed in the concrete, because it is conceived as fused together with its subject the body. "Whiteness," on the other hand, is expressed in the abstract, because it is represented as "taken away from" the bodies in which it was originally known, and as standing by itself. Briefly, a form or act or perfection expressed as just in itself is taken in the abstract; expressed as in its subject, it is taken in the concrete. All the immediate objects of human cognition are sensible things. These, as is shown in natural philosophy, consist of forms in a subject or matter. Forms or acts or perfections, then, are immediately known by us as in the concrete. But the human mind is able to consider the act or perfection just in itself, apart from the subject, as has been seen in the cases of whiteness and being. The mind can think of them in the abstract. The being that the mind immediately apprehends through judgment is always in a subject. That subject is anything whatsoever. Named from the being that is found in it, a thing is called a being, just as Khrushchev is called a man from the humanity that is found in him.

---

[6] ". . . that universal being by which everything formally is." St Thomas, *De Ente et Essentia*, c. V; ed. Roland-Gosselin (reprint, Paris, 1948), p. 38.1. Cf. below, n. 16, and Epilogue, nn. 11–21.

[7] See Hegel, *Logik*, no. 87; Robin G. Collingwood, *An Essay on Metaphysics* (Oxford, 1940), p. 15. Cf. Gerald B. Phelan: "Those who, in spite of all, have tried to look upon being naked and unadorned have been struck with intellectual blindness. And those who have attempted to express it in clear and distinct ideas have sinned against intelligence . . ." *Saint Thomas and Analogy* (Milwaukee, 1941), p. 8.

Being, therefore, is originally known in the concrete but can also be conceived in the abstract. Conceptualized in the concrete, it denotes a subject that exists, a being. In this sense a tree or a stone is a being. In the abstract, it signifies the existential act that is possessed by the tree or the stone or any other such being. In a word, it can designate either subject of being or act of being.[8] As has already been seen, being is ambiguous in regard to real being and cognitional being.[9] It now shows a further ambiguity or equivocity,[10] in its ability to mean either the subject that exists or the act that renders that subject existent. In English, the ambiguity is often not felt, since the indefinite article is used in so many instances where the subject is meant. Expressions like "a human being," and "a thing is a being," leave no doubt that "being" refers to a subject. "A being" in ordinary language would never mean the act of being. Similarly "beings" in the plural will always denote subjects that exist. Used without any article, "being" regularly denotes the act, though it can also mean in the concrete the collectivity of all beings, just as "humanity" can signify the totality of men. With the definite article, "being" can mean either subject or act. You can call a person the laziest being in the world, and you can speak of the being that is enjoyed by a tree. With certain indefinite particles like "any" and "whatsoever" it may be similarly ambiguous. In Scholastic Latin the ambiguity is much more noticeable.[11] "Existence," the alternative for "being," signifies in the abstract, though it may also in the concrete denote the totality; "existent," on the other hand, always signifies in the concrete.

Since metaphysics studies beings insofar as they are beings, it will have being in the concrete as its subject. Common being, then, when it expresses the subject of metaphysics,[12] is taken in the concrete.

[8] St Thomas, *In Boeth. de Hebd.*, c. II; ed. Mandonnet, *Opusc.* (Paris, 1927), I, 171–172. On "esse abstractum" as God, see *De Subst. Sep.* (tr. Lescoe), c. XIII, 71.

[9] See above, Chapter 2, p. 40.

[10] St Thomas, *In IX Metaph.*, lect. 3, no. 1982; cf. *Quodl.*, II, 3c (Latin *ens*). The term "equivocity" in traditional Scholastic usage, as established by Boethius, *In Cat. Aristotelis*, I (PL, LXIV 163C–167A), is not restricted to "equivocals by chance," but extends also to the cases where things have the same name by analogy or by reference. Cf. below, Chapter 6, nn. 13–15.

[11] The ambiguity apparent in the use of the participle *ens* (see above, n. 10) holds likewise for the use of the infinitive form *esse*; see St Thomas, *In I Sent.*, d. 33, q. 1, a. 1, ad 1m; ed. Mandonnet, I, 766; and *In III Sent.*, d. 6, q. 2, a. 2, Resp.; ed. M. F. Moos (Paris, 1933), III, 238. Though acknowledging the accepted use of *esse* to denote a thing's nature (like the French *être* in *un être humain* and the Italian *essere* in *un essere umano*), St Thomas in his own usage regularly takes the infinitive *esse* as meaning the act of being. In repeating Aristotelian or Boethian clichés, though, he may sometimes leave it in the traditional meaning.

[12] See St Thomas, *In Metaph.*, Proem.; *In Boeth. de Trin.*, V, 1, ad 7m (ed. Wyser, p. 30.42). When the subject of metaphysics is expressed in the formula "being qua

Non-generic Character of Being. Ordinarily, common concepts are specific or generic. If individuals like Parmenides, Brutus, Nero, Beethoven, Stalin, and so on, are considered by the mind just according to what they have in common, the specific notion "man" is established. All the individual characteristics of each are left out of consideration. This process of considering things according to what they have in common while leaving out of consideration all that is not common to them, is technically called **"abstraction."** An object of consideration in those things is as it were "taken away from" all non-common traits and details. The things are considered apart from the non-common characteristics. If the consideration does not cut off or expressly exclude the non-common characteristics, it is abstraction **without precision.** The notion "man" leaves individual traits out of consideration, but it does not cut them off or exclude them. Accordingly, "man" can be predicated of any individual man, for it excludes nothing that is in the individual. You can say "Socrates is a man." The identity required for this predication is unharmed by abstraction without precision. But abstraction may also take place **with precision.** It then explicitly cuts oft or excludes or prescinds from the non-common characteristics. What is common to all individual men now appears as "humanity," taken in the abstract as the form or perfection that makes individuals men. It is not exactly the substantial form. This is isolated in natural philosophy, and it is received into a really distinct subject, physical matter. "Humanity," on the other hand, includes both the physical matter and form, but as taken in the abstract. Its subject is the man, while the subject of the substantial form is the physical matter. Humanity or human nature, therefore, is conceived as the formal part of the concrete man. Since it is conceived as a part, it cannot be predicated of the individual. You cannot say "Socrates is humanity, or human nature," any more than you can say "A man is a nose." A man has a nose, and Socrates has human nature. The part does not have complete identity with the subject as required for strict predication.

What is abstracted without precision, then, does not exclude anything from which it abstracts. It includes all, though implicitly and indeterminately. It remains the whole thing. Such abstraction may therefore be called the **abstraction of a whole.** "Man" signifies the whole Socrates or

---

being" or "beings qua beings," the term "being" is similarly understood in the concrete; cf.: "But the first philosopher treats of things in so far as they are beings. . . ." In *VII Metaph.*, lect. 13, no. 1576; "But the primary science is about these in so far as they are beings. . . ." *In XI Metaph.*, lect. 4, no. 2209. Cf. *ibid.*, no. 2208.

the whole Plato, but leaves the individuation of each undetermined. Hence it may be identified with either in predication, as a whole with a whole. Socrates is a man, Plato is a man. What is abstracted with precision, on the other hand, is conceived as only a part, the formal part. The other part is the subject from which it is abstracted, as man is the subject of humanity. This abstraction may accordingly be called the **abstraction of a form,**[13] since it conceives the form as taken away from the subject.

The generic natures are likewise abstracted from the specific either without or with precision. If what is common to man, horse, ox, and so on, is considered apart from, but without exclusion of, the specific differentiae, it is conceived as a whole that is completely identical in reality with each of its species and each of its individuals, even though it does not express any of their differentiae. You can therefore say that man is an animal and that any individual man is an animal. It is again a case of a whole that is identical with a whole, and so allows predication. On the other hand, that generic nature may be abstracted with precision and be conceived as "animality." It is then conceived as a part, and so cannot be predicated as identical with the whole individual or species. You cannot say that a man is animality, even though he is an animal. The higher genera can similarly be abstracted in both ways. Strictly, the species and genera are abstracted without precision, like "man" and "animal." "Humanity" and "animality," as abstracted with precision, are rather the formal principles of the species and the genus.

Since it is the whole, the genus contains its differentiae implicitly and indeterminately. It is the whole conceived as undetermined by any of its specific differentiae. Each differentia is likewise the whole thing, now conceived as determining itself to its specific nature. Genus and differentia unite therefore in the species as whole with whole. But the genus may also be considered as the subject that is determined by the differentia. Their relation then is no longer that of whole to whole, but of subject to quality.[14] Regarded in this way, the differentiae lie outside their genus and are not contained by it.

As one ascends through ever wider predicates of a thing, one finally comes to the widest predicate of all, being. It can be predicated in one way or another of everything. Is it therefore a genus, the highest genus

[13] For the terms *abstractio totius* and *abstractio formae*, see St Thomas, *In Boeth. de Trin.*, V, 3c; ed. Wyser, p. 40.19–21. Cf. *De Ente et Essentia*, c. II; ed. Roland-Gosselin, pp. 11.9–23.7. Cajetan, *In De Ente et Essentia*, ed. P. M.-H. Laurent (Turin, 1934), p. 6 (no. 5), uses the terms "total abstraction" and "formal abstraction," with change in meaning.

[14] See St Thomas, *In VII Metaph.*, lect. 12, nos. 1542–1559; *In X Metaph.*, lect. 10, nos. 2114–2116.

of all? Genera, as has been seen, are established by abstraction, which is cognition in the order of simple apprehension. Being, on the contrary, is not known originally through simple apprehension but through judgment. Unlike a genus, it is not first reached by abstraction, even though it may later be conceptualized not only in the concrete but also in the abstract. Moreover, a genus does not contain its differentiae insofar as they are its specific qualities. But being does contain all its differentiae even in their determining function. If they did not exist they could not determine.[15] Unlike a genus, consequently, being does not have a content in inverse ratio to its extension. Since in its own way it contains all differentiating notes, it has the richest content as well as the widest range.

Common being, therefore, is not a generic concept. Rather, it is supergeneric. It is above all the supreme genera, and unites them all in its embrace. Conceptualized in the concrete, it is predicated of them all, for everything is a being. As an act, it is predicated even of its own differentiae in their qualitative aspect, for to differentiate they have to exist. It is the most common predicate of all. But though the fact is apparent, the difficulty remains. Being, as originally apprehended in sensible things, is highly individualized in time and place. It presents no common nature[16] that the mind at once could conceptualize as in the case of species and genera. Yet it is conceptualized by the mind as common. What basis does it offer for this conceptualization? The answer will have to be sought in an investigation of the nature of being, an investigation to be carried out in the ensuing chapters.

Conceptual Distinction. Enough is clear from this study of the conceptualization of being, however, to show that thing and being are at least two distinct concepts. A "thing" is conceived as subject, "being" is conceived primarily as an act. The concept of "thing" is obtained originally through simple apprehension, that of "being" conceptualizes an act originally grasped through judgment.[17]

Being

[15] See Aristotle, *Metaph.*, B 3, 998b22–27; H 6, 1045b1–7.

[16] St Thomas (*In I Sent.*, d. 19, q. 5, a. 2, ad lm; ed. Mandonnet, I, 492) does refer to being (*ens*), understood in the concrete, as a "common nature" that is present in things in various degrees of perfection. It is constituted by an act that is found as a nature in its primary instance only, and in every other thing as an act other than the thing's nature. Being (*ens*) that is divided into substance and accident, i.e., being as understood in the concrete, is also called a common aspect (*ratio* — *De Malo*, VII, 1, ad lm; ed. Bazzi-Pession, II, 566b) that is found perfectly in one instance and in lesser degrees in others.

[17] Maritain, using the English "being" for "that which exists or is able to exist," i.e., for being in the concrete, and taking "existence" for the being that is originally grasped in judgment, describes as subsequent the formation of the "concept or notion of existence." *Existence and the Existent* (New York, 1948), pp. 27–28, n. 13 (3).

Even when being is taken in the concrete, and so is conceived as "a being," it adds the notion of the act that is attained through judgment. "Thing" and "being," therefore, are conceptually distinct. Whether or not their distinction is more than just conceptual, but is found in reality. independently of the mind's conceptualization, is still an open question. The investigation so far has established only that they are at least conceptually distinct. Does the distinction of concepts reflect a deeper dis-

---

The generic and specific common nature, on the other hand, is constituted by a form that functions as nature in all its instances. On the Thomistic common nature in its historical setting, see J. Owens, "Common Nature: A Point of Comparison between Thomistic and Scotistic Metaphysics," *Mediaeval Studies*, XIX (1957) 1–14.

When abstracted without precision, a specific or generic common nature remains understood in the concrete. In the expression "abstracted without precision," "abstract" is not used in a sense that is opposed to "concrete," for it means "abstraction of a whole," with none of the concretizing elements excluded. Rather, what is abstracted without precision coincides with what is understood in the concrete. This coincidence of "abstracted without precision" with "understood in the concrete" is important for locating the subject of a science. As the subject of metaphysics, "being" (*ens*) is abstracted from its determinations without precision, yet it is clearly understood in the concrete. E.g., no other science treats "of being absolutely understood (*de ente simpliciter*), that is, of being in common, nor even of any particular being insofar as it is a being. . . . For it belongs properly to the metaphysician to treat of any being at all, insofar as it is a being." St Thomas, *In VI Metaph.*, lect. 1, no. 1147. Cf. other texts cited above, n. 12. In this sense of "abstraction of a whole," that is, of abstraction from determinations and individuation without excluding them, abstraction is required in metaphysics as in any other science: "A denial that metaphysics proceeds by means of abstraction would be tantamount to the denial that it is a science . . ." E. C. Garvey, "The Role of Metaphysics in a Catholic Liberal College," *Proceedings of the American Catholic Philosophical Association*, XXX (1956), 92. It is an abstraction that leaves as the subject of metaphysics "being in the concrete."

Being as understood in the abstract constitutes things as beings in the concrete: ". . . being (*esse*) itself is common to all. And in this way things that are from God are likened to him, insofar as they are beings (*entia*), as to the first and universal source of all being (*esse*)." St Thomas, *ST*, I, 4, 3c. "Beings" in the expression "insofar as they are beings" is understood in the concrete. From Suarez (see *Disp. Metaph.*, II, 2, 16; ed. Vivès, XXV, 75b) on, "abstraction" and "precision" have been generally identified in Scholastic circles in a way that tends to understand "being" in the expression "insofar as it is being" as though it meant "being in the abstract." The result is that metaphysics has been regarded as dealing with abstractions, instead of with concrete things. The twofold sense of "abstract" has to be kept carefully in mind. In one sense it excludes the concrete, in another sense it does not. What is abstracted can be taken in the concrete (i.e., abstracted without precision) as well as in the abstract (i.e., abstracted with precision). The notion "abstract" is accordingly ambiguous.

On the all-inclusive content of being, cf.: "Since its comprehension does not involve any particular determination opposed to other determinations, the idea of being does not have a circumscribed or limited content . . ." F. Van Steenberghen, *Epistemology*, tr. M. J. Flynn (New York, 1949), p. 187. "Instead of being the emptiest and most abstract of all notions, it is the richest, for everything which *is* — either material or immaterial — is implicitly included in its content . . ." L. J. Eslick, "What is the Starting Point of Metaphysics?" *The Modern Schoolman*, XXXIV (1957), 259.

tinction that is present in the thing apart from the human mind's activity? In a word, is there a real distinction between a thing that exists in the real world and the existential act by which it so exists? To serve as the viewpoint for a metaphysical study of things, must "being" appear isolated from "thing" not only on the basis of two distinct concepts, but also as really other than the real thing it actuates? Does the conceptual distinction, then, arise merely from the way the human mind knows beings, or is it based upon a distinction present in the thing independently of human cognition?

Résumé. Being, though not originally attained by human cognition through a concept in simple apprehension, is subsequently conceptualized, spontaneously and vaguely as something, technically as an act or perfection. So conceptualized it has the universality required for the subject of a science. The universality, however, is super-generic, allowing it to be applied in different ways to its various instances, both in the abstract and in the concrete. Yet no proper concept of being can ever be formed in this way. The concept remains the concept of act or of perfection, a concept originating in the formal perfections known through simple apprehension. The concept is appropriated to being only through further description, for instance as the act of all acts and the perfection of all perfections. To retain proper content it has to be kept focused on being that is apprehended through judgment.

SUGGESTED READINGS AND REFERENCES

St Thomas Aquinas, *De Ente et Essentia*, cc. I–III; tr. Armand Maurer, *On Being and Essence* (Toronto: Pontifical Institute of Mediaeval Studies, 1949), pp. 26–42. In the English translation of the title, "Being" is taken in the concrete; see tr. Maurer, p. 26, n. 1. It means "that which is," i.e., either the collectivity of beings or any individual thing that exists.

Edward D. Simmons, "In Defense of Total and Formal Abstraction," *The New Scholasticism*, XXIX (1955), 427–440.

L. Ferrari, "'Abstractio Totius' and 'Abstractio Totalis,'" *The Thomist*, XXIV (1961), 72–89.

CHAPTER 5

Accidentality and Priority of Being

Natures and Being. When you say of anything that it is a being, you predicate being in the concrete, without prescinding from any of the thing's generic, specific, or individual determinations. You say that a man is a being just as you say that he is an animal. You are using a predicate that contains implicitly and indeterminately all the narrower perfections of the subject. So far no special difficulty arises. But if through mere simple apprehension you try to prescind being from all generic and specific perfections, you get a notion equivalent to that of nothing. You have no content left. Yet, as was seen in the last chapter, being has to contain all its differentiae even in their determining function. In the abstract, then, being should contain all other perfections. Instead of lacking content, it should have all content. How can it be attained by the human intellect in a way that satisfies this requirement? Humanity and animality and the other specific and generic aspects may be prescinded from their subject and retain their proper content. But no content at all is yielded by immediately prescinding being from the thing that exists.

On the other hand, may a thing be abstracted from its being, and nevertheless retain its content? May what is grasped through simple apprehension in a tree, for example, be considered in abstraction from any existence it may happen to possess? The nature of a tree may have real being in a pine in front of a house, and in any number of other trees in a park or in the woods. It may also have cognitional being in your mind as you think of it, and in innumerable other minds. Of itself, consequently, the nature of a tree cannot include in a determined way any particular existence it may have. If of itself it were determined to be in the tree in front of the house, it could never have being anywhere else. But the nature of a tree, as known through simple apprehension, is not determined or limited to any one of those ways of being. Likewise, it does not of itself exclude any of them. It remains open to them all. Accordingly, it abstracts from them all. But does it prescind from them?

If it could prescind from them, it would exclude itself from being. It would thereby make itself not just actually nothing, but literally nothingness, even in the sense that it could not be given being in cognition. Such precision is impossible. Abstracting from all the ways in which it may be, a sensible thing has of itself no determination either to be or not to be in any one of them. It contains nothing that would exclude one rather than another. All sensible things, therefore, abstract from all their ways of being without prescinding from any of them.[1]

The consequence of this situation is that no knowledge of any sensible thing's nature will lead to knowledge of its existence.[2] You can know what a phoenix or a whooping crane or a unicorn or a dinosaur is, whether or not any exist in reality or in anybody else's mind at the moment. You

[1] "It is false to say that the nature of man as such exists in this individual man, because, if existing in this individual belonged to man as man, it would never exist outside this individual. Similarly, if it belonged to man as man not to exist in this individual, human nature would never exist in it. It is true to say, however, that it does not belong to man as man to exist in this or that individual, or in the intellect. Considered in itself, the nature of man thus clearly abstracts from every act of existing, but in such a way that none may be excluded from it." St Thomas, *De Ente et Essentia*, c. III (ed. Roland-Gosselin), p. 26.1–10; tr. A. Maurer (Toronto, 1949), p. 40. The reason why the nature does not prescind from any particular act of being is implied in the consideration that the nature of man as such does not require non-existence in any designated singular of the species.

This argument from abstraction does not as yet show any real distinction between a sensible thing's nature and its being. The reasoning applies in corresponding fashion to nature and individual. Human nature as such abstracts from Chaucer, Shakespeare, Milton, Tennyson, Browning, and all other individuals. It does not contain explicitly in its notion any individuating principles. If the unity of an individual belonged to it as human nature, it could never be found in any other individual: "Similarly, if unity were contained in its concept, then Socrates' and Plato's nature would be one and the same, and it could not be multiplied in many individuals." *De Ente*, c. III (ed. Roland-Gosselin), p. 25.2–4; tr. Mauer, p. 40. Human nature absolutely considered abstracts accordingly from the individual as it abstracts from being. But that does not at all mean that there is a real distinction between nature and individuality. The two cases differ of course insofar as nature taken in the abstract can prescind from individuality but it cannot prescind from being. "Humanity" prescinds from individuality and still remains an object of consideration; but it could not prescind from being without making itself nothingness and doing away with itself as an object. Another difference in the two cases, as will be seen later, is the requirement of efficient causality for the actualization of nature by being.

[2] "Now, every essence or quiddity can be understood without anything being known of its existing. I can know what a man or a phoenix is and still be ignorant whether it exists in reality. From this it is clear that the act of existing is other than essence or quiddity, unless, perhaps, there is a being whose quiddity is its very act of existing." St Thomas, *De Ente*, c. IV (ed. Roland-Gosselin), p. 34.10–16; tr. Maurer, p. 46. This otherness of nature and being is still not established as a real distinction. It is based as yet merely on abstraction without precision, as noted above, n. 1. The same reasoning would hold for the distinction between nature and individual. You can understand what human nature is without having any explicit knowledge of the individual differences found in Socrates or the Platonic Timaeus.

know that they exist in your own mind, but you know this through a judgment of existence and not through anything seen in the natures themselves. But are not the specific natures of sensible things impenetrable to human intellection?[3] Could not their determinate being pertain to what the intellect misses in their natures? No, the generic knowledge of them as bodies, according to the above reasoning, shows sufficiently in each instance that no one of them is determined of itself to any particular act of existing. This consideration will hold for any sensible thing, regardless of its species.

If being were in the nature of anything, moreover, it would allow only one instance of that nature as a nature. Since being contains all its own differences, it would endow that nature with all possible differentiations and perfections. It would leave no generic or specific or individual determinations by which the nature could be pluralized.[4] It alone, consequently, would be the nature. Did not Parmenides, at the very beginning of Western metaphysics, show in his reasoning that if being is considered as a nature it absorbs everything else into itself and renders itself the one sole existent? This consideration universalizes the tenet that a nature does not contain its being in any determined way, with the only possible exception of a unique being in which all perfections would be contained.

Being, then, could pertain to the nature of one thing only. In all other things, and definitely in all things found in genera and species like sensible things, being lies outside the thing's nature. As only sensible things are immediately knowable to men, they will have to provide the means of demonstrating whether the one thing in which being is nature actually

[3] "But even in the case of sensible things the essential differences themselves are unknown to us; hence, we have to signify them by the accidental differences which arise from the essential, as we designate a cause by its effect. *Biped*, for instance, is given as the difference of man." St Thomas, *De Ente*, c. V (ed. Roland-Gosselin), p. 40.6–10; tr. Maurer, p. 52. A list of other passages where this doctrine occurs in St Thomas is given by Roland-Gosselin, *ad loc.*, n. 2. Cf. Locke's teaching that the real essences of bodies are unknown, *Essay concerning Human Understanding*, III, 3, 18; ed. Fraser, II, 28–29. See also *ibid.*, IV, 12, 8–9; II, 347–348.

[4] "And there can be only one such being, the First Being. For nothing can be multiplied except: (1) through the addition of some difference, as the generic nature is multiplied into species; or (2) by the form being received in different parts of matter, as the specific nature is multiplied in different individuals . . . But, should there exist some being which is simply the act of existing, so that the act of existing be itself subsistent, a difference cannot be added to this act of existing. Otherwise, it would not be purely and simply the act of existing, but the act of existing plus a certain form. Much less can matter be added to it, because then it would not be a subsistent, but a material, act of existing. So we conclude that there can only be one such being which is its very act of existing." St Thomas, *De Ente*, c. IV (ed. Roland-Gosselin), p. 34.16–30; tr. Maurer, p. 46. In "an act of existing plus a certain form," the form would be what existed; i.e., the act of being would no longer subsist.

exists. If that unique thing should exist in reality, it would mean that being is a real nature. In it real being and a real nature would be identical. This would show that being, as an act, is real, and so is a really different perfection from the nature of a sensible thing. For the present, however, the non-inclusion of being, in any determined way, merely shows that it is not grasped in what simple apprehension reaches in a thing. This distinction between being and thing has in fact been regarded as merely conceptual,[5] like the distinction between nature and individual. But at least it lays the groundwork for further investigation.

Accidentality of Being. Whatever there is in a thing outside its nature belongs to it accidentally. Since being lies outside the natures of sensible things, it will accrue to them only in accidental fashion. But the philosophical notion of accident has wide as well as narrow senses. In a narrow sense it denotes the nine categories listed after substance in the Aristotelian logic. In a wide sense it means whatever is not part of the thing's nature,[6] whether or not it belongs to a different Aristotelian category. Being is explicitly not an Aristotelian category, for it is not a supreme genus.[7] It is therefore not an accident in the narrow sense. All predicamental accidents presuppose the substantial nature in which they inhere. But without its being, that nature would be nothing. The nature of a sensible thing cannot be imagined as already there in priority to its being and receiving its being as it receives color or hardness or quantity or other predicamental accidents. Rather, it has to presuppose its being, somewhat as it itself is presupposed by its predicamental accidents. Being is clearly not an accident in the predicamental sense.

Is it then a predicable[8] accident, or could it be a property that flows necessarily from the nature though it is not part of the nature? Risibility in man, for instance, is regarded as following necessarily upon human nature even though it is not one of the parts that constitute man's nature. Human nature consists of generic animality and specific rationality. They

outside Nature

[5] E.g., by Suarez, *Disp. Metaph.*, XXXI, 6, 15; ed. Vivès, XXVI, 246b. On the incomplete character of the argument from abstraction and its continuity with what follows in *De Ente*, see Cornelio Fabro, *La Nozione Metafisica di Partecipazione* (2nd ed. Turin, 1950), pp. 218–219. See also Norman J. Wells, "Suarez, Historian and Critic of the Modal Distinction Between Essential Being and Existential Being," *The New Scholasticism*, XXXVI (1962), 419–444.

[6] "An accident means in a wide sense everything that is not part of the essence; and such is the character of being in created things . . ." St Thomas, *Quodl.*, XII, 5. Cf.: "Whatever is in anything apart from its essence, is in it accidentally." *Comp. Theol.*, c. LXVI.

[7] ". . . since being is not a genus, it is not the essence of anything." Aristotle, *APo.*, II 7, 92b13–14; Oxford tr.

[8] On this distinction of accident from property, see Aristotle, *Top.*, I 5, 101b38 ff.; Boethius, *In Porphyr. Comm.*, Lib. IV (*PL*, LXIV, 130C–134B).

are its parts. Risibility is not one of them. Upon rationality and animality, however, there follows the radical capacity to laugh. Intelligence gives the power to see the incongruous, and the disposition of specifically human[9] organs allows the reaction of laughter. Accordingly risibility is looked upon as a property consequent upon human nature even though it does not form part of the nature. Such a property, of course, is in no way really distinct from the nature. It is only conceptually distinct.

Could being, though not a part of any sensible thing's nature, nevertheless flow from that nature as a property? Could the nature of a sensible thing require that it be, just as human nature requires radical risibility? The difficulty again lies in the priority of being to sensible nature. If a thing were conceived in priority to its being, it would be conceived as nothing. How, then, could it make itself be? It just would not be there to cause its own being. A property follows upon a nature in the order of formal causality,[10] as the equality of its angles to two right angles follows upon the nature of a Euclidean triangle. The nature is presupposed as already there, as having its being, and the property is then regarded as flowing from it. But if being were regarded as a property of the nature, there would be nothing there from which such being could flow! The type of causality required for being is strikingly different. It is not a question of providing a ground upon which some property logically follows when both are already there in being, as risibility is already there in anyone

[9] Since here as elsewhere the specific differences remain unknown (above, n. 3), there is no way of deducing the character of these organs from the definition of man. In that definition the difference "rational" is known from effects rather than from the nature itself. Cf.: ". . . because the substantial differences of things are unknown to us, in their stead those who give definitions sometimes use accidental characteristics, in so far as these designate or make known the essence as proper effects make known a cause . . . and it is likewise in regard to reason, or to what consists in having mind." St Thomas, *De Ver.*, X, 1, ad 6m. "For frequently the substantial differences are taken from accidents instead of substantial forms, which become known through such accidents, as 'twofooted' and 'ambulatory,' and the like; and in this way also 'sensible' and 'rational' are placed as substantial differences." *De Spir. Creat.*, a. 11, ad 3m.

[10] The four types of cause — material, formal, efficient, final — were treated of by Aristotle (*Ph.*, II 3–7, 194b16 ff) in the context of natural philosophy. They received these names in Peripatetic tradition. A special Scholastic treatise on the causes was built up in the seventeenth century by writers like John of St Thomas (1589–1644), *Phil. Nat.*, Pars I, qq. 10–13, and Antoine Goudin (1630–1695), *Physica*, Pars I, disp. 1 & 2. Suarez, *Disp. Metaph.*, XII–XXVII, had given this treatment under metaphysics, and in Neoscholastic manuals it may be found in metaphysics, e.g., Joseph Gredt, *Elementa Philosophiae Aristotelico-Thomisticae*, 7th ed. (Freiburg i. Breisgau, 1937), II, 145–183. On account of its original setting in the physical doctrine of matter and form, its systematic treatment seems better left to natural philosophy. Its metaphysical aspects can be investigated as they are encountered in the course of the present inquiry. For the four causes in natural philosophy, see Francis Collingwood, *Philosophy of Nature* (Englewood Cliffs, N. J., 1961), pp. 139–168, 217–249.

who has human nature. It is a question of making that basic nature be, when it is not already there in being.

Making something be, when it did not exist before, is technically called **efficient causality.** The term is none too happy a choice,[11] but it is traditional and customary. Efficient causality itself is too primal to describe except in relation to its term, being.[12] It is the production of being, it is making a thing be. It is experienced as one thinks one's thoughts and makes one's decisions or other acts of volition.[13] They are new acts, and one experiences bringing them into being. One sees other new things appear in being, it is true, for instance the phenomena of combustion that result from the striking of a match. But in such cases one does not experience or perceive the efficient causality itself by which the new being was caused. What is clear, however, is that being, if caused, comes through efficient causality and not through formal causality. In the exercise of formal causality the being of the nature is presupposed. Its being is prior to any formal causality exercised by the nature and so cannot be the result of such formal causality. Being, therefore, cannot present itself as the property of any nature. As a predicable, it is an accident and not a property.

Priority of Being. The priority of being to all sensible natures emerges sharply enough from the foregoing considerations. If its being were not presupposed, there would be no nature. It would be nothing. But does not being consist in the composition of the nature's parts, as has been emphasized so strongly in a preceding chapter? Does it not arise from the composition of the principles of the nature, and follow upon those principles? How can this be, if the parts themselves presuppose their being? Yet they have to presuppose their being, or they just would not be there to enter into any composition.

This touches one of the most difficult points in the whole problem of being, and demands exceptionally careful thought. The being of sensible things has to be understood as a composition, in the sense of an active composing. It is not a composition that adds any new object of simple

[11] The term "efficient" implies a making *out of* some material. It does not carry in philosophy the connotations of its use in ordinary language. The Aristotelian term was *poiêtikon*, literally rendered perhaps by the obsolete English word "factive."

[12] "It pertains to everything to have an agent cause in so far as it has being." St Thomas, *ST*, I, 44, 1, ad 3m. In Aristotle, efficient cause was regularly defined in terms of motion. It was understood as the cause that originated motion.

[13] The experience of efficient causality is immediate in regard to only the internal acts of cognition and volition. Neoscholastic attempts to generalize these particular experiences into a universal and necessary "principle of causality" have not been convincing; e.g., A. Pechhacker, "Zur Begründung des Kausalprinzips," *Scholastik*, XXV (1950), 529–532.

apprehension whatsoever. It does not consist in such a predicamental relation or order of parts, or in any new aspect added to the thing's nature. From the standpoint of what is attainable through simple apprehension or conceptualization it adds nothing, but consists in composing the nature's parts and is as it were constituted by those principles of the nature. In one way it is undoubtedly determined by the nature it makes be, for the being of a man is different, for instance, from the being of a horse.[14] From that viewpoint the thing's being may be regarded as arising from its nature and as following upon its nature. But these are all secondary aspects under which being is conceptualized. None of them expresses the deepest character of being. What is apprehended first and foremost in being is conceptualized under the aspect of act or perfection. Being is the basic actuality of the thing, the act of all its acts and the perfection of all its perfections. This aspect is therefore that of actuality without qualification, actuality absolutely.[15] It is indeed a composing, and it is determined to a particular nature; but these are only secondary and concomitant aspects. As an existential composing it is absolutely prior in actuality to the nature it makes be. Kant's penetrating thought manifested the priority of synthesis to conceptualization.[16] But, directed by over a

---

[14] "Thirdly, because all the things that are in the one genus communicate in the quiddity or essence of the genus . . . But they differ in being: for the being of a man is not the same as the being of a horse, nor the being of this man and of that man." St Thomas, *ST*, I, 3, 5c. Cf. below, Chapter 7, nn. 6–9.

[15] "And therefore he says that this verb 'is' consignifies composition, because it does not signify it principally, but by way of consequence; for it signifies primarily that which goes with the notion in the manner of actuality without condition. For 'is,' understood absolutely, signifies 'to be in act'; and therefore it signifies in the fashion of a verb. But because the actuality which this verb 'is' principally signifies is in general the actuality of every form or act, substantial or accidental, it follows that when we wish to signify that any form or act whatsoever is actually in a subject, we signify it by this verb 'is,' either absolutely or in a certain respect; absolutely, in the present time, but in a certain respect in other times. And therefore this verb 'is' consignifies composition, by way of consequence." St Thomas, *In I Periherm.*, lect. 5, no. 22. The aspect of composition that takes place in time, therefore, is consignified by the verb "to be." The most basic actuality is primary in its notion. When the verb is used as a copula this aspect remains predominant, as stated in the foregoing quotation from St Thomas. Cf.: "The problem is not to know how *is* has come to signify existence, it is rather to know why it has been singled out to play the part of copula. . . . In short, *is* has correctly been chosen as a copula because all judgments of attribution are meant to say *how* a certain thing actually *is*." E. Gilson, *Being and Some Philosophers* (Toronto, 1949), pp. 199–200.

[16] "It will easily be observed that this action is originally one and is equipollent for all combination, and that its dissolution, namely, *analysis*, which appears to be its opposite, yet always presupposes it. For where the understanding has not previously combined, it cannot dissolve, since only as having been combined *by the understanding* can anything that allows of analysis be given to the faculty of representation." Kant, *Critique of Pure Reason*, B 130; tr. Norman Kemp Smith. Cf.: "Consequently

century of Cartesian introspection as the starting point of philosophy,[17] Kant failed to see that this cognitional synthesis was originally the apprehension of being in its synthesizing priority there in the sensible thing itself outside the mind.

The priority of being to nature is nevertheless an outstanding instance of the truth in Bergson's reflection that metaphysical thinking goes against the natural bent of human intellection.[18] Man's is a sensible nature and he thinks in terms of sensible natures. It is through sensible natures that he has to understand being, as best he can. In their own order these natures are basic. They are the substances, all else follows upon them in role of subsequent accidents. The notion that there is an accident prior to substance in sensible things is repellent to the ingrained human way of thinking. Yet the effort has to be made for the metaphysical understanding of existence. Not substance, but an accident, being, is absolutely basic in sensible things. This has to be understood, however, in a way that does not make being function as the substance. Strictly, it is not the being that is there, but the substance that has the being. The nature cannot take on an adverbial relation to its being. Man cannot be regarded as basically a certain portion of being that exists humanly, or a horse as another portion of being that exists equinely. The man and the horse are not portions of being, but are substances that have being. They, and not their being, have to be expressed substantively, even though their being is prior to their natures. Not the subject, but the predicate, is absolutely basic.

Neither the accidentality nor the priority of being immediately shows any real distinction between being and thing. On the basis of the reasoning so far, they might still be really identical though conceptually distinct. Being could appear as an aspect that was accidental and prior to the aspect of nature, without involving any distinction in the thing itself independently of human thought.

Cause of Being. Nevertheless, the combined accidentality and priority of being raise the question of the real dependence of the thing's being upon something else. What is accidental is dependent upon something. It is not there just in its own right. By its very nature

---

it must previously be thought in synthetic unity with other (though, it may be, only possible) representations, before I can think it in the analytic unity of consciousness, which makes it a *conceptus communis*." *Ibid.*, B 134, note.

[17] See Kant, *Prolegomena to any Future Metaphysic*, 9 (43). Text above, "Historical Introduction," n. 30.

[18] See Bergson, *Introduction to Metaphysics*, tr. T. E. Hulme, ed. Thomas A. Goudge (New York, 1949), pp. 50–51; E. Gilson, *The Christian Philosophy of St. Thomas Aquinas* (New York, 1956), pp. 40–45.

it is dependent upon a substance. Being *in* a substance is not sufficient to constitute it an accident, even though an accident is always found in a substance. Eyes, heart, liver, are in an animal body but are not thereby constituted accidents. Aristotle, accordingly, when describing the notion of substance in the *Categories* (2, 1a24–25), was careful to give the preposition "in" the sense of entitative dependence. Being *in* a subject meant dependence on the subject in a way that prevented the accident from being at all outside the subject. It rendered impossible for it any being apart from the subject in which the accident inhered. An accident is a form or act that perfects a substance in a secondary way. It actuates the substance, though in accidental fashion. The substance, consequently, is in this respect a potency for the accidents. In Aristotelian doctrine the full entitative dependence of an accident is upon the substance it actuates. Such entitative dependence, for Aristotle, is sufficiently expressed by the preposition "in," if the preposition is given the sense assigned it in the second chapter of the *Categories*.

In a philosophy where being is regarded as significantly prior to natural substance, however, the situation becomes more complicated. This priority indicates that the basic dependence of existential act is not upon the subject it actuates. It may inhere *in* that subject, in the sense of actuating it. Nevertheless, it is accepted as prior to it. The primary dependence of existential act, therefore, is not expressed by the preposition "in," as it was for Aristotle. The substance upon which the act of being depends is not the substance that it makes be. It is prior to the substance in which it is found, is presupposed by that substance. It must depend upon another substance. This means that a sensible thing's being is dependent upon some other thing; that is, the thing is made to be by something else. To give being to something is to cause it through efficient causality. Accordingly, everything whose being is other than its nature is produced by an efficient cause that is other than itself.[19] It has its being from something else. Nothing can produce itself or bring itself into being.

[19] "But it is impossible that the act of existing be caused by a thing's form or its quiddity (I say *caused* as by an efficient cause); for then something would be the cause of itself and would bring itself into existence — which is impossible. Everything, then, which is such that its act of existing is other than its nature must needs have its act of existing from something else." St Thomas, *De Ente*, c. IV, ed. Roland-Gosselin, p. 35.6–11; tr. Maurer, p. 47. The latter sentence, introduced by an *ergo*, formulates the causal proposition, in the order of efficient causality. It is presented, not as a self-evident axiom, but as the conclusion of a long and difficult demonstration. In the order of formal causality a sequence may be self-evident, as in the structure of the syllogism. But the notion of a contingent being or of something that begins to exist does not immediately reveal any dependence upon an efficient cause. This was pointed out by Hume, *A Treatise of Human Nature*, I,

The accidentality and priority of being, therefore, show that everything not its own being has an efficient cause. Its being comes and is from another through efficient causality. But even this is not sufficient to establish a distinction in reality between a thing and its being. Many Christian thinkers, who readily admit that all things in the created world receive their being from God, and regard it as contingent to their natures, do not hesitate to deny any real distinction between those things and their being. Nor has the above reasoning presupposed any such real distinction. The distinction between being and nature required in the wording "everything whose being is other than its nature has its being from something else," need only be conceptual. Accidentality and priority endow being with sufficient otherness for the demonstration of the causal proposition, and the accidentality and priority, as has been seen, do not immediately make manifest any real distinction between a thing's being and its nature. No answer to the question of that real distinction, then, has as yet emerged from the reasoning.

External Cause. Are not the foregoing considerations, though, merely a highly complicated way of stating the obvious? How could a thing that comes into being account for its own existence? Is

---

3, 3, and in the Neoscholastic setting by the penetrating scrutiny of Joseph Geyser, *Das Prinzip vom zureichenden Grunde* (Regensburg, 1929), pp. 52–57. In the Aristotelian tradition axioms or principles emerged from sensible things as known. With Descartes (*Principia*, I, 48; A–T, VIII, 22.27–30), however, eternal truths were, as objects of cognition, basically distinguished from things. For Leibniz (*Monadology*, 31–32) our reasonings were based upon two of these principles, that of contradiction and that of sufficient reason. An application of the principle of sufficient reason to the world of contingent things gave the "principle of causality." Against this background the principle of causality was accepted by Neoscholastics as a self-evident axiom and as fundamental for philosophical reasoning. It still seems to be regarded as immediately self-evident by the great majority of Neoscholastic writers, in spite of the insuperable objections repeatedly brought against this stand for over half a century. On the general topic, see E. Gilson, "Les Principes et les Causes," *Revue Thomiste*, LII (1952), 39–63. On the introduction of the "principles-philosophy" into the Neoscholastic tradition, see J. E. Gurr, "Genesis and Function of Principles in Philosophy," *Proceedings of the American Catholic Philosophical Association*, XXIX (1955), 121–133; "Some Historical Origins of Rationalism in Catholic Philosophy Manuals." *Ibid.*, XXX (1956), 170–180.

The causal proposition in a metaphysical context is considerably different from what is understood by the principle of causality or the principle of causation in modern physical science, where it denotes the uniformity of nature. The meaning then is "same cause, same effect." See Mario Augusto Bunge, *Causality* (Cambridge, Mass., 1959), p. 4. This was expressed by St Thomas in the words: ". . . a natural agent acts in the same manner as long as it is disposed in the same way. . . ." *Comp. Theol.*, I, 97. Metaphysically, the causal proposition on the contrary bears upon the existence, not the nature, of the effect. It means that every finite thing or action, whether determined or free, has to have a cause of its being.

it not clearly dependent upon something else for its production, as common sense admits, and so for its reception of being? Plato had long ago formulated that common sense observation, in a context of probable reasoning. Whatever comes to be, he insisted, has to be made by a cause.[20] Yet the common sense basis, no matter how probable, is not sufficient to guarantee universality and necessity to the causal proposition. Except in your own internal acts of cognition and appetition, you do not experience the efficient causality. In other instances you see only the temporal succession. You do not see that they receive their being. You may see them begin, but you do not see their dependence on a cause. Moreover, in the case of hypothetical eternal beings, like the Aristotelian heavens or an angel without temporal beginning, there would be no such succession.

The notion of temporal beginning, therefore, is not sufficient as a means to trace a thing metaphysically to an efficient cause that is external to it. That the thing does not come from itself need not immediately guarantee that it comes from another. Why should the notion of "come from" be read into it at all?[21] The thing has to be analyzed in terms of nature and being, and the accidentality and priority of its being have to be shown. Only then can causal dependence upon an external agent be established universally and necessarily for all things whose nature is not their existence. Only then may the causal proposition function as a step to the further inquiry into the ultimate source of their being.

Résumé. Since the being of a sensible thing is *both* accidental and prior to the thing's nature, it is dependent on something external to the sensible thing itself. This is the same as saying that any sensible thing is caused efficiently by something other than itself. The being of a sensible thing, then, provides the means for reasoning to a cause external to the thing's own actualities.

SUGGESTED READINGS AND REFERENCES

St Thomas Aquinas, *On Being and Essence*, c. IV; tr. A. Maurer (Toronto: Pontifical Institute of Mediaeval Studies, 1949), pp. 43–47.

Francis Xavier Meehan, *Efficient Causality in Aristotle and St. Thomas* (Washington, D. C.: Catholic University of America Press, 1940).

[20] Plato, *Ti.*, 28AC; cf. *Phlb.*, 26E.

[21] See J. Geyser, *Das Prinzip vom zureichenden Grunde*, p. 54. On the Skeptical arguments against causes, see Sextus Empiricus, *Pyrrh. Hyp.*, I, 180–186; Diogenes Laertius, *Lives of Eminent Philosophers*, IX, 97–99. For discussions of modern notions of causality, see the papers in the *Causality* volume of *University of California Publications in Philosophy*, XV (1932).

Joseph Owens, "The Causal Proposition — Principle or Conclusion?" *The Modern Schoolman*, XXXII (1955), 159–171, 257–270, 323–339.
John Edwin Gurr, *The Principle of Sufficient Reason in Some Scholastic Systems 1750–1900* (Milwaukee: Marquette University Press, 1959).
Thomas O'Shaughnessy, "St. Thomas's Changing Estimate of Avicenna's Teaching on Existence as an Accident," *The Modern Schoolman*, XXXVI (1959), 245–260.

CHAPTER 6

Subsistent Being

First Cause. Every sensible thing, according to the reasoning of the last chapter, has its being from something else. In receiving existence it does not acquire any new nature or any addition in the order of nature. Just its own nature is made to be. Its nature, prior to the reception of being from an efficient cause, has no existence at all. Its nature, accordingly, cannot produce its own being. Its being is caused efficiently by an agent other than itself. If that agent in turn exists through an act of being that is accidental and prior to its own nature, it will similarly depend upon another agent for its proper being. It will be a caused cause, in the order of efficient causality. The series of causes will have to continue. Even an infinite regression of these caused causes, however, would not account for the least being in the world. In every instance and in all the instances together there would be only nature that contained no being, nature that merely remained open to receive being from something else. There would be an infinite series of existential zeros. They would never add up to any being at all. In their sum total they would remain from start to finish existentially zero.

This means that for any series of efficiently caused causes there is a first cause. It is first in the sense that it does not have its being from anything else. It has no efficient cause prior to itself. Accordingly it has no cause of its being whatsoever. It is an uncaused cause. Its being, therefore, is not prior to its nature but is simultaneous or coincident with it. Its being is not in any way accidental to its nature but is of its nature and in its nature. Its very nature is to be.[1] The first cause, consequently, is not

[1] "And since every being which exists through another is reduced, as to its first cause, to one existing in virtue of itself, there must be some being which is the cause of the existing of all things because it itself is the act of existing alone. If that were not so, we would proceed to infinity among causes, since, as we have said, every being which is not the act of existing alone has a cause of its existence. Evidently, then, an intelligence is form and act of existing, and it has its act of existing from the First Being which is simply the act of existing." St Thomas Aquinas, *De Ente et Essentia*, c. IV (ed. Roland-Gosselin), p. 35.11–18; tr. A. Maurer, p. 47.

contained within the series of caused causes. It is extrinsic to that series, somewhat as the mathematician remains outside the mathematical series he constructs. However, in the entire series of causes, caused and uncaused together, it is first in order.

Being as Substance. A nature that includes being, as seen in a previous chapter,[2] is itself being and nothing else. It is only being.[3] It expresses no other characteristic. Being, as a nature, absorbs everything else into itself.[4] Other things have being. They are expressed substantively, they are substances that exist. But no one of them is existence. Even though only a conceptual distinction is granted between them and their being — and so far no real distinction between their nature and their being has been established — their being is not explicitly included in their nature. If it were, their nature would be to exist. They could never perish, they could have no other determining characteristic, they could not be a plurality generically, specifically, nor individually. The first efficient cause, on the other hand, does include being in its nature, explicitly. This means that its whole nature is being. Here the substance that exists is being. It is therefore called **subsistent being.**

The technical term "subsistent being" is awkward and misleading. It is meant to signify that in this case being is the substance that exists. Philosophically, "subsistent" is closely connected with substance. "Substance," in its etymology, suggests "standing under," insofar as substance is conceived as sustaining its accidents. "Subsist," meaning "to stand still" or "to support," can hardly avoid the overtones of substance.[5] In regard to the first efficient cause, however, "subsistent" need only mean that here being does not function as an accident. It need not imply that accidents

[2] See above, Chapter 5, n. 4.

[3] St Thomas, *De Ente*, c. IV (ed. Roland-Gosselin), pp. 34.24 and 26; 35.14. 16 and 18; c. V, p. 38.8 and 13. This esse *tantum* is highly individualized by its own nature and is sharply distinguished from common being (*esse commune*), *De Ente*, c. V, p. 38.8–12; cf. *In I Sent.*, d. 8, q. 4, a. 1, ad 1m (ed. Mandonnet, I, 219); *De Pot.*, VII, 2, ad 6m; *CG*, I, 26; *ST*, I, 3, 4, ad 1m. "Common being" allows the addition of generic and specific concepts; the nature that is being alone, on the contrary, allows no such addition.

[4] "Similarly, although God is simply the act of existing, it is not necessary that He lack the other perfections or excellences. On the contrary, He possesses all perfections of all genera of beings; . . . But He possesses these perfections in a more excellent way than all things, for in Him they are one, while in other things they are diversified. The reason for this is that all these perfections are His according to His simple act of existing." St Thomas, *De Ente*, c. V (ed. Roland-Gosselin), p. 38.12–20; tr. Maurer, p. 51. Cf. *ST*, I, 13, 5c.

[5] Subsistence is the characteristic of substance somewhat as inherence is the characteristic of accidents. To subsist, accordingly, means to exist as a substance. Cf. below, Chapter 10, n. 12.

are supported by it or that grades of being are traversed before a halt is made. Though awkward, "subsistent being" seems nevertheless the best term available to describe philosophically the nature of the first efficient cause. It signifies that here the very being of the first cause is *what* exists. It denotes complete identity of being and nature. It allows no intrinsic conceptual distinction between the two, but only an extrinsic one based upon the distinction of being from nature in other things.

Being as Nature. To show that subsistent being really exists is to show that being is a nature in reality. In subsistent being nature and existence are identical. To establish the one is to establish the other. Demonstration reaches its real existence, which is its nature. Being, therefore, is established in this way as a real nature, and not just a conceptually distinct aspect of other natures.

This, however, does not imply that either the existence or the nature of subsistent being is grasped in itself. The existence of a piece of sulphur present in the real world before one's cognition is immediately apprehended through judgment, just as the sulphur's generic nature as a body is known through simple apprehension. Here both nature and being are attained in themselves. The atoms and electrons in the piece of sulphur, however, are not known in themselves but only in the immediately observable phenomena they cause. They are reached through the demonstrations of chemistry and modern physics, as regards both existence and definition. Correspondingly, the nature and existence of subsistent being are known by us not in themselves but in the truth of a proposition[6] that is the conclusion of a metaphysical demonstration from sensible things. We are sure of the truth of the proposition that subsistent being exists. Knowing in this way the existence of subsistent being we know to the same extent its nature. But that is quite different from the way in which we know the existence and the generic nature of a sensible thing. In the sense of direct and adequately proportioned knowledge, we know neither the nature nor the existence of subsistent being, for to know its existence is thereby to know its nature. The thorough identity of existence with nature in this case is far from immediately clear to our minds.

Accordingly, the nature and existence of subsistent being are mentioned with a plural verb, even though we are aware of their strict identity. They

[6] ". . . 'being' is expressed in two ways: in one way, it signifies the act of being; in another way, it signifies the composition of a proposition, which the mind attains in joining predicate with subject. Therefore taking 'being' in the first way, we cannot know the being of God, just as we cannot know his essence; but only in the second way. For we know that this proposition which we form about God is true, when we say 'God exists.' And we know this from his effects . . ." St Thomas, *ST*, I, 3, 4, ad 2m. Cf. *CG*, I, 12.

Man cannot know God
Can know If exists

denote the same characteristic, but are represented by us after the model of nature and being in sensible things. Hence we can use the expression "Subsistent being exists," even though subsistent being, reached as the result of the demonstration from sensible things, means its own real existence. The sentence is tautological to anyone who has in mind the philosophical meaning of subsistent being. It has to be used with proper therapy. It states a truth that is evident in itself and that becomes mediately evident to us through metaphysical demonstration, but which is not immediately evident to human cognition.[7]

As seen earlier,[8] there can be only one instance of subsistent being. In subsistent being, therefore, nature coincides with individual as well as with existence. There cannot be two or more subsistent beings. All effects are from that one source. Any series of agents will lead to the same first cause.

Pure Act. Since being is the act of all acts and the perfection of all perfections, where it subsists it will be perfection in the highest degree. There is no higher act that could make it more perfect. It has, accordingly, no potency to further perfection. This means that as subsistent it has no potency at all. It is pure act.[9] It is pure perfection and so the fullness of perfection without any admixture of imperfection. It therefore contains within itself the perfections of all other things.[10] It contains them as undistinguished in reality from itself, for any real distinction here would involve real potency. A really distinct perfection would mean potency for real composition. But all such potency is excluded from pure act. Even conceptual distinctions that imply potentiality, like generic and specific distinctions, cannot be placed in subsistent being.

Negative Predication. The nature of pure act, then, establishes the presence in it of all perfections without any accompanying imperfections. Any known perfections, therefore, will be

[7] St Thomas, *ST*, I, 2, 1c. St Thomas takes from Boethius' *De Hebdomadibus* (*PL*, LXIV, 1311B) the distinction between propositions that are self-evident to all people and those that are self-evident only to the learned (*per se notae apud sapientes tantum*). Those of the latter type are self-evident in themselves but not to all persons.

[8] See above, Chapter 5, n. 4. Cf. St Thomas, *ST*, I, 3, 3; *CG*, I, 21.

[9] For Aristotle finite form was equated with act, and therefore any form that was separate from matter was act without potency. Accordingly for Aristotle there could be a plurality of pure acts. On this subject see J. Owens, "The Reality of the Aristotelian Separate Movers," *Review of Metaphysics*, III (1950), 319–337; reprinted in *Readings in Ancient and Medieval Philosophy*, ed. James Collins (Westminster, Md., 1960), pp. 75–81.

[10] See above, n. 4. Similarly: "The perfections of all things pertain to the perfection of being . . ." St Thomas, *ST*, I, 4, 2c. Cf. *CG*, I, 28; *In de Div. Nom.*, c. V, lect. 2, no. 661 (ed. Pera, Turin & Rome, 1950), p. 245b.

found in subsistent being, provided that all imperfections conditioning them in other things are relentlessly denied. Pure act will be substance, but incorporeal substance. Substance as directly known to human cognition is corporeal. But anything corporeal, as natural philosophy shows, has matter in its nature. Matter is potency, and so is excluded from pure act. Similarly, substance as pure act cannot be the subject of any accidents. An accident by its nature is imperfect, and as subject of accidents the substance would be in potency to them. In particular, all extension is incompatible with pure act. Extension is not only an accident, but is a corporeal accident, and so is found only in bodies. Subsistent being, then, is unextended. It occupies no space. It is not in any place, in the way definite extension locates a thing. It is not in any genus or species, because these imply potency to further determination; so it has to be unique. It can have no parts, for parts are in potency with respect to the whole. All composition has to be denied it. It is absolutely simple. It is entirely immutable, for mutability means potency to become something else or to be in some other way. It is therefore not subject to motion and so is not measured by time or any other imperfect duration. It has accordingly no past nor future, but has its existence all together. Its duration is an eternal now.[11] Such duration is called eternity. Unlike the being of sensible things, then, it is not spread out in time. Just as it is beyond the conditions of space, it is also above all temporal conditions. Nor has it other limits. Any limitation of existential act would mean its restriction by a potency, for in itself it is not a finite form.[12] Since pure existential act involves no finitude nor potency, it is entirely unlimited. It is infinite.

This negative method of predication has to be used in regard to all other perfections that are seen in pure act. The procedure here consists

---

[11] ". . . the aspect of eternity follows upon immutability, just as the aspect of time follows upon motion, as is clear from what has been said. Therefore since God is in the highest degree immutable, it belongs to him in the highest degree to be eternal." St Thomas, *ST*, I, 10, 2c. The classic definition of eternity was given by Boethius: "Eternity therefore is the simultaneously total and perfect possession of interminable life." *On the Consolation of Philosophy*, V, 6. Cf. St Thomas, *ST*, I, 10, 1c; *CG*, I, 15, arg. 2.

[12] An act that is strictly a form is by its very nature limited. For Parmenides, being was conceived as a form and so as limited. The being that is apprehended in judgment, on the other hand, is not conceived as a form but as a non-formal actuation imparted to a form. It expresses nothing that would involve limit when it subsists. ". . . since we are able in an existential metaphysics to escape from the limitation which is necessarily intrinsic to the order of essence, we are therefore able, through the resources of judgment, to break through to the discovery and consideration of the pure act of existence which is God." Robert J. Henle, "Existentialism and the Judgment," *Proceedings of the American Catholic Philosophical Association*, XXI (1946), 53.

mostly in saying what subsistent being is not. Life is a perfection, and so belongs to subsistent being. But it is life whose activity is substance and not accident, a life that involves no change, no growth, no progress, no process. Intelligence is a perfection, but any distinction of faculty or act from substance and any dependence upon sensation or imagination have to be denied it in subsistent being. Sensation and imagination require corporeal organs, and so are excluded from pure act. The cognitional perfection they exhibit has to be found in pure act in an incorporeal manner. Knowledge is a perfection, and so will be present in subsistent being, but without any process of learning and without any limitation. Will, volition, and love are among the endowments of pure act, but without the requirement of any external object. Power is a perfection, and accordingly will be found there, but in complete identity with substance and without any need of instruments. As everything in the sensible world owes its production and its being, ultimately, to the one first cause, the power of the first cause embraces them all and is productive of all their perfections. In that sense all their perfections **pre-exist** or are **pre-contained** in subsistent being.

These considerations show forcefully enough how the different perfections found in sensible things are to be attributed to their first efficient cause. They belong to it not as different from one another but as merged entirely in the one pure act. Those whose concept can be purged of all imperfections through the process of negative predication may be attributed in their own notion to subsistent being. In the above examples, subsistent being may be called substantial, living, intelligent, productive. These are perfections encountered in the observable world. Because in their proper notion they are not mixed with any imperfection, they may from that viewpoint be called **unmixed perfections** (*perfectiones simpliciter simplices*). In technical language they are said to be in the first cause **formally and eminently.** This signifies that their notion is formally the same in all cases, but is realized in a different and higher way in the first cause. Notions like body, extension, accident, sensation, motion, on the other hand, cannot be deprived of their imperfection and remain the same. Such notions, therefore, cannot be applied formally to subsistent being in any proper sense. They are notions of perfections that are indeed contained eminently in pure act, but only in a causal way. Subsistent being is their first cause, just as it is the cause of everything else. Those perfections, in consequence, are said to be not formally but only **virtually and eminently** in the first cause. Since they are in their very notion mixed with imperfection, they may be called **mixed perfections.** But in both cases a positive perfection is predicated.

Analogy and Reference. Some perfections found in caused things, then, are attributed formally to subsistent being. Are they ever predicated **univocally** in the two cases? In univocal predication all the instances belong to the same species or, at least for the logician, to the same genus. Churchill and Stalin, for example, are instances of "man." The notion "man" expresses human nature in the concrete and is entirely the same, as nature, in each of these two cases. "Date" has exactly the same meaning when predicated of every individual date on the luncheon platter. The definition, as signified by the word, is the same in all instances.

In the opposite extreme, notions predicated **equivocally,** in the full sense of equivocity by chance,[13] are entirely different or diverse in each pertinent instance. "See," for example, may mean either the diocese of a bishop or to perceive by the sense of sight. "Date" may signify a day of the month or the fruit of a palm. The definition as expressed by the one term is different without qualification in each of these instances. Purely by chance or accident of word coinage does the same term signify entirely different notions. They are the opposite of univocals, where the notion is entirely the same.

Between the two extremes are found various types of partial sameness and partial difference. One is **analogy.** The word was borrowed from Greek mathematical vocabulary. There it meant sameness of ratio or proportion between the respective terms of different pairs. "Two is to four as three is to six" exhibits the same proportion or ratio in each pair, that of half. Outside arithmetic the sameness does not have to be equality, for instance: "As a point is to a line so a surface is to a solid," or "As sharp is to the sense of touch, so is shrill to the sense of hearing." The analogous notion is expressible for the first example by the word "extremity," and for the second perhaps by the phrase "sudden, intense, and rather painful sensation." The sameness of proportion in such cases is not equality but merely similarity. It is a likeness in the respective ways in which the terms are related to each other in the two pairs. But the likeness is found in a feature that differentiates the instances. Conversely,

[13] In the terminology that goes back to Boethius (*In Cat.*, I; *PL*, LXIV, 166B) equivocals are divided into equivocals by chance (*casu*) and equivocals by design (*consilio*). Equivocals by chance manifest no common ground for the designation by the same name. They are accordingly the direct opposite of univocals. The etymology of the words "univocal" and "equivocal," however, would not require any difference in meaning for the two terms. "Univocal" indicates "one word" for a number of things. Merely by convention is it applied solely to things in the same species or logical genus. "Equivocal" indicates the use of a "word equally" for a number of things. Conventionally it is applied, in fashion opposite to "univocal," only to things that do not coincide specifically or generically.

the various instances while different in themselves exhibit in that very difference itself enough similarity to require expression in one and the same notion. The one identical notion, accordingly, is partly the same and partly different. Both the sameness and the difference are in the one notion. It is not a question of differentiating a logically generic notion by a further specific differentia. That would be univocity. In univocity one notion, the generic, makes the instances logically the same. Another notion, the specific differentia, makes them different. In analogy, on the contrary, the one and the same feature renders the instances both alike and different. In the above example, the notion "extremity" itself is different when used of a line and of a solid. In the first case it means a point, in the second case a surface. Here is found no univocally common generic notion, like "body" or "quantity." No such notion is a genus for "extremity." Yet a point functions as the extremity of a line and a surface as the extremity of a solid. That likeness of proportion is contained in their very notions, different as those notions are. On account of that proportional likeness, both point and surface may be expressed by the one notion "extremity," and the difference between them may be brought out by adding their respective terms, namely "of a line" and "of a solid." But it is that very difference that shows the proportional likeness. An analogous notion, accordingly, is not divided like a genus into species by added differentiae, but into **analogates** by making explicit its various instances without the addition of any new notion. The notion "extremity," for example, does not submerge in any generic unity its instances in a line, a surface, endurance, rage, and so on.

The analogy described in the preceding paragraph is called analogy of **proper proportionality**, because the analogous notion is found in its proper sense in all the analogates. There is also a type of analogy in which the notion is found in its proper sense in only the principal or **primary analogate.** In a secondary analogate the notion is found merely in a transferred sense. This type of analogy is known as **metaphor.** In the assertion "Lindbergh was an eagle," the nature of an eagle is found just in the bird and not in the man. The notion "eagle," accordingly, has its proper notion in only one of the analogates, and so constitutes the bird the primary analogate in the implied comparison "Lindbergh was to his flying as an eagle to its flying." The properly analogous notion here is something like "superb flier." If plane travel may now be considered a proper sense of the verb "to fly," Lindbergh and the eagle may both be called superb fliers through analogy of proper proportionality. But when the ace of the twenties is called an eagle, the sense of the notion "eagle" is transferred to that of "superb flier." In that transferred or improper sense the notion "eagle" is predicated of Lindbergh through analogy of metaphorical or improper proportionality. The man in this case becomes a secondary analogate of "eagle." There is difference with proportional likeness in ace and eagle as fliers.

Another type of partial sameness and partial difference occurs in predication through reference. The classic Aristotelian examples are "healthy" and "medical." "Health" is the proper disposition of a living organism. It is not formally present in a diet, for example, as such. Yet a diet is called healthy on the ground that it is the cause of health. Exercise is healthy as a preservative of health, and a color is healthy as a sign or effect of health. Neither the food nor the exercise nor the color possesses formally the proper disposition of a living organism. But they are related in different ways to that disposition, as cause, preservative, effect, or sign. They are denominated healthy on account of the reference. "Medicine," the other Aristotelian example, is formally a science possessed by physicians. Yet many things outside the physician's mind, like schools, books, or curative materials, are called "medical" or "medicine" by reason of the relation they bear to medical science.[14]

---

[14] See Aristotle, *Metaph.*, Γ 2, 1003a33–b5; K 3, 1060b32–1061a10. On the analogy of inequality or of genus, that is, on the way a genus may be considered analogically shared by different species, see A. Maurer, "The Analogy of Genus," *The New Scholasticism*, XXIX (1955), 127–144. For a short résumé of the different conceptions that go under the name "analogy," see Gerald B. Phelan, *Saint Thomas and Analogy* (Milwaukee, 1941), pp. 9–20. The union of difference and likeness in metaphysical analogy is cogently expressed by Msgr. Phelan: "This is, indeed, a difference in the very likeness and a likeness in the very difference; not merely a mingling of likeness and difference wherein likeness is based upon a formal identity and difference is based upon a formal diversity." *Ibid.*, pp. 29–30. If this is described as simply (*simpliciter*) different but in some respect or proportionally (*secundum quid, idest secundum proportionem*) the same, as in Cajetan, *De Nominum Analogia*, c. IV (ed. P. N. Zammit, Rome, 1934), no. 36, care has to be taken not to conceive the *secundum quid* sameness in any univocal manner. Both the difference and the sameness are better described as "essential" — "eamdem formam in pluribus inveniri essentialiter dissimilem simul et essentialiter similem." J. Le Rohellec, "De Fundamento Metaphysico Analogiae," *Divus Thomas* (Piac.), XXIX (1926), 89. Neither in reality nor in the mind can the two phases be separated — "ita ut diversi aspectus non possint ab invicem separari nec re nec mente." *Ibid.*, p. 90. No "mental precision" can part the one from the other (p. 672). Le Rohellec (pp. 93–94), however, sees this requirement only in analogy of proper proportionality — "Solius enim proportionalitatis est eodem signo exhibere simul convenientiam et defectum convenientiae" (p. 93).

The total lack of univocal sameness or equality in the proportion between the respective terms, accordingly, does not at all mean that the proportion is based upon a further analogy, thus occasioning an infinite regression. Rather, the analogous notion is of its very nature dissimilar as well as similar, and so does not require anything beyond its own proper notion to explain the dissimilarity. No new four term relation need be or can be set up to explain the dissimilarity in the original proportion between the terms of the respective pairs. The analogy that accounts for

In these Aristotelian examples, the nature signified is seen formally in the primary instance only. But there is no reason why in other cases the nature signified should not be present formally in the secondary instances also, though in a lesser degree. For example, the efficient causality of subsistent being, as has been shown, is the cause of all other efficient causality. The primary instance of efficient causality will therefore be located in the first cause. Yet all other efficient causes will remain efficient in the formal sense of the notion. They may be understood as efficient causes insofar as their efficiency imitates in an inferior way the efficiency of the primary cause. In this way they are regarded as possessing formally and intrinsically a characteristic found in its highest sense only in the primary instance. To that primary instance the secondary instances are related as its effects. Human reason, it is true, may first know and name the characteristic from its secondary instances. But having come to know the primary instance and the relations of the secondary instances to the primary, it is able to regard the characteristic as present by nature in the primary instance, and in the secondary instances as only by participation from the primary. In this way the presence of the characteristic in the secondary instances, though formal and intrinsic, is understood and accounted for through reference to the primary instance. The primary instance of wisdom, as another example, may be located in the first cause, and all other instances of thinking and planning may then be looked upon as wise insofar as they imitate in a lesser way that primary wisdom.[15]

---

the dissimilarity is the very analogy by which the notion itself is predicated of all the analogates. On this topic see Hampus Lyttkens, *The Analogy between God and the World* (Uppsala, 1952), p. 474. Le Rohellec, pp. 91–93, also emphasizes that what is directly signified is the analogously common *perfection* itself. T.-L. Penido, *Le Rôle de l'Analogie en Théologie Dogmatique* (Paris, 1931), p. 26, objects only that precisely as an analogous word the name directly signifies the *analogy*, that is, the likeness of relations between the terms in each pair.

For discussions of analogy from the viewpoint of logic, see Ralph M. McInerny, *The Logic of Analogy* (The Hague, 1961), esp. p. 166, and "The *Ratio Communis* of the Analogous Name," *Laval Théologique et Philosophique*, XVIII (1962), 9–34. In "The Logic of Analogy," *The New Scholasticism*, XXXI (1957), 154, n. 12, McInerny regards as "sheer anachronisms" Cajetan's restrictions of "analogy" to its original use. Idiomatic English, however, might welcome these restrictions.

[15] "For when it is said 'God is good,' or 'wise,' not only is there signified that He is the cause of wisdom or goodness, but that these pre-exist more eminently in Him. Wherefore, in accordance with this consideration, it is to be said that with regard to the thing signified by the name, they are stated of God in priority to being stated of creatures, because such perfections flow from God to creatures. But with regard to the application of the name, by us they are applied in priority to creatures, which we first know." St Thomas, *ST*, I, 13, 6c. Cf. *CG*, I, 34. This type of predication by reference is contrasted in St Thomas (*De Ver.*, XXI, 4, ad 2m) with the type seen in the Aristotelian example of "health," where the denomination is from "something extrinsic," and the notion predicated is the reference itself — "ipse

Predication by analogy and by reference, as well as by other types of

---

respectus est ratio denominationis." Where the denomination is on the contrary from an "inherent form" (*ibid.;* cf. ad 3m), though it is made in reference to something else, the reference is not the notion predicated but gives the cause of that aspect. So: "It is in this way that the creature is called good with reference to God" (*ibid.,* ad 2m; tr. Robert W. Schmidt). — The notion of "healthy" applied to food is the reference that is expressed in "health-giving." The name "health" comes from something *extrinsic* to the food. The notion or aspect of goodness, on the contrary, is *inherent* in the sensible thing. It is not the expression of a reference to the primary instance of goodness. But the sensible thing's goodness is understood as a participation of the primary goodness, and so in reference to the primary goodness as to a cause.

On the priority, from a metaphysical viewpoint, of this type of reference in respect to analogy of proper proportionality, see R. J. Masiello, "The Analogy of Proportion according to the Metaphysics of St. Thomas," *The Modern Schoolman,* XXXV (1958), 91–105. The form or aspect shared analogously has to be considered as present in a definite way and degree in each subject before it can be regarded as proportionally related to each. The *intrinsic* presence of the aspect in each member was stressed by Suarez, *Disp. Metaph.,* XXVIII, 3, 11–17 (ed. Vivès, XXVI, 16–19), in order to eliminate analogy of proportionality from the predication of being in regard to God and creatures and (*ibid.,* XXXII, 2, 12–14; Vivès, XXVI, 322–323) substance and accidents. J. Le Rohellec, "Cognitio Nostra Analogica de Deo," *Divus Thomas* (Piac.), XXX (1927), 305–306, admitting both ways of predication, maintains the absolute priority of analogy of proper proportionality as far as the origin of knowledge is concerned, except in the case of the divine attributes. For John of St Thomas, *Ars Logica,* II, 13, 4 (ed. B. Reiser, Turin, 1930, I, 490a4–13) there is formally in these cases only analogy of proper proportionality, and just virtually predication through reference. This would seem to limit the actual predication to analogy of proper proportionality; see Le Rohellec, *Divus Thomas* (Piac.), XXIX (1926), 82–83.

The texts of St Thomas dealing with analogy are listed in the original Latin, with analytic index, by George P. Klubertanz, *St. Thomas Aquinas on Analogy* (Chicago, 1960), pp. 163–302. A "working bibliography" is added, pp. 303–313. The use of the Aristotelian example "healthy" as an illustration by St Thomas is discussed, and the pertinent texts listed, by W. W. Meissner, "Some Notes on a Figure in St. Thomas," *The New Scholasticism,* XXXI (1957), 68–84. The doctrine that analogy is a foundation of metaphor goes back to Aristotle, *Po.,* 21, 1457b6–30; cf. *Rh.,* III 10, 1411a1–b4; 11, 1412b34–35. "That from analogy is possible whenever there are four terms so related that the second (B) is to the first (A), as the fourth (D) to the third (C); for one may then metaphorically put D in lieu of B, and B in lieu of D." *Po.,* 21, 1457b16–19; Oxford tr. This traditional basis of metaphor in analogy is rejected by R. R. Boyle, "The Nature of Metaphor," *The Modern Schoolman,* XXXI (1954), 257–280. "Metaphor is not analogy. It is, actually, a denial of all analogy. Metaphor is an assertion of identity, not of likeness but of oneness. Hence metaphor, based on *being . . .*" *Ibid.,* pp. 274–275. The identity in being, however, is with what is signified by the word in its *transferred* sense. In "Lindbergh is an eagle" the identity is with what "eagle" signifies in its transferred sense as "flier." The transference of sense is made on the basis of analogy. The analogy makes possible the substitution, and so the identity in being of the subject with the substituted meaning of the predicate.

For a critique of the Thomistic application of analogy to God, see Dorothy Mary Emmet, *The Nature of Metaphysical Thinking* (London, 1946), pp. 169–188. On the epistemological basis of that critique, see Eric Lionel Mascall, *Existence and Analogy* (London, etc., 1949), pp. 175–181.

partial sameness and partial difference, may be called ambiguity or equivocity, but not pure ambiguity or pure equivocity. There is always enough sameness to ground a common notion for all the instances. In analogy and reference, however, as may be seen from the above examples, the difference in the various instances is usually much greater than the sameness. Analogy and reference are the types of this deliberate or systematic ambiguity that are stressed in Scholastic philosophy. In Scholastic terminology predication through reference is called analogy of attribution or analogy of proportion.[16] In contradistinction, a four-term analogy is named analogy of proportionality, either proper or improper according to the distinction explained above. But in either acceptation, analogy does not reach the deepest phases of the way being is predicated of things. There are more fundamental considerations for understanding the systematic

[16] A glance at the history of the Scholastic terminology here may help guard against confusion. For Aristotle, analogy always involved a four-term relation. Predication by reference, since it involved in each instance only a two-term relation, was not analogy for the Stagirite. The standard Latin translation of the Greek term *analogia* was *proportio*, carrying the general sense of comparison or even similitude — see instances in J. M. Ramírez, "De Analogia secundum Doctrinam Aristotelico-Thomisticam," *La Ciencia Tomista*, XXIV (1921), 22, n. 4. As in English, "proportion" could mean a two-term relation, for example, the proportion of two to one is double. From this meaning it came in mediaeval Latin to signify in a transferred sense (see St Thomas, *In IV Sent.*, d. 49, q. 2, a. 1, ad 6m; ed. Vivès, XI, 485a; or *ST*, Suppl., 92, 1, ad 6m; cf. *ST*, I, 12, 1, ad 4m) any relation (*habitudo*) of one thing to another. Accordingly the Aristotelian predication by reference (*pros hen*) was regularly called "analogy" by the Scholastics. In the Latin Averroës, *In IV Metaph.* (Venice, 1574), fol. 66rl, it was called *per attributionem*, and in consequence the designation "analogy of attribution" arose. A new name was required in this setting to distinguish the original four-term analogy from the two-term analogy. The two-term relation was regarded simply as a proportion, and the four-term relation as a likeness of proportions or a proportionality (see St Thomas, *De Ver.*, II, 11c). In accordance with this distinction, analogy of attribution was also called "analogy of proportion" or "analogy of simple proportion," while the four-term kind was named "analogy of proportionality." Through Suarezian emphasis on the intrinsic participation of being, "analogy of intrinsic attribution" arose in distinction from the extrinsic type regularly illustrated by the Aristotelian examples of health and medicine. Where the notion was applied "symbolically" (St Thomas, *ibid.*), and so "metaphorically" as opposed to "properly" (Cajetan, *De Nominum Analogia*, c. III, no. 25), the analogy became technically known as "analogy of improper or metaphorical proportionality" (John of St Thomas, *Ars Logica*, II, 13, 3; ed. Reiser, I, 484b38–40), in contrast to analogy of proper proportionality (*ibid.*). The terminology and divisions of St Thomas Aquinas, however, do not fit any too smoothly into this late Scholastic schema.

Other Aristotelian types of partial sameness and partial difference are the actual and potential (e.g., *Top.*, I 15, 106b13–20), and the essential and accidental (*Top.*, II 3, 110b21–24). Being is predicated in both these ways as well as by reference (*Metaph.*, E 2, 1026a33–b2). For Aristotle, apparently, there is no reason why one type of partial sameness and partial difference should exclude other types in the predication of the one notion.

ambiguity or equivocity of being. These arise from the differences between being in reality and being in cognition, and between being as subject and as act.

Positive Predication. No perfection formally and eminently in pure act can be univocally the same there as in any other thing. The two instances of the perfection can never belong to the same species or logical genus. Life, intelligence, production, and the like, are substantial in subsistent being and accidental in other things. They cannot coincide even in a supreme genus. They may all be referred to, indeed, as being. But being is not a genus. In the first cause, moreover, substance is being; in all other things it is distinct from being. Are the perfections, then, predicated of subsistent being in pure equivocity? Hardly. Subsistent being is the first efficient cause of them all as they are found in other things. At least it offers a ground for receiving denomination from them, through reference, as their cause. The power of the first cause, for example, may be said to have been exercised upon the world during the past century, even though in itself that power has no temporal aspect whatsoever. It continued its exercise throughout the last century because its effects took place all during that time.

Not only aspects that are extrinsic to it, like the temporal, may be predicated of pure act through reference, but also characteristics that in varying degrees are inherent or intrinsic both to it and to other things. It may be denominated being, good, intelligent, wise, productive, and so on, with all perfections that are in it formally and eminently. It turns out, of course, to be the primary instance of all these perfections. Yet these perfections become known originally to men through the secondary instances. Only later are the secondary instances understood in their true status as feeble imitations of the primary instance. But the imitation is sufficiently manifesting to allow the characteristic to be predicated formally of pure act, through reference.

Most of these perfections may also be predicated of pure act by four-term analogy. The two ways of predicating, by reference and by analogy, are not mutually exclusive. By four-term analogy, for example, subsistent being may be likewise denominated a cause. The relation of its proper effect to it corresponds proportionally to the relation of any other effect to its own proper cause. Similarly the wisdom of the first cause may be expected to guide its activity proportionally as human wisdom guides human activity. In this way analogy of proper proportionality enables the human mind to grasp in a proper though analogous fashion the relations of the different perfections to the nature of pure act. Hence emerges the important role of this type of analogy in any study of the supersensible. The analogy presupposes, however, that the nature of the supersensible being is known in some previous way, in order that it may function as one of four terms in the proportional comparison. In pure act, that nature is already understood as being, in the strictest intrinsic identity. Accordingly there is difficulty in using four-term analogy to predicate being of pure act. The intrinsically distinct concepts are only three.

Mixed perfections, present in pure act not formally but only causally and eminently, can be predicated of it by metaphor. Metaphor, it will be remembered, is a type of analogy in which the characteristic ascribed to a thing is formally present only in something else. Since the first cause is incorporeal, it can be denominated only metaphorically by anything that involves corporeity or extension, for instance in the assertion that it overshadows the world, or that it is the rock upon which the universe is built.

Perfections are predicated of pure act, then, neither univocally nor by pure equivocity. Predicated univocally, they would give rise to **anthropomorphism,** for we would be placing the nature and activity of the first cause on the same plane as our own. Predicated in the other extreme by pure equivocity, they would occasion **agnosticism.** They would provide no knowledge whatsoever of subsistent being. Rather, they are predicated through different types of partial sameness and partial difference. The first cause's proper effect, being, carries in its own intrinsic character enough resemblance, distant though it may be, to make the first cause understood as being. The other unmixed perfections formally inherent in man and other terrestrial things similarly provide enough resemblance to allow their prototype or primary instance to be understood and represented in each case as such. These unmixed perfections exhibit their proper intrinsic relations wherever they are found, in the primary as well as in the secondary instances. Once being has been established as subsistent, therefore, its further perfections and activities are open to positive explanation through the analogy they have with their respective subjects in secondary but observable instances. In the secondary instances the distinction between the two terms will often be real, as a man's wisdom is really distinct from his nature. In pure act, on the other hand, the distinction between the two corresponding terms can be only conceptual. The terms in the one pair, moreover, will be infinite, in the other they will be finite. Yet their relations to each other remain proportionally similar. The relation of infinite wisdom to infinite being will resemble, however distantly, the relation of finite wisdom to a finite agent.

Attributes. The nature of the first cause, as knowable by unaided human reason, is found in one characteristic only, that of being. According to the above considerations, however, subsistent being is understood to have a number of **attributes.** These are perfections seen in other things but found also formally and eminently in their first cause. As present in the first cause they may be elucidated through analogy. They bear to subsistent being relations that correspond proportionally to the relations borne to finite substance by the properties or accidents from which they are named. The existence and nature and perfections of the first cause are established by demonstration from their effects. Then, through analogy, many of the perfections can be studied in their complicated relations as attributes. They are known originally as properties or accidents of finite things. They are attributed, purged of all imperfections, to the first cause. They are expressed in concepts that differ from one another intrinsically, but which are just as intrinsically interrelated. The concept of justice, even when represented as infinite, is not the concept of intelligence nor the concept of freedom. Nor is any of these concepts the concept of being. Yet justice is of its very nature related to being, to intelligence, and to freedom. It retains these intrinsic relations even when it is attributed to infinite being. It is understood as following upon other perfections in the same order as it follows upon them in finite things, and so may be investigated according to that same sequence of formal causality.

The intrinsic distinction of concepts, though, does not in any way mean that the nature of the first cause is a potency actuated by attributes. Nor does it represent the attributes as in potency to composition with one another. It allows each and all of them the status of pure act, and emphatically does not make them limited parts of a composition. It does not set them apart in the way genus is set apart from differentia, when the genus is represented as subject or potency to the differentia. The distinction is therefore called a minor virtual distinction, in contrast to the major virtual distinction between differentia and genus. But it is an intrinsic virtual distinction. The concepts it distinguishes represent formally different perfections. The distinction in the first cause between nature and being, on the other hand, is only an extrinsic virtual distinction, since the being of the first cause is exactly what is meant by its nature.

Causal Inquiry. At this stage of the procedure it might be well to stand back for a moment and take a quick glance at the general nature of the inquiry about the first cause. In Gilbert Ryle's simile,[17] should the present task be likened to the work of the detective or to the work of the cartographer? Is it a search for someone who did something, or is it a plotting out of the contours of concepts like those of nature and being? Is it a causal inquiry into the real causes of real events and real things, or is it a dialectic of concepts that consists in making explicit what was all along implicitly contained in the concepts?

The comparison with the detective or with the cartographer may limp in many respects when it is applied to the metaphysician. But its general bearing is clear enough. It is asking if the metaphysician is working in the pattern of the man who starts from certain clues like fingerprints that he finds in the room of the murder, and from such clues strives to pinpoint and describe the murderer that he does not see in the room. Or is the metaphysician merely gazing upon certain concepts before his mind's eye and sketching their outlines and interweavings, just as the cartographer has the outline of the coast before his vision, at least in principle, while he maps out its curvings on paper?

Focused in this way, the comparison definitely makes the metaphysical investigation of the cause of being fall in line with the detective's work. Here the metaphysician is starting from clues that he sees in sensible things, and concluding to the unseen cause that put them there. He is searching out an agent who did something, an agent not to be seen in the sensible things but who can be traced from the evidence left in those things. Like the detective he is concluding, from what he has seen, to the existence and description of an individual that he has not seen. He does not have the individual there before him to sketch his features in the way in which the cartographer has the coast before his mind's eye as he maps its outlines.

Establishing metaphysically the existence and nature of the first cause, therefore, can be called a "process of making explicit what is implicit in the fact of existence"[18] only if the notion "implicit" is forcibly made to include the external efficient cause, in a sense that would enable one to say that the murderer is implicit in the clues he has left. In that case "implicit" would connote all the thing's causes, extrinsic as well as intrinsic. Explication would include every causal inquiry. The difficulty in this view is that the efficient cause is outside the thing produced. It is not implicit in the thing, and cannot be brought to light merely by

[17] Gilbert Ryle, "The Theory of Meaning," in *British Philosophy in the Mid-Century*, ed. Cecil Alec Mace (London, 1957), p. 264.

[18] Maxwell John Charlesworth, *Philosophy and Linguistic Analysis* (Pittsburgh and Louvain, 1959), p. 213. Cf.: ". . . this process by which the implications of the fact of existence are made explicit is, for both Aristotle and St. Thomas, largely negative or therapeutic in character." *Ibid.*

making explicit what is already contained in the thing. It does not emerge in any process of analysis. It has to be reasoned to, as the detective reasons to the murderer. The first cause is implicit in the fact of sensible existence only insofar as it produced that existence in the role of extrinsic efficient cause. The purpose of the argument has not been to prove "something about those things, namely, that they are dependent,"[19] but to prove something about something else, namely about the first cause, that it exists and that it is infinitely perfect. The procedure has isolated being as a real nature, as pure act that is incompatible with any potency in its status as a nature. This should be of prime importance in establishing being as the viewpoint from which metaphysical investigation is to be conducted.

The procedure has also revealed how the notion of supersensible being is reached. Being is known first as sensible. Then, through judgments, every sensible characteristic is denied to it in its primary instance. In this primary instance real being and all unmixed perfections still remain after separation from the sensible through these judgments. The primary instance of being is thereby understood as a real something beyond the whole sensible order. The notion of being is accordingly exhibited as applicable to both the sensible and the supersensible. The process by which it is so established is called **judgment of separation.**[20] Being, though encountered directly only in sensible things, is submitted to judgments like these: "Of its nature as such, being is not sensible, is not quantitative, is not mobile, is not temporal, though it does have those features in observable instances." No simple process of conceptual abstraction can isolate the supersensible in the way notions like "animal" and "body" are obtained. Merely leaving out of consideration feature after feature through conceptual abstraction will not free being from immersion in

---

[19] Charlesworth, *op. cit.*

[20] See St Thomas, *In Boeth. de Trin.*, V, 3 and 4. Cf. tr. A. Maurer, *The Division and Methods of the Sciences* (Toronto, 1958), pp. xx–xxv. Although St Thomas does not treat this problem elsewhere, the doctrine in these two articles is formal and explicit and has to be considered as his definite teaching on the subject. A discussion of the topic may be found in H. Renard, "What is St. Thomas' Approach to Metaphysics," *The New Scholasticism*, XXX (1956), 67–80. A survey of the whole problem and of the recent literature upon it is given by R. W. Schmidt, "L'Emploi de la Séparation en Métaphysique," *Revue Philosophique de Louvain*, LVIII (1960), 373–393. On the Aristotelian background of separation in the subject of metaphysics, see J. Owens, *The Doctrine of Being in the Aristotelian* Metaphysics (Toronto, 1951), pp. 238–240. St Thomas borrowed the term *separatio* from this Aristotelian use, as is clear enough from *In Boeth. de Trin.*, V, 3c (ed. Wyser, p. 41.6–7); V, 4, ad 4m (p. 51.10–11). His notion of separation in this respect, however, is considerably different from the Aristotelian.

the sensible.[21] A direct conceptualization either of the spiritual or of a generic nature really common to both sensible and spiritual does not occur. Only through acts of judgment may being and substance, experienced as they are in sensible things, be separated from sensible commitment. Solely as the result of judgment of separation is the notion "being that is not sensible, not quantitative, not mobile, not temporal" acquired.

In the wake of the foregoing considerations, however, being is now established as an aspect that is not restricted to the sensible and as a real nature that is not present as a nature in sensible things. These considerations are obviously of prime importance for the isolation of being in a way that will allow it to serve as the viewpoint for metaphysical study. In this regard, though, the further question of its distinction from sensible nature still lies open. How is the being that is present in sensible things distinguished from their nature? Is it really other than their nature, apart from any work of the human mind? The answer now should emerge from an investigation of the manner in which finite things participate being from their first cause.

Résumé. The being that is known in sensible things is caused ultimately by the subsistent nature of being. As pure act, subsistent being contains the perfections of all things, not univocally and not in a totally equivocal manner, but in an eminent way that while thoroughly different allows predication of the same perfection in each instance.[22]

SUGGESTED READINGS AND REFERENCES

St Thomas Aquinas, *Summa Theologiae*, I, 2, 1–2.

Thomas De Vio, Cardinal Cajetan, *The Analogy of Names*, tr. Edward A. Bushinski (Pittsburgh: Duquesne University Press, 1953).

Gerald Bernard Phelan, *Saint Thomas and Analogy* (Milwaukee: Marquette University Press, 1941).

James Francis Anderson, *The Bond of Being* (St. Louis: B. Herder, 1949).

[21] Hence arises the all too frequently accepted conclusion: "Existence in its literal sense is always spatio-temporal. . . . When used in any other sense it is used symbolically." Wilbur Marshall Urban, *Language and Reality* (London, 1939), p. 710. As originally grasped by the human intellect, being, though a transcendent aspect, does not at once manifest itself as transcendent. When its primary sense is reached in subsistent being, its literal meaning is seen to extend beyond the sensible and beyond the finite orders.

[22] On the sameness yet unknowability of the perfections in their eminent existence, see below, Chapter 25, nn. 3–17. As precontained in pure act, each perfection is really identified with subsistent being. In consequence it is known in terms of being rather than of nature. You know *that* the perfection is in subsistent being, without knowing in quidditative terms *what* it is when really identical with the nature of being.

Sr. Thomas Marguerite Flanigan, "The Use of Analogy in the *Summa Contra Gentiles*," *The Modern Schoolman*, XXXV (1957), 21–37.
George Peter Klubertanz, *St. Thomas Aquinas on Analogy* (Chicago: Loyola University Press, 1960).
James F. Ross, "Analogy as a Rule of Meaning for Religious Language," *International Philosophical Quarterly*, I (1961), 468–502.
Martin S. O'Neill, "Some Remarks on the Analogy of God and Creatures in St. Thomas Aquinas," *Mediaeval Studies*, XXIII (1961), 206–215.
Joseph Owens, "Analogy as a Thomistic Approach to Being," *Mediaeval Studies*, XXIV (1962), 303–322.

CHAPTER 7

Participated Being

Creation. Since pure act contains within itself the fullness of all perfections, it is a nature that requires nothing else. Nothing in its nature, therefore, could necessitate it to produce something other than itself. From what is known of its nature there is no ground to demonstrate the existence of anything else.[1] Rather, what is known of its nature shows that it gives no ground to reason in that way, for the perfection of subsistent being is already infinite. What it does produce, then, it produces of its own free choice, and not from any necessity of its nature. Freedom of action is a perfection. It is a perfection without any imperfection involved in its proper notion,[2] and so is to be found in pure act. As a matter of fact, other things have been produced. They have provided the ground for reasoning to the existence of the first cause; though the first cause does not in itself, as subsistent being, furnish any basis for demonstrating their existence. Their existence is known through appre-

---

[1] Plotinus (*Enneads*, IV, 8, 6; V, 4, 1), basing his inspiration on Plato's (*Ti.*, 29E) teaching that the demiurge on account of his own unalloyed goodness brought order into the world chaos, maintained that the perfect good could not stay within itself but had to engender the universe in a process necessary down to the last detail. Supreme goodness, accordingly, necessitated the production of other things. For Plotinus, freedom implied indetermination and lack of completeness, and so could not be found on the divine level; see *En.*, VI, 7, 1. Any philosophy that claims to show a necessary sequence of things from their first principle, thereby denies the freedom of the first cause in the production of its effects, at least in any sense of free choice to produce or not produce.

[2] "Further, one who acts through intellect and will is in the order of agents prior to one who acts through necessity of nature; for one who acts through will has set for himself in advance the end for which he acts, while a natural agent acts for an end set for him by someone else. But it is clear from what has gone before that God is the first agent. He is therefore one who acts through will, and not through necessity of nature. Also, it has been shown above that God is of infinite power; he is therefore not determined to this or that effect, but is disposed indeterminately towards all. . . . It is necessary therefore that effects proceed from God according to a determination of will. Therefore he does not act through necessity of nature, but through will." St Thomas, *Comp. Theol.*, I, 96.

hension in judgment, and is traced to the immediate or mediate efficient causality of subsistent being. This means that subsistent being does produce, by efficient causality, things other than itself.

As everything else has to receive its being in one way or another from the unique first cause, no material can be presupposed for the original production of things. There is no possibility of anything out of which the first product could be made, as a table is made of wood by a cabinet-maker. That material would have to be produced previously, and so would be the first product itself. This lack of any material for the original production of things is expressed by saying that they were made out of nothing. "Out of" in this assertion does not signify a material cause, but merely denotes that what preceded was nothing. Whether or not this following upon nothing means that the sensible world had a temporal beginning, cannot be shown on philosophical ground.[3] Both possibilities are open. Cosmic motion could be without beginning and without end in time, as Aristotle's reasoning in the *Physics*[4] has shown. But where subsistent being produces the material as well as the motion, the production can take place in an instant and so would not require any preceding part of time. In that case time and motion would begin in an indivisible instant, and the sensible world would have a definite temporal beginning. On account of the freedom of the first cause in this regard, neither alternative can be demonstrated. In either case, however, the production of things out of nothing is called **creation**, and the product **creatures**.

To forestall any explanation of the original production of things as an emanation of the first cause's own substance, the material excluded in the definition of creation may be stated in further detail. It does not admit any material other than the first cause, and it does not allow what

[3] See St Thomas, *In VIII Phys.*, lect. 1–2; *De Aeternitate Mundi contra Murmurantes*, in *Opusc.*, ed. J. Perrier (Paris, 1949), pp. 53–61. The probative force of the demonstration that being subsists in a first cause, accordingly, does not lie in any impossibility of a mathematically infinite series, but in the dependence of being that is an accident upon being that is not an accident. On the non-mathematical character of the regress, see J. Owens, "Aquinas on Infinite Regress," *Mind*, N.S. LXXI (1962), 244–246.

[4] *Ph.*, VIII 1, 251a17–252a5. Cf.: "Such reasons are efficacious for proving that movement did not begin by way of nature . . . but that it did not begin with the production of things anew as it were by the first principle of all things, as our faith lays down, cannot be proved by these reasons . . . the production of all being by the first cause of being is not movement, whether this emanation of things is taken to be from eternity or not." St Thomas, *In VIII Phys.*, lect. 2 (ed. Leonine), no. 17. Movement can begin not only in a divisible part, as it does when caused by a natural agent, but also in an indivisible instant, through creation. If it began through creation in an indivisible, there would be no preceding part of motion and no preceding part of time. See St Thomas, *ibid.*, no. 20. This means that philosophical reasons cannot prove or disprove that cosmic motion had a temporal beginning.

already exists in the first cause to be used as a material. A material is potency to the finished product, and all potency is barred from pure act. There is nothing in the first cause itself, then, that could be used as material for creation.[5]

Entitative Composition. In creation, nevertheless, a subject has to be produced along with the existential act. In creation a subject has to receive being. The reasoning that led to the first cause was based firmly upon the reception of being from another. The final step was the immediate reception of being from the first cause. There is a subject, then, that receives being in creation, even though that subject's existence is not presupposed by the creative act. What receives a perfection is a potency to have the perfection. The subject that receives being, therefore, is potency to being; and where it receives being in reality, as in creation, it is a real potency. In the product of creation, accordingly, there is composition of act and potency. The thing created is the potency. It is a real potency, because it is a real thing made to exist in reality. The produced act is a real act, because it is real existence. It makes the thing exist in the real world. Both the potency and the act, then, are real.

It could not be otherwise. Being, where it is a nature existent in itself, is infinite and unique. It could not have a second instance. Yet it produces being. That is the effect that corresponds to its nature, and so may be called its **proper effect.** That is the effect upon which the demonstration of subsistent being was developed. Yet when being is produced, it cannot be produced as a nature, for as a nature it is unique and uncaused. It has to be produced as act, for it is always found as act, the act of every other act. It has to be produced, consequently, as the act of something other than itself. Every produced act of being, accordingly, involves its corresponding potency.[6] It cannot be produced except as the act of that potency. Through that potency it provides its own limitation,[7]

[5] "But creation is the production of something in its whole substance, presupposing nothing that is either uncreated or created by anyone." St Thomas, *ST*, I, 65, 3c. Creation, because it produces being absolutely, requires the plenitude of infinite power. There is nothing about it that could be touched by a limited cause. Hence no creature could be an instrument for creation. See *In II Sent.*, d. 1, q. 1, a. 3 (ed. Mandonnet, II, 20–23); *De Pot.*, III, 4c; *ST*, I, 45, 5c; I, 65, 3c.

[6] "Each essence is set up by an act-of-being which it is not and which includes it as its own determination." E. Gilson, *The Christian Philosophy of St. Thomas Aquinas*, tr. L. K. Shook (New York, 1956), p. 36. The original French *autodétermination*, *Le Thomisme*, 5th ed. (Paris, 1944), p. 54, expresses much more strongly the notion that every finite existential act is *self*-determined by a nature *other* than itself.

[7] "To being can be added nothing that is extraneous to it, because nothing is

for reception into a potency, as the function of potency was seen in the argument for the infinity of subsistent being, somehow limits an act.[8] Produced being, therefore, is finite being. It is finite, not because it is being, but because it is the act of a limiting potency. Strict expression, indeed, would require one to say that in the case of finite being what exists is not the existential act, but the something else to which that act gives being. Correspondingly, what is produced is the thing rather than its being. One says that the sun, the galaxies, the universe, were created, and not exactly that their being was created. This way of speaking represents the situation quite correctly, even though not completely. The proper effect of subsistent being is being, but that effect can be realized only in something else. In producing finite being, the first cause thereby produces the potency finite being inevitably involves.[9] Its being maintains the priority, even though, strictly, the thing itself is what is produced. In creation, therefore, the production of the finite existential act is the production of the subject that is made to exist. It does not at all presuppose that any such subject already exists. Rather, viewed from a metaphysical standpoint, it produces the potency in sequence to, and not in priority to, the existential act that is received.

Does the composition of act and potency in a creature, though, mean that they are really distinct from each other? If they are really distinct, they give an affirmative answer to the long drawn out question whether a real distinction and not just a conceptual or verbal distinction falls between a sensible or other created thing and its being. If so, will the real distinction mean that every finite entity is composed of two realities, nature and being? Will their real distinction indicate that they are two different realities? What kind of distinction would then fall between

---

extraneous to it except not-being, which cannot be either form or matter. Hence being is not determined by something else as potency by act, but rather as act by potency." St Thomas, *De Pot.*, VII, 2, ad 9m. With Aristotle, form was equated with act, and matter with potency. For Aristotle, accordingly, formal limiting was always a function of act, never of potency.

[8] On the limitation of act by reception in a subject, see J.-D. Robert, "Le Principe: 'Actus non limitatur nisi per potentiam subjectivam realiter distinctam,'" *Revue Philosophique de Louvain*, XLVII (1949), 44–70. On the historical background of the question, see W. Norris Clarke, "The Limitation of Act by Potency: Aristotelianism or Neoplatonism," *The New Scholasticism*, XXVI (1952), 167–194.

[9] ". . . by the very fact that being is conferred upon a quiddity, not only the being, but the quiddity itself is said to be created; because before it has being it is nothing, except perhaps in the intellect of the creator, where it is not a creature but the creative essence." St Thomas, *De Pot.*, III, 5, ad 2m. ". . . in giving being he produces that which receives the being." *Ibid.*, a. 1, ad 17m. In limiting merely as potency, a nature requires no actuality whatsoever in priority to being.

cognitional being and what it makes exist in cognition? These are questions that all have to be answered if the distinction between thing and being is to be understood. Where the distinction is real, and independent of any consideration by the human mind, the composition between a thing and its being will be a real composition. As a composition between the basic parts or principles that constitute a finite entity, it may be called technically **entitative** composition, and the parts entitative parts or entitative principles.

Real Distinction. The demonstration of the existence of the first cause has shown that being is a nature in the real world. Being is that existence, and so is a real nature. But it is a real nature that includes every perfection, every act, in its own indivisible unity. If it entered into composition with anything else as a nature, it would absorb that thing into itself. It would be what thereby existed, it itself and not the other thing. Parmenides had viewed being as a nature present in sensible things, and from this starting point had shown with flawless reasoning that all being was a single whole in reality. Once being is regarded as belonging to the natures of things, it absorbs all those things into its own nature. It is a real nature itself, and is in fact given to other natures through efficient causality. But it cannot be given to them as a nature, and cannot enter into their natures. It is really given to them through efficient causality, it is really in them as a real act in a real potency. It is really not any of their natures nor part of their natures. It is really other than they, independently of consideration by the human mind. It is an act that is real, but which has to remain really other than the real potency it actuates, under penalty of absorbing that potency into the real nature of being. Being, therefore, is in finite things not a nature nor a note nor aspect of a nature, but is the entitative act of a nature really other than itself. Strictly, the other nature, the stone, the tree, the horse, is what exists. In making it exist, its being remains an act really outside the nature. If its being were contained within the nature, if its being were a note or an aspect just conceptually distinct from the rest of the nature, that being would be present in it as a nature and so would absorb it completely and irretrievably in subsistent being.

In any finite thing in the real world, accordingly, there is a real distinction between the thing itself and its being. Apart from any work of the human mind, the two are distinct in reality. The way of establishing this real distinction has been long and difficult. Only after the demonstration that being is a real nature, that is, after the demonstration that subsistent being really exists, has one obtained sufficient ground to prove a real distinction between a finite thing and its being in reality.[10] Being must first be established as a real nature, before one can proceed to the demonstration of a real distinction between being and thing.

Does this mean, though, that being and nature are two distinct realities in creatures?[11] Hardly. To have a reality other than subsistent being, you

[10] In Neoscholastic writers the consideration that the concept of a finite thing's nature does not contain the notion of its existence in reality is often given as a separate proof for the real distinction between the nature and the existence. In this status its validity has been open to challenge by both defenders and adversaries of the real distinction. See Cornelio Fabro, *La Nozione Metafisica di Partecipazione secondo S. Tommaso d'Aquino*, 2nd ed. (Turin, 1950), pp. 218–219. In St Thomas it occurs independently only in contexts after the existence of subsistent being has been demonstrated. As appears from its place in *De Ente et Essentia*, prior to the demonstration that being is a real nature it is merely one step in the long and complicated demonstration of the reception of being into a distinct subject through efficient causality. In recent decades the tendency among Neo-Thomists has been to give the principal place to the argument from limitation of act by reception into a real potency. This argument is not used in St Thomas to prove the real distinction; see J.-D. Robert, *art. cit.*, pp. 51–52. It takes for granted that existence is in itself a real act. However, that can be known only after the demonstration of subsistent being. Among the older Thomists a favorite argument was based on the necessary character of the esse *essentiae*, as shown by the essential predicates of a thing, in contradistinction to the contingent *esse existentiae*. On the origin of this argument and its introduction into the Thomistic tradition by Capreolus, see Norman J. Wells, "Capreolus on Essence and Existence," *The Modern Schoolman*, XXXVIII (1960), 1–24. Of the eleven arguments assembled by Norbert del Prado, *De Veritate Fundamentali Philosophiae Christianae* (Fribourg, Switzerland, 1911), pp. 29–70, all but the fifth and eighth are variations of the "limitation by subjective potency" argument.

A physical argument, meant to apply only in the case of sensible things, is added by Joseph Gredt, *Elementa Philosophiae Aristotelico-Thomisticae*, 7th ed. (Freiburg i. Breisgau, 1937), II, 109 (no. 705). It argues that existence is always complete, while matter is incomplete and form is incomplete. A material composite is therefore really distinct from its existence, because its parts are really distinct from existence. — This argument does not recognize that existence is the composing of the parts, and not something of the same order as the parts that could be compared with them from the viewpoint of completeness or incompleteness. The composing does not immediately make manifest that existence is an act in itself, with a content other than that of the composite. One has still to prove that being is a real nature. This is not accomplished till one has proven that being subsists in reality in a first efficient cause.

[11] The notion of the real distinction as a distinction between two *res* or realities, conceived in the fashion of the distinction of predicamental accident from substance, seems to have originated about two years after the death of St Thomas Aquinas, in controversies in which the leading names were Giles of Rome (ca. 1247–1316), affirming that distinction, and Henry of Ghent (1217–1293), denying it in favor of his own intentional distinction. It was formulated: "And, just as matter and quantity are two things, so essence and being are two really different things." Giles of Rome, *Theoremata de Esse et Essentia*, XIX; ed. Edgar Hocedez (Louvain, 1930), p. 134.11–13. It is found quite early in the Thomistic tradition as a distinction between *duae diversae res* in the *Totius Logicae Summa*, II, 2; ed. Mandonnet, *Opusc. Spuria*, in *S. Thomae Aquinatis Opusc. Om.* (Paris, 1927), V, 23. It is understood by Cajetan

have to have both entitative components. No finite reality is possible without the two. Without its being, the nature is merely nothing. It is not a reality, unless it is first made to be.[12] Without the limiting nature, any being whatsoever would be subsistent being. Only when an act of being, that is, an existential act, has limited itself by a really distinct potency, is there a finite reality. The real distinction between thing and being, therefore, cannot be a distinction between two realities. It is a real distinction within one and the same reality, a distinction that antecedes metaphysically any finite reality. The thing's being in no way becomes an added thing or an added reality. It accordingly adds nothing to the conceptualization of the thing. It is just that the thing is made to be.

The notion of a real distinction, then, is not to be understood in this case as a distinction between two realities. Nor may the designation "real" exclude the entitative distinction from full application to cognitional being. When a thing exists in someone's cognition it remains just as thoroughly distinct from its cognitional being as from any real being. It is not its cognitional being any more than it is its real being. But a real distinction is understood as a distinction in the real world, not in the cognitional world. How, from this point of view, can the distinction between the thing and its cognitional being appear as a real distinction? Yet the entitative distinction is there. The appellation "real distinction," consequently, falls short of expressing the extent of the entitative dis-

---

as falling between two such realities — *ex duabus rebus realiter distinctis, In de Ente et Essentia*, c. V; ed. M.-H. Laurent (Turin, 1934), p. 161 (no. 102). Bañez defends it under the formula "being is really distinct from essence as thing from thing (*tanquam res a re*)," In *Primam Partem Summae Theologiae*, I, 3, 4; ed. L. Urbano (Madrid-Valencia, 1934), I, 147a. In this guise it was combatted especially by Suarez. Accordingly it may be found among Neo-Thomists described as a distinction between what are "opposed realities in the finite thing, or are really distinct." Arthur Little, *The Platonic Heritage of Thomism* (Dublin, 1951), p. 213. It may even be found understood, with both existence and reality placed on each side of the couplet, as falling between "two realities existent in the real world," J. Gredt, *Elementa Philosophiae*, II, 105 (no. 704, 2). Typical, however, has been the description of them as "distinct, though not separable, realities . . ." R. P. Phillips, *Modern Thomistic Philosophy* (London, 1934–1935), II, 196.

[12] To allow the nature any being apart from its existence, real or cognitional, is to locate the problem in the setting of Avicenna's *esse proprium*, or proper being of the essence itself. This being was understood as identical with the nature of the thing, and somehow distinct from the real or intentional existence it receives. See Avicenna, *Metaph.*, Tr. I, c. 6C (Venice, 1508), fol. 72vl. It was called by the Scholastics the *esse essentiae*, or essential being of the thing; see Henry of Ghent, *Quodl.*, I, 9 (Paris, 1518), fol. 7r. Suarez had no difficulty in showing that essential being (*esse essentiae*) coincided with existential being (*esse existentiae*), and therefore that there was no real distinction between the two. See *Disp. Metaph.*, XXXI, 4, 4–6; ed. Vivès, XXVI, 235b–236b. This leaves untouched the question of distinction between that being and the essence itself.

tinction between thing and being. Along with the danger of being understood in its usual sense of a distinction between two realities, this makes "real distinction" none too satisfactory as a label for the metaphysical doctrine it is meant to express;[13] but it has come to be used in order to emphasize that the entitative distinction is not just a conceptual difference.

Participation of Being. Being, as is clear from the foregoing considerations, is a real nature that is received by other things through efficient causality not as a nature but as an act that is other than nature. This sharing in being is called **participation.** The term is borrowed from Greek sources. It carries overtones of formal causality. Etymologically it signifies "to take part of." The notion is that of something being divided into shares among the participants. Part of it goes to each. So whiteness is participated by thousands of white things, as though each had a share or part of whiteness. The notion works very well in the order of formal causality, where the same form, like whiteness or hardness or animality, is shared by many subjects. The earliest philosophical use of the notion seems to occur in the poem of Parmenides, proclaiming that neither of the basic forms, light (being) and darkness (not-being), can share in the other.[14] The setting was quite definitely formal causality. In Anaxagoras the theme was widely exploited in the all-pervading participation of things like the hot and the cold, the dry and the moist, the great and the small, flesh, bone, marrow, and to a restricted extent, mind. With Plato being was a form (Idea) that was participated by all other forms.[15] Through the Neoplatonic tradition the doctrine of the participation of being, against its background of formal causality, was passed on to the mediaeval Scholastics.

In its application to being, the doctrine of participation has to be purged of any aspect of formal causality. In no sense can you say that part of being goes to each of its recipients. There is here no form to be

[13] St Thomas uses the notion "real" three times in reference to this entitative distinction or composition — *In I Sent.*, d. 19, q. 2, a. 2, Solut. (ed. Mandonnet, I, 471), *De Ver.*, XXVII, 1, ad 8m (ed. Spiazzi, I, 513a), and *In De Hebd.*, c. II (ed. Mandonnet, *Opusc.*, I, 175–176). All three are occasional references, that is, references made on the occasion of treating some other subject. In places where the distinction between thing and being is treated *ex professo*, it is not called "real" by St Thomas. Cf.: ". . . quaecumque distinguuntur realiter, unum eorum est alia res ab alio." *In I Sent.*, d. 9, q. 1, a. 1, *Contra*; ed. Mandonnet, I, 246. Moreover, the term "distinction" is not free from difficulty when used to contrast a potency, immediately knowable only as actuated, with its own actuation; see J. A. Cunningham, "Distinction according to St. Thomas," *The New Scholasticism*, XXXVI (1962), 279–312.

[14] *DK*, 28B, 9.4. This line, however, may be interpreted in a way that eliminates the notion of participation, e.g., tr. Kranz, ad loc.

[15] Plato, *Sph.*, 250A–253C.

divided among different subjects. If being as a nature may be called a form,[16] it is a form that is entirely indivisible and unable to be shared as a nature with anything else. As the first efficient cause it can just make other natures be. In this communication of being, on the side of the first cause, there is no trace of strictly formal causality whatsoever. Being is imparted, from that viewpoint, to creatures only through efficient causality.[17] The finite nature is made to exist, without any addition at all in the order of nature. Nothing of formal nature is shared when being is participated.

It is not so easy, therefore, to transfer the notion of participation from its original habitat in the realm of formal causality. Yet in application to being it has to be transferred entirely to the order of efficient causality. It does indeed mean that the thing participating existence does not contain in itself the totality of existence, as does subsistent being. Yet that does not mean that it has a part of existence. Existence as a nature cannot be portioned into different parts or instances, like whiteness or animality. Participation of being merely means that some *other* nature is brought out of non-existence, is made to exist. No *part* of the shared nature, being, is received when something is brought into existence. Being is communicated, through efficient causality, in an act that is not at all a nature. The existential act of a creature is not a part of the nature of being, even though it is still less the totality of being.

The participation of being, accordingly, means merely that the one nature of being makes all other things be, through efficient causality. It is a causality that may be immediate or mediate. That is exactly what was demonstrated in the process of reasoning that led to the first efficient cause. To call it participation adds nothing more to its notion. The introduction of the term, however, occasions a warning against understanding the communication of being in the sense of a common nature that would be shared by all existents in the manner of formal causality.

Diversity. Even when the participation of being is understood strictly in terms of efficient causality, however, it encounters difficulties in regard to the diversity and plurality of beings. If subsistent being is infinite in all perfections, how does it leave room for anything outside

[16] E.g., St Thomas, *ST*, I, 3, 2, ad 3m. Cf. I, 3, 7c (5o), and below, Chapter 8, n. 3.

[17] "God is not the essential being of all things but the causal being." St Thomas, *In I Sent.*, d. 8, q. 1, a. 2, Solut.; ed. Mandonnet, I, 198. Subsistent being is indeed the exemplar of participated being, but not in the sense of causing any added formal aspect in the finite thing's nature. Efficient causality does not terminate in any added note of the nature. It simply makes the nature exist. Cf. *ST*, I ,3, 8, ad 1m.

itself?[18] If pure act is lacking nothing, how can anything else exist? Is not any being outside the first cause a further perfection added to the sum total of being as soon as it is produced?

There is no doubt that every finite nature is something other than pure act. It is other than being, while pure act is the real nature of being. They do not coincide. Nor is the existential act of any finite thing subsistent being. It is an act that remains other than any nature in which it is found, while subsistent being is its own nature. The existential act of any creature does not subsist, but existence as pure act does subsist. Again the two do not coincide. These considerations emerge clearly enough from the demonstration by which the first cause was reached. Yet how is such diversity possible?

The diversity can hardly be expected to appear if it is approached only from the side of pure act. There is nothing in subsistent being that relates it necessarily to anything else. The relations of sameness and otherness or difference or diversity, especially, are taken from the order of finite things and are not applicable to infinite being. They are categories that can directly categorize only the finite, because they involve limitation. They become meaningless[19] when applied directly to the absolutely infinite. Infinite being, then, viewed strictly from the standpoint of itself, is not different from anything. It includes undifferentiated in itself everything that has the least aspect of perfection. But that does not at all mean that it is the same as any finite thing. Either statement would be literally meaningless.

Approached from the side of creatures, though, diversity is straightway apparent. A finite nature is definitely not the nature of being, and a limited existential act is other than subsistent being. This approach is sufficient to allow the overall statements that there is diversity between subsistent being and participated beings,[20] and that subsistent being is the being of creatures through efficient causality but not formally. There is but one nature of being. It includes in itself the totality of being. That nature is not increased nor extended in any way by the production of other things. A million galaxies mean hundreds of millions of beings in the universe. But they do not mean the least bit more being than there was before anything was caused, or than there would be if they were nonexistent. They just do not add up to subsistent being, for they can

[18] This objection against Thomistic doctrine is emphasized by Paul Weiss, *Modes of Being* (Carbondale, 1958), p. 191 (no. 3.08).
[19] See G. B. Phelan, "The Being of Creatures," *Proceedings of the American Catholic Philosophical Association*, XXXI (1957), 122.
[20] E.g., St Thomas, *ST*, I, 3, 8, ad 3m.

add nothing to the nature of being. "Participation" here does not at all mean that they receive parts or portions of being, as its etymology would imply. It leaves the whole of being intact and unincreased, even though it sets up diversity between the creature and the first cause.

Conservation. Participation of being by finite things means not only that they were created by subsistent being, but also that they are continually sustained in being by their first cause. As an accident, participated being always depends on subsistent being, through efficient causality. The participation does not at all cease once things have been created. It continues as long as they exist. If the participation did not continue, the creature would at once lapse back into nothing.[21] A creature cannot of itself persist in being, for the same reason that it could not bring itself into being. All participated being depends continually on subsistent being. This continued participation of being to a subject that has already received being is technically called **conservation.** It differs conceptually from creation, for creation is the conferring of being upon something that did not yet exist. In both, being is immediately participated from the first cause. Creation and conservation, accordingly, are two different concepts of the participation of being to things. Conservation is the continuance of the participative action that began with their production in being.[22]

The being that is participated through creation and conservation carries along with it certain characteristics that are called transcendental.[23] Since these are concomitant wherever being is found, their investigation pertains directly to the study of being and is required for rounding off the inquiry about the existential act of things.

Résumé. Being, when imparted by efficient causality, gives rise to its own self-specification, namely the thing produced. In actuating a thing, being remains entitatively distinct from the thing itself. It does

[21] "For the being of every creature depends on God, so that they could not subsist even for a moment, but would be reduced to nothing, if they were not conserved in being by the operation of the divine power . . ." St Thomas, *ST*, I, 104, 1c.

[22] ". . . the conservation of things by God is not through any new action, but through the continuance of the action by which he gives being . . ." St Thomas, *ibid.*, ad 4m. In conserving, therefore, the first cause does not continue to create, even though conservation is a continuance of the participation of being that began with creation. On the mediate production of being, see below, Chapters 14, nn. 21–27, and 15, nn. 35–36.

[23] J. Maritain, *A Preface to Metaphysics* (New York, 1940), p. 69, describes the transcendentals as "consubstantial with being." In regard to created things, this expression has to be understood in a way that keeps the transcendentals concomitant with being when being is participated as an accident.

not absorb the thing into the one nature of being. The original imparting of existence, with no subject presupposed, is creation. Once created, the subject requires continued conservation by the first cause in order to remain in being.

SUGGESTED READINGS AND REFERENCES

Louis Bertrand Geiger, *La Participation dans la Philosophie de S. Thomas d'Aquin* (Paris: Vrin, 1942).
Arthur Little, *The Platonic Heritage of Thomism* (Dublin: Golden Eagle Books, 1951).
James Francis Anderson, *The Cause of Being* (St. Louis: B. Herder, 1952).
W. Norris Clarke, "The Limitation of Act by Potency: Aristotelianism or Neoplatonism?" *The New Scholasticism*, XXVI (1952), 167–194.
Joseph Owens, "The Number of Terms in the Suarezian Discussion on Essence and Being," *The Modern Schoolman*, XXXIV (1957), 147–191.

CHAPTER 8

Transcendentals

Predication of Being. In the first cause, being is a nature. In all other things, being is present not as a nature nor part of a nature but as a participated act. Being, accordingly, is found in all things whatsoever. It is predicable of them all. It is not confined to any one of the Aristotelian categories. Rather, it runs *through* all the categories and extends *beyond* them to their first cause. In the sense of both "climbing across" and "climbing beyond" it may be said to "transcend" all the categories. It is therefore called a **transcendental** predicate.

"Transcendental" in this meaning dates from the sixteenth century, though "transcendent" had been used for the notion since the thirteenth.[1] "Transcendental," it is true, has another well-established philosophical signification. It may refer exclusively to what is beyond the world of sense experience. In the present use, however, it denotes a characteristic found in all things throughout as well as beyond the Aristotelian categories. In this sense being is predicated transcendentally.

What permits the transcendental predication of being? Being is diverse in its every instance. Yet in each instance throughout the realm of finite things it actuates a potency in a way that is proportionally common to all.

---

[1] The term "transcendental" in this sense first appears in Suarez. He attributes it, in a way that cannot be verified, to the sixteenth-century Dominican Chrysostom Javelli. See Louis-Marie Régis, *L'Odyssée de la Métaphysique* (Montreal and Paris, 1949), p. 39, n. 47. The understanding of "transcendent" as "climbing across" the categories may be seen in St Thomas: ". . . the multiplicity that is not in any genus, but belongs to the transcendents" and "multiplicity according as it is transcendent," *ST*, I, 31, 3c. "One" (*ST*, I, 30, 3, ad lm) and "good" (*De Virt. in Comm.*, 2, ad 8m) and "thing" (*ST*, I, 39, 3, ad 3m) are similarly classed with the "transcendents." But the term is also used by St Thomas in the sense of transcending time (*CG*, III, 61) and change (*ST*, I–II, 5, 4, ad lm), matter (*ST*, I, 118, 2c), sense (I, 59, 1, ad lm), and imagination (I, 75, 1c), that is, of location beyond the whole order of movement, and similarly by Albert, text above, "Historical Introduction," n. 2.

On the origins of the Scholastic study of the transcendentals, see H. Pouillon, "Le Premier Traité des Propriétés Transcendantales," *Revue Néoscolastique de Philosophie*, XLII (1939), 40–77.

It makes the potency more than nothing, it makes a subject be. This ever present proportion sets up the notion of common being. It accordingly gives rise to an analogous concept, analogous by proper proportionality. In all creatures this common proportion is found. Peter's being does proportionally for Peter what Paul's being does for Paul. A corresponding proportion holds for specific and generic natures, in regard to the being they receive in the mind. Human nature is to its being as equine nature is to equine being.[2] In all these ways the proportion is there. It is too primal to be expressed in any other way than by saying that in every case the existential act makes the creature be. To say that it makes the thing more than nothing is merely a circumlocution; for "nothing" is knowable only as a lack of all being, as has been stressed. The common proportion, then, allows being to be predicated analogously of every creature.

But can this way of predication extend to subsistent being? In subsistent being, nature and existence are not conceptually distinct from each other. Attributes like knowledge and power are conceptually distinct from the nature of pure existential act, and so allow analogous predication. But how could the existence of the first cause be conceived as making its nature be? That nature is already existent as nature, for its very concept is "real existence." There is no proportion between its nature and its existence, but only the strictest intrinsic identity. Yet the common notion of being, conceptualized from the composition apprehended through judgment, is based on that ever present proportion. Clearly, subsistent being is not included in the notion of common being. But it is the cause of everything directly included in the notion of common being, and so may be called the cause of common being. The same reasoning that establishes subsistent being as the cause of all other beings, however, places the nature of being in subsistent being only. In all other things being is an accident. Where being is a substance it is naturally prior to

---

[2] This nature, though universal in regard to the really existent singulars that come under it, is nevertheless particular in regard to the individual intellect in which it is found: "Human nature, then, can have the character of a species only as it exists in the intellect. Human nature itself exists in the intellect in abstraction from all individual conditions, and it thus has a uniform relation to all individual men outside the intellect . . . And although the nature existing in the intellect has the character of a universal from its relation to things outside the intellect, since it is one likeness of them all, nevertheless, as it exists in this or that intellect, it is a certain particular species apprehended by the intellect." St Thomas, *De Ente*, c. III (ed. Roland-Gosselin), pp. 27.10–28.15; tr. Maurer, p. 41. Specific being may be compared with other specific being, just as individual being may be compared with other individual being: ". . . all the things that are in one genus communicate in the quiddity or essence of the genus. . . . But they differ in being; for the being of man is not the same as the being of horse, nor is the being of this man the same as the being of that man." *ST*, I, 3, 5c.

instances in which it is an accident. Its nature is of necessity its primary instance. Even though the being of sensible things is first known by the human mind and through it subsistent being is mediately attained, it cannot serve as the nature to which all other instances are referred; for it is not the nature of being. Often a nature is not attained in itself by human cognition. Electricity, for instance, is not known directly in itself but only through its effects. Yet electricity is the nature in reference to which motors and razors and toasters and all other such instances are denominated electric.

Subsistent being and participated beings, then, are denominated alike beings because the one is the nature of being and the others are, as beings, its effects. All the others are accordingly beings through reference to subsistent being.[3] Among themselves, however, they share being analogously. In this analogous way being extends through all the Aristotelian categories. It extends to features like motion that run through different categories,[4] and to all privations and negations insofar as each of them is

[3] "Creator and creature are brought under one notion, not by community of univocity but of analogy. Such community can be twofold: either because some things participate some one aspect in order of prior and subsequent, as potency and act participate the aspect of being, and likewise substance and accident; or because one thing receives being and aspect from another, and such is the analogy of creature to creator. For the creature does not have being except as it descends from the first being, nor is it called a being except insofar as it imitates the first being." St Thomas, *In I Sent.*, Prol., q. 1, a. 2, ad 2m; ed. Mandonnet, I, 10. The "form" or nature or aspect that is received and so communicated is in this case the thing's very being; cf. *ibid.*, d. 35, q. 1, a. 4, Solut.; I, 819–820. See also *ST*, I, 3, 2c (3o).

[4] Opposition, priority, simultaneity, movement, and possession were treated of by Aristotle in the *Categories* (10–15, 11b15 ff.) *after* the ten predicaments, and so were called *postpraedicamenta* in Scholastic tradition. Each is found in several or all of the categories. Privation and negation were listed under opposition in the *Categories* (*ibid.*, 11b18–19). For St Thomas: "Thus, we call even privations and negations beings, for we say that affirmation is opposed to negation, and that blindness is in the eye." *De Ente*, c. I (ed. Roland-Gosselin), p. 3.3–5; tr. Maurer, p. 27. On their being for Aristotle, see *Metaph.*, Γ 2, 1003b8–10.

In general, accidental being functions in regard to accident as substantial being does in regard to substance: "But, just as from the union of matter and form there results a substantial act of existing, so from the joining of accident to subject an accidental act of existing results." St Thomas, *De Ente et Essentia*, c. VI (ed. Roland-Gosselin), p. 43.4–7; tr. Maurer, p. 55. In detail, however, this four-term analogy seems mentioned by St Thomas only occasionally; e.g.: ". . . as substance is related to the being due to it, so also is quality to the appropriate being of its kind." *In III Sent.*, d. 1, q. 1, a. 1, Resp.; ed. Moos, III, 8 (no. 12). Cf. other texts below, Chapter 11, n. 7. In the Aristotelian tradition, St Thomas seems content to emphasize only the way in which accidents are denominated beings through reference to substance, with the proviso that the transcendental aspects are inherent in all the instances; see above, Chapter 6, n. 15. The four-term analogy of accidents to their respective being, or of substance and accident to their respective being, was not part of the Aristotelian tradition, and was based upon a doctrine of being that was not

given being in cognition. It is predicated in the concrete and in the abstract, and in the cognitional as well as in the real order. Wherever anything is made to be through any kind of efficient causality, the analogous predication of being has its application.

The Principle of Being. Insofar as being actuates any potency, it necessarily makes that subject exist and makes it other than anything else. In every instance it is diverse. In sensible things being is a composing in time and, as actuating the Aristotelian categories, is possessed by a thing in both substance and accidents. The immediate axiom or principle of being, accordingly, is worded with those conditions: a thing cannot both be and not be at the same time and in the same respects. This maxim is so primal that it cannot be proven and needs no proof. It is presupposed by any proof and it makes demonstration possible. It shows that the terms of the propositions may retain their fixed meaning throughout the course of the demonstration, and excludes a wonderland of nonsense in which anything could be said indifferently of anything. For this reason it was known in the Aristotelian tradition as the **first principle of demonstration.**[5] Since it determines a thing to one of the two sides of a contradiction, it is known in modern times as the **principle of contradiction.**[6] It allows no middle state between the two

---

found in Aristotle. But it follows from the doctrine of St Thomas that every finite thing is other than its being. To a substantial composing in being there corresponds proportionally accidental composing in being, according to the order of prior and subsequent that holds for substance and accident. The being of the accident corresponds to the being of the substance insofar as they both make their respective potencies be, the one in an accidental way and the other in a substantial way. This is sufficient to establish four-term analogy among the accidents themselves. Though not in the text of St Thomas, "it is implicit in the various passages that compare and contrast the accidents one with another. . . . It seems reasonable enough to say that the various accidents are analogously accidents by an analogy of proper proportionality." George P. Klubertanz, *St. Thomas Aquinas on Analogy* (Chicago, 1960), p. 132.

[5] See Aristotle, *Metaph.*, Γ 3–4, 1005b11–1006b1. This is the only axiom or demonstrative principle that is absolutely first: ". . . for this is naturally the starting-point even for all the other axioms." *Ibid.*, 3, 1005b33–34; Oxford tr. Cf.: ". . . it belongs to the primary philosopher to consider the first principle of demonstration." St Thomas Aquinas, *In IV Metaph.*, lect. 6 (ed. Cathala-Spiazzi), no. 596. "For what first falls under apprehension is being (*ens*), the notion of which is included in all things whatsoever anyone apprehends. And therefore the first indemonstrable principle is that nothing is to be affirmed and denied at the same time. This is based upon the aspect of being and not being; and upon this principle all others are based, as is said in the fourth book of the *Metaphysics*." *ST*, I–II, 94, 2c; see also *In IV Metaph.*, lect. 6, no. 605.

[6] Leibniz, *Monadology*, 31. It was understood by Leibniz as the principle of essences. Understanding it as expressing the self-identity of a thing in this way, Leibniz was able to use the designation "principle of identity" as an alternate title for it:

sides of the contradiction. This aspect of it is called the principle of **excluded middle.** The maxim itself is but an expression of what is immediately apprehended in the judgment of being, and so provides its own evidence in a way stronger than any proof. It formulates what is known in the immediate apprehension of being. The expressed contrast with not being adds in no way to its content, as not being is known only in terms of being.

In the first cause the necessity of being is absolute. Non-existence is utterly impossible for subsistent being. In it there is no subject that is other than being and that might lose being. It necessarily exists, and exists in every respect in the infinity of perfection, and in all duration simultaneously, that is, in eternity. In other things the necessity expressed by the first principle of demonstration is found in various degrees of caused necessity and contingency. But in every instance the principle formulates a necessity that is involved in the thing's being.[7] In every instance, to be not only means the fact that the thing exists, but also involves the necessity that it cannot be otherwise at the moment and in the same respects. Parmenides was the earliest Western philosopher to emphasize the necessity that being inevitably and everywhere involves.[8] In his failure to see any participation of being by non-being, however, he applied the full necessity of being as a nature to being wherever it was found.

Differences of Being. Because it is transcendental, being, as has already been seen,[9] is predicated of all its differences. But how is being distinguished from these differences? In subsistent being,

---

". . . the Other great Principle of our Reasonings, viz., that of essences; that is, the principle of Identity or Contradiction . . ." *A Collection of Papers which passed between Mr. Leibniz and Dr. Clarke in the Years 1715 & 1716* (London, 1717), p. 163. It should mean, though, against the mediaeval background, that being contradicts non-being.

A more recent designation is the "principle of non-contradiction." This title understands it as meaning that a thing cannot contradict its own self, and so seems to follow upon the conception of it as the principle of identity or of essences. For Maritain the principle of non-contradiction "directly concerns logic not metaphysics, and is but the logical form of the principle of identity." *A Preface to Metaphysics* (New York, 1940), p. 91.

[7] On the combination of necessity and contingency in varying degrees, see J. Maritain, "Reflections on Necessity and Contingency," in *Essays in Thomism*, ed. Robert E. Brennan (New York, 1942), p. 33. Cf. St Thomas, *ST*, I, 86, 3c.

[8] Parmenides, *Fr.* 2.3–5 (DK 28B). Cf. *Fr.* 8.30–31. See St Thomas, *De Pot.*, V, 4c; *ST*, I, 19, 3c.

[9] See Chapter 4, n. 15. "But nothing can be added to being that is extraneous to it, since nothing is extraneous to it except non-being, which cannot be either form or matter." St Thomas, *De Pot.*, VII, 2, ad 9m; cf. *De Ver.*, I, lc.

the distinction can be only verbal; for there is no intrinsic conceptual distinction here between what subsists and its being. The primary instance of being and the nature of being coincide, even conceptually.[10] In all other things, being is related to thing as act to potency, and so when conceptualized in relation to each differing thing it appears as diverse in every individual and different in every genus and species.[11] The existential act, of course, is really diverse in each case as it is apprehended in judgment, and is really other than its subject in real things. But the relation to a different potency in each occurrence allows the common concept of being to be conceptualized in a different respect each time, and so gives rise to a conceptual distinction between the common concept of a being and the many differences of which that common concept is predicated.

It is entirely wrong, therefore, to schematize being as a common notion with two main divisions under it, infinite and finite, or subsistent and participated,[12] somewhat as the nature "animal" is divided into "rational" and "irrational." In a generic notion like "animal," the nature itself is not an instance of the universal.[13] But with being, the nature is the

[10] The primary instance of being is distinguished only by being: "That explains why we find some philosophers asserting that God does not have a quiddity or essence, because His essence is not other than His act of existing. . . . The act of existing which is God is such that no addition can be made to it. Consequently, in virtue of its very purity it is the act of existing distinct from every other act of existing." St Thomas, *De Ente*, c. V (ed. Roland-Gosselin), pp. 37.14–38.4; tr. Maurer, pp. 50–51.

[11] See St Thomas, *ST*, I, 3, 4c; see text above, n. 2. Cf.: "And therefore whenever the form signified by the word is being itself, it cannot belong to them univocally . . ." *In I Sent.*, d. 35, q. 1, a. 4, Solut.; ed. Mandonnet, I, 819. Being, accordingly, is never univocal to any two things.

[12] For Duns Scotus, the concept of being is of itself neither finite nor infinite, but univocal to both, and contracted to each by the appropriate differentia. The concept, though univocal, is not generic, because it is predicated of its own differentiae and of the transcendentals. On this topic see Cyril Louis Shircel, *The Univocity of the Concept of Being in the Philosophy of Duns Scotus* (Washington, D. C., 1942); J. Owens, "Up to What Point is God included in the Metaphysics of Duns Scotus?" *Mediaeval Studies*, X (1948), 165–170. Without this univocity, infinite being would not be naturally knowable. For Suarez, "the first and most essential division of being is into finite and infinite" (*Disp. Metaph.*, XXVIII; ed. Vivès, XXVI, 1a), or divisions that coincide with this though using other terms or concepts. This division for Suarez, however, is analogous, but "according to a common objective concept" (XXVIII, 3, 20; XXVI, 20b; cf. no. 9, pp. 15–16). The one common objective concept permits the use of being as a middle term in demonstration, according to the Suarezian view.

[13] That is why a Platonic Idea cannot be considered as an instance of itself, without giving rise to insuperable difficulties. Cf.: "Proper universals are not instantiations of themselves, perfect or otherwise." R. E. Allen, "Participation and Predication in Plato's Middle Dialogues," *The Philosophical Review*, LXIX (1960), 147. Considered as a species in an individual intellect (see above, n. 2), however, any nature is actuated as a new instance in cognitional being each time it is thought.

primary instance. The primary instance, accordingly, would have to occupy the top place in the schema. Its being is not differentiated by any added concept, and so is not common being. Rather, as already noted, it is the cause of common being. Far from having itself contained under common being, it contains common being under its power and causality. The community of being, in consequence, is twofold.[14] By analogy, being is common to all participated beings. By reference through efficient causality, being is derived from the nature of being to participated instances. In this way it is trancendentally common. As transcendental it is not above all its instances. It does not transcend *to* its primary instance, but transcends *from* it to all others. Subsistent being, accordingly, is not transcendental being, but is the cause of that being. It does not come under transcendental being. On the contrary, transcendental being comes under it. Being, one has to keep in mind, is participated not by formal but by efficient causality.

Properties of Being. On account of its transcendental character, being likewise is predicated of any properties it may have as being. Ordinarily a subject is not predicated of its properties, because the role of a property is qualitative.[15] Yet in order to function in their qualitative role, the properties of being, even under that aspect, have to be. If they are strictly properties, they will accompany being wherever being is found. On that ground they may be called trancendent or transcendental properties of being. As properties they will be in some way distinct from their subject. The type of distinction, however, is best investigated in connection with each of the transcendental properties that makes itself apparent in being.

Unity. A unit means something that is undivided. The being of sensible things consists in a composing or "uniting." Insofar as each thing is a being, therefore, it is a unit. Upon its being necessarily follows unity.

But in the real world, a finite nature like "animal" is not an individual instance of animality, while on the contrary the nature of being is an individual instance of being.

[14] In the type found just among creatures, St Thomas notes only the prior and subsequent sharing of a common inherent aspect, with no mention of four-term analogy: "But analogy is twofold. One type is by coinciding in some one feature that pertains to them in order of prior and subsequent; and this analogy cannot be had between God and creature, just as univocity cannot be had. The other type of analogy is through one imitating the other as far as it can, and not perfectly attaining it; and this is the analogy of creature to God." St Thomas, *In I Sent.*, d. XXXV, q. 1, a. 4, Solut.; ed. Mandonnet, I, 820. Cf.: ". . . between God and creature there is no similitude through coincidence in any one common trait, but through imitation; hence a creature is said to be similar to God, but not vice versa . . ." *Ibid.*, ad 6m; p. 821. See above, nn. 3 and 4.

[15] See above, Chapter 4, n. 14.

Subsistent being is one by the very pureness of its actuality; and in general any simple nature to the extent that it is, will thereby be one. The being of anything whatsoever, accordingly, consists in undividedness.[16] Everywhere unity will follow upon being as a property. Insofar as anything is, it is one. Undividedness, however, is a negative consideration added in the mind to the positive notion of being. It provides the basis for a new concept in the mind, without requiring the addition of anything at all outside the mind to the existential act. Unity is therefore conceptually and not really distinct from being. To say that a thing exists and to say that a thing is one, is to express the same actuality first from a positive and then from a negative viewpoint, in two different concepts.

Transcendental unity, of course, is not the same as numerical unity. Numerical unity belongs to one category of being, quantity. The unity that is a property of being transcends all the categories. Because it is merely a negative consideration, transcendental unity may be said to follow upon the substance or nature of a thing.[17] Strictly, though, unity follows rather upon the thing's being. Unless the nature is represented as in some way existing, it cannot at all be conceived as a unit.[18] Because transcendental unity is a property of being, it cannot be regarded as a division of being, as though being were divided into one and many. Rather, being necessarily implies only the first of the two, unity; and because each instance of participated being is a unit, multiplicity arises.[19]

Truth. Truth is what the mind strives to attain in its own endeavors. It is reached when the intellect knows something as it actually is. The truth about a crime, for instance, is had when you know who the criminal really is. To have merely the notions "criminal" and "murder" is not enough to have truth. You have to know that murder *is* a crime, or that this man *is* the murderer. In a word, truth is reached in a judgment,

[16] "Hence it is clear that the being of any thing whatsoever consists in indivision." St Thomas, *ST*, I, 11, 1c.

[17] ". . . unity is indifferent in regard to its bearing upon essence or being. Hence the essence of a thing is one by itself, not on account of its being. And so it is not one by any participation, as happens in regard to being and goodness." St Thomas, *De Ver.*, XXI, 5, ad 8m. Cf. *ST*, I, 11, 1, ad 1m.

[18] Cf.: "Then it has no being even so as to be one, for if it were one, it would be and would partake of being . . ." Plato, *Prm.*, 141E; tr. H. N. Fowler. In abstraction from being the nature can have the unity neither of a particular nor of a universal: "If someone should ask, then, whether the nature so considered can be called *one* or *many*, neither should be granted, because both are outside the concept of humanity and both can be added to it. . . . unity and community belong to the notion of a universal. Now, neither of these belongs to human nature considered absolutely." St Thomas, *De Ente*, c. III (ed. Roland-Gosselin), pp. 24.10–27.2; tr. Maurer, pp. 40–41.

[19] See St Thomas, *ST*, I, 11, 1, ad 2m; 2, ad 4m.

when the judgment reflects the actual being of a thing. It is not attained in simple apprehension, where the nature and not the being is grasped. Truth, therefore, is grounded upon the being of a thing, not on its nature.[20] Where there is being, truth can be had by an intellect capable of knowing that being. Truth accordingly follows upon being, when being is considered in relation to any intellect that can know it. The being may be called true, because it is able to ground the truth that is in the intellect. The truth of a being, then, is merely the being itself considered as knowable or intelligible. It adds no new reality to the thing, but is expressed in a new concept. Truth, in consequence, is conceptually and not really distinct from being.

The being of creatures, however, is not related to the intellect of the first cause in the same way as it is to other intellects. The first cause produces other things not by necessity of nature but by free choice. This means that the first cause knows what it chooses to create. Its knowledge is causative in regard to the being of other things. The truth in the intellect of the first cause, therefore, grounds the being of all else. Things are true primarily in relation to the intellect that grounds their being, and only secondarily in relation to the intellects for which their being is the ground of truth. In any of these cases, though, truth is being as conceived in relation to intellect.

Because truth is what intellection achieves, it is said to be formally in the intellect rather than in things. The intellect in its activity gives the thing it knows cognitional being. The terminus of the intellect's endeavor, accordingly, is within. The intellect has reached the truth when the correct judgment is formed within itself. Formally, then, it is the judgment that is true. A statement or proposition is true, because it expresses a true judgment. Since the being of the thing is the cause of the correct judgment, that being is said to be causally true. It is denominated true from its effect. In relation to the first cause, however, the situation is the reverse. Truth remains formally in the intellect of the first cause, but the truth of participated being is its effect, somewhat as the lines of a building are true because they were correctly designed by the architect.

When things are called true, then, it is always in relation to an intellect that knows their being. True gold is such that it grounds the judgment "This *is* gold." Pyrite is called fool's gold, because it does not provide ground for the scientific judgment that it is gold. Its intelligibility is not that of gold. Its own truth is furnished by its intelligibility as a sulfide.

[20] ". . . the aspect of truth is based upon being, and not upon quiddity." St Thomas, *In I Sent.*, d. 19, q. 5, a. 1, ad 7m; ed. Mandonnet, I, 489. Cf. *De Ver.*, I, 1, ad 3m in contr.

That intelligibility grounds the judgment that it is a sulfide. Since all things are accordingly intelligible in terms of being, truth is transcendental. It is a transcendental property of being.

Goodness. Natural philosophy shows that everything known occasions a reaction in some appetitive faculty. If what is known appears as a perfection for the knower, it is desired when absent and enjoyed when possessed. The presence of appetite or desire is known through consciousness in one's own self. It is seen in its effects in other animals and in plants and even in inanimate things. Each of these tends to preserve its own identity and being. If it is a living thing, it strives to develop itself along set grooves and seek the circumstances best adapted to its existence and activity. Its activity consists in efficient causality, which is the production of new being. A thing in its whole nature and activity, therefore, is meant for being, and through its faculties it works to conserve its own being and to bring its potentialities and required effects into existential act. In this way it always tends toward the ultimate actuality or perfection that consists in being. Because being is a perfection and an ultimate perfection, it is appetible. Insofar as it is appetible, it is called good.

Goodness, accordingly, is being when considered in relation to appetite. It adds nothing real to being, for it is merely being itself, now conceived as appetible. This is a new concept, and so gives rise to a conceptual distinction between goodness and being, but not to a real distinction. All created things are appetible primarily in their relation to the will of subsistent being, which produced them through free choice. Secondly, they are appetible to other things that seek them. Some appetibility, therefore, always follows upon being, and being is always the ground of the appetibility. Goodness, then, follows upon being as a transcendental property.

Unlike truth, goodness is found formally in the thing sought or enjoyed, and not in the appetite that seeks it. Appetite does not give a thing new being within itself, as intellect does. Rather, it is a tendency toward what is in the thing that constitutes its object. In the thing, then, is the goodness located. Only insofar as it happens to be itself something sought is an appetite formally good, as for instance when one would like to have a good appetite for food. Except in that case, an appetite is denominated good only insofar as it is specified by a good object. From this viewpoint arises a difference between goodness and being that is described in terms of the Aristotelian categories. A thing is absolutely a being through its substance, and in particular respects through its accidents. A thing is good, on the contrary, in a certain respect through its substance, but absolutely through its accidents. A horse is absolutely a horse as long as it is just alive, but is it a good horse if it lacks sight, hearing, and sound limbs? Hardly. The reason is that goodness is based upon perfection, and accidents are necessary for the perfection of anything finite. If all the required physical perfections are present, the thing is **physically good.** A lack of a required physical perfection is called a physical evil, like blindness in man. The required moral perfection in human conduct is called **moral goodness,** and its privation moral evil.

Because every existent has at least substantial being, it can function as the object of appetite. But if through lack of required accidents it is physically or morally evil, the appetite may be denominated bad. An urge to overeat may be physically bad, and the deliberate will to satisfy it may be morally evil. But as long as any object exists, there is always some good in it, because there is some being; and on account of that goodness, it is appetible. Anything evil, therefore, is desired only on account of some goodness it possesses. The transcendental character of goodness extends to all evil things insofar as they are beings. Everything is transcendentally good. Only a metaphysics that gives nothingness a status equal to being can see it hanging as a veil over all things.[21]

Mathematical and logical constructions are good by reason of the cognitional being they possess. In themselves they have their own appeal for the pure mathematician and for the logician. But logic is also useful for other sciences, and mathematics for manipulating sensible things. The **useful** is what is desired not for itself, but as a means to other goods. Because it is desirable it is a good, but though it attracts on account of its usefulness it does not terminate any appetite. The appetite that seeks it as useful tends thereby to a further good sought for its own sake. Any good sought for itself[22] terminates a particular appetite, as enough food satisfies hunger and sufficient rest quiets the desire for sleep. But just as all finite beings are caused by subsistent being, so all finite goods are subordinate to the infinite good that follows upon infinite being. A particular good like nourishment or health may indeed be sought for its own sake and not just as a means. As a good it contributes to the well-being of the animal. The well-being of animal nature helps in its own turn

[21] See Heidegger, *An Introduction to Metaphysics*, tr. Ralph Manheim (New Haven, 1959), p. 203.

[22] A good sought for itself is called an end (*finis*), or goal. On the axiom that every agent acts for an end, see G. P. Klubertanz, "St. Thomas' Treatment of the Axiom, 'Omne Agens Agit Propter Finem,'" in *An Etienne Gilson Tribute*, ed. Charles J. O'Neil (Milwaukee, 1959), pp. 101–117. The axiom is called "the principle of finality." On the subordination of finite goods, as goods, to the infinite good, see St Thomas, *De Ver.*, XXI, 5c; *ST*, I, 6, 4c.

toward spiritual life. Each particular good in this way serves toward a higher. Only the good that is infinite absolutely terminates all appetite. It alone is perfectly good, just as it alone is perfectly being. Insofar as any good affords pleasure or enjoyment it is called **delectable.** In the infinite good, the greatest delectability coincides with the greatest appetibility.[23] In other things they frequently differ, for instance as seen in the sacrifice of pleasure in order to fulfill the duty of looking after an aged parent.

Beauty. Of all the transcendentals, beauty is the most evasive and the most difficult to understand. It has given rise to discussions and treatises that are legion. The controversies have resulted in disagreement and in no generally accepted explanation.[24] A sufficiently penetrating treatment of the beautiful would perhaps require a man who was at the same time a great artist and a keen metaphysician, a combination not readily found. Beauty is undoubtedly something perceptible by the intellect. It corresponds directly to the cognoscitive rather than to the appetitive faculties. It seems to consist in an effulgence of actuated form.[25] In its perception it gives an elevated pleasure and deep satisfaction. Accordingly it in-

[23] See Aristotle, *E N*, I 8, 1099a24–31; *E E*, I 1, 1214a1–8. A good sought as an end distinct from the pleasure it affords is called in Scholastic Latin a *bonum honestum:* "That which is sought as an ultimate, entirely terminating the movement of the appetite, as something towards which the appetite tends of itself, is called 'honestum,' because what is desired of itself is called 'honestum.'" St Thomas, *ST*, I, 5, 6c. The term "honestum" is difficult to render in English. It came into Scholastic tradition from the Stoics through Cicero and St Augustine. Like the Greek *kalon,* it was meant to express both the beautiful and the morally good. On this history of the term, see H. Pouillon, "La Beauté, Propriété Transcendantale chez les Scolastiques (1220–1270)," *Archives d'Histoire Doctrinale et Littéraire du Moyen Age,* XXI (1946), 268–271. Including as it does the moral good and the beautiful, the notion of *bonum honestum* does not fit any too neatly into the regular Scholastic grooves.

[24] On the divergence among the Neoscholastics, see Pouillon, *art. cit.*, pp. 263–265. On the transcendental character of the beautiful, see J. Maritain, *Art and Scholasticism,* tr. J. F. Scanlan (New York, 1930), pp. 23–32; *Creative Intuition in Art and Poetry* (New York, 1953), pp. 160–163; Francis J. Kovach, *Die Ästhetik des Thomas von Aquin* (Berlin, 1961), pp. 183–214. Kovach (*ibid.*, pp. 183–185) studies the different meanings of the term "transcendent" in St Thomas, and (pp. 5–27) gives a critique of the Neoscholastic efforts in developing a doctrine of the beautiful. For non-Scholastic views, see bibliographies in Susanne K. Langer, *A Theory of Art* (New York, 1953), pp. 417–423, and in *Modern Art,* ed. Charles McCurdy (New York, 1958), pp. 431–464.

[25] "But the beautiful is related to the cognoscitive faculty; for things that please when seen, are called beautiful. Hence the beautiful consists in due proportion, because a sense delights in things duly proportioned . . . And because cognition takes place through assimilation, and similitude is concerned with form, the beautiful properly belongs to the notion of formal cause." St Thomas, *ST*, I, 5, 4, ad 1m. ". . . the beautiful is the same as the good, differing only in notion." *ST*, I–II, 27, 1, ad 3m. Difference in notion is a conceptual distinction.

volves the appetitive side of one's nature, even though formally it is something perceived. In order to be perceived as beautiful, a thing has to have already the integrity conferred by goodness. Insofar as a thing is physically or morally evil, it is defective and is to that extent lacking in beauty. There is a sense, then, in which goodness sets up the beautiful. This may be called the goodness that is proper to beauty. There is also of course the common way in which goodness characterizes beauty and the enjoyment to which the beautiful gives rise, just as it characterizes truth and everything else and renders them all appetible as goods.

In sensible things beauty does not as a rule appear too readily or too forcefully. Often it does not appear at all, or only in weaker degrees that in English may be called interesting or pleasing or attractive. Usually it requires the skill of the artist to make it appear in a really striking way, by the disposition of colors or sounds in an order and harmony that let form radiate its native splendor through the sensible media. Sight and hearing, consequently, are the senses through which perception of the beautiful takes place in bodily life. Through these senses the arts of painting, sculpture, and music make their appeal. Through the imagination the beautiful is presented in poetry and literature. In human activity it appears in the virtues and in the sublime and heroic, as in different ways an outstandingly courageous end in battle or a saintly giving up of soul amidst prayerful surroundings is called a beautiful death. In an occasional sunset or landscape or human person it may break forth spontaneously in all the fullness usually associated with it by the English word "beauty."

Beauty seems therefore a splendor that emerges from actuated form. It should be present wherever form is actual, that is, wherever anything exists.[26] To be esthetically (i.e., sensibly) beautiful, however, a thing

[26] ". . . but every form, through which a thing has being, is a participation of the divine splendor; and this is what he adds, that 'all things' are 'beautiful according to their proper notion,' that is, according to their proper form." St Thomas, *In De Div. Nom.*, c. IV, lect. 5 (ed. C. Pera), no. 349. Msgr. Phelan comments: "The relational character of beauty is thus rooted in existence, in being. It belongs to all things which are, in any manner whatsoever. Its degrees and kinds are determined only by the degrees of being." G. B. Phelan, "The Concept of Beauty in St. Thomas Aquinas," in *Aspects of the New Scholastic Philosophy*, ed. Charles A. Hart (New York, etc., 1932), p. 131. Emerging in this way through form, for St Thomas the beautiful pleases by objectively formal causality, while the good attracts by final causality. Nevertheless, the beautiful is said to follow upon the good, since the splendor and proportion that constitute it come under the good: "Although the beautiful and the good are identical in subject, because both splendor and harmony are contained under the aspect of good, nevertheless they differ in notion; for the beautiful adds, over and above the good, a relation to the faculty that knows the good is so." St Thomas, *op. cit.*, no. 356. This doctrine means that the perception of the beautiful is a further way of knowing the good. Wherever the good is found, then, the beautiful follows. Hence the simplicity of pure being is beautiful

requires the proper disposition of colors or sounds and of the quantity that becomes sensible through those qualities. Just as a thing may be transcendentally good without being physically or morally good, so it may be transcendentally beautiful without being esthetically beautiful. That the beautiful is not everywhere apparent to the senses and often requires great artistic elaboration to make it appear, therefore, need not exclude beauty from the ranks of the transcendentals. As a transcendental property, beauty like truth and goodness is conceptually but not really distinct from being. Subsistent being is in its simplicity beauty itself, and the cause of the harmony that conditions beauty in sensible things.

Thing. Whatever exists is a thing. The notion "thing," accordingly, is transcendental. But it can hardly be considered a property of being. In finite things it is rather a potency to being. Every act of existence that proceeds from the first cause inevitably requires its proper potency, which is other than itself. In that way a thing is proper to every finite existential act. But this is a rather different sense of "proper" from

---

in itself. It is indeed the primary instance of beauty, without any call for "virtual multiplicity." Nor does the requirement of proportion make the beautiful consist formally in the entitative composition of nature and being. Umberto Eco, *Il Problema Estetico in San Tommaso* (Turin, 1956), p. 62, while admitting that this "places beauty on an extremely rarified metaphysical plane," nevertheless proposes as an original comment: "A thing *is* in the act of composition between essence and existence, and this act is a *proportio*, a concordance, a harmonizing; and proportion is constitutive of beauty. Every being, therefore, insofar as it *is*, is beautiful because it *is* in virtue of a harmony." — Yet subsistent being is beautiful in itself, without any such composition. As a requirement for beauty, proportion conditions the good. If anything simple is good in itself, accordingly, it is beautiful in itself. On the causal attribution of beauty to the first cause, see St Thomas, *ST*, II–II, 145, 2c.

Of its nature, beauty satisfies the rational appetite: ". . . it pertains to the notion of beauty that in beholding or knowing it the appetite be satisfied." St Thomas, *ST*, I–II, 27, 1, ad 3m. While presupposing the goodness that properly constitutes it (i.e., splendor and harmony), the beautiful is also appetible in the way truth or anything else is. On this "twofold goodness" in beauty, see G. Phelan, *art. cit.*, p. 136. On the description of esthetic contemplation as "disinterested," see John Leonard Callahan, *A Theory of Esthetic according to the Principles of St. Thomas Aquinas*, 2nd ed. (Washington, D. C., 1947), pp. 72–75.

Because it is an aspect of being, beauty like the other transcendental properties is not to be considered as a value, but as something real. Gilson notes: "St. Thomas Aquinas' doctrine is a realism; according to him, beauty is being itself considered under one of its transcendental aspects. Modern idealism begins by turning the transcendentals into 'values' . . ." *Painting and Reality* (New York, 1957), p. 191, n. 22. A list of texts from St Thomas on the beautiful is given by G. Phelan, *art. cit.*, p. 145. To these Msgr. Phelan later added: *ST*, I–II, 49, 2c; 2 ad 1m; 4c; 52, 2c (cf. 50, 1c); 54, 1c; II–II, 103, 1, ad 2; 141, 2, ad 3; 145, 2; 180, 2, ad 3; *CG*, II, 64; III, 139. The Thomistic texts are listed in chronological order by Kovach, *Die Ästhetik*, pp. 270–272. Cf. list by Germain G. Grisez, "References to Beauty in St. Thomas," *The Modern Schoolman*, XXIX (1951), 43–44.

that found in the sequence of unity, truth, and goodness upon being. Though a transcendental, then, it should not be called a transcendental property of being, unless a different sense is first explained for the term "property." In subsistent being, moreover, it can in no sense be considered a property, for there the thing that exists and the existence are not even conceptually distinct. The one cannot follow upon the other as a property. In all other things the two are entitatively distinct. The entitative distinction serves as the basis for conceiving the same object first as a thing and then as a being. In this way there is a conceptual distinction between a thing and a being, for being is now conceived in the concrete.[27] The basis for distinguishing a thing and a being, consequently, does not at all correspond to the basis for distinguishing the other transcendentals.

Other Claimants. The five top genera listed by Plato included sameness. Everything was at least the same as itself.[28] In modern times this identity of a thing with itself has been considered a basic principle in metaphysics.[29] Yet no finite thing is perfectly identical with itself. In every instance it is composed of itself and its being, which is other than itself.[30] The only case of perfect self-identity is subsistent being, where the existent is completely identical with its existence. But here the notion of sameness does not apply directly. As has already been seen, sameness presupposes two things. These coincide in one or more respects. The notion, accordingly, is taken from finite things. It can be applied only indirectly and negatively to subsistent being, insofar as no finite thing is the same as it.

The notion of otherness, also found among the top Platonic genera, has a better claim to the title of transcendental. For Plato it meant not-being, in the sense that everything is not what is other than itself. In finite things it follows upon unity. Insofar as each finite thing is a unit, it is distinguished from all other things, and so is other than anything else. In this way otherness or "something (else)"[31] is a transcendental. It con-

---

[27] "It is clear from the already stated reason, not only that they are one in reality, but that they differ in aspect . . . the term 'thing' is applied from the quiddity only; the term 'a being' is applied from the act of being; and the term 'one' from order or undividedness. But it is the same thing that has essence, and that is undivided in itself. Hence these three, thing, a being, one, signify entirely the same reality, but accordingly to different aspects." St Thomas, *In IV Metaph.*, lect. 2, no. 553.

[28] Plato, *Sph.*, 254D.

[29] On the origin of the "principle of identity," see above, n. 6. On some different formulations of it, see J. Maritain, *A Preface to Metaphysics* (New York, 1940), pp. 92–94.

[30] See St Thomas, *Quodl.*, II, 3, arg. 1m.

[31] *Aliquid*—"quasi aliud quid." St Thomas, *De Ver.*, I, lc; ed. Spiazzi (Turin and Rome, 1953), I, 3a.

ceptualizes the thing in a new and distinct way. But to subsistent being it applies only indirectly, on the ground that all finite things are other than pure act.

Finally, there are a number of pairs that have been called transcendental, because together the two members cover the whole range of being. Such pairs are found in the necessary and contingent, pure act and actuated potency, motion and rest, substance and accident. Each member of the pair has to present a positive notion, and not merely express the contradictory of the other; for every pair of contradictories, in virtue of the principle of excluded middle, leaves no being outside its scope.[32]

Résumé. In the full sense of the expression, then, the transcendental properties of being are unity, truth, and goodness, and presumably, though it is but rarely obvious to human cognition, that of beauty. Thing is indeed transcendental in notion, but is the subject rather than a property of being. The transcendental properties are conceptually and not really distinct from being. A thing and its being, on the other hand, have emerged from the whole preceding inquiry as entitatively distinct, and in things in the real world, as really distinct. Being is a real nature. When participated by any other nature, it cannot coalesce but remains distinct regardless of consideration by the human mind. In this way being has been isolated as one of the two entitative components of every finite thing. It is a distinct principle of things, in the sense in which "principle" means cause and not maxim.[33] So isolated, it can serve as a viewpoint from which things may be investigated according to their being, as required by a science of metaphysics. From the viewpoint of being, the other entitative principle of finite things — the nature or the thing itself — is called essence. In that light, as proper potency to being, it presents the next object of metaphysical inquiry. Through it being is participated, and so finite beings are constituted. Along with being, then, essence is a constitutive metaphysical principle of any creature. After being, it is the most fundamental constitutive principle. In a metaphysical study, accordingly, it finds its place immediately after the initial treatment of being. Being, as nature in subsistent

[32] On the "disjunctive transcendentals" and their importance in Bonaventure and Duns Scotus, see Allan Bernard Wolter, *The Transcendentals and their Function in the Metaphysics of Duns Scotus* (Washington, D. C., 1946), pp. 128–161. On their role in the background of Francis Bacon's "first philosophy," see Robert McRae, *The Problem of the Unity of the Sciences: Bacon to Kant* (Toronto, 1961), pp. 27–28.

[33] Actuation of essence by being is called "formal or intrinsically activating causality," by Jacques Maritain, *The Degrees of Knowledge*, tr. G. B. Phelan (New York, 1959), p. 437. Here "formal" means actuating but not specifying. Specification is by the essence. The actuation by being eludes Aristotle's schema of the causes.

being and as an act other than nature in finite beings, is, absolutely speaking, the first principle of things as they have been considered so far in the science of metaphysics. As essence, however, the potency by which each act of participated being determines itself is also a first principle of finite things. But it is a first principle only in the order of formal causality, functioning in subordination to the causality initiated in the order of being. The two entitative principles of finite things, therefore, are not in a strict sense coordinate, even though both are positive principles. Being is absolutely primary. Essence, as actuated by being, is primary in a particular order of causality, that of finite determination.

SUGGESTED READINGS AND REFERENCES

St Thomas Aquinas, *Truth*, I, 1–3, tr. Robert W. Mulligan (Chicago: Henry Regnery, 1952), I, 3–14.

Gerald B. Phelan, "Verum Sequitur Esse Rerum," *Mediaeval Studies*, I (1939), 11–22.

Elizabeth G. Salmon, *The Good in Existential Metaphysics* (Milwaukee: Marquette University Press, 1953).

——— "Metaphysics and Unity," in *Progress in Philosophy*, ed. James A. McWilliams (Milwaukee: Bruce, 1955), pp. 47–60.

Joseph Owens, "Unity and Essence in St Thomas Aquinas," *Mediaeval Studies*, XXIII (1961), 240–259.

BEING

UNITY
TRUTH
GOODNESS
BEAUTY
} TRANSCENDENTAL PROPERTIES

conceptually distinct from Being
NOT
really distinct

PART TWO . . . ESSENCE

CHAPTER 9

Essence Absolutely Considered

Etymology. The potency that corresponds to being and is actuated by it is, as has been seen, the thing itself or the thing's nature. The technical name given to thing or nature in the function of proper potency to being is essence. The term is derived in a rather peculiar fashion from the Latin infinitive esse, "to be." As is the case with so many other metaphysical terms, its use in the technical sense requires considerable elucidation. The morphology of the word "essence," indeed, is especially misleading in view of what it has come traditionally to express. A non-existent participle *essens* is presupposed as though formed from the infinitive esse, like *patiens* from *pati*, and is given the ending of an abstract noun in the form *essentia*. In English, this word appears as "essence." According to its form it should mean the very nature of being, that is, beingness, if such a derivative were permissible in English. But in point of fact it was coined to translate the Greek term *ousia*, a word that in Aristotelian logic was used to denote the subject of predication. In this logical context *ousia* was regularly and without difficulty translated "substance." Its alternate translation "essence," consequently, became quite easily established in the sense of the subject of being, the potency to existence.

Morphologically, then, "essence" should denote existential act; but technically in traditional use it has come to mean the opposite entitative principle, the potency to being. Only when used of subsistent being does essence coincide with existence, and then only in virtue of the absolute identity there of nature and being. In all other instances it sets up a contrast with existence. The morphology of the term, accordingly, should not be allowed to influence its accepted meaning. The etymology serves, though, to connect it with being, and to show that it is treated in metaphysics from the viewpoint of being.[1] The term describes nature or thing as a potency to being, in spite of its incongruous morphology.

[1] ". . . essentia dicitur secundum quod per eam et in ea ens habet esse"—"through which and in which a being has its act of existing." St Thomas, *De Ente*, c. I (ed. Roland-Gosselin, p. 4.15–16); tr. Maurer, p. 28. On the origins of technical terms for a being (*ens*) and essence and existence, see E. Gilson, "Notes sur le Vocabulaire de l'Etre," *Mediaeval Studies*, VIII (1946), 150–158.

Essence as Nature. Sensible things, the only direct objects of human cognition, are all individual as they exist in themselves in the real world. But they are known by the intellect in abstraction from their designation in a particular matter. So abstracted they are still composed of matter and form, but lack designation in definite dimensions that could be pointed to with the finger.[2] In this way they are conceptualized with a content of matter and form in general, but not in particular. They abstract from any indication by which they could be marked off or designated as it were by the finger in dimensions of length, breadth, thickness, and at a particular time. In so abstracting from the particular they abstract from place and time, and exhibit their natures under an aspect that is found in all the individuals and that is timeless. So abstracted, the nature when considered as a potency to its being is called the thing's essence.

When the essence is abstracted with precision, it does not fully coincide with the thing. As will be remembered,[3] "precision" in that connection is taken in its etymological signification of "cutting off." The term is rather awkward in this meaning so remote from its ordinary English use; but a technical name is required for the type of abstraction denoted by the original Latin word, and it is the best available. Since the essence abstracted in that way prescinds from or excludes the individuality, it represents only a part of the thing. It and the individuality go together to compose the thing, as parts. Since a part is not predicated of a whole, the essence when abstracted with precision cannot be predicated of the thing. You cannot say that a man is his humanity, any more than you can say that he is his arm, as already noted. Rather, he has his humanity and he has his arm. In this sense, then, a thing is not its own essence, but has its essence. Its essence is not itself, but one of its principles, when the essence is abstracted with precision.

HAS possesses vs IS

Essence as Thing. But the essence can also be abstracted without precision.[4] Abstracted in this second way it excludes

---

[2] On the history of this way of indicating the individual, see Marie-Dominique Roland-Gosselin, *Le "De Ente et Essentia" de S. Thomas d'Aquin*, reprint (Paris, 1948), pp. 11, n. 1; 58–60. For Aristotle, the universal includes both matter and form in general. See *Metaph.*, Z 8, 1033b24–26; 10, 1035b27–31; 11, 1037a5–10. ". . . man or animal is the compound of both taken universally" — *ibid.*, 1037a6–7; Oxford tr.

[3] See above, Chapter 4, n. 13.

[4] "And this is why we sometimes find the word *essence* predicated of a thing (for we say that Socrates is a certain essence), and sometimes denied (as when we say that Socrates' essence is not Socrates)." St Thomas, *De Ente*, c. II (ed. Roland-Gosselin), p. 23.4–7; tr. Maurer, p. 38. On the way in which "being" or "existent" (*ens*) is predicated of an essence in precision from the individual, see St Thomas, *De Ver.*, XXI, 4, ad 4m; *ST*, I–II, 55, 4, ad 1m.

nothing in the thing, but contains the individual designation implicitly and indeterminately. So considered it can be predicated of the thing in complete identity, even though it itself focuses the mind's consideration only on the nature that is common and timeless. A man, therefore, is his own essence when the essence is abstracted without precision. Essence and thing are here identical. It is equally correct to say that the essence exists or that the thing exists, when the abstraction of essence does not prescind from individuation.

Essence as Common. The essence can exist in reality and in the human intellect. In reality it exists in individuals, as humanity exists in millions of men. The same essence, humanity, is found separately in every one of these many individuals. It is common to them all. The same essence, moreover, can exist in your intellect or in the intellect of anyone else who thinks of it. In this cognitional existence it is no longer individual but specific. It is the universal species "man," or human nature in its universality. As a universal, it represents all individual men in the one concept. It has a unity of its own as universal, just as in any particular man it has a unity that is individual. Of itself, however, the essence can have no unity. If it had of itself the unity of an individual, it would always be that individual. If humanity had of itself the individual unity of Plato, all humanity would be united in the individuality of the one Greek philosopher and could not be found as an essence or nature in any other individual. Correspondingly, if the essence had of itself the all-embracing unity of a universal, it could never be found in a plurality of individuals. But the same essence is found in many individuals and in the universal concept. It is common to all. It is a common nature.[5]

Abstraction from Being. But how can an essence have no unity? Unity follows upon being as a transcendental property. If the essence in itself entirely lacks unity, it must entirely lack being. As has already been seen,[6] every finite nature abstracts from being

[5] The expression "common nature" is used frequently by St Thomas, rarely by Duns Scotus, to designate the essence that is rendered individual in real things and universal in the mind. The doctrine that the common nature is formally distinct in reality from the individuating entity, as nature from mode, is fundamental for Scotus. For him the common nature has a unity of its own outside the mind, called minor unity, and so it has its own corresponding entity or essential being. It is a reality or entity that combines with another reality or entity to constitute the individual. See Op. Ox., II, d. 3, qq. 5 and 6, nos. 9–15; ed. M. F. Garcia (Quaracchi, 1912–1914), II, 264–270 (nos. 285–289). It is not identified with the singular in the way required for predication, and so it cannot be predicated of the individual. For St Thomas (text below, n. 18), on the contrary, the common nature is what is predicated of all the individuals.

[6] See above, Chapter 5, n. 1.

without prescinding from it. Does this mean that a finite essence is of itself totally devoid of being? The answer has to be affirmative. If the essence of itself contained any being whatsoever, it would come under the control of the first principle of demonstration, the principle of being. It would be a unit in itself, cut off from thoroughgoing identity with anything else. It would be just itself. Yet the essence of man is identified as a whole with Caesar, with Pompey, with Mark Antony, with Raphael, with Paderewski, and with every other individual man that ever lived or has been thought of. The whole essence is found in every individual. Caesar was a man, Pompey was a man, and so on. Each is the essence man, when the essence is abstracted without precision. If the essence "man" had any being of its own as an essence, it would not allow predication of anything but itself. "Man is man" would be the one permissible predication.[7] Only an essence completely devoid of being can be predicated of many individuals in thoroughgoing identity with each.

This means that there is no "essential being" that would be either really or conceptually distinct from existence.[8] The only "essential being" is existence. Of itself a finite essence is nothing.[9] All its being, therefore, comes to it from its efficient cause, from outside itself. When it is said to receive being, or to enter into composition with being, it is not thereby imagined to have already, of itself, enough being to function as a presupposed subject or component. It is not presupposed as already there

[7] On the topic of identical predication, see Plato, *Sph.*, 251AC. It is attributed by Aristotle (*Metaph.*, Δ 29, 1024b32–34) to Antisthenes. On the problems encountered in predicating the whole nature of each individual, see Plato, *Prm.*, 131AC.

[8] In the long Scholastic controversy on the distinction between essence and existence, beginning about two years after the death of St Thomas, essence was understood as essential being (*esse essentiae*) and existence as actual existential being (*esse existentiae actualis*). Suarez (*Disp. Metaph.*, XXXI, 4, 4–6; ed. Vivès, XXVI, 235b–236b) showed conclusively that there was no real distinction between the two. In seeking to establish a conceptual distinction, Suarez (*ibid.*, 6, 13–14; pp. 246a–250b) had to change the terms. Actual essence and actual existence were the terms he showed to be really identical, while non-actual essence was the term he established as conceptually distinct from actual existence. On this topic, see J. Owens, "The Number of Terms in the Suarezian Discussion on Essence and Being," *The Modern Schoolman*, XXXIV (1957), 147–191; J. Gómez Caffarena, "Sentido de la Composicion de Ser y Esencia en Suarez," *Pensamiento*, XV (1959), 135–154.

This controversy does not touch the doctrine of St Thomas, where the entitative distinction falls between the essence and any being whatsoever the essence may possess. If the expression *esse essentiae* is to be used, the distinction of St Thomas will fall between the *esse* and the *essentiae* — all *esse* that belongs to the essence is entitatively distinct from it. The only being of the essence is existence.

[9] ". . . so that whatever aspect of being anything has, it has only from God; but the deficiency of being is from itself." St Thomas, *In II Sent.*, d. 37, q. 1, a. 2, Solut.; ed. Mandonnet, II, 946. Cf.: "Therefore, necessarily, it would be according to its own nature a non-being, unless it had being from God." *Ibid.*, d. 1, q. 1, a. 5, ad 2m in contr.; ed. Mandonnet, II, 38.

in itself, waiting to receive a further act or perfection of existence, or to enter into a new composition. If it were already there, it would already exist.[10] A further "existential being" could not confer upon it an existence it already had, and so would be superfluous and impossible. Rather, the existential act is prior to the essence, and endows it with all the being it possesses. The caused existential act has to involve its own limiting principle, a principle other than itself, a principle whose entire being it does not presuppose but confers. How can it be received into something that is not already there to receive it? How can it enter into composition with something which as yet has no being? The answer to such questions lies in the priority of existential act. If the subject or the other component already had being, there would be no room for that priority. The whole function of existential act is to make the essence be. Its only role is to make its own subject be, to confer being upon the limiting principle with which it is composed. In priority to that participation of the nature of being through efficient causality, absolutely no being is there. An essence can have no being whatsoever of its own, except in the unique case of the nature of being itself, whose essence is subsistent being and not participated being.

Ground of Particular Instances. But if a finite essence is totally devoid of being, what becomes of the truth that a rose is eternally a flower whether or not a rose ever existed in reality or in human cognition? The individual of a species presupposes the common nature of the species as its ground, and human cognition presupposes the real individuals from which it abstracts the universal. Every individual rose, therefore, is a particularization of a certain plant nature, and every individual man is a particularization of human nature. The common essence undoubtedly has its special priority to its instances. But does that priority involve being? Does it require that the essence itself be in any way, prior to its reception in an individual in reality or in a universal in the mind? On the contrary, that priority abstracts from all being. If the common essence had any being of its own, it could not be each of the individuals and the universal, as is required when it receives existence in reality or in the mind. Its priority of community and timelessness, rather, demands that it have no being at all of its own.

[10] This approach, modeled on the pre-existence of matter to change as studied in natural philosophy, occasions the difficulty in understanding how existence can actuate a subject really distinct from itself: "For how can an act be impressed upon that which is nothing?" Suarez, *Disp. Metaph.*, XXXI, 4, 5; ed. Vivès, XXVI, 234b. Cf. below, n. 20. The much used example of the rose goes back to Abelard, *Glosses on Porphyry*, in *Selections from Medieval Philosophers*, ed. Richard McKeon (New York, etc., 1929), I, 219–220.

Yet does this not give an essence that lacks being priority to being, if being is found only in individuals or in cognition? And how can a rose *be* a flower eternally, if prior to the individuals and cognition it has no being whatsoever? Has the common essence itself any prior ground, a ground that involves being and so could ensure the absolute priority of being? The considerations that have already emerged from the investigation of the first efficient cause show there is such a prior ground of finite essence. The first cause creates through free choice, not through necessity of nature. It has to know and choose what it creates. This means that the essences of all things exist eternally in its knowledge. There the essences have being, but their being is the being of the first cause. There they are not creatures, but the creative essence.[11] In this way the essences as they exist in the first cause are the ground of the common essences that abstract from all being. The common essence in its turn is the ground of the individuated nature; and the individuated nature as well as the nature absolutely considered is the ground of the universal that exists in human cognition.[12] Being remains absolutely prior to essence, and timelessness is assured to the common essence without requiring that it have any being as such. A rose is eternally a flower because the abiding ground of its essence is the eternal knowledge of it in the first cause. If it did not exist in some individual, therefore, or in some knowledge, it would not at all *be* even a flower. It would coincide with nothing. Because in itself it has no being, it can exist by the divine being, by real created being and by cognitional being. The divine being is prior to it in every respect, while in the order of formal causality it itself is prior to the other two ways of being.

Formal Causality. Even though an essence just in itself is completely devoid of being, and so is actually nothing, nevertheless its potentiality distinguishes it from utter nothingness. Though actually nothing it is able to be something in reality, for it is able to receive real existential act. It is a potency to real existence, while nothingness, conceived as a nature, has no potency to real existence. Essence, there-

[11] ". . . because before it has being, it is nothing, except perhaps in the intellect of the creator, where it is not a creature, but the creative essence." St Thomas, *De Pot.*, III, 5, ad 2m.

[12] ". . . hence the first consideration of any caused nature whatsoever is as it exists in the divine intellect; the second consideration is of the nature itself absolutely; the third as it has being in the things themselves or in the angelic mind; the fourth as it has being in our understanding. . . . the divine understanding is the reason of the nature considered absolutely and in singulars; and the nature itself considered absolutely and in singulars is the reason of the human understanding, and in a certain way its measure." St Thomas, *Quodl.*, VIII, 1; ed. Spiazzi (Turin, 1956), pp. 158–159.

fore, is properly a potency to real existence, not just to cognitional existence. Accordingly, negations like nothingness, contradictions like a square circle, and privations like blindness, are not essences. They can receive cognitional being, but not real being.[13] They cannot exist in the real world, but only in the constructions of human reason. Human reason can take the positive notion of being, negate it, and so set up the notion "nothingness" as though it were an essence. Similarly, reason can take the notion of sight in a man, retain the subject but deny the form and set up in place of the form of sight its privation. In this way the privation blindness is conceived as though it itself were a form and so an accidental essence. But properly, an essence has to have a positive formal aspect of its own.

On account of this formal aspect the essence determines the existential act. It exercises formal causality in its regard. In natural philosophy, form is always seen to determine as act. It is the act of a matter, and as act determines the matter. But in regard to existential act, form determines only as potency.[14] It is the potency that limits the existential act, and in so limiting it determines it to the existence of a tree, a stone, or whatever the essence happens to be. Because it determines only as potency, the essence does not have to have any actuality in priority to the reception of its existential act. For this reason it is able to determine and limit without requiring any actuality in priority to being. As the subject of existence it calls for no prior being of its own, and as the determining principle of existence it demands no actuality. It receives its actuality from the existential act it determines.

In the order of formal causality, then, essence determines being, and the form of the thing is in this sense the cause of the thing's being. The efficient cause of its being is extrinsic to it, but the formal cause is intrinsic. As formally caused by the essence, its being may be said to flow from the essence and to follow upon the essence. In this way every nature is essentially a being,[15] because an essence is of its very notion a potency to being and formally demands being. This formal requirement, of course, is not enough to make anything be. The efficient causality of an

[13] See St Thomas, *De Ente*, c. 1 (ed. Roland-Gosselin), p. 3.7–12. A being of reason (*ens rationis*, see above, Chapter 2, n. 19), like nothingness or a square circle, has accordingly no essence. Similarly privations, relations of reason, and second intentions as such, do not have any essence. On relations of reason, see below, Chapter 13, nn. 29–32.

[14] "Hence being is not determined by anything else in the way a potency is determined by an act, but rather as an act by a potency." St Thomas, *De Pot.*, VII, 2, ad 9m.

[15] ". . . any nature whatsoever essentially is a being." St Thomas, *De Ver.*, I, 1c. Cf. *ibid.*, XXI, 1, arg. 1; *ST*, I, 6, 3, arg. 2.

agent has to make that formal causality actual.[16] But in any production of being, even in creation, the agent has to function through the formal causality of the essence its efficient causality brings into being.[17] That is the only way it can produce finite being, and all caused being is finite. A finite essence, therefore, though of itself it is nothing, is nevertheless different from nothingness. It is a potency to real being, while nothingness is no such potency. Without existential act, finite essence is nothing. Yet it is able to be actuated existentially, and in that very actuation it functions as formal cause. It is here the formal cause, not of a potency like matter, but of an act that is other than itself. It can never prescind from being, for in its very notion it is a cause of existential act, not efficiently, but formally. Although an essence does not include real being, it nevertheless does not exclude it. Nothingness, on the contrary, excludes real being.

Absolute Consideration. But if finite essence of itself is nothing, how can it be known as such? If a nature as common has no being whatsoever, how can it be spoken about and treated of metaphysically? The preceding paragraphs have as a matter of fact been discussing it and using it as a subject of predication. Clearly it cannot be known directly. If it is of itself nothing, it cannot in itself play the role of an object of cognition. It can be attained directly only where it exists. It exists in real individuals and in the universal that is brought into being in the mind. These may be known immediately, the individuals by direct perception, the universal by reflexion. Comparing the various existences of an essence, say humanity, the intellect sees that the essence of itself is not bound to cognitional existence nor to existence in any real individual. It can be in the one or in the other indifferently. There is nothing in humanity that requires it to be present in any particular individual or in any universal cognition. Since no one of these existences is necessary for it, it may be considered as freed from them all. This is called essence in its absolute consideration. It is only a consideration, not a way of being. It is the result of a difficult reasoning process, and not an object of direct perception. Its referents are the real individuals and the universal. In strict language the essence absolutely considered is not an "it," in the

---

[16] ". . . being follows of itself upon the form of a creature, presupposing, however, the influx of God." St Thomas, *ST*, I, 104, 1, ad lm.

[17] ". . . God produces natural being in us through creation, with no efficient cause as a means, but by means nevertheless of a formal cause; for the natural form is the principle of natural being." St Thomas, *De Ver.*, XXVII, 1, ad 3m. ". . . God created natural being without any efficient means, yet not without a formal means. For he gave to everything the form by which it would be." *De Caritate*, a. 1, ad 13m.

sense of a subject able to receive predication, for it is not a being. Therapy, accordingly, has to be practiced in its use.

The essence absolutely considered, of course, is what is predicated of each individual.[18] It alone is able to be predicated, because of itself it abstracts from any being that would keep it united with one subject and exclude it from others.[19] Yet as directly known in any instance, it is known as existent. The copula, expressing its being, precedes it. The common nature "man" is known in the particular applications "John is a man," "Paul is a man," and so on. In the universal it is given cognitional existence as a subject of predication, as "Man is mortal." These uses presuppose that the nature "man" is common. If the nature were not common, it could not be predicated in those ways nor be conceived as a universal. But that implicit community does not manifest directly the lack of being it involves. This is brought to light only by careful metaphysical investigation. Predication was used long before men became metaphysicians. For its explanation in logic, individuality and universality suffice. The third or absolute consideration is from the viewpoint of being, and is proper to the metaphysician. It is the conclusion of a demonstration, and not a direct perception. In it essence abstracts from individual, universal, and being.

An essence, then, is individual when existent in reality, universal when existent in the human intellect, but common and not existent when considered absolutely. Essence as common nature, essence in its absolute consideration, and essence as contrasted with existence coincide.[20] All

[18] "Considered in itself, the nature of man thus clearly abstracts from every act of existing, but in such a way that none may be excluded from it. And it is the nature considered in this way that we predicate of all individual beings." *De Ente*, c. III (ed. Roland-Gosselin), p. 26.8–11; tr. Maurer, p. 40. Cf. *ibid.*, II, pp. 20.12–21.1.

[19] The Scotistic common nature, accordingly, cannot be predicated of the individual. It has its own proper entity, and this renders it incapable of such predication. What is predicated for Scotus is the universal in the full sense. The common nature "is not actually universal, because it lacks that indifference through which the universal is universal in a completed fashion, that is, through which it — as the same by a certain identity — is predicable of each individual in such a way that each is it." *Op. Ox.*, II, 3, 1, no. 9; ed. Quaracchi, II, 231 (no. 238). Cf. *Quaest. Metaph.*, VII, 18, no. 6; ed. Vivès, VII, 456–457.

The utter novelty of St Thomas' doctrine that essence is wholly devoid of being and is made to be by an existential act other than itself, has been expressed by a modern writer as follows: "Aquinas invented a new kind of nonexistent and a third use or meaning of 'being.' The new nonexistents are called *natures.*" Gustav Bergmann, *Meaning and Existence* (Madison, 1960), p. 192.

[20] Therefore essence as "objective potency" and as "receptive potency" or "subjective potency" coincide. The essence that receives being has no actuality whatsoever prior to the reception of being. It specifies and determines only as potency. See above, n. 14.

three denote the essence that may be brought into being by existential act, either in reality or in cognition. Because it is completely devoid of being, the essence so considered is able to be common to many individuals and to the universal, and leave all being whatsoever on the "existence" side of the "existence-essence" couplet. But because the essence is in itself not directly knowable, its distinction from its being cannot be directly represented in cognition. One can only reason that the distinction has to be there.

Entitative Principles. In essence, the second of the two entitative principles of beings is found. Metaphysics aims to investigate beings insofar as they are beings. To understand them from the viewpoint of being, it has to explain them in the light of their entitative principles. It isolates these principles as being and essence. Together these constitute finite realities. Neither of the two entitative principles can be represented by the human mind as just in itself. The origin of human cognition lies in sensible things, and all other knowable objects have to be represented by the mind in their light. Sensible things are composite, known simultaneously in their essence by simple apprehension and in their being by judgment. Every other knowable object, accordingly, has to be represented as something that is. The two entitative principles are no exception. The first, being, is shown to exist as a nature in the first efficient cause of things, and as an act that is not a nature in all things else. As an existential act that is not a nature it has to involve its own limitation, an essence that is other than itself. In this way it confers being upon a man, a mountain, or a star. Strictly, what exists is not the existential act itself, but the limiting essence that has being in virtue of the existential act. The limitation is not a negative cutting off of further being, but a positive thing like the man or the star. A limitation of being is a thing that exists.

To be understood at all, then, essence has to be approached from the viewpoint of existence. Of itself it is nothing and so cannot make itself intelligible. If it is proposed in itself as the starting point of its own explanation, it leads to hopeless tangles. It would have to be considered as already there and so enjoying some kind of being in itself, while waiting to receive another kind of being called existence. But the possession of any being at all in its own nature would prevent predication and render superfluous and impossible the reception of the alleged existential being. To ask how that which is not can receive an act if it is not already there to receive it, or how it can enter into real composition if it does not already have being of its own, is to set up essence as a fully constituted starting point in its own right. Regarded as a self-completed nature instead of a principle that has its being and its intelligibility from an act other than itself, it occasions insoluble problems. But when it is given the status of mere potency to being, it is conceived as a principle that has its being and its intelligibility from its existential act. Made actual by existence, it has a specific intelligibility showing *what* the thing is, in contradistinction to the intelligibility in the judgment that the thing exists. In this way it functions as a positive "intelligible opposite"[21] of being.

In the light of these two opposite principles, being and essence, finite things lie open to metaphysical investigation. Continued therapy, however, has to be practiced, since finite existence is unavoidably represented as "something," even though in itself it is not a reality nor a thing. Correspondingly, finite essence is represented as though it were a thing in

---

[21] In this way being has an intelligible opposite, namely essence. Sidney Hook, "The Quest for 'Being,'" *Proceedings of the XIth International Congress of Philosophy* (Amsterdam and Louvain, 1953), XIV, 18, would "banish the term 'Being' from the vocabulary of philosophy," because he finds no such opposite for it. "In ordinary discourse every significant word has an intelligible opposite. Being, however, as an all inclusive category does not seem to possess an intelligible opposite." *Ibid.* Yet the intelligibility of *what* a thing is seems obviously different from the intelligibility expressed in the judgment *that* it exists, as is apparent in the example of St Thomas that you can know what a phoenix is without knowing whether it exists in reality. The two are opposite in the full sense of the opposition between act and potency, even though the actual intelligibility of essence is brought about by existence. The opposition between them from this viewpoint does not at all mean that a created essence has enough actuality of itself to be intelligible, while it needs a superadded act to exist in reality. "Essential being," distinct from existence, would confer this intelligibility of its own upon essence, as may be seen for instance in Giles of Rome (ca. 1247–1316): "For we say that a created nature, although it is of sufficient actuality to be understood in itself, is not of sufficient actuality to exist in the real world, unless an actuality that is commonly called 'being' is superadded to it." *Quodl.*, V, 3 (Louvain, 1646), p. 273a. Giles seems to have been the first known writer to place a real distinction between essential being and existential being, and to insist that they are two different realities. On the origins of the centuries-long controversy regarding the real distinction between essence and existence, see P. Mandonnet, "Les Premières Disputes sur la Distinction Réelle entre l'Essence et l'Existence 1276–1287," *Revue Thomiste*, XVIII (1910), 741–765; J. Paulus, "Les Disputes d'Henri de Gand et de Gilles de Rome sur la Distinction de l'Essence et de l'Existence," *Archives d'Histoire Doctrinale et Littéraire du Moyen Age*, XV–XVII (1940–1942), 323–358. On the introduction of the doctrine of "essential being" into the Thomistic tradition, see Norman J. Wells, "Capreolus on Essence and Existence," *The Modern Schoolman*, XXXVIII (1960), 1–24. "Essential being" may likewise appear in modern philosophy, e.g.: "And though a term may cease to exist, it cannot cease to be; it is still an entity . . ." Bertrand Russell, *The Principles of Mathematics* (Cambridge, 1903), p. 471 (no. 443). Cf.: "Again every term is immutable and indestructible." *Ibid.*, p. 44 (no. 47).

In contrast to negation, the positive character of essence is described by St Thomas: "Nothing however is found affirmatively asserted in absolute fashion in the case of every being, except its essence, according to which it is said to be." *De Ver.*, I, 1c.

itself. Yet without its being it cannot function at all as a direct object of intellection. Both principles, accordingly, have to be represented as existentially actuated realities, even when one is considered in opposition to the other. But the necessity of representing each in union with the other should not be the occasion of allowing any being to finite essence just in itself, nor of thinking that finite existence just in itself is a thing or a reality. Every finite reality has to be constituted of both principles.

Résumé. Essence is the proper potency to being. When abstracted without precision, it coincides with the thing that exists, and is predicated of the thing in thoroughgoing identity. This is possible because essence abstracts from all being. In its absolute consideration, essence is prior to its existent instances as found in reality and in created intelligences, but is subsequent to its existence in the divine mind. Through formal causality it specifies its existential act. In this way it is the second of the two entitative principles of finite things.

SUGGESTED READINGS AND REFERENCES

St Thomas Aquinas, *On Being and Essence*, c. I; tr. A. Maurer (Toronto: Pontifical Institute of Mediaeval Studies, 1949), pp. 26–29.

Gerard Smith, "Avicenna and the Possibles," *The New Scholasticism*, XVII (1943), 340–357.

Joseph Owens, "Thomistic Common Nature and Platonic Idea," *Mediaeval Studies*, XXI (1959), 211–223.

CHAPTER 10

Substance

Divisions of Essence. Often the word "essence" is used in express contrast to the accidental. The essence of comfort might be considered by someone, for example, to consist in informality, with other requirements more or less accidental to it. In philosophical usage, however, every real accident has its own essence. Size, color, time, place, and so on, present distinct objects of simple apprehension, over and above the nature they modify. That nature remains the same nature while changing in such accidents. A man remains the same man as his color changes from white to a deep tan with the course of the summer's sun. The color is an accidental essence that changes while the nature it qualifies remains the same. Every accident, accordingly, is in its own way an essence. Nevertheless, the use of "essence" in contrast to the accidental is not without its ground. Accidents are always modifications of some other essence.There is always a more basic essence prior to an accidental essence. The divisions of essence, therefore, will not be univocal but will follow an order in which one type of essence will be basic and primary. The other types will have reference to it as its modifications. This condition grounds predication through reference,[1] while the proportional relation that every essence has to its proper existential act establishes analogy among the various types of essence.

The divisions exhibited in these ways by essence are called **categories** or **predicaments.** The terms are borrowed from logic. In Greek, "category" meant first a legal accusation, then the broader notion of something asserted or said of anything, and finally in the Aristotelian logic it took on the technical signification of a predicate. It became traditional in the sense of a column of predicates one placed over the other until the highest was reached. "Man" was predicated of Socrates, "animal" of "man," "living thing" of "animal," and so on in ever widening range until the

[1] "But substance is a being absolutely and through itself; and all kinds other than substance are beings in a certain respect and through substance." St Thomas, *In VII Metaph.*, lect. 1 (ed. Cathala-Spiazzi) no. 1248. Cf. *ibid.*, nos. 1247–1259, and *In IV Metaph.*, lect. 1, nos. 535–539.

highest univocal predicate in this series, located as "substance," was reached. Each category was named from its highest listed predicate. "Categories" in this acceptation were, accordingly, the supreme genera. Nothing higher could be predicated univocally. The first category having been called "substance," the other categories, each with its own name, were grouped under the overall designation of "accidents." This sense of the term "category" was translated into Latin as *praedicamentum*, occasioning the English word "predicament." Since predication is grounded upon reality, it allowed its broad divisions to be applied without too much difficulty to the real order.[2] The more important names for the divisions of predicates became in consequence the terms used for the basic divisions of essences and things.

Dependence and Independence. The broadest division of all follows upon the independence or dependence in being that an essence enjoys. This independence in being is not meant to exclude dependence upon an extrinsic efficient cause. Every essence in a category is finite, and so has its being from something else. The dependence or independence that distinguishes essences refers not to the reception of being but to the way in which that being is possessed. If it is possessed only through modifying something else, it is accidental. The sun tan has its few months' being each summer only as a modification of a human skin. It could not exist independently of the man in whom it is found. The man himself, on the contrary, is not a modification of any more basic essence. In the order of essence, he is the most basic of all. His size, color, relations to his environment, actions, and so on, all presuppose that he is there to possess them. The way they have their being is "in dependence upon" him. They are modifications superadded to his nature, and so are not essences in themselves but essences of or in some other essence, in the sense of accretions belonging to that basic essence. The man, on the contrary, does not belong to his size, his color, his relations to the things around him, or his actions. He is not a modification of any of them. In this sense he has his being in an independent way. Anything that has being in this independent way is called a **substance**. Whatever has its being in dependence upon a substance, on the other hand, is known as an **accident**.

There are, of course, many ways in which a substance is dependent upon its accidents. A man may be dependent upon his sun tan to keep his

[2] There are, however, a number of significant differences in the Aristotelian application of the categories to the logical and to the real orders, especially in regard to primary and secondary substance, and to action and passion. On this topic, see J. Owens, "Aristotle on Categories," *The Review of Metaphysics*, XIV (1960), 83–86.

skin from getting burned, upon his digestion for continuance in bodily life, upon his faculties for knowledge and enjoyment. But none of these ways is the way in which he has his being. None of them makes him receive and have his being as a modification of something else. Even though he is dependent upon them in many other ways, he does not receive his being through them, as they receive theirs through him. He could not live without a good number of them, but he does not exist as a dependency of any of them.

As essences, then, substance and accidents are by no means on a par. The priority of substance in being is too striking to need defense in a metaphysical context, that is, when approached from the viewpoint of being.[3] Existence can be imparted to the modification of a thing only on condition that the thing being modified exists, at least as far as the regular exigencies of accidental natures show.[4] Substance, accordingly, is an essence or nature that calls for being through itself and not through another,[5] in the sense just explained. Etymologically, the word may mean "standing under"; but it translates a Greek original whose signification was in terms of being. The pristine designation of the first category was ousia, the abstract noun for "being." The nature of being was located by

[3] Approached from the viewpoint of mathematical logic, all entities are reduced to the same abstract level, and the difference in order between substance and accident is obliterated. So considered, any entity or term "is, in fact, possessed of all the properties commonly assigned to substances or substantives." Bertrand Russell, *The Principles of Mathematics* (Cambridge, 1903), I, 44 (no. 47). Without substance there is no subject for real change. Change, in the sense of one thing becoming another, accordingly disappears: "Change, in this metaphysical sense, I do not at all admit." Russell, p. 471 (no. 443).

Similarly in logical positivism: "Logical analysis shows that what makes these 'appearances' the 'appearances of' the same thing is not their relationship to an entity other than themselves, but their relationship to one another. The metaphysician fails to see this because he is misled by a superficial grammatical feature of his language." Alfred J. Ayer, *Language, Truth and Logic*, 2nd ed. (London, 1946), p. 42.

[4] In the Eucharist, the accidents retain their natural aptitude to exist in their proper substance, even though that substance itself no longer exists. If the merely natural order were not transcended, their existence would require the existence of the substance. Since being does not enter into the definition of any finite thing, substance and accident are described by the exigencies of their natures rather than by their being: "Substance is a thing whose natural requirement is to be without being in another; but an accident is a thing whose natural requirement is to be in another. Hence it is clear that, although an accident should miraculously have being that is not in a subject, it still does not attain to the definition of substance . . . for its nature still remains such that it should require being in something else." St Thomas Aquinas, *Quodl.*, IX, 5, ad 2m.

[5] This notion is expressed in Scholastic Latin by the phrase *per se*. Hence the characteristic of substance is *perseitas*, which is sometimes translated into English as "perseity."

Aristotle in the first category. For him, all other instances were denominated being through reference to that nature.[6] In his explanation, the priority in being of the first category could not be more manifest. The being that is referred to in an accident is always the being that is found in the first category, according to this view. To say that there is green color would mean that *a body is* — green. The being that is referred to is that of the body. This Aristotelian explanation locates the nature of being in finite form, and is unacceptable in a metaphysics for which the first instance of being is pure existential act. Yet it illustrates how priority in being and not any "standing under" accidents is the distinguishing characteristic of the first category.

The independence of substance, then, is not to be conceived primarily in terms of "standing under" or supporting accidents. It is not that of an elephant carrying a load of baggage.[7] It is independence in the way substance receives and has its being. Substance does not receive its being through any other essence as a modification of that essence. Finite substance will always be dependent upon something else in the order of efficient causality for its being,[8] but, in the order of essence, it is not a modification of anything else. In receiving being it is not dependent on any other finite essence as a principle through which being pertains to it. When it is called the subject of the accidents, it is conceived as the basic essence of which the accidents are modifications and through which they receive their being.[9]

[6] The primary instance of being is expressly introduced as a nature (*physis*) by Aristotle at *Metaph.*, Γ 2, 1003a34.

[7] ". . . if he were demanded, what is it that solidity and extension adhere in, he would not be in a much better case than the Indian before mentioned who, saying that the world was supported by a great elephant, was asked what the elephant rested on; to which his answer was — a great tortoise: but being again pressed to know what gave support to the broad-backed tortoise, replied — *something, he knew not what.*" Locke, *An Essay concerning Human Understanding*, II, 23, 2; ed. Fraser, I, 391–392. This is the notion of substance that has been vigorously — and rightly — combatted during the last couple of centuries. Cf. instances above, n. 3.

[8] Descartes, defining substance in terms of existence rather than nature, gives a notion that in its strict sense applies only to divine being: "By *substance* we can understand nothing else than a thing that so exists as to be in need of no other thing for its existence. And indeed, a substance that has entirely no need of anything, can be understood as one solely, namely God." *Principia Philosophiae*, I, 51; A–T, VIII, 24.21–25 (IX, 47). On the Cartesian elimination of natures in the sense of essences, see E. Gilson, *Etudes sur le Rôle de la Pensée Médiévale dans la Formation du Système Cartésien* (Paris, 1930), pp. 158–168, 243. Spinoza, *Ethics* I, Def. 3 and Props. 1–14, shows on this basis of complete independence that there can be no substance other than God.

[9] The notion of an accident being "*in* a subject" was carefully explained by Aristotle, when introducing it, as entitative dependence: "By being 'present in a subject' I do not mean present as parts are present in a whole, but being incapable of existence apart from the said subject." *Cat.*, 2, 1a24–25; Oxford tr.

Substantial Principles. In all sensible things, as is shown in the Aristotelian natural philosophy, the substance is composite. It consists of two components or intrinsic principles, matter and form. The matter is entirely potential, and so is of itself undetermined to any particular form. In this way it is the principle of change, since it is able to lose the form it has at the moment and acquire another one. It makes possible substantial change. It is also the principle that allows a substance to be spatially extended. Imparting no formal or other actual determination, it can play the role of substantial basis for increase in size without any substantial change in the thing. The form, on the other hand, is the principle of specification. It determines the substance to be of a definite kind — water, iron, tree, man, or whatever else it happens to be. In contrast to addition of matter, which takes place without causing change in nature, any addition in form would change specifically the nature of a thing.

As principles of a sensible thing's nature, matter and form are called its elements or intrinsic causes. In Scholastic terminology the matter is known as the material cause of the thing, and the form as its formal cause. This terminology may not conform any too well with the ordinary English acceptation of "cause." Ordinarily, in English, wood is not called a cause of a table. Nor is the shape of the table regarded as one of its causes. Yet the philosophical tradition of calling them causes goes back to Aristotle, and is too well established and too meaningful to be disregarded from the standpoint of technical language. A table is a table because of the wood and because of the shape, and not only because of the carpenter's work and because of the purpose of dining or writing. As intrinsic causes, matter and form are contrasted with the two extrinsic causes of a thing. The extrinsic causes are the efficient cause or agent, like the carpenter in regard to a table, and the final cause or purpose, like dining or writing. In English, the word "cause" is used regularly of the agent. The purpose or motive may likewise be termed the cause of one's actions, though this usage is now quite restricted, as in the expressions "to have good cause for joy," "to have no cause for grief," or "to fight for a good cause." But with respect to the intrinsic causes, matter and form, the application of the word "cause" is entirely technical.

Form as Cause of Being. The function of any essence as an entitative principle is to determine formally and so limit existential act. A composite substance may exercise this function only through its form, since matter is not capable of providing any formal causality. The form may from this viewpoint be named the cause of being, in the order of formal causality. A sensible thing, therefore, may be said to have being through its form. Nevertheless, what exists is the composite of matter and form. What is placed directly in the category of substance is the composite sensible thing — the man, the tree, the metal. The two substantial principles, the matter and the form, are placed in the category **reductively** or indirectly. They are the components of what is placed in it directly.

Substantial Being. Still less is the existential act of a finite substance placed directly in the category. It is not a "something." The existential act is not what exists. It is prior to the substance, but it is not the substance. Yet it is not a predicamental accident. All predicamental accidents are subsequent to the basic category. The existential act of a substance, therefore, cannot be placed in any of the categories of accident. Rather, since it is formally determined by a substance and to that extent is specified by a substantial form, it cannot be regarded as other than substantial in character. It pertains to substance insofar as it actuates substance in priority to any predicamental accident. For this reason it is said to belong reductively to the first category. The existential act of substance is accordingly called esse *substantiale*, "substantial being."

When matter loses one substantial form and acquires another, it becomes the material principle of a new thing. The first thing perishes, the second comes into being. Since the form is the cause of being, each existential act lasts only as long as the form that determines and limits it. When the composite is what exists, then, the thing is of its very essence perishable. It is an essentially "mobile" being, a being that is changeable. In metaphysical language, it is a **contingent being.** Again, the technical term is none too enlightening. Etymologically, it means "touching together." It conveys the notion that thing and being are in fact found together, but with no permanent binding link. They as it were merely touch each other, they do not necessarily require union. The association is one that can be dissolved. Applied to the union of a sensible thing with its being, it means that the thing is of such a nature that it can lose its being. The reason is that the material principle renders the thing perishable.

The perishable nature of sensible things helps show why their being is said to follow upon the composition of their essential principles and to flow from that composition. The form, as the specifying principle, is the cause of being and orientates things toward being. It renders every nature essentially a being. The matter, on the other hand, renders every non-spiritual nature perishable. Each of the two substantial principles exercises its own proper causality. Because of its form, the nature is essentially a being. Because of its matter, it is essentially perishable. Arising from the composition of the two substantial principles, the being of the thing bears the marks of both. To it rather than to not-being is the thing essentially orientated through the form. Yet it is contingent being, because its union with the thing is dissoluble on account of the other substantial principle, the matter. Any sensible thing, therefore, has to be considered metaphysically from the two sides. By its form it is orientated to being, by its matter it is disposed to its own not-being. The opposed tensions make possible a cosmos, or ordered universe of change.

If a finite nature had no matter in its essence, it would not be a contingent being. Only the essential orientation of form to being would be present in it. In itself there would be no potency to destruction, and so no potency to not-being. It would be, therefore, as far as its nature is concerned, a necessary being. Outside itself it would in a way have potentiality to not-being. It has its being from the first cause through efficient causality. On the cessation of that efficient causality it would at once lapse back into nothing. Such a withdrawal of efficient causality, by which a thing would not change into something else but fall directly into nothing, is called **annihilation.** Since the first cause freely created things and freely conserves them in being, it has absolutely the power to withdraw the conservation and so annihilate them. Its efficient causality is never necessitated by its nature, but always proceeds and continues by way of free choice. The power of the first cause, when considered in this absolute way, that is, without reference to any other attributes, is called its **absolute power.** In the absolute power of the first cause, then, all necessary finite beings may be said to have a potentiality to not-being.[10] When the power of the first cause, however, is considered not just in itself but in conjunction with the other attributes, it is called its **ordinate power.** One of these attributes is wisdom. In creating a nature meant only for being, the wisdom of the first cause would intend to conserve it perpetually in being as its nature requires. The ordinate power of the first cause, accordingly, causes the necessity of a finite spiritual being. Such a being is a necessary being

[10] "Hence the potency to not-being in spiritual creatures and the heavenly bodies is rather in God, who can withdraw his influence, than in the form or the matter of such creatures." St Thomas, *ST*, I, 104, 1, ad 1m. Cf. *De Pot.*, V, 3c. On the Thomistic doctrine that spiritual substances and the Aristotelian heavenly bodies are necessary, and not contingent beings, see C. Fabro, "Intorno alla Nozione 'Tomista' di Contingenza," *Rivista de Filosofia Neoscolastica*, XXX (1938), 132–149; T. B. Wright, "Necessary and Contingent Being in St. Thomas," *The New Scholasticism*, XXV (1951), 439–466; A. Maurer, "Henry of Harclay's Questions on Immortality," *Mediaeval Studies*, XIX (1957), 79–89. In later Scholastic tradition, however, all beings other than subsistent being have been regarded as contingent.

that has a cause of its necessity. The only being that is necessary without having any cause of its necessity is subsistent being.

Complete, Incomplete Substance. Both matter and form, the constituents of sensible natures, belong reductively to the category of substance. They are without hesitation called substantial principles. May they also be named substances? Certainly neither is a complete substance. Together they constitute but the one essence, and receive but the one act of being, at least in the substantial order. There is in each instance but the one substance that exists. Yet the matter and the form are really distinct parts of the sensible substance. They are parts that enter into composition to make up the complete nature. From that viewpoint they may be regarded as prior to the whole nature itself. Seen in this priority each appears as it were a substance in its own right, even though an incomplete substance. Accordingly each of the two substantial principles was called nature by Aristotle (*Ph.*, II, 1); and form and in a secondary way matter were described by him as substance (*Metaph.*, Z 3).

In traditional Scholastic terminology, then, matter considered alone may be called an incomplete substance. Substantial form considered alone may likewise be classed in that way. They may from one angle be regarded as incomplete substances that are joined together to make the one complete substance. There is a standpoint from which they may be viewed as prior to the whole substance itself. On the other hand, integral parts like hands, feet, or eyes, which include in themselves the one substantial form of the whole composite, really presuppose the complete substance. They are regarded by Aristotle (*Metaph.*, Z 16, 1040b5–8) as potencies to substance, and on occasion by St Thomas (*ST*, III, 16, 12, ad 2m) as a certain type of individual substance. But the substance found in each of them is that of the whole living organism. There is no other substance of their own. They are more easily understood, then, if they are called with St Thomas (*ST*, III, 2, 2, ad 3m) not substances but parts, and so are not considered to be substances in themselves at all, even incomplete substances. Only when cut off from the whole living body and endowed with other substantial forms may they be regarded as substances themselves. But then they are equivocally hands, feet, and so on, if they lack life. At best, like a cornea for transplanting, they may be actuated by a vital form different from their original one.

Incomplete substances are possible solely on condition that one of the two is pure potency. If each had its own existential act, each would thereby be shut off in itself as a substance, receiving all other acts only as accidents.

If each had formal act in itself, each would have its own distinct formal cause of being, inducing its own existence as a complete substance. This means, then, that there can be only one substantial form in any substance.[11] If a form is incomplete as a substance, the co-principle that completes it in the substantial order has to be entirely potential. Correspondingly, the wholly potential matter is incomplete in itself as substance but gives rise to a complete substance when it receives its first formal act. Any finite form added to the already completely constituted substance is thereby accidental, for it is added to something that already has substantial being. Doctrines that allow an entitative act of its own to matter, as in Duns Scotus or in Suarez, pertain to types of metaphysics in which being is not kept entirely on the "existence" side of the essence-existence couplet.

Subsistence. When a substance exists directly through the real being that corresponds to its nature, it is said to **subsist.** A halt as it were is made in the requirements for its existing. Such a halt is never made in the nature of an accident. Because an accident is a modification of a substance, it looks to the further nature of that substance in which it may have existence. Nor can the material principle of sensible substances be said to subsist. It is a substantial principle; but it is not subsistent, for it does not directly have being in itself. It has being only as a principle of an existent substance, and so only indirectly, just as it belongs to the category of substance only indirectly. What directly exists is the sensible composite. For the same reason a non-spiritual substantial form is not subsistent. It again is not what exists. It is only a principle of an existent substance. Further, cognitional being does not suffice to make a thing subsist. A thing does not have cognitional being in itself, but only in a knower. Cognitional being is being in something else, and so does not confer subsistence. Universals, accordingly, cannot subsist. Subsistence belongs only to individual substances, and is had when they are actuated by the being that corresponds directly and properly to them.[12]

[11] "Hence in order that any things should become actually one, it is necessary that they all be brought together under one form, and that they do not have each its own form by which they are in act. Therefore it is clear that if a particular substance is one, it will not be made up of substances that exist actually in it." St Thomas, *In VII Metaph.*, lect. 13, no. 1588. On the theological difficulties encountered by this doctrine of one substantial form to one substance, especially in regard to man, and the mediaeval controversies concerning the plurality of forms, see E. Gilson, *History of Christian Philosophy in the Middle Ages* (New York, 1955), pp. 416–420.

[12] The notion originally conveyed by the Latin verb *subsistere* was "to halt." But as a technical term it was used, according to Boethius (*Liber de Persona et Duabus Naturis*, c. III; *PL*, LXIV, 1344B), to translate the Greek *ousiôsthai* "to be endowed

To explain subsistence, no added essential mode[13] is necessary, as though a mode were required to complete and close off the essence and so keep existence and accidents from mixing with the thing's nature. The existential act itself is the completion (*complementum*)[14] and closing off of the thing's nature, for it composes the principles of the nature into one being. As existence, it cannot enter into any finite nature, and so of itself remains other than the nature it actuates, without the need of any mode to set up a barrier.

Supposit, Person. When a complete nature subsists, it is called a **supposit.** A supposit, accordingly, has to be an existent. It is something that really acts. To it all the individual's actions are attributed. Existence in this way pertains to the supposit, even though existence is not included in the supposit's nature or notion.[15] The being that pertains to a finite supposit, therefore, remains other than the supposit itself. The supposit is the individuated nature considered as sub-

---

with being." The corresponding Greek noun was *ousiôsis*, rendered in Latin by *subsistentia*. Substantial being was meant — "existing by itself and not in another" (St Thomas, *De Pot.*, IX, 1c).

[13] Such a mode would have to pertain to the order of essence, not the order of being, in terms of the distinction between essence and being. The modes of being to which St Thomas (*ST*, I–II, 85, 4c; *De Ver.*, XXI, 6, ad 5m) refers are finite essences in general, both accidental and substantial, insofar as essences are limitations of being. On the controversies concerning this topic, see G. Duggan, "The Teaching of St. Thomas Regarding the Formal Constitutive of Human Personality," *The New Scholasticism*, XV (1941), 318–349; T. U. Mullaney, "Created Personality: The Unity of Thomistic Tradition," *The New Scholasticism*, XXIX (1955), 369–402; J. B. Reichmann, "St. Thomas, Capreolus, Cajetan and the Created Person," *The New Scholasticism*, XXXIII (1959), 1–31, 202–230. ". . . St. Thomas never did make use of the term 'mode' in referring to the problem of supposit." Reichmann, p. 220. From a strictly philosophical viewpoint, the controversies have been quite sterile. At best they serve to focus attention on real existence as the completion of essence. In theology the issues are important for countering objections against the Trinity and Incarnation.

[14] ". . . complementum substantiae existentis." St Thomas, *CG*, II, 53; cf. *Quodl.*, XII, 5. See E. Gilson, "Cajétan et l'Existence," *Tijdschrift voor Philosophie*, XV (1953), 267–286, on Cajetan's requirement of "a recipient already fully constituted" (p. 274) for the reception of existence.

[15] "Not everything that accrues to something apart from the notion of its species is determinative of its essence, so that it has to be placed in its notion, as has been said; and therefore although being itself is not in the notion of a supposit, nevertheless because it pertains to the supposit and is not in the notion of its nature, it is clear that supposit and nature are not entirely the same wherever a thing is not its own being." St Thomas, *Quodl.*, II, 4, ad 2m. A supposit, therefore, is not an individuated nature abstracted without precision from its being, but is the individuated nature considered as existing (*De Pot.*, IX, 2, ad 13m) or subsisting (*ST*, III, 16, 12, ad 2m). When it is contrasted with the nature, however, "nature" is usually taken in a formal sense, prescinding from the individuating notes; e.g., *Quodl.*, II, 4c. Supposit means "an individual subsisting in that nature." *ST*, III, 2, 2c.

sistent. If the individuated nature is considered in abstraction from its being, it is not called a supposit. The supposit is ordinarily the recipient of predication.

If its nature is intellectual, the supposit is called a **person.**[16] Since all human actions are attributed to the person, and the responsibility for them rests on the person, and unlimited possibilities of cultural development and moral dignity spring from the person, its notion plays a tremendous role in ethics, law, and the philosophy of man (philosophical anthropology) in general. It is understood in various ways, however, in the many different personalist and existentialist philosophies.

Subsistence, though always required for personality, is not sufficient just alone to constitute a person. A complete individual substance is also necessary. There is no question of matter subsisting in itself, because it would lack any formal act through which it could receive being. But the possibility of a form subsisting as an incomplete nature lies open. As a formal act it might be able to function alone in some way as cause of being. Such a form, though subsistent, would not be considered a supposit or person.[17] It would not be complete as a nature. To perform actions in a natural way, it would require completion by its co-principle, matter. According to the traditional Scholastic condition of complete nature for a supposit, the form of any matter, even if it were a subsistent form, could not be called a person.

The characteristics of subsistence and completeness round out the notion of person in rendering it the notion of something incommunicable. Because subsistent, a person cannot be assumed into a higher unity in the existence of something superior to itself, as hands and feet and other members are actuated by the existence of the human body. Because complete, it cannot communicate itself to any other substantial principle,

---

[16] The name "person" seems to have come over into philosophical use from its designation of characters playing parts on the stage. See Boethius, *Liber de Persona et Duabus Naturis*, c. III; *PL*, LXIV, 1343D. It was considered to have arisen from the notion of "sounding through" a mask, though the change from the short "o" of *sono* "sound" to the long "o" of *persona* has not been explained. Boethius' (*ibid.*, 1343C) definition of person became classic: "Person is an individual substance of rational nature." In accepting this definition, St Thomas understands "individual substance" to mean an existent or subsistent individual substance: ". . . not any individual whatsoever in the genus of substance, even in rational nature, has the aspect of person, but only that which exists by itself . . ." *ST*, III, 2, 2, ad 3m; cf. 3, ad 2m. A nature can be individuated, as the human nature in the Incarnation, and still not be a finite person. The human nature of Christ is not subsistent because it is not actuated by any human existence, the existence that would correspond properly to it as a nature.

[17] "The soul is a part of the human species . . . And so neither the definition nor the name of person belongs to it." St Thomas, *ST*, I, 29, ad 5m.

as a form communicates itself to matter. Because it is incommunicable in these ways, it represents what is ultimate in the order of substance. It is in the full sense what lives and acts and has being. Because it is able to initiate action and freely dominate its own conduct, it is in this incommunicability an origin of what is most precious in the whole universe: ". . . person signifies that which is most perfect in the whole of nature, namely, a subsistent in rational nature."[18]

Résumé. The sole absolutely basic essence in any finite thing is called its substance. A substance has being in itself and not as a modification or a dependent of some other essence. If it exists in reality through the being proper to it, it is said to subsist. A complete subsistent substance is called a supposit, while a person is a supposit of intellectual nature.

SUGGESTED READINGS AND REFERENCES

Aristotle, *Categories*, 5, 2a11–4b19.

Armand Maurer, "Form and Essence in the Philosophy of St. Thomas," *Mediaeval Studies*, XIII (1951), 165–176.

Jacques Maritain, "On the Notion of Subsistence," in *Progress in Philosophy*, ed. J. A. McWilliams (Milwaukee: Bruce, 1955), pp. 29–45. Republished in Appendix IV of *The Degrees of Knowledge*, tr. Gerald B. Phelan (New York: Scribner's, 1959), pp. 434–444.

Edward Rousseau, "Essence and Supposit in the Angels according to St. Thomas," *The Modern Schoolman*, XXXIII (1956), 241–256.

James B. Reichmann, "St. Thomas, Capreolus, Cajetan and the Created Person," *The New Scholasticism*, XXXIII (1959), 1–31; 202–230.

[18] St Thomas, *ST*, I, 29, 3c. "Rational" in the Boethian definition has to be understood in the wider sense of "intellectual" (*ibid.*, ad 4m), just as "individual substance" in the definition has to be understood as subsistent and incommunicable individual substance. The basic explanation of subsistence, however, has to be given in terms of existence rather than of incommunicability; see Jacques Maritain, *The Degrees of Knowledge*, tr. Gerald B. Phelan (New York, 1959), p. 438. Further, purely metaphysical considerations do not require any distinction between a complete individual substance and a supposit, though they are able to provide the distinction when necessary for problems arising in a Christian milieu. This reservation may be applied to the statement "A doctrine of the distinction of nature and person has no place in philosophy." D. J. B. Hawkins, "On Nature and Person in Speculative Theology," *The Downside Review*, LXXX (1962), 4.

CHAPTER 11

Accidents

Etymology. The notion implied by the original Aristotelian term (*symbebêkos*) for predicamental accident was "going along with" or "occurring with" something else. Size and color, for example, go with bodies. They presuppose the bodies of which they are merely the modifications. They can change, while the body's nature remains the same. Sapling and tree do not differ in substance, in spite of changes in size, shape, and color. The same individual man passes through the different stages of embryo, fetus, childhood, youth, maturity, and old age, changing in many ways in size, shape, color, activities, place, time, but remaining identical in substance. These accidental characteristics are real, for they occur in the real world. They are really distinct from the substance, for they really change without involving substantial change on each occasion. Their being, accordingly, is other than the being of the substance, regardless of any consideration by the human mind. They are distinct realities that occur to, or belong to, a substance. The etymology of the Latin term *accidens*, "falling upon" or "happening" expresses this notion quite vividly.

Dependence. Changes like those in color and size reveal the accidental character of such features. But change is not the essential trait of an accident. An accident may remain the same during the whole course of its subject's existence, as do the intellectual faculties in a man. What necessarily distinguishes an accident from substance is the dependent way an accident has its being. Whatever being it has, it has through the being of something more basic, the substance it modifies. It is a nature too weak to have being just through itself. Whiteness could not exist in reality except through a body that is white. It is called a nature, because it is conceptually intelligible.[1] It is essence, because it is a potency to the being that corresponds to it; it is able to be in its own way. But it does not have its being in an independent way like substance. Like every

[1] For the traditional Boethian application of the term "nature" to accidents, see above, Chapter 3, n. 9.

finite nature, it can exist only through an existential act that is other than itself and other than any finite nature. Unlike substance, however, it requires also a finite nature other than itself through which to receive and have its being.

This dependence in the order of essence and not just in the order of being is the distinguishing trait of an accident. It is an essence that depends upon another essence in its very role of essence, that is, as a potency to being. Because of this thoroughgoing dependence in the order of essence, it is not at all on the same level as substance. It is an essence, not just through itself, but through a substantial essence. Redness is an essence only because a primary instance of essence, a body, can be red. It may be called an accidental essence, or an accidental nature, to distinguish it from essence meant absolutely, that is, from substance. It is true that an accident mentioned entirely alone has to be represented as a substance. A color or a quantity has to be spoken of as though it were a thing by itself, with the grammatical form of a noun. Just as participated existence has to form a subject of discussion under a substantive construction as though it were a reality in itself, so an accident conceived apart from its substance has to be represented as a substance. Its nature is not only too weak to stand alone in reality, but is correspondingly too tenuous to be conceptualized alone as an accident. It is accordingly represented alone as a substance. But no more than in the case of participated existence should one be deceived into thinking that it is really something in itself, in the way for instance that Locke[2] described the primary qualities. The

[2] ". . . not imagining how these simple ideas can subsist by themselves, we accustom ourselves to suppose some *substratum* wherein they do subsist . . ." *An Essay concerning Human Understanding*, II, 23, 1; ed. Fraser, I, 390–391. Locke regards the simple ideas of the qualities as adequate and determined in themselves in the Cartesian setting of clear and distinct ideas. In the Aristotelian tradition, on the contrary, an accident cannot be conceived except through and with the notion of substance. Substance, though really different, enters the notion and definition of an accident. No concept of an accident can ever be "clear and distinct" in the sense of excluding its opposite, the notion of substance. Cf.: "For as the other categories do not have being except through their being in a substance, so they are not able to be known except insofar as they share something of the mode of cognition of substance . . ." St Thomas, *In VII Metaph.*, lect. 1, no. 1259. Both being and cognoscibility in creatures belong to substance primarily and to accidents only secondarily and through substance. According to the very nature of an accident, being is predicated of it through reference to substance. Correspondingly, it is defined through substance: "But an accident is defined through something that is outside its essence, that is, through its subject, upon which it depends in its being. Hence, what is put in its definition, in place of a genus, is the subject." St Thomas, *De Pot.*, VIII, 4, ad 5m. Cf. *Quodl.*, IX, 5, ad 1m. As subject, substance has the role of potency to the act or form which is the accident, for it "is subjected to the accident as a potency of an active principle; hence also an accident is called a form." *De Virt. in Comm.*, 3c.

required therapy is to be practiced in understanding an accident as a nature that has its being through another nature, even though human thought can isolate it only by representing it as a substance. You say that the color changes, for example, when a body changes in color.

Inherence. The dependence in being that is characteristic of an accident was described by Aristotle in the *Categories* (2, 1a24–25) as being *in* a subject. From this viewpoint the very nature of every accident is such that it is meant for being *in* something other than itself, that is, in a substance.[3] In more metaphysical language, an accident is an actuation of a potency. It is the accidental act of a subject. It actuates a substance in a secondary way. Redness, for instance, makes actually red a face that in itself was just *able* to blush. Accordingly, it actuates a potency to redness. The potency here is the substance. Redness is one of its accidental forms or acts. Every accident, then, is *in* a subject that is a substance, and every accident actuates a substance. Is every accident therefore an inherent form?

The more basic accidents, like quantity and qualities, are undoubtedly forms intrinsic to the thing they actuate. A color inheres in a body, adding a new form to the thing's intrinsic constitution. But do accidents such as where and when a thing is add any inherent form? There seems to be no intrinsic addition to the reality of a pie when it is brought from the pantry into the dining room. Yet there is a real accidental difference accruing to it from the new and really different place. The possibility of non-inherent accidents, accordingly, is to be kept open. Each category of accident is a supreme genus of being, an original mold in which existential act is cast. One type of accident, therefore, is not to be conceived as modeled on another. Accidents such as where and when need not be expected to conform to the type found in quality. There is the possibility that some accidents may actuate a thing extrinsically, that is, without effecting any change in its intrinsic constitution, as in the case of the pie being in different places. If the non-inherent accidents presuppose the inherent ones, however, there is a sense in which accidents may be said in general to inhere, as substance is said to subsist. Yet while every accident is dependent on and in this sense *is in* a substance, some accidents need not be inherent.

---

[3] "It pertains to the quiddity or essence of an accident, however, to have being in a subject." *ST*, III, 77, 1, ad 2m. Cf. *Quodl.*, IX, 5, ad 2m. Inherence, though, pertains to substantial forms as well as to accidents: ". . . 'this particular thing' may be taken in two ways: in one way, for any subsistent whatsoever . . . it excludes the inherence of an accident and of a material form." *ST*, I, 75, 2, ad 1m. On non-inherent accidents, see below, Chapter 14.

In the case of inherent accidents, the substance through which they have their being is the substance in which they inhere. By actuating their substance these accidents have their being through it. By making a body white, whiteness has its being as a modification of the body. In the case of participated existence, as has been seen, the situation is different. The existential act inheres in[4] or actuates the essence it makes be. It belongs to that essence, it is an accident of that essence. But what it depends on primarily is an agent other than that essence. It is through another substance, the extrinsic efficient cause. The essence it actuates depends upon it for distinction from mere nothing. The existential act is accordingly prior to the corresponding essence. The predicamental accident, on the other hand, is subsequent to what it actuates, and so has its being through the nature in which it inheres. It requires also an efficient cause, for it involves new being. Its efficient cause may be the substance in which it inheres, as in the case of an act of intellection, or an agent other than that substance, as in the case of the electric plate heating the water.

An inherent predicamental accident, accordingly, has a substance as the proper subject in which it is present. It may be called a form that has substance as its corresponding matter. It has therefore no matter in its own nature, as sensible substance has. It requires something outside its own nature, namely substance, to function as its subject or matter. It is called an accidental form, to distinguish it from the substantial form that inheres directly in primary matter. As the subject of accidents, however, a material substance may be referred to as matter in a secondary sense. From this viewpoint it is called secondary matter. Such is the matter that is treated of in the modern physical sciences, when matter is contrasted with mind or with energy. In the accident itself, though, there is no matter whatsoever, either primary or secondary. The inherent accident is just a form, absolute or relative, that is found in substance as its proper subject. Unlike dependence on a substance, however, inherence is not necessarily required for an accident. Where and when a thing is, for instance, are really accidental to it, yet are not inherent forms. They *are in* the thing in the sense of dependence on it in being; but they do not, like size or whiteness, add to the intrinsic constitution of the thing.

A Being of a Being. Just as an accident may be termed a nature or an essence or a form, but always in a secondary

[4] ". . . in which being is not subsistent but inherent." *De Pot.*, 7, 2, ad 7m.

sense of those words, so it may be called a thing or a quiddity or a being, likewise in a secondary sense. These terms denote *what* exists, and what exists is primarily a substance. A tree or a stone is unhesitatingly called a thing, but the term is applied only with misgivings to a color or a sound or a size. Yet each of these is something. In some diluted sense, therefore, a color or a sound is a thing. You may ask *what* a size or a smell is, thereby designating it as a quiddity. But any such accident is always a quiddity that belongs to another quiddity, the substance. In this sense it is a quiddity of a quiddity. In a corresponding secondary way, every accident may be termed a being, insofar as it has existence. Since it has existence only through a substance, and belongs to a substance, it is rather a being of a being (*ens entis*) than a being simply so called.

When a substance acquires more quantity in growth or a new color from the sun's rays, the added quantity or color really comes into existence. In each case a new being, in the sense of a being of a being, comes into existence in the real world. The existential act that constitutes it a being in this way will likewise be existence in only a secondary sense, when compared with substantial being. The primary being of a finite substance is its substantial existence. This is its being simply so called. Accidental being is termed rather *being in* (*inesse*), to distinguish it from substantial being. When you ask about a thing's being, your question when unqualified is understood in regard to something like a metal or a hill or a house, and not like a color or a sound. "Being" needs qualification, accordingly, when applied to the existential act of an accident.

Distinction of Accidental Being. Quite evidently, accidental existence is distinct from substantial existence. Accidental existence is *being* in, substantial existence is not. In regard to real accidents this is a real distinction. The substantial being of a man really continues, while the accidental being of his sun tan perishes with the autumn months. The substantial being endures in reality without that accidental being, independently of all consideration by the human mind. But even where the real distinction cannot be shown through accidental change, it emerges from the real dependence of accidental being upon substantial being, in contrast to the independence of substantial being in regard to anything that is not its efficient cause. An accident really exists as a modification of a really existent substance. Only in real dependence upon substantial existence can the accidental existence be had. An identical existence could not be really dependent and really independent in the same respect. The one has to be really distinct from the other.[5]

On the other hand, is the accidental existence as evidently distinct from the accidental essence it immediately actuates? The reason why existence has to be entitatively distinct from any finite nature is that otherwise it would absorb the finite nature into the infinity of subsistent being. *What* existed would be subsistent being itself. A real accident, however, is a real limited nature, and by definition it cannot subsist. It is really other than subsistent being, and in consequence really distinct from its proper existential act.

A conceptual distinction from an accidental essence would indeed suf-

---

[5] "For in us, relations have dependent being, because their being is other than the being of substance. Hence they have their own way of being in accordance with their own character, as is also the case in the other accidents." *CG*, IV, 14, Leonine manual no. 7c. The accidental being is superadded to substantial being just as accidental essences are superadded to substance: "For, since all accidents are certain forms superadded to the substance, and caused by the principles of the substance, their being has to be superadded upon the being of the substance, and dependent on it." *Ibid.* Substantial being, accordingly, is distinct from accidental being in the same way substance is distinct from accident. To interpret this text and similar ones in any other sense than a real distinction can hardly avoid implying the denial of a real distinction between finite substance and its being, e.g.: "We can consider the being as existing determined by its primary distinction from mere potency — its essence; and, considering it in that light, we attribute to the being an *esse substantiale.* If, on the other hand, we consider the being as existing in a manner further determined by its accidents, we attribute to it an *esse accidentale.*" J. S. Albertson, "The *Esse* of Accidents according to St. Thomas," *The Modern Schoolman,* XXX (1953), 274.

Since in contrast to substantial being, accidental being is not "being" (*esse*) but "being in" (*inesse — De Ver.,* VIII, 2, ad 3m; *De Pot.,* VII, 7c; *Quodl.,* IX, 5, ad 1m; *In VII Metaph.,* lect. 1, no. 1253; *ST,* I, 28, 2c), St Thomas can say simply, in contexts where he is taking "being" properly in the sense of substantial being, that an accident does not have being (e.g., *ST,* I, 90, 2c). The "being in" of an accident, however, is called "being" in the texts in which the being of accidents is characterized as "being in," and the being of creatures "is divided into the being of substance and the being of accident" (*CG,* I, 26). The being of an accident is a secondary type of being: "Hence, the supervening accident . . . causes a certain secondary act of existing . . ." *De Ente,* c. VI, (ed. Roland-Gosselin, p. 43.25–28; tr. A. Maurer, p. 56). Cf. *Quodl.,* IX, 3c. The accident has its own being that depends upon substance: ". . . its being and its unity depend upon that in which it inheres." *In I Sent.,* d. 9, q. 1, a. 2, Solut.; ed. Mandonnet, I, 248. Being, accordingly, follows upon accidental form as it follows upon substantial form: "It is clear that all being is from some inherent form, just as being white is from whiteness and substantial being is from substantial form." *In I Sent.,* d. 17, q. 1, a. 1, Solut.; I, 393. Cf. *ibid.,* ad 6m, p. 396. So, while the substantial being remains the same, "color and taste are distinguished by the one and the other accidental being." *In I Sent.,* d. 24, q. 1, a. 2, Solut.; I, 578. Because their existence is accompanied by substantial existence, accidents may be classed nevertheless with other concomitants of substance as "coexistent" and "concreated" (*ST,* I, 45, 4c). On accidents as forms, see *ST,* I, 77, 6c; *Comp. Theol.,* I, 90.

fice for establishing the finitude of accidental existence.[6] Anything accidental is thereby the act of a potency, and so is limited in its very notion as accidental. Substantial existence, on the contrary, is not so limited in its notion. In subsistent being it is infinite. In other real things, it requires a real distinction from essence to establish its finitude. In the case of accidents, however, the notion of their existential act already includes finitude. But can the restriction "accidental" be added to existence without already presupposing its real distinction from the accident itself? Existence means the difference between nothing and something. Just in itself it is subsistent and infinite. To be considered as finitized, it has to be regarded as an act entitatively distinct from a finitizing potency. As restricted to accidental existence, it is already represented as participated and so as entitatively distinct from the accidental essence. Where the accidental existence is real, the distinction will have to be real. Once it is considered as accidental existence, it would manifest its finitude sufficiently through a conceptual distinction; but in fact it cannot be accidental existence unless the much stronger entitative distinction is there to ground the conceptual difference.

---

[6] ". . . because they do not subsist, it does not belong to them properly to be; but through them the subject *is* in a certain way. Hence they are properly called 'of a being' rather than 'beings.' And therefore for something to be in a category of accident it does not have to be composed in real composition, but only in the notion's composition of genus and differentia." *De Ver.*, XXVII, 1, ad 8m. Actually, the composition of genus and differentia in an accident presupposes real composition with the substance, since substance enters the accident's definition in place of the basic genus; cf. above, n. 2. In the reply to the third argument of the same article of *De Veritate*, the being of the accident in question, grace, is caused by the accidental form as substantial being is caused by substantial form: "For the natural form is the principle of natural being. And similarly God produces gratuitous spiritual being in us without the mediation of any agent, but with the mediation nevertheless of a created form, which is grace." *De Ver.*, XXVII, 1, ad 3m. Being "cannot be the essence of substance or accident." *ST*, III, 77, 1, ad 2m. Not only in substance but in every genus does being lie outside the content of the quiddity: ". . . in every genus there has to be indicated a certain quiddity, as has been said, and to its notion being does not pertain." *In I Sent.*, d. 8, q. 4, a. 2, ad 2m; I, 222–223.

In spite of the many texts in which the "being in" of accidents is called "being" and is distinguished from the accidental essence just as substantial being is distinguished from substantial essence (cf. also texts below, n. 7) a number of present day commentators maintain that the doctrine of an accidental being, really distinct from the accident's essence and from substantial being, was unknown to St Thomas. E. g., C. Fabro, "L'Obscurcissement de l' 'Esse' dans l'Ecole Thomiste," *Revue Thomiste*, LVIII (1958), pp. 460–461. For other instances, see Albertson, *art. cit.*, pp. 271–272, n. 14. From this viewpoint, any existential act seems regarded as substantial being; e.g., "This second *esse* is not a second act of existing; that would make the accident into a substance joined to another." C. G. Kossel, "Principles of St. Thomas's Distinction between the *Esse* and *Ratio* of Relation," *The Modern Schoolman*, XXIV (1947), 93, n. 4.

Analogy and Reference. The existence of each accident, then, is entitatively distinct from the accident's essence, just as substantial being is proportionally distinct from substantial essence in finite things. In every case the accident's being (*inesse*) will be proportioned to the accident's nature, and will be specified by that nature just as any existential act is limited and determined by the formal causality of the essence it actuates. Accidental existence, accordingly, will correspond exactly to every different category of accident and pertain reductively to it. The existence of a quantity will be of a different type from the existence of a quality or of a relation. The difference will arise from the different types of accidental essences. With all real accidents, moreover, the existential act will be really distinct from the existential act of the substance.

This means that in every instance throughout the categories the existential act is proportional to the nature of the essence, either substantial or accidental. As substantial existence is to substance, so the existence of a quality is to the quality itself, and so on in the case of every other accident.[7] Analogy of being extends through the whole range of the categories. Here, however, the analogy does not exclude predication in reference to a primary instance. Substance, as has been seen, is the primary instance of predicamental beings.[8] As its modifications, and so essentially in reference to it, are accidents beings. On this ground alone they could be denominated beings, as in fact they were by Aristotle.[9] Of the two grounds, though, analogy penetrates much deeper than reference; for in predicamental beings it lays bare their entitative structure, while reference accepts without examination that structure as already complete.

The priority of substance in the order of being, nevertheless, shows how a substance may be actuated as a potency by an accident without undergoing any change in its own nature. The substance is primarily a potency to its proper existential act, that is, to substantial being. When

[7] Cf. *In III Sent.*, d. 1, q. 1, a. 1, Resp.; ed. Moos, III, 8 (no. 12), text above, Chapter 8, n. 4. "Also, just as a substantial form is related to the being of nature, so is charity to the being of grace." *In I Sent.*, d. 17, q. 1, a. 3, arg. 2; ed. Mandonnet, I, 400. ". . . just as substantial being is other than accidental being, so it is clear that substantial form is other than accidental form." *De Ver.*, XXI, 6, ad 9m; cf. 1, ad 6m; 5c. ". . . in it a twofold being has to be considered. For, since form is the principle of being, a thing having form is necessarily said to be in a certain way according to every form it has." *In Boeth. de Hebd.*, lect. II; ed. Mandonnet, *Opusc.*, I, 174.

[8] See above, Chapter 10, n. 1. Subsistent being, because it is unlimited, is not predicamental being and does not come under the category of substance; see St Thomas, *In I Sent.*, d. 8, q. 4, a. 2; ed. Mandonnet, I, 221–223. Cf. *ST*, I, 3, 5c.

[9] See above, Chapter 6, n. 14; Chapter 8, n. 4.

completed by this existential act of its own substantial order, its nature is sealed off from any essential addition or change. The composing of its essential principles, that is, its existential act, is its completion (*complementum*) as a nature. Any further actuation cannot make an essential difference in it, for no such actuation can enter into its completed nature. It is primarily a subject for its own existence, and only secondarily a subject for predicamental accidents. It receives predicamental accidents, then, but does not allow them to enter into its nature and effect any essential change or addition. Correspondingly, all accidents are acts of a substance; but the primary act of the substance is its own being, while the predicamental accidents are acts of a subsequent order that leave the basic substantial nature unchanged in itself. The substance is therefore a potency primarily to existence, and only secondarily to predicamental accidents. It has to be first completed by its substantial being before it can be regarded as a potency to them.

Completed by substantial being, however, the substance can be actuated in secondary ways and accordingly can *be* in secondary ways. From this viewpoint of being does the understanding of accident take place on the level of metaphysics. Since accidental being is a secondary way of being for substance, accidental essence will be a secondary type of essence for substance. It will be an essence belonging to another essence. It will depend upon substantial essence and may inhere in it. It will be a secondary way in which the substance exists. As being in composite things is always a joining and uniting, so accidental being is an existential joining of the accidental essence with the substance. It effects a composition of accidental form with substance, a composition on a secondary plane of being. When accidents are the subject of thought and discussion, they have to be represented unavoidably as though they were substances. Yet the effort should always be made to keep from regarding them as beings in their own right. If they are approached from the viewpoint of their being, they will keep manifest the imperfection in their very notion: "For the notion of accident contains imperfection; because the being of an accident is being in and being dependent, and effecting composition with its subject as a consequence."[10]

---

[10] *In I Sent.*, d. 8, q. 4, a. 3, Solut.; ed. Mandonnet, I, 224. It is hard to see how the *inesse*, dependence, and composition of the accident's existential act could be real if the existential act were really identified with substantial existence, as in the position: "The accident is a new nature which participates in the act of existing of substance. But we predicate esse always through essences; and since the essence of substance does not include accidents we must predicate a second time, give a second *esse*, to indicate this accretion of being to substance." Kossel, *loc. cit.* In the Aristotelian doctrine, being is indeed predicated of accidents quite in this way, that is,

Résumé. An accident is a secondary essence or form that has being dependently on substance. It is accordingly a being of a being. It may be either an inherent or an extrinsic actuality. Its being is correspondingly secondary in type, and other than the accident itself, and other than the being and essence of the substance on which the accident depends.

SUGGESTED READINGS AND REFERENCES

Aristotle, *Metaphysics*, Z 1–5, 1028a10–1031a14.

St Thomas Aquinas, *On Being and Essence*, c. VI; tr. A. Maurer (Toronto: Pontifical Institute of Mediaeval Studies, 1949), pp. 55–59.

——— *Commentary on the Metaphysics of Aristotle*, Book VII, Lesson 1, nos. 1247–1259; Lesson 3, nos. 1309–1326; Lesson 4, nos. 1331–1355. Tr. John P. Rowan (Chicago: Henry Regnery, 1961), II, 489 ff.

John of St Thomas, *The Material Logic of John of St. Thomas*, IV, 14, 4; tr. Yves Simon *et al.* (Chicago: University of Chicago Press, 1955), pp. 208–213.

K. K. Berry, "The Relation of the Aristotelian Categories to the Logic and the Metaphysics," *The New Scholasticism*, XIV (1940), 406–411.

---

solely through reference to substance. But according to the texts and the overall metaphysical principles of St Thomas, each act of participated existence is specified by its own corresponding essence. An accident comes into being by specifying a new existential act, an act that is thereby really other than the existential act specified by substance. On this topic the Aristotelian doctrine is in full solidarity with its own general metaphysical principles, and the doctrine of St Thomas is likewise fully coherent with its own basic teachings.

CHAPTER 12

Absolutely Inherent Accidents

Absolute Inherence. Of its very nature every predicamental accident is conceived as relative to the subject on which it depends. In its notion as accident it is a modification of a substance. Some accidents, however, bring the substance into relation with other things. The location of a substance, for instance, presupposes and involves a number of relations to the environment. The action of driving puts a man into relation with a car and a road. Two kinds of accidents, though, when regarded just in themselves are not relative to anything outside the substance in which they are found. Size, considered in abstraction from references for the further accident of place, does not by itself relate a substance to anything else. Color, just as color, does not express any new relation to something outside the substance. These accidents modify the substance absolutely, that is, regardless of things external to it. They may therefore be called absolutely inherent accidents. Sometimes, too, an accident may modify a substance absolutely, and yet of its nature be conceived as relative to an external object. A science like chemistry, once mastered, remains with a chemist regardless of external things. Yet fundamentally the science of chemistry bears of its nature on the constitution of bodies. It is conceived as relative to them. Since the absolute phase is obviously more basic in accidents of this dual type, they are more conveniently grouped with the absolutely inherent accidents.[1]

Quantitative, Qualitative. The absolutely inherent accidents fall into two categories, the quantitative and the qualitative, or quantity and quality. In calling these accidents "quantity" and "quality," one is thereby representing them as substances. This way of designation is unavoidable in philosophic treatment. In any study of them, the accidents have to be placed before the mind as subjects for

[1] See Aristotle, *Cat.*, 9, 11a20–38. On the notion "absolutely inherent," cf. "inest ei per se et absolute," St Thomas, *In V Metaph.*, lect. 9 (ed. Cathala-Spiazzi) no. 892; "absolute inhaerens rebus," *De Pot.*, VII, 9c.

discussion. This means projecting them with substantive force and designating them with substantive words. The original terms that Aristotle used to name the accidental categories, however, were not substantive in form, even though Aristotle himself glides frequently enough in his actual discussions into the abstract noun "quality" and the like. The proper designation of the category of quantity, for instance, was *to poson*, the quantitative. That of quality was *to poion*, the qualitative. Corresponding to these adjectival forms, adverbial and verbal forms were used to name the other categories.

Use of the title "the quantitative" helps keep in mind that it designates not something self-contained and as it were standing in its own right, but rather a way in which a substance happens to be. What is there is something quantitative, and not any detached "quantity." Be that as it may, the frequent use of the abstract nouns quantity, quality, relation, and so on, is inevitable perhaps even more in English than in Greek. All one can do is try to keep in mind, while using the substantive designation, that the accidents should be represented adjectively or adverbially or with a form of the verb. This therapy is constantly necessary in order to avoid understanding the accident as something self-contained, when actually it is just modifying something else.

a) THE QUANTITATIVE

Continuous, Discrete. Everything in the sensible world has size or extension. Any sensible object is spread out in the three dimensions of length, breadth, and thickness. Sensible objects, moreover, may be counted in terms of one, two, three, four, and so on. These two features, extension and number, are called technically their quantity. Extension is termed **continuous quantity**, because it consists of parts joined each with the next in common extremes, and so of parts that are continuous with each other. Number is called **discrete quantity**, because it is made up of units separate from or divided from one another (*discreta*). Contiguous parts, that is, parts that touch each other without having common extremes, are discrete. Extension and number, accordingly, are the two highest divisions in the category of quantity.

Not Substance. Extension manifests itself as a different nature in reality from the substance of the extended thing. The extension or size can change, while its subject retains substantial identity. The animal remains the same animal as it grows from foal to horse. It undergoes real change in size, but remains really the same in substantial nature. The substantial nature, moreover, is found whole and entire in every part of its extension. Every part of a man's body is human, every part of the iron is equally metal. Its extension, on the other hand, is not found whole and entire in each part. Rather, one part is not found in another, but outside the other. Every part of the human body will possess the same substantial nature as any other part, but not the same extension. The parts really coincide in nature substantially; but they do not coincide in their extension, for each part really lies outside the others. The substance, then, is really different from each part and so from the totality of the parts that constitute the thing's extension or quantity. These two facts, namely growth in plants and animals, and identity of nature throughout really differing parts, establish sufficiently the real difference between substance and quantity.[2]

A corporeal nature just in itself, therefore, is not extended. But it is a nature that is *capable* of extension in the three dimensions. The capability or potency to extension belongs to its very essence, and distinguishes it radically from supersensible substance. A material nature is necessarily composed of the two physical principles, matter and form. The matter allows the formal principle to be spread through parts outside parts without any formal increase whatsoever. In this way it renders the nature itself potentially extended. But that potentiality can be actuated only through an accident, the accident of quantity. Not even the matter, just in itself, is extended.[3] The matter is only the substantial basis of extension, insofar as it makes a formally identical nature capable of spread by a superadded accident through parts outside parts. The parts may be homogeneous, as in the case of a metal like iron, or heterogeneous as in animals where the same animal nature is spread through bone, marrow, muscle, nerves, and other such dissimilar parts.

Continuous quantity, then, is an accident of corporeal nature, and not a substance. It is not primarily what exists, but is only an accidental mode under which corporeal substances exist. Still less does discrete quantity exhibit itself as the substance of anything. It rather presupposes extended substances and enumerates them. It is accordingly subsequent to continuous quantity, and so is even more manifestly of the accidental order. Its species are one, two, three, and all the other numbers that are found in reality. Each number constitutes a different species of discrete quantity.

[2] Descartes, on the ground that there was no "clear and distinct idea" of corporeal substance apart from extension, maintained that the two were identical in reality. See *Principia Philosophiae*, II, 4–9; A–T, VIII, 42.4–45.16 (IX², 65–68).

[3] Quantity is expressly denied to the ultimate matter by Aristotle, *Metaph.*, Z 3, 1029a20. What is understood in the modern sciences by "matter" is something that is already quantitative, the Scholastic "secondary matter" as opposed to "primary matter."

Though the notion of discrete quantity is attained originally from things of the sensible order, immediately susceptible as they are of enumeration, the notion itself is unhesitatingly applied to immaterial things. You speak of two or three or any number of supersensible substances, for instance of Platonic Ideas or of Aristotelian separate entities, or of angels. They are different beings, each with its own transcendental unity. Because each is a unit in the same way it is a being, they may be regarded as constituting a particular number of units. This is called transcendental number, or transcendental multiplicity,[4] because it is based upon the transcendental unity of each of the things concerned. Supersensible entities, however, have no formal quantity, because they have no matter in their substantial natures. But on account of the transcendental unity of each, they may be enumerated as though they did possess quantity, and so may be said to come virtually under the notion of discrete quantity, that is, of number. The technical term for this capacity of enumeration in immaterial things is accordingly **virtual quantity**, even though the enumeration is made on the basis of transcendental and not of extended units.

Basic Corporeal Accident. Any accident present in a material thing is found spread throughout its parts. A color, for instance, is always perceived as extended over a certain space. All sensibly perceptible qualities are similarly attained as spatially extended. Any corporeal activity or movement is also located in extended parts, and has as its principles corporeal qualities that are already extended. Upon quantity and actions and movements depend the relations of bodies to other things. Upon these inherent accidents depend the categories that arise from extrinsic denomination, such as where and when a thing is. This means that quantity is the ground through which all other corporeal accidents are sustained in being by their substance, for they all require a substance that is already extended.

Quantity, however, does not properly become the subject in which the other accidents have being. Not having being in itself, it cannot function as the basic essence that sustains other essences in being, as required in a proper subject of accidents. Through quantity, nevertheless, the other corporeal accidents are sustained in being by substance in such a way that if the quantity is kept in being the others are able to be conserved in

[4] For the use of "transcendent" in this regard, see St Thomas, *ST*, I, 30, 3c, and ad 2m. For "virtual quantity," see *ST*, I, 42, 1, ad lm, etc. A. Krempel, *La Doctrine de la Relation chez Saint Thomas* (Paris, 1952), p. 205, n. 1, notes that St Thomas gradually restricted the latter expression to the realm of causality. Krempel, p. 84, finds quantity reduced through modern physics to quality.

being in their natural sequence upon it. In this remote way quantity may loosely be regarded as a kind of mediate subject for the other corporeal accidents. In exact terminology, however, quantity is the ground for the other corporeal accidents without properly becoming a subject for them.

Quantitative Change. A thing may change in quantity either by increase (augmentation) or decrease (diminution). In living things increase in quantity is called growth. The unity of vital activity that continues in spite of change in size is sufficient to guarantee the identity of the substance throughout the additional parts, for instance in the same person growing from child to man. In non-living things, as when one piece of iron is fused with another, unity of substance is not so clear. The specific natures remain unknown in themselves, and the accidents do not clearly manifest whether the individual is found in the molecule or in a larger aggregation.

Quantitative change is not properly from opposite to opposite. In the category of quantity, strictly speaking, there are no contraries.[5] Large and small are not opposed contrarily, but only relatively. In discrete quantity, correspondingly, many and few are only relatively opposed.

Mathematical Abstraction. In real things quantity is always found immersed in sensible qualities. It gives a thing the three dimensions of length, breadth, and thickness. It inevitably makes the thing a solid. A real solid has weight, color, and many such qualities that affect the human senses. If it entirely lacked those qualities, it would not at all be perceptible to man.[6] Since it is perceptible only through the sensible qualities, real quantity may be called sensible quantity. The human mind, however, can leave the sensible qualities out of its consideration and regard the quantity in abstraction from them, as when it considers a line or a surface apart from the real solid, or when it states that one and one are two regardless of any particular sensible instance of a one or a two. Quantity so considered apart from all sensible qualities is called abstract or mathematical quantity. A line, a surface, and a mathematical solid are species of abstract quantity taken as continuous, with the endlessly varied mathematical figures constituting subdivisions. Discrete quantity in the abstract has also species that are not found in the real order, for instance the irrational numbers. A point is not formally quantity, because it is not spread out in parts. But it pertains to quantity because it is the terminus of a line, and so is placed in the category of

---

[5] See Aristotle, *Cat.*, 6, 5b11–6a18.

[6] Cf. above, Chapter 1, n. 2.

quantity reductively. Correspondingly, zero is regarded as a number in modern mathematics, because from it mathematical succession begins.

Does mathematical quantity abstract also from substance? A moment's reflection will show that such an abstraction is impossible. Substance enters into the very notion and definition of any accident. In its very essence any accident, including quantity, is a modification of a substance. It could not abstract from substance without thereby obliterating its own self. Because it is spread through parts outside parts, even mathematical quantity requires some kind of matter to allow the same formal notion, like a line or a surface, to remain formally the same while differing in extension. Likewise there can be many mathematical twos and threes, just as there are many real pairs and trios. The multiple individuation of the formal mathematical notions shows accordingly the presence of matter. As abstract, this matter is not perceptible by the senses. It is known only through the intellect. It is therefore called intelligible matter,[7] as distinguished from sensible matter.

In what does the intelligible matter of mathematical abstraction consist? It must in some way be material substance, for that is the only subject in which quantity can inhere. Without the notion of material substance, quantity cannot even be understood. As the first accident of material substance, however, it can be understood in abstraction from the subsequent accidents. Among these are the sensible qualities, the qualities that render material substance sensible. By those qualities matter becomes sensible. Without those qualities it is only intelligible. Intelligible matter, accordingly, is material substance considered in abstraction from sensible qualities.[8] Since specific differentiae are indicated only by the sensible qualities and subsequent accidents, they do not at all appear in this abstract matter. Mathematical quantity, therefore, is indifferent to both substantial and sensible qualities.

b) THE QUALITATIVE

Accidental Quality. As quantity makes a thing be of a certain size, so quality[9] makes it be of a certain kind. Anything,

[7] The expression "intelligible matter" is Aristotle's, *Metaph.*, Z 11, 1037a4–5. It was also used of the genera as matter for the species, *Ibid.*, H 6, 1045a36. At *ST*, I, 78, 3, ad 2m, St Thomas calls quantity the "proximate subject" of the sensible qualities. Substance, however, is what sustains all accidents in being; see *In I Sent.*, d. 17, q. 1, a. 2, ad 2m (ed. Mandonnet, I, 398); *Quodl.*, III, 1, ad arg. in contr.; *De Virt. in Comm.*, 3c.

[8] See St Thomas, *In Boeth. de Trin.*, V, 3c; ed. Wyser (Fribourg & Louvain, 1948), p. 39.21–37; tr. Maurer (Toronto, 1958), p. 29. Cf. *ST*, I, 85, 1, ad 2m.

[9] The term "quality" seems to have been introduced by Plato, *Tht.*, 182A. The Presocratics did not distinguish effectively physical qualities from substance.

however, is already of a certain kind by its substantial nature. A man is human, a horse is equine, a plant is vegetative. This type of qualification pertains to the category of substance. It is the determination given by the substantial nature itself, when that nature is conceived as the specific differentia. A specific differentia is accordingly a substantial quality.[10] Besides its substantial qualification, however, every sensible thing is further qualified in accidental ways. It has for instance colors, figure, weight, temperature, and hardness. In all these it can change while remaining the same in its substantial quality. A man, besides being human through his substantial nature, may also be cultured, ruddy, and stout. He could be a man without being any one of these latter. They are therefore accidental to him. Since they make him to be of such and such a kind, they have full right to the technical name "qualities." Since they are accidental, they have to be placed in a category different from substance. Accidental qualities, accordingly, are ranged in a special category, with four main subdivisions.

Habits and Dispositions. The first subdivision in the category of quality is known as "habits and dispositions." "Habit" in this sense means a permanent way in which a nature is disposed toward a definite type of activity. The medical art acquired by a physician during his years of training and study is such a "habit." It is a quality that enables him to treat and cure the sick or injured. Once acquired it remains with him during all the years of his practice. The same holds proportionally for any science, art, or craft, and for the moral virtues. These are "habits" in the philosophical sense of the term. The philosophical sense, as can be readily seen, is somewhat different from the meaning of the word in ordinary speech. It does not at all signify a rut that someone has drifted into. It denotes rather possession and control. It means a definite way in which a person "has" himself disposed (*habitus*) in permanent fashion. Such possession of one's self in regard to a way of acting implies intelligent control. However, health is classed as a habit, but as an "entitative habit"[11] to distinguish it from habits that dispose a person toward activity. These latter are called operative habits.

[10] St Thomas, *In V Metaph.*, lect. 22, no. 1122 (ed. Cathala-Spiazzi). Cf. Aristotle, *Cat.*, 5, 3b18–21.

[11] The expression "entitative habit" is of recent use, but the contrast with operative habits is traditionally Scholastic and was referred back to Aristotle, *Ph.*, VII 3, 246b4–8, where he ranged health, beauty, and strength among the habits. See St Thomas, *ST*, I–II, 50, 1c. These habits were regarded as dispositions to being, instead of dispositions to operation. Philosophically the notion is vague and of little practical importance, but in theological study it takes on crucial significance in locating sanctifying grace as the basic supernatural habit in the soul. See St Thomas, *ST*, I–II, 110, 2c & 4c.

Knowledge, accordingly, is a habit, because it has a sure and abiding grasp of its object. It enjoys the permanent character required in a habit. Opinion, on the other hand, is variable in its grasp of its object. It lacks the permanence of a habit, for it can keep changing as new information becomes available. Yet it qualifies a person through the cognition it gives him, just as knowledge does. It disposes its subject as does a habit, but without the characteristic of permanence. It is therefore called simply a disposition. A disposition qualifies a person in regard to some type of activity, but it lacks the notes of permanence and security of possession. With a mere disposition a person does not "have" himself definitely and firmly disposed toward the particular type of activity. A man who dabbles occasionally in fixing things is not thereby a mechanic. He is disposed to that kind of work, but he does not inspire the secure confidence that is placed in the trained professional. His disposition is not constant in regard to the range and character of work expected from a mechanic. He may be able to do a few odd jobs well enough, mostly of the easier sort. But he lacks the steady and understanding orientation to mechanical work. He has therefore only a disposition, not a habit, in that regard.

Habits and dispositions are acquired by acts, and so can be destroyed by contrary acts. Because of its note of permanence, a habit is comparatively difficult to remove, a disposition comparatively easy. From this viewpoint a habit is said to be "removable with difficulty" (*difficulter mobilis*), while a disposition is "easily removable" (*facile mobilis*). Habits usually begin with dispositions. By study and practice and training these dispositions gradually acquire the status of a habit. Accordingly habits and dispositions are classed under the one subdivision of the category of quality. Though absolute accidents in their own nature, they have also a relative aspect on account of their specification by an external object. From the standpoint of logic they may therefore be classed also as relatives.[12] Viewed metaphysically, however, they belong definitely to the category of quality. In themselves they are primarily ways in which a subject is qualified, for instance, as learned, cultured, or virtuous.

Abilities and Debilities. A second type of the qualitative is found in a nature's capacities for its various operations. The capacity of a man to know and to think, for instance, is called his intellect. Intellective capacity follows upon human nature itself, even though the capacity may be perfected by various habits and dispositions or may be almost completely impeded by brain damage. The capacities to will, to see, to breathe, to digest food, to walk, to grow, to reproduce,

[12] Aristotle, *Cat.*, 9, 11a34–38. On the relative, see below, Chapter 13, n. 31.

all come under this type of the qualitative, whether or not they are capacities that can be trained through habits. They are called faculties or powers. They qualify a man by making him be of a certain kind, namely intellective, appetitive, ambulatory, and the like. Capacities of inanimate things, for instance to resist pressure, to impart motion, to cohere and adhere, and so on, likewise come under this subdivision of the category.

In the traditional Greek and Latin philosophical vocabulary the faculties or powers, though capacities to *perform* actions, were designated by the same term as the capacities to *receive* forms or acts. They were known as "potencies." Since they were potencies to operation, the faculties were regarded as active potencies, in contrast to merely passive or receptive potencies like primary matter or essence. The latter are potencies for receiving or undergoing something, while an active potency is a power to do something. But in this regard the traditional terminology became rather confusing. Cognitive potencies, like sight, hearing, or intellect, are clearly capacities for operation. Yet they have been traditionally regarded as passive potencies, because they are as it were passively informed by the object of cognition in the cognitive operation itself. But all faculties, even the cognitive ones, are active in the sense that they are powers for operation.

When the power is comparatively weak in respect of the operation it is able to perform, like the power of resistance in soft things, or the power of a sickly person to withstand inclement weather, it was designated rather incongruously in the Scholastic tradition by the term *impotentia* or incapacity.[13] Such potentialities may be too weak to deserve the name of powers or abilities. Yet they belong to the same overall type of the qualitative, and are placed in the same subdivision, with the understanding that they are debilities in contrast to the full abilities to perform their actions.

The presence of active powers in substances is not known immediately. Experimental psychology rightly refuses to have anything to do with faculties.[14] All that is known immediately, through consciousness, is the activity. According to the various kinds of activities are classified the

[13] The original Aristotelian *adynamia* "debility" signified weakness in contrast to strength. See *Cat.*, 8, 9a14–27. The Oxford translation, however, renders it by "incapacity" or "lack of . . . capacity."

[14] Nor are they popular in metaphysics; e.g.: ". . . the ghosts of the old 'faculties,' banished from psychology, but still haunting metaphysics." Whitehead, *Process and Reality* (New York, 1941), p. 27. On the historical background against which the doctrine of St Thomas on the operative powers is sketched, see Aimé Forest, *La Structure Métaphysique du Concret selon Saint Thomas d'Aquin* (Paris, 1931), pp. 258–274. Though conceived as relative to action, a faculty is for St Thomas an "absolute form" — *De Pot.*, II, 2c.

various powers to perform them. A man is conscious of his own intellection, but not of his intellect. Having performed acts of intellection, however, he can reason that he has the power to do so. Even where you see only the effect, you can reason to the power in the cause, as when watching a tree grow you reason that it has the power to develop in size. So far there is no special difficulty. But a further question at once arises. Are those powers identical with the substantial nature of the agent, or are they accidents distinct from and superadded to the substance? There is no immediate intuition of the powers to settle the problem. A reasoning process that turns out to be quite difficult is required for its solution. The problem itself, however, is clearer when it is approached not in the terminology of "faculties," which tend to be represented as distinct entities, but rather of "abilities" to perform operations. The question whether these abilities are really distinct from the substance then becomes more pointed.

The starting point of the reasoning is the accidental character in the operations of a finite substance. Activities like thinking or talking or walking begin and end, while the substance remains permanent. They change, while the substance stays the same. They are, then, accidental acts that are able to be performed but are perhaps not actually being performed by a substance at a given moment. The substance therefore is somehow in potency to them. But is it of its own nature, immediately, a potency to those actions? Is it an immediate potency to operate as well as to receive? Without doubt a finite substance is of itself a potency to *receive* both existence and accidents. This is clear from its role as essence and substrate. In the case of action, however, the question is not about its receiving something but about its *doing* something. Its other accidents and its own existence are given to it. Through some other activity they are caused efficiently and determined to be what they are. But in action the substance itself takes the initiative and is an originating cause in the order of efficiency and of determining an effect. Because of the operating substance, determined effects like ideas, heat, or light, come into being. To operate, then, belongs to a new order of actuality, different from the order of acts that are merely received. It is accordingly more than just to be, whether "to be" is taken in the sense of existing as a finite substance or of existing in accidental ways like being large or being green. To operate is to produce being, not just to receive or possess it. Since all created being is received from something else, there is for creatures a sense in which being may be distinguished from its own production. The production, as causing the being, will appear in this light as higher in actuality than its effect.

Operation in finite things is, consequently, a further type of actuality than being that is merely received and not produced by the thing. To express the contrast, this being of a finite thing is called in Scholastic vocabulary "first actuality" (*actus primus*), and its operation is called its "second actuality" (*actus secundus*). The sharp difference between doing something and just possessing or receiving something renders them obviously distinct orders of actuality in finite things. The second actuality presupposes and follows upon the first, giving rise to the traditional adage that "operation follows upon being."[15]

Can a finite substance, then, be of itself a potency to its second actuality, as it is to its first actuality? Actuated by its substantial being, it is of course closed off to further actuation in the order of substance. But it is still open as a substrate to further actuation by accidental forms like size or color or other characteristics on the level of first actuality. These require no further potency, over and above the substance itself, for their inherence. If they did, they would set up an infinite regress. Rather, a body, because it is a body, is able to be extended and colored. But is it able to operate, just because it is a body?

If a body or any other finite substance could be actuated immediately by any of its operations, it would of itself be immediately a potency to second actuality. Just as it is necessarily a being, so it would necessarily be operative. When actuated it would be put in operation by the very act that puts it in being. It would be always and essentially in operation just as in being. This was the way Descartes conceived the human mind.[16] Somewhat similarly Aristotle regarded a form as active of itself to the full extent of its capacities. The reason why it was not always producing its effects was for Aristotle some impediment or a lack of contact with the patient.[17]

If a substance were actual of itself, in Aristotelian fashion, to be and to operate would have to coincide in its regard. But if its proper actuation, being, is other than itself, the substance is immediately a potency to being.[18] If its being coincided with second actuality, a finite substance could have only one operation, in the same way as it has only one

[15] Accordingly, "each thing's way of operating follows upon its way of being." St Thomas, *ST*, I, 89, 1c.

[16] See Descartes, *Quintae Responsiones*, A–T, VII, 356.23–357.6, and *Ad Hyperaspistem*, August, 1641; A–T, III, 423.16–17. Cf.: "For according to its essence the soul is actuality. If therefore the essence of the soul were an immediate principle of operation, what has a soul would always have activities of life in actuality, just as what has a soul is always in actuality something living. . . . And so the soul itself, insofar as it is a subject for its power, is called first actuality, related to second actuality." *ST*, I, 77, 1c.

[17] See *Ph.*, VIII 4, 255a34–b24.

[18] St Thomas, *ST*, I, 54, 3c. Cf. *Quodl.*, X, 3, 1(5); *De Spir. Creat.*, a. 11. Cf. A. Rozwadowski, "Distinctio Potentiarum a Substantia, secundum Doctrinam Sancti Thomae," *Gregorianum*, XVI (1935), 272–281.

existence. Its operation would not only be continuous, but would always be specifically the same. Yet, besides having operations that begin and cease, finite things have different and often contrary types of activities.[19] No operation, therefore, can immediately actuate a finite substance that is other than its being and that in either of these ways has accidental operations. Because it can operate, a finite substance has indeed potency to second actuality; but such potency or potencies will, like its operations, be accidental to it. They will be outside its essence, and superadded to the essence. Wherever the activities are specifically different, there will be different potencies corresponding to the specific differences of the actions.[20] If the operations are accidental, then, the potencies to the operations will likewise be of the accidental order.[21] But every operation of a creature is contingent upon a preceding motion by an efficient cause, as will be seen in the study of the category of action.[22] All actions of creatures, accordingly, are accidents, and no creature is an immediate potency to any of them. A creature is of its essence a potency to be determined, passively. But just of itself it cannot be a potency to cause and to determine, efficiently. It is operative through faculties that are its accidents. No creature is immediately operative.

As accidents, of course, the powers inhere directly in the substance. They are caused in it efficiently by the producer of the substance. They are required by the thing's essence, and in this way flow from the essence in sequence of formal causality. They are therefore properties and not predicable accidents, even though they are predicamental accidents. They enable the finite substance not only to be a substrate for its operations, but to perform them. For all accidents other than operations, the substance is indeed of itself a substrate. It is operative, however, only through superadded powers.

---

[19] St Thomas, *Quodl.*, X, 3, 1(5); *De Spir. Creat.*, a. 11; *Quaest. de An.*, a. 12, So Plato had distinguished the different parts of the soul, *Rep.*, IV, 436AC.

[20] St Thomas, *ST*, I, 77, 3c. Cf. L.-M. Régis, *Epistemology* (New York, 1959), pp. 180–181.

[21] St Thomas, *In I Sent.*, d. 3, q. 4, a. 2, Solut.; ed. Mandonnet, I, 116. *ST*, I, 77, 1c. *Quaest. de An.*, a. 12. The potencies to accidents in the order of first actuality may also be considered, though reductively, to belong to accidental genera: 'But with regard to passive potency, it is clear that a passive potency to a substantial act is in the genus of substance; and that which is to an accidental act, is in the genus of accident by reduction, as a principle and not as a complete species . . . Hence what is potentially a man is in the genus of substance, and what is potentially white is in the genus of quality." *Quaest. de An.*, *ibid.* The principle "act and potency divide being and every genus of being" has therefore a special meaning when first actuality and second actuality are considered as two genera. In this case it means that the potency to second actuality has to be *directly* in the category of quality.

[22] See below, Chapter 14, nn. 19–23.

Affections and Affective Qualities. The qualities most apparent are the kind through which the external senses are immediately affected. Colors, hardness, sounds, odors, tastes, and the like, qualify sensible substances. They make them be of a certain kind. Through them, primarily,[23] all else in the sensible world is known. If they were not really inherent in the thing, the other accidents and the substance and existence of the sensible thing could not be attained by human cognition. They are accordingly as real as any other accidents in a body.

If the color or other primarily sensible accident was something of a merely passing nature, like the redness of a blush, it was called in traditional Aristotelian terminology a passion (*passio*). This is the name given also to another Aristotelian category. The same term was used in both cases, seemingly without regard for neat systematization in philosophical vocabulary. In designating the subdivision of the qualitative, it implied that the subject underwent or suffered something in having this kind of quality, as happens for instance in the case of a blush. It may be rendered in English technically as "affection." If on the other hand the quality was of a lasting character, as redness in a ruby, it was called a *patibilis qualitas*. This notion may be expressed in English as "affective quality." Here the designation meant that these qualities affect the senses.[24] The notion is perhaps better expressed by the alternate name "sensible quality."

Form and Figure. There does not seem to be any significant difference of meaning in these two words used traditionally to designate the fourth subdivision of the qualitative. Examples given by Aristotle are straightness and curvedness, triangularity and quadrangularity.[25] These answer questions about the *kind* of line or figure. They are accordingly qualitative and not quantitative descriptions. A triangle and a quadrangle could have the same size, though they are different types of figures. This is clearer in the case of three dimensions. A lump of plastic material, for instance, retains the same quantity as it is changed from the shape of ball to the shape of a cube. The external form or figure of anything, therefore, pertains not to the category of the quantitative but to that of the qualitative. Sometimes form may be distinguished from figure by making the one term stand for the two-dimensional and the other for the three-dimensional, or the one for the artistic and the other for the natural. Such distinctions, however, lack sanction in traditional usage.

Two characteristics peculiar to the qualitative are contrariety, as justice

[23] See below, Chapter 15, especially pp. 220–221.
[24] Aristotle, *Cat.*, 8, 9a35–b14.
[25] *Ibid.*, 10a11–16.

is the contrary of injustice, and variation of degree, as a thing becomes colder or whiter. Some qualities, however, like figures, may not have contraries and may not be susceptible to degrees of intensity. Motion in the category of quality is called alteration.

Besides the four subdivisions just listed, Aristotle allowed the possibility of other types of the qualitative. He claimed, though, that the four cover pretty well all its principal instances.[26]

Résumé. Absolutely inherent accidents are those that are in a substance regardless of its external environment. They are the quantitative and the qualitative. The quantitative may be continuous or discrete, while the qualitative consists, principally at least, in habits, faculties, sensible qualities, and figures. Both the quantitative and the qualitative terminate and specify motion.

SUGGESTED READINGS AND REFERENCES

Aristotle, *Categories*, 6,4b20–6a35; 8,8b25–11a38.

John of St Thomas, *The Material Logic of John of St Thomas*, IV, 16 & 18; tr. Yves Simon *et al.* (Chicago: University of Chicago Press, 1955), pp. 251–305; 367–387.

Richard J. Blackwell, "The Methodological Function of the Categories in Aristotle," *The New Scholasticism*, XXXI (1957), 526–537.

[26] *Ibid.*, 10a25–26.

CHAPTER 13

The Relative

Notion of the Relative. A relation consists in the referring of a thing to something else.[1] The equality, for instance, of one sugar cube to another refers the first to the second, on the basis of coincidence in size. The one cube is equal to the other. The thing that is referred, namely the first sugar cube, is the **subject** or substrate of the relation. The thing to which it is referred, here the second sugar cube, is the **term.** The cause of the relation, in this case the size in which the coincidence takes place, is the **ground** or basis (*fundamentum*) of the relation. The reference of the subject to the term, that is, the equality, is the **relation** or relative character itself. Even if complete identity is considered a relation, these four factors will be present. When a thing is said to be identical with itself, it is considered first as the subject, then is set up in another concept under the word "itself" and made the term, while coincidence in substance is taken as the ground for the relation. The relation is then the identity of what is represented in the first concept with what is represented in the second.

In the latter example, the question of reality for the relation does not arise. The one thing is distinguished as subject and term only through the working of human reason. In reality there is no distinct term to which the subject could be referred. The relation, accordingly, does not antecede the activity of human thought. Hence it is a product of human reason. It is a being of reason (*ens rationis*).[2] Yet in it the notion of

[1] As a supreme genus, relation cannot be analyzed into any simpler notions. Descriptions of it merely repeat the same notion in other words, as "reference" in English or in Latin "ordo" or "se habere," e.g.: "relatio . . . consistit tantum in hoc quod est ad aliud se habere . . ." St Thomas, *In III Phys.*, lect. 1, no. 6 (Leonine ed.). The point to be stressed is that it consists entirely in the reference, and not in anything absolute. The history of the philosophical notion of "relation" is sketched briefly in A. Krempel, *La Doctrine de la Relation chez Saint Thomas* (Paris, 1952), pp. 1–4.

[2] See St Thomas, *ST*, I, 28, 1c. Cf.: "There is nothing to prevent a thing from having a reference to another thing, even though no relation is really in it. Thus the knowable is referred to knowledge . . ." *Comp. Theol.*, I, 212; tr. C. Vollert (St Louis, 1947), p. 238.

relation is found in its entirety. Since a being of reason has no essence,[3] there is understandably considerable reluctance in calling relation, as such, an essence or a quiddity or a nature, though these terms may without hesitation be used of a relation that has reality outside cognition.[4]

In characterizing relation in general, then, a word that can apply to both types is preferable. In Scholastic Latin, *ratio* serves the purpose admirably.[5] In English, there does not seem to be any corresponding and satisfactory designation. "Notion," if it is given the objective sense of what is known, as in "animality is one notion, rationality and whiteness are other notions," may be allowed as a substitute. But in speaking of relation as a notion, one has to be careful not to let the term exclude the reality of some relations, just as in calling whiteness a notion one does not imply that a thing cannot be really white. The sense has to permit things to be really related, or really relative.

Since every relation presupposes a subject and a term as somehow constituted in themselves or absolutely, or else as existing in human intellection, the relative always presupposes the absolute.[6] In this contrast with the relative, the absolute means something like substance, quantity, or quality. The notion of these absolutes just in itself does not express reference to anything further, even though as accidents quantity and quality are represented as relative to substance, and any finite being as relative to subsistent being. But are these relations real, or are they the work of the human intellect?

Real Relations. The two sugar cubes, in their real being, are equal to each other regardless of any consideration by the human mind. If they are both white, moreover, they are like each other in color without the human intellect's help. They are therefore related to each

[3] See above, Chapter 9, n. 13.

[4] Cf. St Thomas: ". . . id quod est per essentiam suam relatum, posterius est absoluto: . . ." *ST*, I–II, 16, 4, ad 2m. ". . . ipsa natura relationis, per quam constituitur in tali genere, est ad aliud referri: . . ." *In I Sent.*, d. 33, q. 1, a. 1, ad 1m; ed. Mandonnet, I, 766. ". . . pro quidditate vel ratione quam significat definitio" (i.e., definition of relation). *In III Sent.*, d. 8, a. 5, ad 2m; ed. Moos, III, 294 (no. 63). Like any accident, a relation is an accidental form, and so may be regarded as a form: ". . . relatio autem, sicut et quaelibet forma . . ." Quodl., XII, 1; cf. *ibid.*, ad 2m.

[5] See Krempel, pp. 307–312; C. G. Kossel, "Principles of St. Thomas's Distinction Between the *Esse* and *Ratio* of Relation," *The Modern Schoolman*, XXIV (1946–47), 24–36; 93–107.

[6] "But a relation is always founded on something absolute . . ." St Thomas, *De Ver.*, XXVII, 4, arg. 4 in contr. A relation cannot have another relation as its subject: "No relation is referred by another relation . . ." *De Pot.*, III, 3, ad 2m. Other texts are listed in Krempel, pp. 150 and 190. On the referring of one relation to another, see below, nn. 13–14.

other in reality as equal and as similar. Their equality and similarity are accordingly real relations. Real relations, of course, add no absolute reality to their subject, but they do add relative reality. They make the subject really related to something else, as the cubes are really equal to each other and really like each other in color. From the viewpoint of absolutely inherent reality, the subject is in no way increased by the addition of real relations. There is no more absolute reality with the relations than without them. But there is new relative reality, for these relations really do relate the things to each other, without requiring any help from the activity of the human intellect.

Subject of Real Relation. The subject or substrate of a real relation is always a substance.[7] A real relation is something that accrues to some absolute nature. It is therefore an accident. Because it is something real, then, it is a real accident. But only a substance can properly be the subject of a real accident. To sustain an accident in being, the subject has to have the independent way of being that is proper to substance.[8] If it did not have that independence, not it but something else as substrate would make the accident be. Further, a real relation is not something extrinsic, like place or time. As an accident, therefore, a real relation inheres in its subject. It is accordingly an inherent accident, though not an absolutely inherent one like quantity or quality. It depends also on something outside its subject, that is, on its term.

As a real accident, this type of relation is necessarily distinct in reality from its subject.[9] The relation may come and go, while the substance remains. A man is a man, for instance, before he acquires the relation of fatherhood, and the sugar would be sugar even though it ceased to be equal to the other cube.

Ground of Real Relation. The immediate (*per se*) causes of a real relation are two, quantity on the one hand

---

[7] For St Thomas, relation is "of substance" (*In I Eth. Nic.*, lect. 6, ed. Pirotta no. 80) and requires the priority of substance in being just as do the other accidents.

[8] "For, since no accident subsists by itself (*per se*), it cannot sustain another." St Thomas, *De Virt. in Comm.*, 3c. "Of itself (*per se*) an accident cannot be the subject of another accident, because it is not 'of itself.' " *ST*, III, 77, 2, ad 1m. Cf. texts of St Thomas listed above, Chapter 12, n. 7.

[9] "In the other real relations, which exist in creatures, the being of the relation is other than that of the substance that is related; and therefore they are said to 'exist in,' and insofar as they 'exist in,' they bring about the composition of accident with subject." St Thomas, *In I Sent.*, d. 33, q. 1, a. 1, Solut.; ed. Mandonnet, I, 765. The subject is *alia res* — *ST*, I, 28, 2, ad 2m.

and action or passion on the other.[10] Quantity is the ground of relations of equality and of more or less, as in the case of the equality and similarity of the sugar cubes, or in the case of the more or less if one were larger or whiter than the other. Action is the ground of relations like fatherhood. It gives rise to corresponding relations in the patient, in this example in the children. Incidental (*per accidens*) grounds of relations are substance and quality.[11] Because substance and quality can be quantified and because they are principles of operation, they are able in an indirect way to ground relations. So unity in a quality[12] or greater or less in a quality ground the relations of similarity and of degrees of likeness. As subject of the relation, the substance cannot help but be one of its grounds, even though indirectly. No real relation, though, can be the ground of another real relation, since of its nature it is real reference and so can do of itself all the referring to which it may be extended.[13] It does not need any other real relation to refer it to something else, and could not allow itself to be referred in reality by anything else. Relations of reason, on the other hand, because constructed by the human intellect, may be multiplied indefinitely one upon the other.[14] They

---

[10] So St Thomas interprets Aristotle: "Every relation, according to the Philosopher, V Metaph., is based either on quantity or what is reduced to the genus of quantity, or on action and passion." *In III Sent.*, d. 5, q. 1, a. 1, Solut. 1; ed. Moos, III, 187 (no. 22). Cf.: ". . . a real relation cannot be understood except as following upon quantity or action or passion . . ." *De Pot.*, VIII, 1c. See Krempel, pp. 195–225; C. G. Kossel, "St Thomas's Theory of the Causes of Relation," *The Modern Schoolman*, XXV (1948), 153–158.

[11] "But through substance and quality a thing is related to itself only, and not to another except incidentally, that is, insofar as the quality or substantial form or matter has the aspect of active or passive power, and insofar as some aspect of quantity is considered in them, as unity in substance gives rise to sameness, and unity in quality to the similar, and plurality or multiplicity to the dissimilar and diverse among them, and to the dissimilar insofar as something is considered greater or less than another, for in this way something is said to be whiter than something else." *De Pot.*, VII, 9c.

[12] ". . . unity in quantity causes equality, and unity in quality similitude . . ." St Thomas, *CG*, IV, 14 (7c). This unity, however, does not mean any unity in either essence or being: ". . . there is not the same quantity in essence, but only in commensurateness; and similarly there is one quality in species . . . Hence there can be said to be one quantity where the being is not one; but there cannot be said to be one essence absolutely except where there is one being, and this is where the essence is numerically the same." *In I Sent.*, d. 19, q. 1, a. 1, Solut.; ed. Mandonnet, I, 461.

[13] ". . . relations themselves are not related to anything else by another relation but by themselves, because they essentially are relations." *De Pot.*, VII, 9, ad 2m. Cf.: *In I Sent.*, d. 31, q. 1, a. 1. Solut.; ed. Mandonnet, I, 719. CG, II, 18. *ST*, I, 45, 3, ad 2m.

[14] "It is not inadmissible that the relations which follow upon the acts of reason or intellect be multiplied ad infinitum." *In II Sent.*, d. 3, q. 3, a. 3, ad 3m; ed. Mandonnet, II, 122.

have diverse existence in every individual intellect that elicits them, and in every new act of intellection by which they are brought into being.

Since a real relation is not absolutely inherent, while its grounds are, it is an accident really distinct from them.[15] The relation can really perish, while the ground really remains. The ground would really remain in the sugar cube, for instance, if every other similar sugar cube in the world had perished. The sugar cube, however, would no longer be similar in reality to any other. The real relation of similarity would have perished, while the ground would still really endure.[16] The absolute reality of the ground and the relative reality of the relation, accordingly, cannot really coincide. It is true that all the absolute reality concerned is in the grounds. The leaning tower of Pisa would acquire no new absolute reality if an exactly corresponding tower were built somewhere else. But it would acquire a new relative reality, for it would then be really similar to something else. All the absolute reality necessary would be there in the grounds for the relation, but only on the coming into being of the term would the real relation of similarity arise.

Term of a Real Relation. The term of a real relation, therefore, has to be something really existent. As long as no other leaning tower exists, the one at Pisa is not really similar to any. The sugar cube could not be really equal to any other, if no other really existed. Besides the subject in which it inheres, then, a real relation demands a really existent term. If the term perishes, the relation thereby perishes. It is essentially dependent upon its term.[17]

---

[15] "Every relation really existing in things is acquired from something that is diverse from the relation itself, as equality from quantity, and similitude from quality." St Thomas, *De Pot.*, III, 3, arg. 7.

[16] Many writers in the Scholastic tradition, ancient and modern, deny any distinction in reality between a relation and its ground. On this question, see Krempel, pp. 248–254. The outstanding figure in the real identification of predicamental relation with its ground is Suarez. While claiming that a predicamental relation is a real form intrinsically denominating its subject, Suarez maintained that "it is not any reality (*rem*) or mode distinct by its nature from all absolute form, but is in reality an absolute form taken not absolutely but as regarding another form that the relative denomination includes or connotes." *Disp. Metaph.*, XLVII, 2, 22; ed. Vivès, XXVI, 792b. The real identity of relation and ground is implied in any explanation that denies they are two really distinct entities, one relative and the other absolute, or that requires the activity of the intellect for the completion of the relation's *ratio*; e.g., "The very presence of two quantified objects in the same universe is all that is required for the reality of the relation between them. The mind merely takes their mutual measure and completes the *ratio* of relation in its proper species of equality, inequality, and so on." C. G. Kossel, "St. Thomas's Theory of the Causes of Relation," *The Modern Schoolman*, XXV (1948), 166.

[17] ". . . on the destruction of the term, the relation is done away with." St Thomas, *Quodl.*, IX, 4, ad 2m. "So its proper being, which it superadds to the substance, de-

In this way the real relation is not absolutely inherent in the subject. It can go out of existence without any change, substantial or accidental, in the absolute reality of the subject. It inheres therefore not absolutely but in dependence upon its term. It can likewise come into being without any change in the absolute reality of its subject, as when a man becomes an uncle through the birth of a nephew about which he knows nothing. In these cases there is real change in the way the subject is related. The one subject really ceases to be equal, the other really becomes an uncle. In each case there is difference in relative reality, even though in neither is there any difference in the absolute reality of the subjects. The subjects change relatively, in independence of human intellective activity.

A relation is said to be specified by its term.[18] It is of course remotely determined by the kind of subject in which it inheres, and by the grounds upon which it follows. But the ultimate specification comes from the term. A father is denominated ultimately from a child, a grandfather from a grandchild. The sugar cube is equal to one of the same size, but larger than one of lesser size. In every case the term gives the final specification. Multiplication of the specifically same term, however, does not multiply a real relation.[19] The numerically same relation of equality refers the sugar cube to every new cube of the same size that comes into existence. The same relation merely acquires more individual terms. It does not become plural itself. A man does not have two different real relations of fatherhood because he has two children. The one real relation of fatherhood, rather, extends to two individual terms. The one real relation extends to all terms specifically the same, as they come into existence. Relations of reason, on the other hand, can be multiplied

---

pends not only on the being of the substance, but also on the being of something external." CG, IV, 14 (7c).

[18] ". . . and therefore the special notion of the relation is distinguished insofar as it is related to one thing or another." *In I Sent.*, d. 29, q. 1, a. 3, ad 4m; ed. Mandonnet, I, 694. "A relation is specified according to the object in regard to which it is expressed." *De Ver.*, XXI, 1, arg. 9. "For relations, like movements, are specified in accordance with their term." *ST*, III, 2, 8, arg. 1.

[19] " . . . because the quantity by which I am equal to several others is one, there is in me only one real relation of equality, a relation having reference to several terms. Similarly, because I was engendered from a father and a mother in the one birth, I am said to be the son of both by the one relation of sonship, although the references are pluralized." *Quodl.*, IX, 4c. Any multiplication of the same relation in regard to different terms is the work of human reason. The one real relation is thereby referred separately to various terms by relations of reason. The one real relation of paternity, for instance, is referred separately first to the eldest child, and then to the younger children one by one. This gives rise to several relations of reason, but does not multiply the real relation.

indefinitely, as already noted, and so can be repeated with each new individually distinct term.

Since subject and term are at opposite ends of the relation, they may in a certain sense be both called its terms (*extrema*).[20] The subject is in this respect the term (*a quo*) from which the relation proceeds, and what is called simply the term is in contrast that to which (*ad quem*) the relation is directed. If either is lacking, the relation cannot exist. They are therefore said to be **simultaneous** in time and in cognoscibility. Both have to exist at the same time and both are required in the knowledge of the relation. Every relation, consequently, is in some sense reciprocal. It involves a corresponding relation in the opposite term. But the nature of the relations need not be the same. In one term it may be a real relation, in the other a relation of reason. In creation, for instance, the relation of creature to creator is real, while that of creator to creature is only a relation of reason. Similarly the relation of knower to thing known is real, but that of the thing known to the knower is not.[21] Since in being related the two terms find themselves at opposite ends of the relation, they are said to be **relatively opposed** to each other.[22] Simultaneity and opposition, accordingly, are regarded as properties of a relation's terms, in this sense in which "term" applies to both the subject and the thing to which the subject is related.

---

[20] ". . . since a relation requires two terms (*extrema*) . . ." St Thomas, *ST*, I, 13, 7c.

[21] "Since God therefore is outside the whole order of creatures, and all creatures are directed to him and not vice versa, it is clear that creatures are really related to God himself, but in God there is not any real relation of himself to creatures, but only according to reason." *ST*, I, 13, 7c. "For in all things that are referred to one another in some respect, and one of them depends on another and not vice versa, a relation is really found in the one that depends on the other, but in the second only a relation of reason, as is clear in the case of knowledge and the knowable, as the Philosopher says." *De Pot.*, III, 3c. In these relations, now called in Neoscholastic circles "mixed," the mutual reference was regarded by St Thomas as *non ex aequo*, in contrast to relations ex *aequo*. In relations ex *aequo*, the terms are reciprocally related by real relations, or reciprocally related by relations of reason. In this type the reciprocal relations, whether real or merely conceptual, are on an equal footing. In mixed relations (*non ex aequo*), on the other hand, the reciprocal relations are not on an equal footing, for one is a real relation and the other a relation of reason: "For some things are mutually related on an equal basis, as master and servant, father and son, large and small. . . . But others are relative not on an equal basis, but one of them is said to be relative not because it is referred but because something is referred to it, as happens in the case of knowledge and the knowable." *In X Metaph.*, lect. 8, nos. 2087–2088; cf. lect. 9, n. 2103. The immediate ground for the *non ex aequo* relations is always action-passion, never quantity. See St Thomas, *De Pot.*, VII, 10c; *ST*, I, 13, 7c. Cf. Krempel, pp. 474–475.

[22] "A reference of one thing to another belongs to the notion of relation, in which the one is opposed to the other relatively." *ST*, I, 28, 3c.

Being of a Real Relation. As a really inherent accident, a relation like any other accident is made to be by an existential act other than itself. A reality identical with its existence would be subsistent being. But is the existential act of a real relation a different act from the existence of its subject and its ground? As accidental, the existential act of a relation is "being in" (*inesse*), and so cannot be really identified with the substantial being (*esse*) of its subject.[23] Nor can the relation's being coincide with the being of its ground, in the sense of real identity. The being of its ground can continue, while the relation itself ceases to be. This happens when the term, but not the subject nor ground, is destroyed.[24] A sugar cube would cease to be equal, if everything to which it is equal were to perish.

A real relation, accordingly, is itself a real accident really distinct from its subject and from its ground and from its own being. Its own being, moreover, is really distinct from the being of its subject and the being of its ground, as well as from the subject and the ground themselves. As with the absolutely inherent accidents, there is correspondingly with real relation a new essence and a new existence, really distinct from and proportional to each other. Neither can be really identified with anything in any other category.[25]

The really distinct and proportional being of a real relation has been a stumbling block for many Scholastic writers. They fail to see how any real being can be acquired or lost by a subject without real change in something absolutely inherent in the subject itself. Yet a real relation in the subject ceases to be merely through a change in something extrinsic, the term of the relation. In this regard they seem to conceive

[23] See above, Chapter 11, nn. 5–6.

[24] ". . . the relations come and go without any change in that which is related." *In I Sent.*, d. 26, q. 2, a. 1, ad 3m; ed. Mandonnet, I, 632. Cf. texts above, n. 17.

[25] "For in us relations have dependent being, because their being is other than the being of a substance. Hence they have their proper way of being according to their proper notion, as happens also in the other accidents." *CG*, IV, 14 (7c). Cf. *ST*, I, 28, 2c; *De Pot.*, VIII, 1, ad 4m & ad 5m. St Thomas acknowledges fully that the esse in the Boethian version of Aristotle's definition of relation means nature or quiddity or essence; see *In I Sent.*, d. 33, q. 1, a. 1, arg. 1 and ad 1m; ed. Mandonnet, I, 763 & 766. Yet he can maintain that this traditional esse is not the esse signified by the accident's *inesse*: ". . . cum relatio sit accidens in creaturis esse suum est inesse; unde esse suum non est ad aliud se habere; sed esse huius secundum quod ad aliquid, est ad aliud se habere." *De Pot.*, VIII, 2, ad 12m; cf. ad 11m. Krempel, pp. 353–354, avoids admitting a *real* distinction between essence and existence, on the ground that the relations between them, because relations of reason, do not *require* "des extrêmes objectivement distincts" (p. 354).

For St Thomas, the being that a relation has makes it other than its subject: ". . . a relation that has being in a creature has other being than is the being of its subject; hence it is something other than its subject." *In I Sent.*, d. 20, q .1, a. 1, Solut.; ed. Mandonnet, I, 505. Cf. text above, n. 9.

real being as absolutely inherent being. Because there is no new absolutely inherent being in the case of a real relation, they maintain that there is no real being at all. From this viewpoint, the stand that the being of a relation is minimal[26] being becomes a deceptive overstatement. It is easily and mistakenly understood as minimal in the order of absolutely inherent being. Relative being, so regarded, would not even be minimal. It adds no absolutely inherent being whatsoever. It is of a different order of being. It merely makes its subject *be* related to something else. Accordingly, the absolutely inherent being of a thing is in no way increased when its relations come into existence, nor in any way decreased when they cease to be.[27] The absolutely inherent being in the subject and ground is such that when the term comes into real existence the relation begins to exist in reality, and when the term goes out of existence the relation ceases really to be. The efficient cause of the relation's being is the efficient cause of the subject and ground. The efficient cause has produced what will be really relative once the term comes into existence. The relation can come into existence without any new efficient causality brought to bear upon its subject or ground, because it adds no absolutely inherent being. It only makes what is already there be related in reality to something else.[28] Some efficient causality and consequent real change is of course required for new relative being. But the efficient causality required need bear only upon the term. The change in absolutely inherent being may take place just in the term, and not at all in the sub-

[26] "... relation has the weakest of being (esse *debilissimum*), which belongs to it only." *De Pot.*, VIII, 1, ad 4m.

[27] "... nothing prevents this accident from ceasing to be without change in the thing in which it is, because its notion does not come to completion insofar as it is in the subject itself, but insofar as it reaches over to something else." *De Pot.*, VII, 9, ad 7m. Insofar as the relative adds no absolute being to its subject, St Thomas can say that as relative it does not result in a composition (*De Pot.*, VII, 8c); and also that insofar as it is an inherent accident it does result in a composition with its subject (*In I Sent.*, d. 33, q. 1, a. 1, Solut.; ed. Mandonnet, I, 765 — text above, n. 9).

[28] "Hence it must be said that if someone through change in himself becomes my size, while I undergo no change, this equality was somehow in me beforehand, that is, in its root, from which it has real being. For, from the fact that I have such a size, it pertains to me to be equal to all those who have the same size." *In V Phys.*, lect. 3, (ed. Leonine) no. 8.

It is therefore incorrect to say that "a man's first act of generation produces a real relation of paternity . . ." T. T. Paine, "Paternity and Predicamental Relations," *The Heythrop Journal*, III (1962), 251. Rather, the act produces the offspring to whom the man is thereby related. The fear that really distinct relations may "increase the population of real entities in the universe in a rather alarming way . . ." (p. 249) is quite unfounded. As these relations add no absolutely inherent being whatsoever, they cannot result in any such cosmic population explosion. The ordered universe requires and is fully capable of sustaining its myriad relations.

ject of the relation. Relative being is being in regard to something else, and so can come and go with change in the absolute being of that other thing. To understand it otherwise would be to understand it as absolutely inherent being, even though as minimal. Just as the difficulties in grasping the real distinction of accidental existence from substantial existence arise from conceiving all existential act as substantial, so the difficulties in understanding the real distinction of a relation's existence from the existence of its subject and ground spring from representing all existential act as absolutely inherent.

Relations of Reason. Because it has no essence, a relation of reason lacks in itself the necessary condition for any direct place in a category. But because it fully manifests the notion of relation, it may be placed reductively under the category of relation, in the way that beings of reason in general may be brought by reduction under a category to which they in some way correspond.[29] A relation of reason comes into being only in and through the activity of the intellect. The relation of the word "frigidaire" to a particular device for keeping food cool is found neither in the word nor in the object signified. It is found only in the minds of English-speaking people who make the word stand for the cooling device. Such is the case with all words and names and mathematical and other conventional symbols. The human intellect relates them to their objects, by conceiving them as signs for the objects. In conceiving things under generic and specific aspects, it sets up the logical relations of individual to species and species to genera, and of subject to predicate and premises to conclusion. These logical relations are attributed to the subject as it exists in the intellect.[30] Other

[29] See Krempel, pp. 497–499. The negation of a relation, clearly an *ens rationis*, also pertains reductively to the category of relation: ". . . non-relatio est in genere relationis . . ." St Thomas, *In I Sent.*, d. 28, q. 1, a.1, ad 3m; ed. Mandonnet, I, 674. St Thomas (*De Ver.*, I, 5, ad 16m) lists four ways in which a relation of reason is occasioned: 1) because the two terms coincide in reality; 2) because the subject of the relation is itself a relation; 3) because in a mixed relation the relation is really in only one of the terms; and 4) because the relation bears upon a term that has no real existence. Cf. *In I Sent.*, d. 26, q. 2, a. 1, Solut. (ed. Mandonnet, I, 631); *De Pot.*, VII, 11c; *ST*, I, 13, 7c.

A relation of reason is often called today a "logical relation." This is not to be understood as restricting relations of reason to the realm that constitutes the object of logic. It means rather that the relation of reason is a *logos* or concept as opposed to a reality.

[30] Relations attributed to something as it is in the intellect, whether the relation is to a term existing in reality or to a term existing in intellection, are regarded by St Thomas (*De Pot.*, VII, 11c) as "devised " (*adinvenit;* cf. *inventae* — *ibid.*, ad 2m) by the intellect itself. The meaning seems to be that the intellect as it were first sets up these relations and then attributes them to the thing as understood, as "individual" to Socrates or "species" to man.

relations of reason, however, are attributed to the subject as it exists in reality, for instance the relation of creator to God, or the relation at the right or at the left to a column, or the relation of knowable to a real tree.[31] Even the relation of a real relation as accident to the subject in which it inheres, is a relation of reason.[32]

Just as a real relation is really other than its existential act, so in corresponding fashion is a relation of reason entitatively distinct from the intentional existence that endows it with being. It has the existence of a being of reason (*ens rationis*).

Résumé. Because it is a referring, a relation requires a subject, ground, and term. Where it is real, it inheres in its subject, but depends also upon ground and term in both its notion and its being. It is specified by its term. As a real accident, it is really distinct from its own being as well as from its subject, and its being is really distinct from the being of the substance in which it inheres. A relation of reason, on

---

[31] Some of these are regarded by St Thomas (*De Pot.*, VII, 11c) as not "devised" by the intellect, but as following with a kind of necessity upon the intellect's way of understanding things. Matter, essence, faculties, for instance, though absolute, can be understood only as principles, and so only in relation to substance, to being, to operation. The intellect cannot conceive these principles except as related by reason to their corresponding actualities. It does not as it were "devise" the relations and then attribute them to their subjects, as it attributes the relation of species to an already known "man," but has to conceive the subjects as related in its very first notion of them as subjects. In later Scholasticism this situation gave rise to the mistaken concept of a "transcendental relation," that is, of a real relation really identical with an absolute reality. It was called transcendental because it was regarded as really present in various categories. It became solidified in the Thomistic tradition through John of St Thomas (1589–1644). It makes the impossible identity of absolute reality and relative reality in creatures. On its history, see Krempel, pp. 645–670; cf. pp. 4, 170–179, and 361–366.

For St Thomas, a real relation in creatures is confined to the one category of relation: ". . . every real relation is in a determined genus; but non-real relations can make the circuit of all being." *De Ver.*, XXI, 1, ad 3m. For him, something relative *secundum esse* is a relation, either real or merely conceptual; while something relative *secundum dici* is not a relation, but is something absolute that is related to something else either by a superadded real relation or by a relation of reason. See *In I Sent.*, d. 30, q. 1, a. 3, ad 4m (ed. Mandonnet, I, 709); *De Pot.*, VII, 10, ad 11m. These expressions have given rise to what Krempel, p. 394, calls a "tragi-comédie" of interpretations through the centuries.

[32] ". . . as when it says a relation is accidental to the subject; hence such a relation of a relation to anything else is only of reason." St Thomas, *De Pot.*, VII, 11c.

In modern philosophical vocabulary, relations required by a thing's nature are called "internal relations," while relations that do not pertain to or necessarily follow from its nature are regarded as "external relations." On the philosophical backgrounds of this division of relations, see C. G. Kossel, "The Problem of Relation in Some Non-Scholastic Philosophies," *The Modern Schoolman*, XXIII (1946), 68–81. Cf. "External and Internal Relations," in George Edward Moore, *Philosophical Studies* (London, 1922), pp. 276–309.

the other hand, has only being of reason, but may be brought reductively under the category of relation.

SUGGESTED READINGS AND REFERENCES

Aristotle, *Categories*, 7,6a36–8b24.

St Thomas Aquinas, *Summa Contra Gentiles*, IV; 14, tr. Charles J. O'Neil, *On the Truth of the Catholic Faith*, Book Four, Salvation (New York: Image Books, 1957) pp. 97–104.

——— *On the Power of God*, VII, 8–11; tr. English Dominican Fathers (London: Burns Oates & Washbourne Ltd., 1932–1934), III, 46–65.

——— *Summa Theologiae*, I, 13, 7, and 28, 1–4; tr. English Dominican Fathers (London: Burns Oates & Washbourne Ltd., 1911–1925), I, 164–168 and II, 14–28.

John of St Thomas, *The Material Logic of John of St. Thomas*, IV, 17; tr. Yves Simon *et al*. (Chicago: University of Chicago Press, 1955), pp. 305–366.

A. Krempel, *La Doctrine de la Relation chez Saint Thomas* (Paris: Vrin, 1952).

CHAPTER 14

Other Categories

Extrinsic Denomination. The quantitative and the qualitative do not in themselves bear upon anything extrinsic to the subject in which they are present. From an absolute viewpoint a thing could be really quantitative and really qualitative even if there were no other real finite thing to which it was related. On the other hand real relation, though an inherent accident, consists wholly in a reference to something else. Along with these categories, however, are found still other accidents that are not relations, yet are denominated from something extrinsic to their subject.[1] Their natures are known and described in terms of things outside themselves. Denomination from something extrinsic, though, need not prevent them from being real accidents, nor even in a couple of instances from being inherent in the substance they characterize.

The general heading "denominated from something extrinsic," then, is not to be understood as incompatible with real inherence. Nor does it distinguish these categories from real relation, which is also specified by an extrinsic term. The categories, as supreme genera of beings, cannot be described in essential notions simpler than themselves. Groupings of them under a heading like "inherent" or "denominated from something extrinsic" are not based upon any prior and higher genera. "Inher-

[1] In contrast to substance on the one hand, and on the other to quantity, quality, and relation, the remaining categories, six in number, are grouped by St Thomas under this third heading. "For it must be realized that a predicate can regard the subject in three ways. . . . In the third way, so that the predicate is taken from what is outside the subject: . . ." *In V Metaph.*, lect. 9, (ed. Cathala-Spiazzi) nos. 891–892. Cf. ". . . when something extrinsic is predicated of anything by way of a certain denomination: . . ." *In III Phys.*, lect. 5, (ed. Leonine) no. 15. Since each category determines a different way of being, any grouping of a number of them under a positively descriptive heading can hardly hope to be satisfactory. Accordingly in the middle ages these last six were grouped under the uninformative title "the six principles," from the *Liber de Sex Principiis*, attributed (wrongly, it now seems) in the second quarter of the thirteenth century to Gilbert de la Porrée (ca. 1075–1154).

ence" may characterize real relation and other categories as well as quality and quantity, while specification by an extrinsic term is found in relation as well as in one of the predicaments grouped under "denominated from something extrinsic." This predicament is expressed by the Greek infinitive *poiein* "to make," "to do," by the Latin *agere* "to act," and in English by the infinitive "to act," or more loosely and conveniently by the noun "action."

a) TO ACT (ACTION)

Real Accident. The actions by which the pitcher throws a ball and by which the catcher gets hold of it, obviously require the movement of the ball. The carpenter's action in building a house has to terminate in the house. If the ball were not being moved, there would be no pitching nor catching. If the house were not being built, there would not be the action of building on the part of the carpenter. Building and pitching and catching are instances of what are known in general as actions. They require a term in which their nature is expressed. They are accordingly known by the human intellect through something that is extrinsic to them. Without their term, the intellect would have no means of identifying and describing them. Even actions like seeing and hearing, though they do not produce anything, are specified by objects that are extrinsic to themselves. Try to form a concept of building or running in abstraction from the effect produced, or of seeing or thinking in abstraction from the object seen or thought. You find that it is impossible.

An action, therefore, is specified by something over and above the action itself. It is a real accident, because it may really come and go while the substance of the agent remains the same. You may commence and cease to chat, to walk, to think, to engage in business activities, to play golf, or to sing. You remain really the same person, while really changing in these actions. The actions add real accidental being to yourself, even though their specific determination comes from something extrinsic to them, namely from their objects.

Production of Being. Of all the categories, action is perhaps the most difficult to understand. It consists in the production of new being, for instance the movement of the ball or the form of the house. But how can any finite thing, limited by its nature to its own finite self, produce something other than itself? How can it be the cause of new being, if it itself is limited to its own being? It is just its own finite self, it does not contain actually within itself the new being it produces. Yet apparently it does produce the actuality of the new being. You are conscious of producing your own thoughts. You see the acorns growing on the oak, and the flame following upon the striking of the match. Everything looks as though the finite substances produce the effects. Yet how can a thing give what it has not got? Evidently the production of a new being cannot be explained in terms of subtraction and addition. The process eludes mathematical logic.[2] It is not just a question of rearranging entities already there, but of bringing into being entities that did not exist before.

So great is this difficulty that it has given rise among both Arabs and Christians to types of explanation called Occasionalism. In an Occasionalism no creature is allowed to produce anything whatsoever. The creature does not really act at all, but has merely the role of an *occasion* though which the first cause, subsistent being, directly and solely produces the effect.[3] Though this reduction of all creatures to the status of inert puppets seems difficult or impossible to reconcile with the infinite wisdom of a creator who has endowed them with the equipment for acting, it serves to emphasize the distinguishing feature of action from the other accidents. In action a creature does not just receive something or have something, passively, but really does something, or produces something, actively. The problem of accounting for the new being of the accident cannot be thrown back upon the efficiency of another cause, at least entirely, but has to be explained somehow in terms of an efficiency that is the creature's own.

Immanent and Transient Action. Another difficulty arises from the two different ways in which an action may terminate. The action may have its term essentially in itself, as in seeing or thinking or enjoying. These actions, of course, have objects. Yet they do not produce the objects in real being. The only real being that is produced is the being of the actions themselves, or of the concepts where necessary. All this real being remains immanent in the agent. No new external being is produced. Actions of this type may therefore be called immanent actions or immanent operations.[4] They are indeed speci-

[2] "Brutus killed Caesar" expresses merely a relation, as far as mathematical logic is concerned. See Bertrand Russell, *Introduction to Mathematical Philosophy* (London & New York, 1919), p. 141.

[3] See Malebranche, *Entretiens sur la Métaphysique*, VII, 1–13.

[4] St Thomas uses the verbs *manere in* and *transire* respectively to describe the two types of action: ". . . action (*actio*) is of two kinds, one that passes over (*transit*) to external matter, as to heat and to saw; the other that remains in (*manet in*) the agent, as to understand, to perceive, and to wish. The difference between them is this, that the first action is not the perfection of the agent that imparts the

fied by objects other than themselves, or at least by themselves not as activities but as objects when the agent reflects upon his own actions or enjoys them. Are they, then, to be categorized as inherent qualities,[5]

---

motion, but of the thing that is moved, while the second action is the perfection of the agent." *ST*, I, 18, 3, ad lm. Cf. *ST*, I, 54, 2c; *De Pot.*, III, 15, Quarta; *De Ver.*, VIII, 6c; XIV, 3c; *CG* II, 23. In all these texts, *actio* is the term used for both the transient and the immanent in the formal division of the notion into its types. It is regularly illustrated by infinitives, and so precludes any distinction of *actio* as action in this twofold sense from *agere* as the category.

Operatio is used in an exactly synonymous way for both types of action, e.g.: "There is a twofold operation (*operatio*) of a thing, as the Philosopher lays down . . . one that remains in the thing operating . . . the other that passes over to an external thing . . ." *CG*, II, 1. Cf. *CG*, I, 100; III, 22. Joseph de Finance, *Etre et Agir dans la Philosophie de Saint Thomas* (Paris, 1945), p. 210, n. 3, remarks that sometimes St Thomas reserves the proper sense of the term "action" for immanent action: e.g., "For to act (*agere*) is used properly for the operation that remains in the agent and does not pass over to an external matter, as to understand and to perceive and the like." *In XI Metaph.*, lect. 7, no. 2253. Cf. *CG*, II, 1, Prima igitur. In contrast, transient action is "to make." At other times (e.g., *De Ver.*, VIII, 6c), "action" is properly transient, and "operation" is properly immanent, even though "action" may be used for both. Ludwig Schütz, *Thomas-Lexikon* (Paderborn, 1895), pp. 10 and 542, lists *actio* and *operatio* as synonyms in the vocabulary of St Thomas. For a discussion, see M. Miller, "The Problem of Action in the Commentary of St. Thomas Aquinas on the Physics of Aristotle," *The Modern Schoolman*, XXIII (1946), 140–145.

[5] Yves Simon, *Introduction à l'Ontologie du Connaître* (Paris, 1934), p. 97, n. 1, acknowledged the lack of any texts in Aristotle or St Thomas assigning immanent action to either category, yet claimed that nothing of the Thomistic doctrine on knowledge could be preserved if immanent action is assigned to the category of action. An indication of this, he maintained, is that the "grands thomistes" unanimously assert that immanent action is a quality, while the "petits thomistes et les parathomistes" generally hold the opposite. — The tenet that immanent action is a quality and not properly an action does indeed go far back in the history of Thomism. The *Summa Totius Logicae*, probably of the latter half of the fourteenth century, states explicitly: "But this immanent action is not directly in the predicament of action . . ." Tr. VI, c. 2; in *S. Thomae Aquinatis Opusc. Om.*, ed. Mandonnet (Paris, 1927), V, 55. The reason was that according to Aristotle action constituting the predicament is identical in reality with passion and motion; immanent action, on the other hand, is not an efficient cause producing something in actuality, but is identical with being in actuality (*idem quod esse in actu* — *ibid.*). Capreolus (1380–1444), *In I Sent.*, d. 35, q. 1, a. 1, C, ed. Paban-Pègues (Turin, 1900–1908), II, 366a, refers to intellection as a quality. He (*ibid.*, B, p. 356ab) is taking the expression from the mid-fourteenth-century Franciscan John of Ripa, who in his *Determinationes*, II, 2, 1o, ed. André Combes (Paris, 1957), pp. 183–184, refers it back to unnamed opponents, with the source in Duns Scotus, *Ordinatio*, I, 3, 3, 4, no. 601, ed. Balić (Vatican City, 1950 —), III, 354, and *Quodl.* XIII, 1–2, ed. Vivès (Paris, 1891–1895), XXV, 507. From a fourteenth-century Franciscan viewpoint (see Combes' note, *loc. cit.*) the teaching of Duns Scotus was that intellection is a quality, while for St Thomas intellection was in contrast an action (*agere*). The sixteenth-century Thomists, however (see Yves Simon, *loc. cit.*), speak of immanent actions as qualities and not predicamental actions. Suarez (1548–1617), *Disp. Metaph.*, XLVIII, 2, 21, ed. Vivès (Paris, 1856–1877), XXVI, 879b, regards second actuality (*actus secundus*) as a quality that intrinsically terminates action. Cf. *De Anima*, III, 5, 5; v. III, p. 631b.

or as belonging rather to a new predicament called action?

On the other hand, an action may produce something distinct from itself, as a house or a color or the movement of a ball. In this case the action originates in the agent and terminates in something else. Because of this "passing over" from the agent to the patient, it may be called transient action.

In both transient and immanent action, however, the distinctive feature as action is the production of new being. In both, the agent *does* something. Both consist in the second actuality (*actus secundus*) of the agent. In contrast, the accidents previously considered, including qualities, all consisted in first actuality (*actus primus*). Is second actuality, then, the distinguishing characteristic of the category of action? If so, then all actions, whether immanent or transient, belong to this new category rather than to quality.

Observability. A further difficulty is concerned with the question of observability. The actuality of immanent operations is observable through reflection. You are conscious that you are seeing, thinking, enjoying — that is, you are conscious that you are performing these actions. But you are not conscious of the passing of a transient action to its external effect. You see the effect, like the table or the color, coming into being. But do you see the passage of your action to the product? In the external world you see the motions in the agent and the patient, as when you strike a match and see the cigar become lighted. But you do not see the causality of the one passing over to the other. That is rather a deduction, as has already been noted.[6] Transient action, as such, is not immediately observable. It is transient, not at all in the sense that something actually existing in the agent passes over to the patient,

The seventeenth century saw the notion worked out doctrinally into a type of quality under the new name "metaphysical action," with predicamental action, described as "physical," opposed to it. John of St Thomas (1589–1644), on the ground that an immanent operation is, like existence, an act informing a potency rather than originating something, so established it as formally a quality. He allowed it to be virtually an action only because it sometimes can produce something else, as intellection produces a concept: "Therefore to understand is likened by Divus Thomas to existence itself or being . . . and so those acts are directly qualities by way of disposition. Yet because it also pertains to an immanent act sometimes to produce, it is called virtually an action . . ." *Ars Logica*, II, 19, 2, in *Cursus Philosophicus Thomisticus*, ed. B. Reiser (Turin, 1930–1937), I, 627a16–22. Cf. *Phil. Nat.*, I, 14, 3, in *Cursus*, II, 309a41–44; IV, 6, 4 (III, 196b); and IV, 11, 1 (III, 344 ff.). In his wake others (e.g. Gredt) have placed immanent actions in the subdivision of quality entitled "habits and dispositions." A. Krempel, *La Doctrine de la Relation chez Saint Thomas* (Paris, 1952), p. 441, attempts to distinguish *l'agir* as the category from *action*, and places transient action as well as immanent action in the predicament of quality. Against this, see above, n. 4.

[6] Above, Chapter 5, nn. 13 and 19.

but in the sense that something new and other than the agent is brought into being.

Historical Difficulty. There is also considerable trouble arising from the approach that has been given in history to the category of action. In Aristotle, form of itself gives being. Accordingly, a thing "energizes"[7] to the full extent of its capacities, as far as it itself is concerned. It produces its effect if there is no hindrance and the patient is in contact with it.[8] Nothing more is required. For Aristotle, then, action adds no new absolutely inherent being in the agent. For him, the only new reality that comes into being is the motion in the patient. The action is therefore identical in reality with the motion, and is located in the patient that is undergoing the motion.[9] From it, as its source, the efficient cause is denominated an agent, and the category of action is set up.

Such is the doctrine of Aristotle, in which finite forms account for all the being in the universe without any need of an infinite creator from whom they receive being. In the Aristotelian doctrine, "action" denoted the same reality as motion, in the sense of the movement or change that took place in the patient. St Thomas frequently uses the term "action" in this traditional meaning. So understood, he locates action in the patient.[10] But just as pointedly he speaks of action as being in the agent and as a perfection of the agent.[11] In this meaning he quite evidently understands by it something very different from what takes place in the patient.

[7] *Metaph.*, Θ 8, 1050b29–30.

[8] See *Ph.*, VIII 4, 255a1–b24. The model seems to be something like fire (b7), regarded as a substance that just of itself burns anything that comes in contact with it, provided there is no hindrance. In this Aristotelian conception, fire as a substance requires a *generans* to produce it. In changing something else into fire the *generans* gives it its nature and so determines it actually to burn. The fire requires no other movent. Of itself it burns till it is changed into some other substance. The soul of the first heaven, correspondingly, moves the cosmos throughout eternity without having any need of a higher efficient cause.

[9] *Ph.*, III 3, 202a13–b22; *De An.*, III 2, 426a4–10.

[10] "For it is clear that both action and passion are movement: for both are identical with movement." *In III Phys.*, lect. 5, (ed. Leonine) n. 3. So *passim* in the Aristotelian commentaries, and also, as a report of Aristotle's doctrine, at *ST*, I, 28, 3, ad 1m. On the divided school interpretations, see Krempel, p. 443.

[11] "An action that is not the substance of the agent is in it as an accident in a subject: hence also action is numbered as one among the nine predicaments of accident." *CG*, II, 9, Adhuc. See other texts listed in Krempel, p. 443, and discussion in M. Miller, *art. cit.*, pp. 207–224. Although he signalizes the role of immanent action as a perfection of the agent in distinguishing it from transient action (texts above, n. 4), St Thomas is not adverse to calling transient action, which is intermediate between finite substance and product, a perfection of the agent: ". . . since the intermediate action itself is a certain proper perfection of the agent." *De Pot.*, VII, 10, ad 1m.

Inherent Accident. For St Thomas, in contradistinction to Aristotle, every finite substance is immediately a potency to a corresponding existential act that is other than itself. This existential act pertains to the order of first actuality (*actus primus*). It completes the substance in such a way that all further acts, including second actuality (*actus secundus*) and operative potencies, lie outside the substance as accidents.[12] The finite substance is immediately a potency to receive, but not immediately a potency to do anything. Between it and its action comes a real accident, its operative potency. Its action, accordingly, is not part of its substantial nature nor of its substantial being. Its action, however, is real, for it really operates. The action therefore is an accident really superadded to the substance, and is something that is a second actuality in the agent. From that viewpoint, action is an inherent[13] accident. But "inherent" tells only one part of the story, and not the part that is properly characteristic of action. To act does not mean to inhere passively like the quantitative and the qualitative and the relative, but rather means doing something. Hence there is a certain reluctance in describing action as inherent.[14] Though truly inherent to the full extent of its being, an action is emanating from or issuing from its subject. It is not merely *in* the substance but is *from* the substance. It might be better described by the obsolete English word "egredient," translating the Scholastic Latin *egrediens*. However, though properly "egredient," it is also entirely inherent in its substance in the full sense of an inherent accident.

From one viewpoint, action adds no "formal content"[15] over and above its corresponding operative potency, somewhat as existence adds no conceptual content to entitative potency. Rather, it is the act of operative potency just as existence is the act of essence.[16] Accordingly, it is expressed by a verb like to build or to run or to think, just as existential

---

[12] On existential act as the *complementum substantiae existentis*, see above, Chapter 10, n. 14. On *actus secundus*, see above, Chapter 12, nn. 15–21.

[13] ". . . by way of action, that is, as it is issuing (*egrediens*) from the substance and inhering in it as in a subject." *In I Periherm.*, lect. 5, (ed. Leonine) no. 5.

[14] ". . . nothing prevents a thing from being inherent, though it is not described as inherent, as also action is not described as in the agent but as from the agent, and yet it is clear that action is in the agent." *De Pot.*, VIII, 2c.

[15] See B. Lonergan, "St. Thomas' Theory of Operation," *Theological Studies*, III (1942), 378–380; 400.

[16] "Just as being itself is a certain actuality of essence, so operating is an actuality of operative potency or power. In this regard both of them are in act: essence by way of being, potency by way of operating." St Thomas, *De Spir. Creat.*, 11c. The analogy with being, however, does not warrant the conception of operation as a quality that is received rather than as something that is done. On this presentation in John of St Thomas, see above, n. 5.

act is signified by the verb to be. Yet an action is a limiting nature. To walk or to build is something specific. Though second actuality, an action is an essence limiting the existential act that makes it be. So actuated by its corresponding existential act, it itself is actuating an operative potency and bringing the agent from first actuality to second actuality.[17] Its specification, of course, in the sense of its "formal content," is always known from something extrinsic to itself, its object. The *kind* of action building consists in is understood through observing the house being built, and the type of science or art is determined through acquaintance with the scientific object or the artistic product.

Concurrence. There remains the problem how a finite substance, limited to its own actuality, can produce new being that it did not contain actually. Certainly the actuality of an action and its product is really more than the potency to perform the action. The actual production of autos, for instance, is something more than just having the plant, the materials, the capital, and the labor. These could be idle, and there would be no actual production.[18] A finite substance, of course, is provided with its operative powers by the agent that in generation first gave it being. So endowed, it has the potency to operate, but it does not thereby have the actuality of the operations. It has to be moved into second actuality, which it does not have of itself. Since whatever is being moved is being moved by something else,[19] the finite agent in doing anything has to have something done to it by another agent. It has to be moved by something else in order itself to operate.

This means that in the operation of every creature there are at least two efficient causes at work. There is the agent that is performing the action, and there is a prior agent that is acting upon it in moving it to action. The filament in radiating light is being heated by the electric

[17] Operation is the ultimate actuality on the "essence" side of the "essence-existence" couplet. Like any other finite essence, however, operation exists through its corresponding act of being. See J. de Finance, *Etre et Agir*, p. 235.

[18] The Aristotelian conception of *energeia* "act" seems to have been in fact modeled on something like a mine in operation as distinguished from the same thing when idle. See instances of the adjective *energos* in Liddell and Scott, A *Greek-English Lexicon*, s.v.

[19] Aristotle regards this proposition not as a self-evident principle but as a conclusion to be demonstrated. See *Ph.*, VII–VIII. Cf. St Thomas, *In VII Phys.*, lect. 1, (ed. Leonine) nos. 2–6; *CG*, I, 13; *ST*, I, 2, 3c. It applies wherever action is a new accident inherent in the agent: "For the newness of an effect can indicate a change in the agent, insofar as it shows the newness of the action; for there cannot be a new action in the agent unless it be moved in some way, at least from idleness to act." *CG*, II, 35. "And therefore those that are in potency, whether they are acting or undergoing, are being moved; because they are both undergoing in acting and are being moved in imparting motion . . ." *In III Phys.*, lect. 2, (ed. Leonine) no. 6.

current from the battery or generator. The filament, not the battery or the current in the connecting wires, is doing the radiating, yet only as it is made actually incandescent by the electricity. Such a prior moving cause is required by the action of every agent that is not its own second actuality, and so by every action of every creature. As with the causing of being, so with the causing of action the series of efficient causation has to originate in the unmoved first cause, which, lacking all potency, alone is its own ultimate actuality.

In being moved to second actuality, however, the finite agent is not passively receiving a form like quantity or quality, but is being made to act and itself produce new being. Both the finite agent and the cause that moves it to action are operating together. For that reason the activity of the prior cause was termed in later Scholasticism a "concurrence." Since from a metaphysical viewpoint the activity that moves the agent to action is prior, it was called "preceding concurrence" (*concursus praevius*), in spite of the apparent incongruity of the expression.[20] "Preceding concurrence" means therefore a causality that is exercised directly upon the agent, and not directly upon the operation or the product. It moves the *agent*, and not directly what issues from the agent. This concurrence of the first cause reaches to every creature that is acting, and does so either immediately, or mediately through the series of intermediate agents.

The same considerations that require the immediate or mediate causality of the first cause to move a finite agent to operation, likewise call for the continuance of that causality in the production of the new accident's being, and in transient action for the production of an effect that is other than the operation itself. Ultimately new being can be accounted for only from an agent that is infinite being and so precontaining the actuality of all possible effects. The operation of the first cause, therefore, has to continue in imparting being to the new entities, that is, to the action of the creature and its product.[21] In this regard the concurrence of the first cause is said to be "simultaneous" (*concursus simultaneus*) with the operation of the creature. Accordingly it is always exercised directly upon the new entities that come into being, and not

[20] It is also known as *praemotio physica*, "physical premotion," in the later Scholastic controversies. The prefix "prae" is tautological, since the imparting of movement is metaphysically prior to the movement itself, and is signified by the active sense of *motio* without requiring the prefix. "Physical" in the expression is meant in contrast to "moral," and does not make the movent belong necessarily to the sensible world.

[21] ". . . nor does anything bring something into being except through the power of God. For being itself is the most common effect, the first, and more intimate than all other effects; and therefore such an effect belongs to God alone from the standpoint of proper power." St Thomas, *De Pot.*, III, 7c.

upon the agent that elicits or produces them. It is always immediate, because no finite intermediary could precontain the *actuality* of the new being that is other than itself, that is, the being of the finite agent's operation and product. "Simultaneous concurrence," however, is not to be represented according to the model of two horses drawing one carriage. Though simultaneous, it is not coordinate with the creature's operation. It is of a higher order, and only in virtue of it does the finite agent produce new being.[22] In this way the first cause is always operating in the actions of every creature.[23]

Secondary Causes. The above considerations show that both the first cause and the finite agent are immediate causes of the same effect.[24] In essence, the effect corresponds to the nature of the finite agent, as oak produces oak, man generates man, or engineer imposes rational design upon the materials that are being made into a bridge or a motor. In being, the effect corresponds to the nature of the first cause, which is being itself. The equality in essence of the finite cause to the nature of its effect allows the finite cause to be the origin of the effect from the viewpoint of specification. It is accordingly a *principal cause* of its own actions and their products. The first cause also is a principal cause of these effects, for through preceding and simultaneous concurrence it is in an even higher sense their origin. The finite agent, consequently, though a principal cause, can be only a secondary cause (causa

[22] "Being is therefore the proper effect of the first agent, that is, of God; and all things that give being are able to do so insofar as they act through the power of God. Besides, in what a secondary agent can do, the ultimate in goodness and perfection is what it can do through the power of the first agent. . . But what is most perfect in all agents is being . . . Therefore being is what secondary agents bring about through the power of the first agent." CG, III, 66, Adhuc.

[23] "Thus therefore is God the cause of the action of everything insofar as he confers the power of acting, and insofar as he conserves it, and insofar as he applies it to action, and insofar as through his power all other power acts . . . it will follow that he is operating immediately in everything that operates, while not excluding the operation of will and nature." *De Pot.*, III, 7c. Cf.: "For these three functions appear to belong to the notion of the efficient cause: that it give being, impart motion, and conserve." *In De Div. Nom.*, c. IV, lect. 5, (ed. Pera) no. 352. See also *In II Sent.*, d. 1, q. 1, a. 4 (ed. Mandonnet, II, 23–27); CG, III, 66–67; *ST*, I, 105, 5; *Comp. Theol.*, I, 129–130 & 135.

[24] "So therefore if we consider the agent supposits, each particular agent is immediate with regard to its effect. But if we consider the power by which the action takes place, the power of the superior cause will in this way be more immediate to the effect than the power of the inferior one; for the inferior power is brought to bear (conjointly) upon the effect only through the power of the superior." *De Pot.*, III, 7c. ". . . it is not inadmissible that the same effect be produced by the inferior agent and by God, immediately by both, though in different ways." CG, III, 70. Cf. *ST*, I, 36, 3, ad 4m.

secunda), since it can operate only in virtue of the concurrence of the first cause.[25]

Instrumental Causes. But no creature can be a principal cause in the communication of being as being. Being is the nature or essence of only one cause, the first cause. Only subsistent being is adequately proportioned to the being of an effect. The finite cause produces the effect, thereby giving it being. To produce the effect means to make it be. The finite agent, therefore, is truly a cause of being.[26] But it cannot be a principal cause of the effect's being. It can give being only in the way a brush gives artistic design to the canvas. The principal cause of the artistic design is the rational agent, the painter. The brush is only his **instrument** in communicating the rational design to the product. The brush exercises its own proper causality in spreading the pigments, but here that causality is instrumental in producing the picture. Similarly every finite agent exercises its own causality in producing its effect, but its causality is only instrumental in producing the effect's being.

Both first cause and creature, therefore, produce the whole effect. Both are the efficient causes of the finite agent's operation and product. There can be no question of one producing the existence and the other the essence, for every finite reality is constituted by both essence and existence together. But the finite agent is the principal cause of the effect from the viewpoint of essence, and instrumental cause from the viewpoint of being.[27] The origin or principal cause of new being, accordingly, is not

[25] "Nevertheless God also is the cause of these, operating in them more intimately than the other movent causes; because he is giving being to things. The other causes are as it were determining that being . . . but being is more intimate to every thing than that by which being is determined . . ." *In II Sent.*, d. 1, q. 1, a. 4, Solut.; ed. Mandonnet, II, 25. The order of causes corresponds to the order of effects: "But being is what is caused first . . . Therefore the proper cause of being is the first and universal agent, which is God. Other agents are not the cause of being absolutely, but the cause of *being this*, like man or white." CG, II, 21, Adhuc.

[26] "But first in all effects is being: for all other things are certain determinations of it. Therefore being is the proper effect of the first agent, and all other agents produce it insofar as they are acting in the power of the first agent." CG, III, 66, Item. In calling God "the unique cause of the being of things," or "the *sole* cause of being" (M. J. Adler, "The Demonstration of God's Existence," *The Thomist*, V [1943], 204), one has to understand the phrase in the sense of principal cause. Unlike the artist with the brush, however, the principal cause in the imparting of being has to be immediate to the effect in supposit as well as in power.

[27] "It is also clear that the same effect is not attributed to the natural cause and the divine power as though it is made partly by God and partly by the natural agent, but the entire effect is by each in a different manner . . ." CG, III, 70, fin. ". . . so upon a natural thing could be conferred its proper power, as a form remaining in it, but not the power by which it produces being as the instrument of the first cause . . ." *De Pot.*, III, 7, ad 7m. "But secondary agents . . . produce as their proper effects the other perfections, which determine being." CG, III, 66, Item.

the limited actuality of the finite agent, but the infinite actuality of subsistent being, which precontains all possible effects. In the production of a new being, however, the nature of the finite agent corresponds to the nature of the effect, while the nature of an instrument like a paint brush does not correspond to the nature of the artistic product. The instrumental cause of being, therefore, can be the principal cause of the whole effect, from the viewpoint of its essence.

Distinct Category. Action, accordingly, is an inherent accident that is the second actuality of creatures. Nevertheless it is always specified by something extrinsic, its object. Unlike the other categories, it is a doing, and not just a way of being in first actuality. Being in second actuality is a distinctive way of being for a creature, and so constitutes a distinct category. If second actuality is regarded in this way as the distinctive characteristic of action, then both immanent and transient operation belong to this category. In it consists the ultimate actuality or perfection of a creature, as the very being of a creature is on account of its operation.[28] Limited to itself by its essence, the creature extends beyond itself by its operation, even to knowing and loving and serving its first cause. The category of action provides the ultimate reason why the goodness of a creature, from an absolute viewpoint, is found not in its substantial but in its accidental being. The good of a creature is something to be achieved by operation.

If on the other hand one insists, in the Aristotelian framework, that the category of action denotes something really identified with movement and located in the patient, one thereby excludes immanent operations from this category. Some other category has to be found for them. In consequence, second actuality as a distinctive way of being comes to be dissipated, and its peculiar importance in a metaphysics where essence is really other than being can easily be lost. The same reason given[29] for placing immanent operation in the category of quality, namely that like existence it is an inherent actuation of a potency, applies likewise to transient action.

Upon predicamental transient action there follows a real relation that continues as long as the effect exists in the real world, even though the

[28] See St Thomas, *ST*, I–II, 3, 2c.

[29] See above, n. 5. What the difficulty amounts to, is that *actio* in the Scholastic vocabulary has two very different meanings. *Actio* can signify a) second actuality in the agent — e.g., "actus secundus, qui est ipsa actio," John of St Thomas, *Phil. Nat.*, I, 14, 4, in *Cursus*, II, 310b30–31; or, b) the reality in which movement consists, that is, in the change that takes place in the patient — "actio identificatur cum motu," John of St Thomas, *ibid.*, p. 311a20.

action itself has ceased.[30] The carpenter, for instance, remains the builder of the house years after he has finished building it. The real relation vanishes only when either its subject or its term loses real existence.

b) TO UNDERGO (PASSION)

Every transient action causes a patient to undergo something. Building, for instance, makes the materials take on the artificial form of a house. The change from one form to another is what the patient undergoes, when acted upon by an agent. The undergoing, accordingly, is the motion or change in the patient, considered as caused by the extrinsic agent. Technically called passion, from *pati* "to suffer" or "to undergo," it is in reality identical with the movement or change. Movement, when viewed just in itself, is defined in natural philosophy as an imperfect act, an act of something in potency insofar as it is in potency[31] to further act and not as stabilized in the actually existing act itself. Regarded merely in itself, the motion or change is specified by its term and is placed reductively in the category to which the term belongs (substance, quantity, quality, place), or is looked upon as a postpredicament. Regarded in general as always caused by an agent, it constitutes the special category of passion.

Passion, accordingly, is change or movement denominated from something extrinsic, namely from its efficient cause.[32] As movement, in which its reality consists, it is an accident really inherent in the patient. It is obviously a different type of reality from action, as can be seen in a boxer undergoing the ministrations of his seconds between rounds, and the same boxer going into action at the sound of the gong. Even in change in which there is no continuous movement and so no imperfect act, as in generation and corruption, there is properly passion because a subject, primary matter, is undergoing change from one form to another.[33] In creation, however, there is properly no passion, because there is no subject to undergo any change.[34]

[30] "For when movement is taken away from action and passion, nothing remains except a relation . . ." *ST*, I, 45, 3c.

[31] Aristotle, *Ph.*, III 1, 201a10–11. Cf. 2, 201b31–32 and VIII 5, 257b8–9 for motion as "imperfect act."

[32] "So therefore insofar as something is denominated from an agent cause, there is the predicament of *passion* (*passionis*), for to suffer (*pati*) is nothing else than to undergo something from an agent; . . ." St Thomas, *In III Phys.*, lect. 5 (ed. Leonine), no. 15.

[33] In generation and corruption the change is instantaneous, and therefore does not come under the definition of movement in the strict sense; see St Thomas, *In V Phys.*, lect. 2 & 4.

[34] See St Thomas, *ST*, I, 45, 2, ad 2m.

Passion gives rise to a real relation of the patient to its efficient cause.[35] The relation remains as long as both subject and term continue in real existence. A house, for instance, retains its real relation to the builder, even though it is no longer in the process of being built. Passion, like action, is properly expressed in verbal forms, as in general to undergo, and in particular to be built, to be struck, to be transported, and the like. Both action and passion admit of contraries and of variation in degree.[36]

c) WHERE (PLACE)

Quantity spreads a thing in parts outside parts, grounding relations of distance in each part from every other part and from every other body in the same material universe. This allows the surfaces immediately surrounding any body to be related in distance to other bodies. In natural philosophy these immediately surrounding surfaces are regarded as immobile and in this way constituting the *place* in which the body is.[37] Extrinsic in consequence to the included body, place as a sort of measure determines *where* the body is, thereby setting up a new category. As in any measure, the starting point is either arbitrary or conventional. "Here" and "there" are indicated through reference to the speaker. A location halfway between New York and Chicago is determined in relation to those two cities. Similarly a thing may be situated so far from the north pole or from the equator, or from moon or the sun, or in a galaxy beyond Andromeda.

Where a thing is, is something very real for it. To be in London is really different from being in Paris or in Bombay. To be in a plane twenty thousand feet in the air is really different from being on terra firma, as a pilot who runs out of fuel at that altitude would probably be the first to admit. Where a thing is, is not a relation in it, even though determined by relations of distance. The whereabouts of a thing is a distinct category. Like any supreme genus, it cannot be analyzed into any simpler generic notions. It does not consist in any actuality that is intrinsic to its subject. To be here does not mean that you have any more inherent being than when you are there. To be in Manhattan does not imply any more intrinsic actuality than to be in Brooklyn. But it does give you a different extrinsic actuality (*actus extrinsecus*)[38] that is

[35] See St Thomas, *De Pot.*, III, 3c.

[36] Aristotle, *Cat.*, 9, 11b1–7.

[37] Aristotle, *Ph.*, IV 4, 212a20–21.

[38] "Hence local motion does not mean emergence from potency to any internal actuality of the thing, but to an extrinsic actuality (*ad actum extrinsecum*)." St Thomas, *In III Sent.*, d. 22, q. 3, a. 1, ad 1m; ed. Moos, III, 679–680 (no. 105).

very real. So real is this extrinsic actuality that it serves as the terminus of a real type of motion, local motion. A journey from New York to Los Angeles is something quite real, not something that exists just in intentional being. When you are in one place you have the potency to be in other places. That potency is actualized through continuous real motion that fully satisfies the Aristotelian definition as an imperfect act, or the act of something in potency insofar as it is in potency. Quantity when real is of such a nature that it grounds in each particular body relations of distance in regard to every other particular body within the same material universe. Lacking these relations to any other body, the universe as a whole is nowhere.

Two mistakes are therefore to be avoided regarding the present category. One would be to conceive it as an absolute way of being, based upon something like a Platonic receptacle or absolute Newtonian space or a Kantian apriori form. This view represents space as something that is there in itself or at least in priority to bodies. It is a view that is not reconcilable with what is now known of the relativity of space, nor with the traditional Aristotelian conception that material substance is the fundamental constituent of the sensible universe. Where a thing is or may be, rather, is grounded upon quantity insofar as quantity sets up relations of distance. The "where" does not ground the relations of distance,[39] but presupposes them.

The other mistake would be to view the "where" not as real being but as merely an extrinsic denomination existent in the human mind. Regardless of any consideration by the mind, each particular body is in its own place and is somewhere. The whereabouts of a thing is real, even though it is an actuality that is extrinsic to the thing and is denominated from extrinsically surrounding surfaces. It is not an inherent accident, like a quality or a real relation. *Is* it then *in* its subject, in the sense in which any accident has to be in (*inesse*) a substance? Yes, for "being in," as accidental being, means to have being in dependence upon something else in the order of essence.[40] In the full sense of this dependence, where a thing is is in the thing as in a subject. If there were not the subject to be somewhere, there would not be the "where," even though the actuality is extrinsic.

Because a particular body is in place through surrounding surfaces, it is technically said to be located circumscriptively. Each of its parts

[39] See Krempel, pp. 437–440. For Gredt, on the contrary, this category "is the ground of the relations of distance and lack of distance (presence)," *Elementa Philosophiae Aristotelico-Thomisticae*, ed. 7a (Freiburg i. Breisgau, 1937), I, 162 (no. 195).

[40] See above, Chapter 10, n. 9.

corresponds to a part of the extrinsic surface. A substantial form, for instance the human soul, is located wherever the body of which it is the form happens to be. But it is whole and entire in each part, instead of corresponding part by part with the locating surfaces. Likewise a spirit may be said to be wherever it is operating upon anything corporeal. The first cause, accordingly, is everywhere because of its conserving and concurring action. On account of the lack of part to part correspondence with surrounding surfaces, these latter are **non-circumscriptive** ways of being in place.

d) POSTURE

Since quantity extends in all static directions, it permits a thing to dispose its parts in different order while remaining roughly in the same place. A man can remain in the same room, and roughly in the same place, while sitting, standing, or lying down. He really changes his posture without changing his place. His members, of course, change place. Posture therefore presupposes the category "where," somewhat as discrete quantity presupposes continuous quantity, and follows upon it as a further determination of the way a thing is in place. There is no doubt about its reality, as the above examples show. But whether it should be regarded as a distinct category, or merely as a differentiation of the category "where" — i.e., where the parts are in relation to the whole — is not too important. The traditional examples refer only to living bodies. The designation by the Greek infinitive *keisthai*, and the Latin noun *situs*, should indicate situation, in the sense of the place where a thing is found. The examples, however, clearly show that what is meant is the disposition of a thing's parts in place, and not where the thing itself is. The English word "position" keeps the vagueness of the traditional terms. Sitting or standing, as well as where a thing is, may be called its position.

e) WHEN (TIME)

Besides being somewhere, a particular sensible thing exists at some time. It has an existence that is one by continuity, but which is not all together. Rather, its existence is determined by a mobile nature, and on account of the motion is spread out in terms of before and after. The measuring or numbering of motion in terms of before and after, as natural philosophy shows, is called time.[41] Its spread is unilinear, from past through present to future. It is a continuum in which but one

[41] See Aristotle, *Ph.*, IV 11, 219b2.

indivisible is actual, namely the present. The past instants have perished, the future ones do not yet exist. The present instant, accordingly, marks the one indivisible that is actual in the existence of any sensible thing. Hence the present moment coincides for everything that is actual in the material universe, no matter where it stands in the continuum of each thing's entire existence. The present moment may be in your twentieth year and in my sixtieth, but for both of us it is the present. The reason is that time is not something absolute in Newtonian fashion, nor a form prior to sensible phenomena as in Kant, but is consequent upon sensible existence. The one actual indivisible that each sensible existence has determines the present time. To presuppose that this indivisible in any particular thing is earlier or later than the present, is to presuppose that it is not actual.

The unit of time, like any other accepted unit of measure, is conventional. The most convenient are the daily revolution of the earth on its own axis, and its yearly revolution around the sun. Any indivisible may be chosen conventionally as the starting point for the temporal measurement, for instance around the founding of Rome or around the birth of Christ. As a measure in this way, time exists extrinsically to the sensible thing that it measures. "When any sensible thing exists," therefore, is a category taken from something extrinsic. It follows upon the relations of before and after in the unilinear spread of sensible existence. "When the thing exists," however, is something very real for it. To be in 1965 is really different from being in 1265. A seventy-year life-span is really longer than a thirty-year one. This means that "when" is a category of real being, though denominated from an extrinsic measure, time. It is a distinct actuality of the sensible thing, although like "where" it is an extrinsic actuality that adds nothing to the internal constitution of the thing. It is an actuality that is necessarily given to every sensible thing through existence conditioned by movement, just as a place is necessary for every particular thing in a quantitative universe. As in the case of where a thing is, two mistakes are to be avoided. On the one hand, when a thing exists is not to be regarded as something absolute or as an inherent mode. On the other hand, it is not to be viewed as a denomination existent merely in the human mind. It is a real accident, really in the subject in the sense of dependence upon it in its being, even though all its actuality is extrinsic.

Since time is the measure of motion, it does not apply to immobile or purely spiritual natures, any more than does place. As it is unilinear in direction, it cannot permit variation in the relative disposition of its parts. No category corresponding to posture, in consequence, follows upon it.[42] As in the case of "where," the category "when" follows upon relations instead of grounding them.[43]

f) STATE

The external things with which a man is in contact and of which he makes use, serve to constitute him in one state or another. In the traditional examples, he may be armed, shod, clothed. A new category is thereby set up, grounded, as can be seen from these instances, upon quantity and action and relations like those of proximity and ownership. This category was named by Aristotle *echein* "to have" and accordingly was called in Latin *habitus*. The Greek verb, however, as the Aristotelian examples show, was used here in its sense of being in a certain state or disposition. The Latin translation misses this meaning, and is confusing on account of the use of the same term *habitus* to translate the Aristotelian *hexis*, or "habit" in the first subdivision of the category of quality.

State is quite evidently a real way of being, as the examples make manifest. It is consequent upon relations, and denominates a man from extrinsic things like weapons, shoes, or clothes. Properly it pertains only to man, on account of his dominion over material things, but reductively states of animals domesticated by man are brought under it, as when a horse is ornamented, saddled, or barbed.[44] Though denominated from what is extrinsic, it is in the subject in the sense of an accident's dependence in being. Without the subject there could not be the state. Whether the category extends to states like wealth, slavery, power, or marriage, is not determined in Aristotelian tradition. In common with the three preceding categories, state is not an inherent actuality in its subject, and is consequent upon relations instead of grounding them.[45]

Résumé. Though radically different categorical schemata have been devised, for instance by Kant or by Hegel, these ten Aristotelian predicaments are a satisfactory and workable division of the ways of being. While open to development, they are fundamentally sound both as categories of predication and as corresponding categories of being.[46] The quantitative and the qualitative cover the absolutely inherent

[42] See St Thomas, *In III Phys.*, lect. 5, (ed. Leonine), no. 15.

[43] For Gredt, *Elementa*, I, 163 (no. 199), the category is on the contrary "the ground of the relations of temporal simultaneity, priority, and posteriority."

[44] See St Thomas, *In III Phys.*, lect. 5, (ed. Leonine), no. 15.

[45] "But the other genera follow upon relation, rather than being able to cause relation." St Thomas, *In V Metaph.*, lect. 17, (ed. Cathala-Spiazzi) no. 1005.

[46] "But the ways (*modi*) of being are proportional to the ways of predicating . . .

accidents of sensible substance, the one required by its matter, the other following in the line of form, in first actuality. Action covers its second actuality and its influence upon external things through efficient causality, while passion includes what it undergoes from them. Relation covers its real references to other things, where and when give its being in place and time, posture the way in which its parts are disposed in relation to one another, while state expresses how it is categorized by things outside itself. These headings seem to cover pretty well all the ways in which a sensible thing may be, both from within itself and from outside itself. Particular ways of being that are not covered by them may be reduced quite easily to one or the other category, as the relative disposition of parts in inanimate things may be reduced to the category of posture as readily as being saddled is reduced to the category of state, or as being wealthy and being married may be regarded as states, at least reductively, according to the model of being armed or being shod.

Under the categories, therefore, are brought all essences, or measures in which being is really imparted. The other way in which being is imparted, that is, intentionally, is the topic that next requires consideration.

SUGGESTED READINGS AND REFERENCES

St Thomas Aquinas, *On the Power of God* (*De Potentia*), III, 7; tr. English Dominican Fathers (London: Burns Oates & Washbourne Ltd., 1932–1934), I, 123–135.

——— *Summa Contra Gentiles*, III, 66–70; tr. Vernon Bourke, *On the Truth of the Catholic Faith*, Book Three: Providence, Part I (New York: Image Books, 1956), pp. 218–236.

John of St Thomas, *The Material Logic of John of St Thomas*, IV, 14, 5; tr. Yves Simon *et al.* (Chicago: University of Chicago Press, 1955), pp. 214–218.

Sr. M. Marina Scheu, *The Categories of Being in Aristotle and St Thomas* (Washington: Catholic University of America Press, 1944), pp. 89–95.

Alexander Marc, "Being and Action," *The Modern Schoolman*, XXVIII (1951), 175–190.

the ten genera of being are called the ten predicaments." St Thomas, *In III Phys.*, lect. 5, (ed. Leonine), no. 15. A recent tendency is to reduce the categories to very few, e.g. to substance, quality, and relation, as the categories of real being (Krempel, pp. 84–85), or to simple qualia and relations (cf. D. Williams, "Mind as a Matter of Fact," *Review of Metaphysics*, XIII [1959], 203). For Aristotle, presence in one category did not exclude the presence of the same thing in another category; see *Cat.*, 9, 11a37–38. For the Scholastics, on the contrary, a thing could in reality be in only one category. ". . . among creatures it is not found that any things belonging to diverse genera coincide in real identity." St Thomas, *In I Sent.*, d. 33, q. 1, a. 3, ad 4m; ed. Mandonnet, I, 773. Cf. *De Pot.*, VIII, 2, ad 1m. Similarly with Duns Scotus, *Quodl.*, XIII, no. 1 (ed. Vivès, XXV, 507a), the genera are "impermixta."

PART THREE . . . KNOWLEDGE

CHAPTER 15

Cognition

Metaphysical Inquiry. The two entitative principles in the light of which metaphysics gives its penetrating account of things are, as the preceding chapters have shown, being and essence. These two principles have furnished the means of explaining the real world from the viewpoint of its being. They have shown that in the real world subsistent being is absolutely primary. From subsistent being other things have either mediately or immediately all their existence, substantial as well as accidental. The real world, however, is known in human cognition, both in ordinary life and in metaphysical or other scientific study. So known, it exists intentionally or cognitionally in the mind of everyone who happens to perceive it. The same world that exists in reality is the world that is known in thought. Otherwise, not it but something else would be known; and that "something else" would be what acquired new being in human cognition and presented itself with characteristics in every way indistinguishable from what men call the real world. The situation would parallel the proof that Shakespeare was really another man by the same name.

These considerations do not at all preclude serious questions regarding the being of the real world. An Idealist may claim to admit fully the everyday world in which men live, and yet deny that it has any being outside cognition. The point at present is to determine where such questions belong. Do they pertain to a separate science that has knowledge itself as object, or do they come under metaphysics as questions concerning a thing's intentional[1] being?

[1] On the notion "intentional," see above, Chapter 2, nn. 3–5. In the wake of Locke's *Essay* and Kant's *Critique*, the study of knowledge has been separated from metaphysics and set up as a special branch of philosophy; see above, "Historical Introduction," nn. 29 and 47. The title "epistemology" became current for the new branch through James Frederick Ferrier's use of it in *Institutes of Metaphysic* (Edinburgh and London, 1854). "Theory of Knowledge," following the German *Erkenntnistheorie* or *Erkenntnislehre*, is also an accepted designation. *Gnoseologia*, used in Italian, has been

Quite obviously, a thoroughgoing phenomenology of human cognition is called for in answer to this query. The contents of human cognition as a matter of fact exist in the mind. They can be examined as they actually are there in their cognitional existence. But even elementary scientific procedure requires that they be investigated without prejudice as "what appears," as the *phainomena*. If what "appears" in sensible things actually seen and touched is that the things exist externally to the cognition, the fact that they are perceived to exist in reality has to be numbered among the contents distinguished by the phenomenology. Real existence "appears" at least as authentic as mental existence. To that extent the real existence of things cannot be "bracketed" without prejudicing, on a purely apriori basis, the whole of the investigation. Rather, the mind should be left frankly open to see what actually does "appear" when it examines its own contents throughout its various acts of simple apprehension and judgment. What "appears" may well be more than just the eidetic. It may be that through judgment the existential "appears" just as primitively and just as irreducibly.

In answer to the present question whether the study of knowledge pertains to metaphysics or to a special science that has knowledge as its object, one fact "appears" very clearly. A thing or essence has to remain unchanged in itself in being known. Otherwise not it but the some-

---

attempted, without lasting success, in its English equivalent "gnosiology." In Neo-scholastic circles *Logicae Pars Critica* (Tongiorgi), *Critica* (Gény), *Critique de la Connaissance* (Tonquédec), *Criteriologia* (San Severino), *Critériologie* (Mercier), and *Ontologie du Connaître* (Simon), have also been in use. Sometimes one or the other of these titles has been restricted to a part of the new science in contradistinction to the science as a whole. There is no general agreement about the exact limits or divisions of its field. It often includes considerable logic and occasionally some psychology. In the early decades of the twentieth century it occupied the leading place in many philosophies. Enthusiasm for it died down toward the middle of the century, but has since been revived on a less comprehensive scale.

For a history of the many and varied Neo-Thomist epistemologies, see Georges Van Riet, *L'Epistémologie Thomiste* (Louvain, 1946). A survey of a number of recent non-Scholastic views may be found in Thomas English Hill, *Contemporary Theories of Knowledge* (New York, 1961). On the impossibility of a critique of knowledge in priority to a realistic metaphysics like that of St Thomas, see Etienne Gilson, *Réalisme Méthodique* (Paris, 1936), pp. 11–15; *Réalisme Thomiste et Critique de la Connaissance* (Paris, 1939), pp. 156–183. The opposite view is strongly expressed in the Louvain circle, e.g.: "This double reflexive analysis, we added, precedes logically a definitive metaphysics and in particular it precedes every ontological theory of knowledge . . ." Léon Noël, *Le Réalisme Immédiat* (Louvain, 1938), p. 281. "It is possible, and today it is absolutely indispensable, to expound Thomism in a way which will satisfy the strictest requirements of a critical and systematic philosophy. In an exposition of this sort epistemology must occupy the first place." Fernand Van Steenberghen, *Epistemology*, tr. Martin J. Flynn (New York, 1949), p. ix; cf. pp. 97–98, 258, 295. Cf. also Léon Veuthey, *La Connaissance Humaine* (Rome, 1948), p. 15.

thing into which it changed would be known. Cognition, in order to be cognition, has to leave unchanged the essence of what it knows. If any change occurs for the thing, the change can be only in the order of being. Anything new added to the thing will consist entirely in the being that is received in cognition. Cognition as a knowable object, distinct from its contents, is not a new essence. The way cognition itself "appears" solidly establishes this fact. In order to be known or perceived, a thing has to remain inviolate in essence, otherwise not it but something other would be known.

Cognition, therefore, cannot be explained in terms of essence or nature. It has to be dealt with in terms of being. It comes under metaphysics, the only science that treats of things from the viewpoint of being. Other sciences like psychology or natural philosophy study the various senses and cognitional acts from qualitative and quantitative and other essential viewpoints. But they all have to take cognition itself for granted. Only metaphysics can hope to explain it.

Phenomena of Cognition. Upon examination the basic contents of human cognition, from which all else in it is derived, appear without exception as sensible things and human activities specified by sensible things. Try to think of anything in other terms. You find you cannot do so. All immaterial things are found represented through notions experienced in the sensible. The concept of an immaterial thing retains the notion of thing while removing the notion of materiality. Subsistent being is represented as existence identified with substance. Here the notions of both substance and existence are taken from the substance and existence of material things, with materiality and all other limitation denied them. What is known immediately through simple apprehension turns out in every instance to be a sensible nature, or a cognitional act specified by a sensible nature. From the viewpoint of essence, a phenomenological survey shows, all appearances or phenomena in human cognition are sensible in their origin.

But do essences or natures exhaust what "appears" in a survey of the contents of human cognition? Far from it. Nothing appears through simple apprehension as a nature without at the same time appearing through judgment as an existent. A nature without existence would not "appear" at all. A nature in its absolute consideration is not a phenomenon but the conclusion of a reasoning process. Without appearing as existent a nature just could not appear. In the phenomena there is no possibility whatsoever of bracketing existence. The objects appear to exist at least in cognition during the phenomenological examination.

But does real existence "appear" in any of them? Could not all the sensible objects in which human cognition originates have merely intentional being? When this question was encountered in the second chapter of the present book, it found a decisive answer in the radically different ways in which things appear existent. The canary in the cage before your eyes as you look at it appears to your judgment as really existent, while the roc you read about in fairy tales does not appear in that way. The sensible things actually seen or touched or perceived through the other external senses appear in their real existence. Their real existence is immediately apparent through judgment. Psychological investigation shows, moreover, that the data for all sensible things you imagine come originally from things perceived in real being.

The real existence of sensible things outside one's cognition is accordingly among the most primitive data that "appear." To bracket it in any seriousness would be to bracket the origin of all human cognition and to preclude a study of knowledge based on its actual source. A cognition not stemming from really existent sensible things is nowhere found among the contents of the human mind. A phenomenology of human cognition, carried on without prejudice, reveals no such datum. To cut off things in their intentional being and set them up as an independent starting point for the investigation of human knowledge is not only a highly artificial procedure of Cartesian inspiration, but is totally unjustified by the actual phenomenology of the human mind. An Eleatic precision of appearance from being is not possible. What appears is existent at least in cognition as long as it appears, and the being of things is apparent through judgment. Their being "appears." It is not just "affirmed." This being is real in things actually seen and touched and heard, and intentional in things imagined or reflected upon. Real existence and cognitional existence are primitive, irreducible data. Neither, in finite things, can be reasoned to from the other.

Starting Points. The facts from which a metaphysical inquiry into cognition has to start, therefore, are clear and definite. An identical thing is found to exist in two different ways. It exists in reality, and it exists in your cognition as you know it. In the real world it subsists; it exists in itself. In you it exists not in itself but in the activity that is your cognition. The differences between the two ways of existing are very pronounced, even though the thing undergoes no change whatsoever in essence when it is known. Complete identity in essence and individuality, sharp difference in being — these are the starting points for the explanation of cognition. The tree you look at in front of your cottage in summer has real existence there. While you are watching it, it has also cognitional being in yourself. You turn away from it, forget about it, and it loses the cognitional being, though without anything happening to its real being. In winter miles away in the city you think of it, and it has being again in your mind. It is always the same individual tree, for if the tree that you see or remember is not the same tree that really exists in front of your cottage, you are not at all thinking of that tree or seeing it. Yet your seeing the tree or remembering the tree does not do anything at all to the tree in its real existence. Your cognition does not effect any change in its real being, just as it does not produce any change in its nature.

However, cognition makes the tree exist under considerably different conditions. In the real world, it stays in the one place summer and winter. In your cognition, it travels around with you, and is where you are. In real existence, it occupies many cubic feet of space. In your cognition it does not. Nor does it increase your weight, nor make you have leaves. Such differences in the two ways of being, especially the last mentioned, should open a path for the metaphysical investigation of knowledge.

Immateriality. The color green cannot really exist in the lawn without making the grass in which it exists green. Only by qualifying the grass does it have being. When you see it or think of it, however, it does not make you green. It exists in you cognitionally, but without qualifying you as green. It is not in you the way a quality is in its substance. The grass is the subject of the color green, functioning as the matter qualified by the accidental form. Such reception of anything is called material reception. If what is received is an accidental form, the substance is modified by it. The substance becomes colored, heated, thickened, or affected in some other way. If what is received is a substantial form, the primary matter takes on the nature of the form, human, equine, plant, mineral, or whatever it may happen to be. But in seeing a horse you do not become equine, nor in studying a metal do you become metallic. In cognition, then, you do not receive anything as a matter receives a form. You receive the object known into your cognition without being characterized by its nature. Negatively expressed, this means that you receive the thing **immaterially.**[2]

[2] The explanation of cognition as immaterial reception of forms originates in Aristotle's description of the senses as receptive of "sensible forms without the matter" (*De An.*, II 12, 424a18–19). The Stagirite explained this as meaning that a sense is affected through different colors or flavors or sounds, but is indifferent to the kind of substance in which these qualities are found (a19–24). Each sense, in a word, distinguishes its proper sensibles but not the secondary matter in which

Accordingly, the size of the thing known does not increase your size when you receive it into your cognition. Its place and its time in the real order do not locate you in that place and time as you remember it. There is no material reception at all when things are received into one's cognition. Immaterial reception or immaterial possession is the necessary condition for cognitive activity. The thing known is in the knowing subject without being a modification of the subject. If reception by way of modifying a subject may be termed subjective reception, according to later Scholastic vocabulary, cognitional reception and possession of a thing may in contrast be named objective reception and possession. The thing remains an object. It does not become a subjective modification, even though it exists in the knower.

How is such immaterial reception or possession to be understood? Nothing parallels it in the observable world. In physical activities, whenever a form is received it imprints its nature upon its subject, and with it constitutes a composite of matter and form. In cognition no such composite is possible. Yet the thing known is received into the knowing subject. There can be no question here of mere juxtaposition, like a picture in a frame, for the thing known receives new being in the cognition

---

those sensibles are found. Yet Aristotle went on to state that plants do not have sensation because they cannot receive forms in that way, but undergo change "with matter" (b3). St Thomas accordingly interprets these assertions to mean that in sensation the form of the sensible thing is received through an assimilation that is formal and not material (*secundum formam et non secundum materiam*), in intentional being (*In II De An., lect.* 24, ed. Pirotta, no. 553), as distinguished from "material transmutation" (no. 557). The difference lies "in the way of receiving" a form (no. 552); cf. lect. 5, no. 283. The "nature of cognition" consists in receiving something immaterially (*De Ver.*, II, 2c). Cf. *De Ver.*, XXIII, 1c; *ST*, I, 14, 1c; *Q. de An.*, 13c.

The "formal reception" or "reception of forms" or "immateriality" in cognition refers accordingly to the manner of receiving, and not to the constitution of the thing received. Not just the form, but the composite of matter and form, comes to exist intentionally in the knower when a sensible thing is perceived. Material things as known remain material things, though as known they exist not in their physical matter but in the knower. It is in this way that their forms are received not materially but immaterially in cognition. They themselves do not become immaterial in the process. The intellect, for instance, "does not attribute to the things understood the manner in which it understands them; just as it does not attribute immateriality to the stone, although it knows it immaterially" (*CG*, I, 36). "Immateriality" is therefore open to misunderstanding in this regard. So Yves Simon, *Introduction à l'Ontologie du Connaître* (Paris, 1934), pp. 16–17, emphasizes intentional existence as preferable to immaterial reception in explaining cognition. Nevertheless, the notion of immaterial reception seems indispensable for understanding how something can be received into something else without giving rise to a third thing or product. On the general question of immateriality in cognition, see Maurice R. Holloway, "Abstraction from Matter in Human Cognition according to St. Thomas," *The Modern Schoolman*, XXIII (1946), 120–130. On the persistence of the perceived thing's individuality, see below, n. 16.

of the knower. The thing known has to be in fact in the knower, but without entering into any composition. Composition would make the reception material. But to be in the knower without the duality of composition is to be identical with the knower. The identity is not substantial, for it is not made in the real substance of the knower. It is made in his cognition, and so is effected in and through an activity. However, the knower is the one who is performing the cognitive actions. Accordingly it is the knower himself and not just his activity that becomes identical with the thing known. This is in no way a physical identity, for the tree and the man remain in every manner just as physically distinct as they were before the act of cognition took place. It is an identity that occurs only in the cognitive act, and then not physically but in a way that can be described just as a cognitional or intentional identity. Because it is an identity found in cognition alone, it cannot be explained positively by any parallels. It has to be reasoned to from the presence of the known object in the knower and from the immateriality of the object's reception and possession. Through that identity the knowing subject *becomes* and *is* the thing known, not physically, but cognitionally or intentionally.[3]

Object Known. All human cognition, the phenomenological survey has shown, originates with sensible things. Only the objects touching the sense organs, however, are immediately perceived through external sensation. What is immediately seen is just the object that

[3] ". . . cognition is accomplished in this way, that the known is in the knower not indeed materially but formally. Just as to have something in one's self formally and not materially — in which consists the notion of cognition — is the most excellent way of having or containing anything . . ." St Thomas, *In Lib. de Causis*, lect. 18, (ed. C. Pera) nos. 338–339. The reason is, that while material reception of a form gives rise to a third thing, the composite of matter and form, formal reception makes the one the other without any third thing arising from their union. On this union see Joseph Gredt, "De Unione Omnium Maxima inter Subiectum Cognoscens et Obiectum Cognitum," in *Xenia Thomistica*, ed. Sadoc Szabó (Rome, 1925), I, 303–318. Cf.: ". . . what is understood in actuality becomes one with the intellect in actuality, insofar as the form of what is understood becomes the form of the intellect insofar as it is the intellect in actuality, not that it is the very essence of the intellect . . . because the essence of the intellect remains one under two forms as it understands two things successively . . ." St Thomas, *In IV Sent.*, d. 49, q. 2, a. 1, ad 10m; ed. Vivès, XI 486a. Aristotle (*De An.*, III 2, 425b25–31; 4, 430a2–9; cf. *Metaph.*, Λ 7, 1072b21–23) notes the fact of the identity of subject and object in the act of cognition even though they are otherwise different from each other, but gives no explanation. For St Thomas, the explanation lies in the distinction between essence and existence. The same thing or essence can have different existential acts, one real and the others intentional. Accordingly "cognition does not mean an efflux from the knower upon the known, as is the case in physical actions, but means rather the existence (*existentiam*) of the known in the knower" (*De Ver.*, II, 5, ad 15b).

touches the retina, what is immediately felt is the inner surface of the skin in contact with the nerve ends, what is heard immediately is only the sound within the ear, and so on. These are all objects really distinct from the knowing subject. They are not subjective modifications of him as the knower. They are modifications of bodies immediately in contact with and reacted upon by the sensory organs. They are in the bodies that constitute the sustaining media of colors, sounds, odors, tastes, temperature, hardness and softness, and so on. Through habits of touch in conjunction with sight the perception of distance is gradually acquired, and through similar habits the immediately perceived data are interpreted, on the basis of groupings and changes, in terms of different natures like stones, plants, animals and men. In these ways there is complicated mediation in human knowledge of external things. But that mediation is from body to body, from substance to substance, and not from accident to the notion or existence of substance. What is perceived immediately in sensation is not color, nor sound, nor odor, nor taste, but something colored, something audible, something odorous, something tasty. Color, sound, taste, and so on, are abstractions of the intellect, and as such are not perceptible by the senses. The senses can attain only a concrete thing, a substance, insofar as the substance is colored, sounding, odorous, and the like.

From a metaphysical viewpoint, what is immediately attained by sensation does not coincide exactly with the sense's object as considered by the physicist or the experimental psychologist. From their viewpoints the sentient organ always reacts upon the thing perceived. In this respect the sense does change the thing somewhat in the physical process that accompanies, and in its own way causes, perception.

Understood in terms of being, however, cognition takes place from start to finish in a different order from that in which all physical action and reaction is brought to completion. It begins when the real order, which is the only order considered by the physicist or the experimental psychologist, is left. A new order of being, the intentional, is entered. The physical action and reaction take place in the order of real being. They result in a real physical object that is known, but which is not reacted upon by anything in the intentional order. Being known does not change that object physically. If it were changed physically, then not it, but the product of the reaction, would be what was known. This in turn would be changed by being known, and so on in infinite regress. In actual fact, however, the things known remain stable while being thought over and discussed. The new cognitional acts do not make them different things.

What is immediately known in external sensation is accordingly the end product of the physical action and reaction. It is still something extended, colored, hot or cold, and the like. Though it may be within the body of the knower, it is nevertheless external to him as a knower, as sentient. It is outside his cognitive activity. It is not perceived as his ego, but as something extended that is other than himself. Even though what is immediately felt is inside the cuticle, and what is immediately seen is inside the eye, it is still something outside the properly sentient subject. In this manner it is trans-subjective to a corporeal knower.

Through the external senses, of course, the specific nature of a substance is not attained. The object is perceived merely as something colored or something hard, with no penetration into its substantial nature. That task is left for the intellect. The intellect takes the data given it through sensation, "something colored, something hard," and so on, and on the basis of the data distinguishes substance from accident and strives as best it can to determine the nature of particular substances by means of their accidental modifications. Genuine aquamarine and a good imitation are each perceived through sensation as something sea-green and hard. The expert knowledge of the jeweller is required to distinguish them as different kinds of substance.[4] But this does not give any literal justification to the statement: "Only accidents are perceived by the senses, and not the substance of the thing." If the statement is understood in the meaning that substance is not contained in the data reached through the senses, an impossible situation arises. The human intellect knows only what is attained in sensation. If substance is not attained somehow in sensation, the intellect has no means of knowing it.

The existent thing, then, is perceived through external sensation, insofar as that thing is modified by sensible qualities. It is the thing itself that becomes and is identical with the knowing subject through sensation. The nature of the thing, at least in its general aspect as a body, is in this way present to the simple apprehension of the intellect. The real being of the thing is correspondingly judged by the intellect in the really existent object perceived by the senses. No reasoning process is either necessary or possible from data perceived through external sensation to their own real existence or the real existence of the substances that sustain the accidents in being.

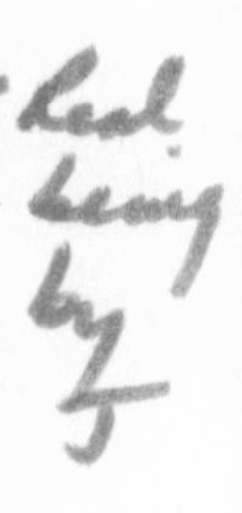

[4] Real specific essences are not immediately attained by human cognition; see above, Chapter 5, n. 3. Cf. J. Le Rohellec, "Utrum, iuxta Sancti Thomae Doctrinam, Essentiae Rerum Sensibilium Statim in Simplici Apprehensione Percipiantur," *Xenia Thomistica*, I, 285–302; R. B. Gehring, "The Knowledge of Material Essences according to St. Thomas Aquinas," *The Modern Schoolman*, XXXIII (1956), 153–181.

Knowing Subject. By the same token, there is no necessity nor possibility of a "bridge" from sensation to intellection in the knower. Strictly, it is not the sense that perceives, but the knowing substance through the sense.[5] Only a substance can perform an activity of any kind, though exercising the activity through its faculties or powers. A sense is one such faculty. Similarly, it is not the intellect that knows, if strict language is observed, but the knowing substance through the intellect. Both cognitional operations are performed by the same supposit, the same person. The knower is one and the same in sensation and in intellection. He becomes intentionally the colored thing through the sense of sight. He thereby is that thing cognitionally. He attains it as colored through sight, as corporeal through simple apprehension, as really existent through judgment. He was identical with the thing cognitionally from the start, and so is able to penetrate it still further in that identity through his other cognitional faculties.

It is practically impossible, of course, and not at all desirable, to discard the shorthand symbols "the senses perceive," and "the intellect knows," or "color is seen," and "a thing's existence is known." But as so often in metaphysical contexts, the requisite therapy has to be practiced. In every instance of external sensation, it is a supposit that perceives a thing. The priority of substance to accident does not allow an accident to be perceived without a substance, nor does it at all permit a faculty to go into operation unless the substance is performing the activity. Accordingly no question of a passage from accident to substance nor of a corresponding passage from sense knower to intellective knower is admissible. Substance and accident are together from the start. The intellective knower is identical with the sense knower. The one knower becomes and is the thing known, in various degrees of cognitional penetration.

---

[5] "It is doubtless better to avoid saying that the soul pities or learns or thinks, and rather to say that it is the man who does this with his soul." Aristotle, *De An.*, I 4, 408b13–15; Oxford tr. Cf. St Thomas, *In I De An.*, lect. 10, (ed. Pirotta) no. 152. Similarly: ". . . properly speaking, neither sense nor intellect knows, but a man by means of both, as is clear in *I De An.*" *De Ver.*, II, 6, ad 3m. "For we say that a man sees with his eye and feels with his hand . . . It can therefore be said that the soul understands as the eye sees, but it is more correct to say that a man understands through his soul." *ST*, I, 75, 2 ad 2m. ". . . the man . . . through his sensitive powers has particular cognition of what is abstracted through the agent intellect." *De Spir. Creat.*, 10, ad 15m; cf. 2, ad 2m. On Gredt's dislocation of the object of human knowledge into a physical world (object of the senses) and a metaphysical world (object of abstract intellection), and the requirement of mediation between the two corresponding acts of cognition, see E. Gilson, *Réalisme Thomiste*, pp. 186–194.

Reflection. Since the knowing subject and the object known are intentionally identical in the act of cognition, the one could not be known without the other being thereby in some way known. The one is the other in the cognitive act. In external sensation, and simple apprehension and judgment concerning the thing so perceived, attention is focused solely upon the sensible object in the real outside world. Yet in perceiving it the knower is himself intentionally identified with it and is therefore aware of himself in a concomitant way to which no direct attention is given. If the term "consciousness," which means "knowing together with," may be applied to this awareness of self that accompanies every act of cognition, it will denote the concomitant grasp of self that has to go with any cognition of an external object on account of the intentional identity of knower and thing known.[6] To focus attention on the self so known, however, a new and different act of cognition is required. Of this act the knower himself and not the external thing is the object. He is known, accordingly, as he is in his own activity of cognition, and also in his own appetitive reaction that follows upon cognition of the thing known.

This cognition of one's self in one's cognitional and appetitive acts may be described as a "bending back" of cognitional activity upon itself, and so is called **reflection.** The direct object of human cognition taken as a whole is an external sensible thing. Sweeping back upon itself that cognition makes itself the object of a new act of knowing. Sensible things, therefore, remain the origin of all human thought. Human thought attains itself and its active subject in their intentional identity with the external thing. Only in the cognition of a sensible thing can it come to know itself.

Cognition of self, consequently, is immediate but indirect. It is immediate, because the self is present to one's cognition in its intentional unity with the external thing. It is not the object of any mediate knowledge, that is, of a reasoning process, at least in regard to its existence. Further knowledge of its nature, however, can be attained by reasoning from the data immediately though reflexively known. Accordingly, the direct object of human cognition is external reality, and its indirect object or the object of its reflexive cognition is itself with its own activi-

[6] "He states therefore, first, that the passive intellect is intelligible, not through its essence, but through an intelligible form (*speciem*), like other intelligible things. He proves it from the fact that what is understood in actuality and the one who is understanding in actuality are one, just as he said above that what is sensibly perceived in actuality and the sense in actuality are one." St Thomas, *In III De An.*, lect. 9, (ed. Pirotta) no. 724. In later Scholasticism the concomitant consciousness was called consciousness *in actu exercito*, and the reflexive was consciousness *in actu signato*. Cf. below, Chapter 17, n. 11.

ties. As knowledge of self, reflexive cognition is **consciousness** in the full sense of the term. In it attention is focused upon self and not upon the external thing with which the self is intentionally united. The concomitant consciousness that accompanies every act of cognition does not in regular Scholastic terminology give its name to the act. Only when the self is the object that specifies the cognitive act does occasion arise for designation of the act itself by a special term, consciousness. In modern philosophies, though, "consciousness" is used loosely for all cognition.

The Cartesian revolution failed to take account of the difference between physical union of things and cognitional union of knower and thing known. Physically, nothing can be more present to a thing than itself.[7] Cognitionally, something else is directly present and the self only indirectly. Physically, one thing unites with another as a part. It does not become the other, it is not the other. Cognitionally, one thing unites with the other not as a part, but immaterially. The thing known is in the knower, yet is not a part of the knower. This can only mean that it is the knower in the act of cognition, not physically, but in another way that is called intentional or cognitional. Aristotle, accordingly, could say that the soul is in a certain way all things.[8]

Intentional Being. Physically, then, or in reality, the perceived sensible thing may be other than the knower. Intentionally, it is identical with the knower. Is this compatible with the principle of being, the principle of contradiction? Yes, for the two are not same and other in the one respect. In physical or real being, they may not in fact coincide. In cognitional being, they do coincide. The being they have in reality may make one not the other. The intentional being they have in cognition does make one the other. Each of the two ways of being carries its own necessity. They make the things different in reality but identical in the cognitive act. It is not at all a question of sameness and otherness following upon the one act of existence. Real existence is had in the thing's own substance. In its real existence the perceived thing subsists. It has intentional existence not in its own substance, but in the cognitional activity of a knower. It presupposes for intentional being the real activity and the real subsistence of the knower. There is no "halt" just in its intentional being and so no subsistence.

[7] This notion of physical presence was transferred quite uncritically to the cognitional order: "So, by this word 'idea' I understand here nothing other than that which is the immediate object or the closest to the mind when it perceives some object." Nicolas Malebranche, *Recherche de la Vérité*, III, 2e partie, c. 1, no. 1.

[8] *De An.*, III 8, 431b21–23. Cf. 5, 430a11–12. See St Thomas, *ST*, I, 84, 2, ad 2m.

Intentional being, though, can be traced back to the first cause of being as its original source. It is genuine being, and has to be caused efficiently, directly by the activity of the immediate knower, and ultimately by the first efficient cause of all things. In this way beings of reason, such as negations and privations, and even sin,[9] have subsistent being as the first cause of whatever being they possess. The being they possess is of course not real being but cognitional being.

Specification of Intentional Being. But how is intentional being a different *kind* of being from real being? "Kind" should denote specification. All the specification of being, however, comes from essence. It is only the essence that limits it as formal cause. Yet it is the same essence, metal, oak, or dog, that has real being in the external world and intentional being in cognition. The specifying essence is the same in both cases. How, then, can there be any difference in being?

Certainly any differences between real being and cognitional being will arise somehow from essence. The differences themselves are manifest. The real being of a stone consists in a composing of physical parts, matter and form. The cognitional being of the same stone when it is known by a human mind consists in a synthesis of whole with whole. Not only individual, species, and genera, but also thing known and knowing subject, are united in the one intentional existence. In its real being the stone exists in itself, in its cognitional being it exists in the activity of a mind. In the real world it endures as long as its own substance continues there. In intentional being, it lasts not as long as its own substance or the substance of the knower remains in real being, but only as long as a particular cognitive act persists. These are notable differences between real and intentional being. They have to be explained on the basis of essence. How?

For a thing to have being distinct from subsistent being, a limiting essence is required in which a thing may participate being. If the thing has its own being just in that essence itself, it subsists. It has real being, formally determined by its essence. It thereby has a different kind of being from the being it possessed from all eternity in the first cause. There its being was not in itself but in its creative cause. That being was not finite nor created, but subsistent; and in that being it itself was

---

[9] ". . . and thus the deformity (of sin) is said to exist, not because it has being in reality, but because the intellect composes privation with subject, in the manner of a form . . . and insofar as it has being in reason, it is manifestly from God." St Thomas, *In II Sent.*, d. 37, q. 1, a. 2, ad 3m; ed. Mandonnet, II, 947. Cf. arg. 3, p. 945.

not a creature but rather the creative essence.[10] As it exists or pre-exists in the first cause, it has a being that is the being of an infinite essence. As known by the first cause, therefore, it has being that is appropriate to the knower. When known by a finite knower, its intentional being is correspondingly conditioned by the essence and activity of the knowing subject. The intentional being conferred upon it in human knowledge is accordingly of a human type.[11] Nothing of the human essence enters into the essence of the thing known, but the human essence and activity do make its intentional being a special kind of being. It is being in the human mind, and not in external matter. It is being in an activity and not immediately in a substance. It is not a composing of physical parts, for the mind in knowing the stone does not make it be in reality. The human essence and the nature of its activity, therefore, make the intentional being conferred upon a thing by the human mind a different kind of being from the being of the thing in the real world.

The essence of the thing known, however, remains unchanged in its nature under both kinds of being. The stone itself does not in the least way become human when it is known by a human mind, even though the intentional being it receives is conditioned through and through by human cognitive activity. The intercontinental ballistic missile is not at all made human because it is designed by a human intellect. Inside and outside the mind the stone is the same stone and the missile is the same missile. But each of the two ways of being is different. They are different not by reason of the essence of the thing known, but by reason of the essence of the knower. The difference, accordingly, like any specification of being, is accounted for by essence. Further, the specification by the knower makes the intentional being that is given in sensation a different kind from that given in intellection, and similarly with the different senses. Being seen is different from being heard, and both are different from being understood.

While real being, then, is specified solely by the essence that it makes be, cognitional being is also specified in a certain way by the knower in which it is produced. Human cognition of a stone, as has been seen, differs from divine cognition of the same stone. Human cognition gives the stone a different *kind* of cognitional being than does the divine cognition. Correspondingly, cognitional being is individuated by each cognitive act. When you look at the lake in which you swim during

[10] St Thomas, *De Pot.*, III, 5, ad 2m; text above, Chapter 9, n. 11. Because of itself it has no being whatsoever, an essence is able to *be* as the *creatrix essentia*.

[11] ". . . the thing itself is in the soul in the manner (*modum*) of the soul, and not in its own manner . . . not according to its proper being, but in the manner of the soul, that is, spiritually." St Thomas, *De Ver.*, XXII, 10c.

the summer, and when you recall the same lake in your daydreams during the winter, you give it individually different acts of intentional being. This individuation comes evidently from the cognitive activity, not from the thing known. The thing known, for example, a tree, remains specifically and individually the same both in reality and in cognition. No change whatsoever is effected in it on the "essence" side of the existence-essence couplet. The acts by which the thing is given intentional being, however, receive further specification and individuation from the cognitional actions, without any addition to or change in the thing itself from the viewpoint of its essence.

Human cognition, consequently, is human because of the knower. But all further specification and gradation and distinctions come from the things known. These are originally sensible things. Through knowing them the knower is able to know himself. Human cognition, therefore, is to be judged and criticized in the light of sensible things. It is known by man only in and through the cognition of the sensible world. Strange though it may sound at first hearing, the critique of knowledge itself has to be carried on in the light of real things, and so has to presuppose the *knowledge* of those things. Sensible things in their real existence are known in priority to any knowledge of knowledge. They necessarily retain methodological priority in the critical study of cognition.

Production of Intentional Being. But how could a sensible thing pass from real being into cognitional being? Could the process be like an osmosis that takes place when the thing is in immediate contact with the sense organ? Does it then pass over from reality into cognition? In osmosis the liquids or gases retain their same physical being as they pass through the porous membrane. They leave one place and enter another. In sensation, the thing in its physical being remains entirely in the outside world. It does not pass over in any literal way, but remains exactly where it was. Yet it is given new being in and by the knower. Through the external senses a stone, for instance, is perceived as there in itself in the outside world, and not in any image expressed internally by the senses of sight or touch. But even when through higher faculties it is imagined or remembered, it is still something that remains other than anything produced by the knower, and other than the knower himself. It is in that case known in an internal image, but it itself is obviously something other than the image as a cognitional object. It, and not the image, is the object directly known. Always it remains something other than the cognition or what is produced in the cognition. It is in the cognition, but in a way that allows it to remain something other than the cognition and its subjective accidents. It does not therefore exactly pass over from reality to cognition, but if really existent it remains in the outside world. At the same time, it is brought into new and distinct being in the cognitional activity of the knower. In an etiquette that goes back to Aristotle,[12] this is expressed by saying that the form of the thing known is in the knower. Actually, it is the thing itself that is in the knower; but the form is the principle that specifies the cognitive activity, for the matter is in itself unknowable.

Cognition, accordingly, is always an activity of a knower. Yet in man it has clearly a passive aspect. The human cognitive faculties are, by themselves, like matter without form. They do not provide their own object.[13] This is shown through the arguments that establish the origin of all human cognition in the experience of sensible things. The forms of something colored, something hard, something sour, and so on, all have to come from the things in contact with the sensory organs. These things, while remaining where they are in their real being, are given new intentional being as they physically act and are reacted upon along the surface of the organ. There is efficient action and reaction in the contact with the sensory organ, yet the causality the things exercise on the cognitive act is in the realm of formal determination. Impinging upon the sense and acting efficiently upon it they determine it and they cause the cognitive act to have intentionally their own formal natures. They are the external formal cause[14] of the cognition, in the manner in which

---

[12] See above, n. 2. To this extent Aristotle can accept the Platonic description of the soul as a "place of forms," at *De An.*, III 4, 429a27–29. For him the cognitive soul is only potentially the forms, and so cannot provide them of itself. The sensible universe has to play the role of the *dator formarum*, as L.-M. Régis, *Epistemology* (New York, 1959), p. 197, remarks.

[13] For Aristotle the human mind is as "a writing-tablet on which as yet nothing actually stands written . . ." *De An.*, III 4, 430a1–2; Oxford tr. Cf. 429a13–24, where sensation is included under this doctrine, and 429b30–31. With the knower providing nothing of the thing known, the epistemological problem "is not a question of the objectification of thought but the objectification of thing. In other words, the question is: How does a thing become an object? How does what *is* in physical existence (a thing), become existent in intentional existence (an object)?" G. B. Phelan, "Verum Sequitur Esse Rerum," *Mediaeval Studies*, I (1939), 15.

[14] "Formal cause outside the thing" (*causam formalem extra rem*) is contrasted with intrinsic formal cause by St Thomas, *In I Sent.*, d. 8, q. 1, a. 2, ad 2m; ed. Mandonnet, I, 198. The thing's form, when existing outside the thing itself, can have two functions: "But the form of a thing existing apart from it can have two purposes; either that it be the exemplar of the thing of which it is called the form; or that it be the source of its being known, insofar as the forms of the knowable things are said to be in the knower." *ST*, I, 15, 1c. In causing formally the specification of the cognitive potency, "the object . . . has in a way the aspect of form, insofar as it specifies." *ST*, I–II, 18, 2, ad 2m. As a type of formal causality, exemplar causality

the thing known is said to be the form of the knower in the union of the two in intentional being. As an operation, therefore, sense cognition and all other cognition is active. As receptive of something external to it, sense cognition is passive. It is exercised efficiently by the knower, it is specified formally by the thing known.[15] The efficient causality of the sensible thing, however, is exercised only upon the principle of the cognitive act. It is not part of the cognition.

There is indeed something in this process that cannot be adequately understood by the human mind, but it is no more mysterious than the imparting of new existence in the real order. The activity of the generative faculties imparts the specific form of the agents to a matter distinct from themselves. It gives that matter a new form, and thereby brings a new individual into being. Through generative activity new being and new form are given to a different individual from the agents. Observed facts indicate this causality throughout the physical world, and permit the ascertaining of the conditions under which it takes place and can be predicted. But how can an existence that the agents do not possess as an act, be given by them to something else? Like all giving of existence, it can be traced back metaphysically to the activity of the first cause. But to understand, from within as it were, the giving of being to something else, one would have to understand the nature of being itself. One would have to understand the very nature of subsistent being. To understand how new being is produced, in the way one understands how equality of its angles to two right angles follows from the nature of a triangle, would require an understanding of the infinite nature of being that would be comparable to one's understanding of the triangle's nature.

Such understanding of being is of course not possessed by the human intellect. Metaphysics can only collect the observed facts, show what actually does happen in sense cognition, and analyze it in terms of being

---

is contrasted with inherent formal causality, *ST*, I, 5, 2c. The other type of extrinsic formal causality, the above texts imply, would be the causality exercised by the object as object. Hence there is a Scholastic division of extrinsic formal causality into exemplar and objective. Suarez (*Disp. Metaph.*, XII, 3, 17; ed. Vivès, XXV, 393b) would reject the tenet that the specifying object is a formal extrinsic cause, on the ground that it does not specify by any real influx, but only by the relation of the faculty to it. He restricts the causality of the object to the efficient causality by which it imprints its species. Suarez' view makes it difficult or perhaps impossible to show that the external thing's content can undergo no change in being known.

[15] See St Thomas, *De Ver.*, XVI, 1, ad 13m; *ST*, I, 77, 3c. Regarding the efficient causality exercised by the sensible thing in impressing its species upon the knower, see *Quodl.*, VIII, 3c; cf. André Hayen, *L'Intentionnel dans la Philosophie de Saint Thomas* (Brussels & Paris, 1942), pp. 138–140. On its "objective causality," see Hayen, pp. 239–240.

as the imparting of new intentional existence to the thing that is in contact with the sensory organ. But how new being is given to it, human metaphysics cannot explain any better and does not explain any worse than it accounts for the imparting of real being to a new individual. Metaphysics can trace, ultimately, any being to the first cause of all being, and can complete its task by showing the reasons why the human mind cannot penetrate any further. Those reasons are the infinite nature of being and the finite capacity of the human cognitive faculties.

Enrichment in Being. Through cognitional activity a knower is continually increasing in being. He keeps adding to his form the forms of other things. The accidental forms acquired in physical being become subjective forms of the agent and of nothing else. But the forms, accidental and substantial, that are received in intentional being remain the forms of things other than the knower. In this way the knower enriches his being in becoming many other things.[16] Most of the accidental forms acquired in real being succeed one another in the myriad changes of daily life, through complementary anabolic and catabolic processes. But the forms acquired in cognitional activity remain after the activity itself has ceased. They can be recalled again in memory. They provide a permanent enrichment of the knower's being. In a man this enrichment can continue to increase throughout the middle years of his life, long after his physical strength has passed its peak. It makes him be innumerably good and beautiful things that he cannot possibly become in real existence.[17] It is his basic means of developing his personality to the full.

Résumé. Basically, then, the approach to the study of cognition is metaphysical. The study is necessarily an investigation from the viewpoint of being. Human cognition presents itself in reflection as an activity specified ultimately by sensible things in their real existence.

---

[16] Reception in real matter is not required for the preservation of the sensible thing's individuality when it is being given intentional existence: ". . . as things are in the soul without their own matter, yet with the singularity and individual conditions that follow upon matter." St Thomas, *Q. de An.*, a. 13c. Though usually calling matter the principle of individuation in sensible things, St Thomas at times attributes individuation to being (e.g., ". . . everything has being and individuation in an identical way." *Q. de An.*, a. 1, ad 2m) or to form (e.g., ". . . every form is an act, and in consequence it is the reason of the unity by which something is one." *De Spir. Creat.*, a. 3c). See texts listed in A. Krempel, *La Doctrine de la Relation chez Saint Thomas* (Paris, 1952), pp. 294, 587–588. On form as individual of itself for Aristotle, see W. Sellars, "Substance and Form in Aristotle," *The Journal of Philosophy*, LIV (1957), pp. 691–692; 698–699.

[17] "And in this way it is possible for the perfection of the whole universe to exist in one thing." St Thomas, *De Ver.*, II, 2c. Cf. *ST*, I, 14, 1c.

Like any other finite action, it produces being. But unlike production of real being, it does not in its immediate activity in man produce any new essence or any new thing. Rather, in its immediate activity it makes something already existent in the real world exist anew in the knowing subject. It imparts a new existence, intentionally, to the same essence that already enjoyed real existence outside cognition.[18] Knower and thing known are united in an immaterial way that does not result in any third thing. Since cognition accordingly produces no addition in the order of essence but only in the order of being, it presents a distinct object of study solely from the viewpoint of being. It provides no new essence that would specify a new and separate science.[19] Nor does it place in-

---

[18] As Yves Simon (*Ontologie du Connaître*, p. 19) notes, one cannot emphasize too strongly that intentional being is a problem not of essence but of existence. This metaphysical viewpoint radically differentiates the Thomistic doctrine of the union of knower and known from the "epistemological monism" of the Neo-Realists. In epistemological monism "the content of knowledge, that which lies in or before the mind when knowledge takes place, is numerically identical with the thing known," as stated in *The New Realism*, cooperative volume by Edwin B. Holt *et al.* (New York, 1922), p. 34. The "independence of things known and the knowing of them" (*ibid.*) was defended on the basis of relations, and so within the order of essences. This explanation, when pressed, did not succeed in accounting for error nor in escaping the "ego-centric predicament," that is, "the impossibility of finding anything that is not known" (p. 11). For a synopsis of the polemic against the New Realists, see J. A. Ryan, "Two Essays on American Critical Realism," *Revue de l'Université d'Ottawa*, VI (1936), Section Spéciale (V), 109*–111*. For longer discussions, see René Kremer, *Le Néo-Réalisme Américain* (Louvain & Paris, 1920); *La Théorie de la Connaissance chez les Néo-Réalistes Anglais* (Louvain & Paris, 1928); and Sister Mary Verda, *New Realism in the Light of Scholasticism* (New York, 1926). The strictly metaphysical viewpoint of the one thing and its diverse existential acts, one real and the others intentional, is required to explain how the real object, existing apart from any perception, may be numerically one with the perceived object at the moment of perception.

[19] In St Thomas himself the strictly metaphysical viewpoint in the study of knowledge is uncontested. E.g., ". . . his doctrine on knowledge and truth. This doctrine the Saint develops as an integral part of his metaphysics, not as an autonomous *Erkenntnistheorie*, outside of and preliminary to the same. The reason is that he regards knowing as a particular manner of being . . ." Leo W. Keeler, *The Problem of Error from Plato to Kant* (Rome, 1934), p. 83. Cf. Joseph Maréchal, *Le Point de Départ de la Métaphysique*, 2nd ed. (Brussels & Paris, 1939), V, 33–39. While admitting the fact, many Neo-Thomists maintain that every metaphysics, including that of St Thomas, presupposes a theory of knowledge by its trust in human cognition. E.g., Gaston Rabeau, *Species Verbum* (Paris, 1938), p. 7. Instead of basing scientific certitude entirely on the being of things, they seem to want a separate guarantee on the side of the knower. In the wake of Jaime Balmès (1810–1848), some required three primitive and immediately known truths for the solution of the critical problem, namely one's own existence as the first fact, the principle of contradiction as the first principle, and the aptitude of the mind for knowledge as the first condition. E.g., Paul Gény, *Critica* (Rome, 1927), pp. 108–116. The concern in this regard is with certitude, a problem that will be examined below, Chapter 18. The difficulty facing the requirement of any prior knowledge of mind is that human cognition has no

tentionally existent things in any priority that would set up a separate starting point for the study of cognition. Sensible things in their real existence are known directly. In knowing these sensible things the knower indirectly knows himself and his cognition. The actual genesis of human cognition, as rendered manifest through reflexive examination, makes the double starting point mandatory for its philosophical study. The real existence of sensible things and the existence of cognition are irreducible

---

such prior nature or structure. The knower, the cognitive faculties, the cognitive acts, all have their own real natures; but each of these natures is knowable only through and from its objects ". . . through the species not indeed of itself but of the object, which is its form; from which it knows the nature of its own act, and from the nature of its act the nature of the knowing power, and from the nature of the power the nature of the essence . . ." St Thomas, *In III Sent.*, d. 23, q. 1, a. 2, ad 3m; ed. Moos, III, 703. This nature, for instance, of the intellect, means accordingly "that it be conformed to things" (*De Ver.*, I, 9c). Cf. *In III De An.*, lect. 7, (ed. Pirotta), nos. 680–682. Cognitionally, therefore, the only form of the cognitive faculty is the form of the thing known. Kant, however, to safeguard universal and necessary knowledge, required a Copernican revolution in viewpoint, in which the object was to conform to the constitution of the knowing faculty (*Critique of Pure Reason*, B xvii). Maréchal, *op. cit.*, V, 33–34, proposes to overcome the resulting agnosticism on the basis of its own Kantian principles. On the impossibility of this task, see Gilson, *Réalisme Thomiste*, pp. 146–155. G. Rabeau, *Le Jugement d'Existence* (Paris, 1938), pp. 70–71, suggests that he himself is following Maréchal in seeing a cognitional apriori in the differences of one cognitive faculty from another. Yet, as has been seen, these differences serve only to specify the different kinds of intentional *being*. They do not contribute anything to the *nature* of the known thing. They furnish no help in structuring the object, since their knowable forms come only from a thing that is known. Bernard J. F. Lonergan, *Insight* (New York, 1957), seeks an "insight into insight" (pp. ix; xxvii; 3) that is "concerned not with the existence of knowledge but with its nature, not with what is known but with the structure of the knowing" (p. xxiii; cf. p. xxix), and that "heads through an understanding of all understanding to a basic understanding of all that can be understood" (p. xxviii). The result is a conception of philosophy in which "cognitional theory" is the basis, and the "pronouncements on metaphysical, ethical, and theological issues" (p. 387) are the expansion. In it, consciousness "is not some inward look but a quality of cognitional acts" (p. 326; cf. p. 320). The method places "the discussion of Self-affirmation prior to the discussion of the Notion of Being" (p. 374). According to it, "objectivity is conceived as a consequence of intelligent inquiry and critical reflection" (p. 388), and things "are concrete syntheses both of the object and of the subject" (p. 267). The aim accordingly is "a philosophy of philosophies" (p. 268). This can only mean that philosophies are to be judged by a philosophy that has philosophy itself as its object, rather than by a metaphysics that bears directly upon things. The zeal to reach "the lost sheep" (p. 745) by use of epistemological techniques in which modern readers have been trained has undoubted apologetic value, for in practice it does as a matter of fact make converts. From a strictly philosophical viewpoint, however, Neoscholastic efforts to proceed from consciousness to things can hardly avoid the aspect of the "nightmare" so vividly described by Régis, *Epistemology*, pp. 74–80. With each new effort, Fr. Régis (p. 74) remarks, the resemblance to the Idealistic original increases.

On phenomenological trends, see Herbert Spiegelberg, *The Phenomenological Movement*, 2 v. (The Hague, 1960).

to each other, even though the knowledge of one's own cognition, because indirect, presupposes the direct knowledge of really existent sensible things.

SUGGESTED READINGS AND REFERENCES

St Thomas Aquinas, *Truth*, II, 2c; tr. Robert W. Mulligan (Chicago: Henry Regnery, 1952), I, 59–66.

Gerard Smith, "A Date in the History of Epistemology," *The Thomist*, V (1943), 246–255.

Louis-Marie Régis, *St. Thomas and Epistemology* (Milwaukee: Marquette University Press, 1946).

Yves R. Simon and J. L. Péghaire, "The Philosophical Study of Sensation," *The Modern Schoolman*, XXIII (1946), 111–119.

Edward MacKinnon, "Atomic Physics and Reality," *The Modern Schoolman*, XXXVIII (1960), 37–59.

Joseph Moreau, "The Problem of Intentionality and Classical Thought," *International Philosophical Quarterly*, I (1961), 215–234.

W. S. Haymond, "Is Distance an Original Factor in Vision?" *The Modern Schoolman*, XXXIX (1961), 39–60.

A. J. McNicholl, "Epistemology and Metaphysics," *Angelicum*, XXXVIII (1961), 200–212.

Cornelius Fay, "The Importance of Count Domet de Vorges in the Return to the Theory of Immediate Realism," *The Modern Schoolman*, XXXIX (1962), 123–134.

CHAPTER 16

Intelligence

Range. Although human intelligence is specified by the quiddity of material things,[1] and so is investigated in natural philosophy, it has aspects that rise above the material order and require treatment in metaphysics. Human intelligence, for instance, can think in terms of being as being. It has been doing so throughout the present study. Being as being, however, extends far beyond the confines of the material order. It extends to the supersensible, as is seen in the demonstration of subsistent being. The scope of human intelligence, therefore, is not limited to the order of material quiddity. Because of the manner in which it apprehends material things in their being through judgment, and not just in their quiddity through simple apprehension, it is able in one way or another to know anything that has the aspect of being. It is in fact into what has the aspect of being that it resolves all its notions,[2] even though it originally grasps that aspect only in material things. As intelligence, then, it has as its object being; for as true all being is intelligible. As human intelligence, it has as its specifying object the quiddity of material things. For it to be human means that in its cognition it proceeds from a form that is the form of a designated matter. It is on a level to which informed matter corresponds as proper object.

What the human intelligence immediately grasps, therefore, is the quiddity and being of sensible things. Yet it is not confined to their range. As intelligence, it attains things under the aspect of being and accordingly extends its scope to all things whatsoever in as much as they have that most universal of all aspects. There is a sense, then, in

[1] "The proper object of the human intellect, which is joined to a body, is the quiddity or nature existent in corporeal matter . . ." St Thomas, *ST*, I, 84, 7c. For Duns Scotus, the first object of the human intellect includes also the immaterial, though this cannot be known except through divine revelation; see *Ordinatio*, Prol., I, 1, no. 33, in *Opera Omnia*, ed. C. Balić (Vatican City, 1950 —), I, 19.12 ff. On the problems involved here, see E. Gilson, "L'Objet de la Métaphysique selon Duns Scot," *Mediaeval Studies*, X (1948), 30–36.

[2] St Thomas, *De Ver.*, I, 1c; ed. Spiazzi, I, 2b.

which the human intellect has unlimited range. However, it is at its ease when dealing with objects that are proportional to its nature as human intelligence, and experiences discomfort when it endeavors to treat of supersensible things.

Universality. Yet even in dealing with sensible things, human intelligence functions in a way that goes beyond the activity of something merely material. Physical matter, as present in the real world, individuates the natures and the activities of which it is a principle. Every act of sensation, though it involves as cognitive the immaterial reception of an object, takes place through a sense organ. In the organ matter is a principle, and conditions the cognitive activity. As a result, sensation attains its objects as individual. What you see is an individual stone or tree, what you hear is an individuated noise. You do not see universal color with the eye, nor do you hear universal sound with the ear. Insofar as the object remains object and does not become a subjective modification of the percipient, the reception of the object into the sense activity is of course immaterial. But in sensation the immaterial way of reception does not prevent the object from remaining individual. Any cognition through a faculty intrinsically dependent on physical matter, as is shown in natural philosophy, attains its object as singular.

The human intellect in its simple apprehension, however, attains in the individual sensible thing an object that extends far beyond the singular. It knows an individual oak tree, for instance, in a way that can leave out of consideration the individual designation and predicate the object known in that singular of any other oak whatsoever. It can further leave out of consideration the specific differentia and apply the generic notion "tree," as known in the oak, to a maple or a pine or a cedar or any other species of tree. In the abstraction in which it exercises its cognitive activity it attains its object universally, and not just individually. This way of knowing rises above the limitations imposed upon a faculty by intrinsic dependence on matter. Its treatment accordingly comes under the scope of metaphysics rather than of natural philosophy.

Necessity. In attaining an object as universal, the human intellect also grasps it as necessary and timeless. By abstracting from individuating matter, the intellect leaves out the element of contingence and change. It knows a tree, for instance, just as a tree. In this knowledge it passes over the designated matter that is the principle of change and time, and so has an object that is timeless. It knows the tree as something living, as a body, as a substance. Regardless of any particular time, a tree is of a nature that possesses those predicates.[3] Its nature is grasped by the intellect in abstraction from time. The designated matter is similarly the principle of contingence in the thing. It is the element that can acquire a new form. It allows the tree to perish into smoke and ashes and so lose its being.[4] With it left out of consideration, the intellect has an object that is necessary. A tree is necessarily something living, a body, and a substance.

Knowledge of Cause. The universality and necessity under which intellection attains its object make possible scientific knowledge. Scientific knowledge has to be of the universal.[5] It requires, for instance, that what is known of a particular piece of sodium in an experiment holds for all such pieces of sodium.[6] It means that what is seen in one individual can be applied to all individuals of the species. When in a Euclidean plane triangle the equality of the angles to two right angles is demonstrated of an individual figure drawn on the board, it emerges as a truth of universal applicability. On the other hand, if a merely individual occurrence is considered without question of any further applicability, it is not yet an object of science. The fact is simply recorded, for instance that the Titanic sank at 2:20 a.m., April 15, 1912. Only when it is considered under an aspect that can be applied to other cases, for example that ships can be sunk by icebergs, does it come under scientific consideration. Universality, and the necessity involved in universality,[7] have to be manifest in a scientific object. These are the characteristics that allow procedure from things known to other things that are as yet unknown.

The basis of universality and necessity in any material thing is its formal cause.[8] This becomes apparent from the functioning of the other causes. The material cause is the principle of singularity and contingence

---

[3] Cf. St Thomas, *Quodl.*, VIII, 1, ad 3m, and text above, Chapter 9, n. 12.

[4] Though contingent, the being of sensible things is known universally by the intellect: "A sense does not know being except as here and now, but the intellect apprehends being absolutely, and for all time." *ST*, I, 75, 6c.

[5] The formula is Aristotle's, *Ph.*, II 5, 417b22–23; *Metaph.*, B 6, 1003a14–15; K 1, 1059b26; 2, 1060b20. The reason is: "If there were no universal, there would be no middle term, and so no demonstration." *APo.*, I 11, 77a7–8. Cf. *Top.*, VIII 14, 164a10–11.

[6] Universal knowledge is accordingly described as potential by Aristotle, *Metaph.*, M 10, 1087a10–17. For his simile that it brings order into a rout, see *APo.*, II 19, 100a12 ff.

[7] On this topic, and its basis in formal causality, see Suzanne Mansion, *Le Jugement d'Existence chez Aristote* (Louvain & Paris, 1946), pp. 18–107.

[8] So Aristotle describes the definition of a thing as "of the universal and of the form." *Metaph.*, Z 11, 1036a28–29.

in the thing.[9] The efficient cause, if it acts necessarily, derives the uniformity of its action from its substantial form. If it acts freely, there will be either no predictability or else the statistical predictability that is based upon the way in which men from their habits and dispositions usually act. The final cause also has its determined nature from its form. To know a singular thing insofar as it gives rise to universal and necessary knowledge, that is, to know it scientifically, is therefore to know it from the viewpoint of its form. Universal and necessary knowledge of sensible things, grounded in this way upon their formal causes, is accordingly knowledge through cause.[10] It can be either direct or reflexive, and so of either the first or the second intention.

First Intention. Any sensible thing, directly known, is grasped as a unit in its real being. It is one thing in its transcendental unity. But it can be represented by the human mind through a series of concepts that widen from individual to highest generic notion, and then into the supergeneric notion of a being. As first the individuation and then the higher differentiae are left out of consideration, the same thing is represented successively under new concepts. Socrates is known as Socrates, as a man, as an animal, as a living thing, as a body, as a substance, and, on the basis of judgment, as a being, in a process by which he is seen respectively in comparison with other men, other animals, other living things, other substances, and other beings.

All these aspects, of course, are present in the sensible individual as first known. No positive content whatsoever is added by any of the further specific and generic concepts. Rather, the composite of them all is first grasped as a unit,[11] that is, as synthesized in the real existence which is prior to their natures. The wider aspects are isolated through the process of abstraction, by successively leaving the differentiae out of consideration. In all these abstractions the sensible thing is what is

[9] For references to discussions on matter as the principle of contingence, see above, Chapter 10, n. 10.

[10] The Platonic background of this doctrine may be seen in the *Meno*, 97D–98A.

[11] Cf.: "It is a complete mistake to ask how concrete particular fact can be built up out of universals. The answer is, 'In no way.' The true philosophic question is, How can concrete fact exhibit entities abstract from itself and yet participated in by its own nature?" Alfred North Whitehead, *Process and Reality* (New York, 1929), p. 30. On the other hand, any corporeal nature is such that when really existent it requires individuation in sensible matter: "It belongs to the notion of this nature that it exist in some individual, which is not without corporeal matter; just as it is of the notion of a stone's nature that it be in a particular stone, and of the notion of a horse's nature that it be in a particular horse, and so with regard to the others. Hence the nature of a stone or of any other material thing cannot be completely and truly known, except as it is known as existing in the particular." St Thomas, *ST*, I, 84, 7c. Cf. Aristotle's texts, above n. 6.

directly known, as Socrates, a man, an animal, and so on. The gaze of the intellect is still focused upon the sensible thing itself. The direct gaze of the intellect upon the thing itself throughout these various abstractions is called technically the **first intention.**

"Intention" in this sense, it will be remembered, came into the Scholastic vocabulary as a translation of an Arabic term meaning concept or notion. It implies nothing mysterious or more difficult than concept or idea. It is merely the intellectual grasp of the thing under a definite aspect. It makes the thing an **object**[12] of cognition. The one real thing becomes a number of different objects, as it is known successively under the various aspects it presents to human cognition. The first intention is accordingly an intellectual attaining of the thing in its real existence, no matter under which concept it represents the thing as object. Under each concept, though, it gives the thing a new intentional existence.

[12] See above, Chapter 15, n. 13. On "object" in St Thomas, see Louis-Marie Régis, *Epistemology* (New York, 1959), p. 176 ff. No matter how abstract the aspect is, it is always apprehended in its reference to an existent thing, for in simple apprehension the intellect "apprehends the quiddity of the thing in a certain comparison with this thing, for it apprehends it as the quiddity of *this* thing." St Thomas, *CG*, I, 59, Amplius. On this "continuation" of human intellection with sense cognition, see André Hayen, *l'Intentionnel dans la Philosophie de Saint Thomas* (Brussels and Paris, 1942), pp. 249–250.

Since the object of the intellect's simple apprehension is always universalized in being known, it does not include the singular directly but only "as though by a certain reflection." St Thomas, *ST*, I, 86, 1c. Because it is abstracted from singulars, the material nature cannot be known as something subsistent in itself but only as something taken from a singular. Known always in a phantasm, it makes the knowledge of the intellect bear upon the thing represented in the phantasm (*De Ver.*, II, 6c), that is, upon a singular thing, and permits the application of the universal to the particular (*ibid.*, ad 3m; cf. X, 5). Through this reflection on the phantasm the singular is indirectly the object of the intellect's simple apprehension. The real being that is the object of the intellect's judgment is of course always individual, since "universals are not subsistent things, but have being in singulars only" (*CG*, I, 65, Ostensum). On the judgments of the singular, see Peter H. J. Hoenen, *Reality and Judgment according to St. Thomas*, tr. Henry F. Tiblier (Chicago, 1952), pp. 217 ff. In sense cognition there is no distinction between the act by which the thing is attained in its qualitative nature and in its existence. The one act of sensation corresponds to the combined acts of simple apprehension and judgment in the intellect. See St Thomas, *In III De An.*, lect. 12, (ed. Pirotta) no. 767. In the act of sensation something existent is attained, for a non-existent could not be the immediate object of any cognition. The senses, of course, cannot consider the being in separation from the nature, as the intellect can. But they do attain the being of the thing in its composition with the accidental essences, and distinguish the being of something red, for instance, from the being of something green. St Thomas, accordingly, speaks without apology of the "judgment of sensation." See list of passages in Hoenen, p. 331, n. 1, and discussion in Hayen, pp. 143–147. There is no need to consider this an improper use of the term "judgment," since it is an apprehension of being, even though the apprehension does not take place under the aspect of being. St Thomas calls the "proper operation" of a sense a "judgment" (*Quodl.*, VIII, 3c), and distinguishes between aspects (not operations) of apprehension and judgment in it (*De Ver.*, I, 11c).

Second Intention. The intellect is also able to reflect on its own activities and processes. It is able to see that what is one in real being has become multiple in cognitional being, as the one real man is represented separately as Socrates, as man, as animal, as living thing, as body, and as substance. The same thing is seen as several objects, each object having its own separate act of intentional being. These objects of simple apprehension are common natures. Each just in itself has no being, but is able to be either in reality or in cognition. Each is seen by the intellect, first in its real existence, and then, through reflection, in its intentional being. Considered separately as it is in intentional being, each appears as a representation through which the real thing is known.

As the intellect in its reflexive gaze views each of these representations separately, it sees them as ever widening objectivations of the same real thing. It compares them with one another. It sees that the object "man" leaves out of consideration the individual characteristics of Socrates, and so can be found identified equally well in reality with Plato, Caesar, Kennedy, Castro, and innumerable other instances. Understood in this way, the object "man" is technically called a lowest universal or a **species.** The predication "Man is a species" may be made. From the same viewpoint, Socrates, Plato, and the other instances are technically known as **individuals.** You may accordingly make the predication "Socrates is an individual." In a corresponding manner the intellect may leave out of consideration the specific differentia of man and have an object, "animal," that can be seen identified in reality equally well with horses and elephants and hundreds of other species. So understood, the object is technically called a **genus,** and allows the predication "Animal is a genus." The higher genera are subject to the same process. They are the higher universals.[13]

---

[13] Cf. Aristotle, *APo.*, II 19, 100a10–b3; St Thomas, *De Ente et Essentia*, c. II, (ed. Roland-Gosselin) p. 10.15 ff. The ascending series of universal natures became known in later Scholasticism as "the metaphysical grades" — *gradus metaphysici*, John of St Thomas, *Ars Logica*, II, 3, 6; ed. B. Reiser, I, 337a40–b2. "Metaphysical" here seems meant to signify abstraction. "Universal" in application to the abstract natures has given rise to much confusion in Scholastic tradition. For Suarez (*Disp. Metaph.*, VI, 8, 3–4; ed. Vivès, XXV, 232–233), the existent nature itself is called the physical universal (*in re, materialiter*), and distinguished from the metaphysical universal (*ante rem*) and the logical universal (*post rem*). The physical universal, however, has for him formal unity of its own. For John of St Thomas (*Log.*, II, 3, 5; I, 333a42 ff.) the nature itself is the metaphysical universal, and is called the material universal as it is in the thing, but fundamental universal when considered with absolute unity of precision. In Neoscholasticism the Thomistic common nature is sometimes called the "direct universal"; e.g., Joseph de Tonquédec, *La Critique de la Connaissance* (Paris, 1929), p. 156; cf. p. 160. In so naming it, one should keep

In all this reflexive activity the intellect is gazing not directly at the thing in its real existence, but at that thing as already objectified in various intentional existences. The view is now of a different kind from the first direct way of looking at the thing in the real world. It is now reflexion, and not direct cognition of a real thing. It is a second gaze at the thing, but now at the thing as found in a new intentional existence. This second or reflexive gaze at the thing in any of its various representations or objectivations is accordingly called the **second intention.** The reflection, of course, could be continued *ad infinitum,* and each new concept would be the concept of the preceding concept. Each new reflexive gaze, however, would be called simply another second intention.

Objects of First and Second Intention. Two different types of predicate, therefore, may be applied to a sensible thing. On the one hand, there are the specific and generic natures that characterize the thing wherever it is found, and the accidents that it has in the real world. These are predicates of the first intention. "Socrates is a man, is an animal, is a body, is pale, is cultured, is running," are instances of predication in the first intention. Even when Socrates is just imagined to be running or to be in a trance, the predicates are still of the first intention. The essential predicates go with the thing in whatever being it may happen to have.[14] The nature of real accidents is to characterize a thing in its real being. Their natures keep them predicates of the first intention, even when applied in imaginary cases. On the other hand, there are predicates that of their nature apply just to a thing in its intentional being. These are characteristics that arise only when the thing receives cognitional being in the knower.[15] As the object of the intellect's reflection, Socrates appears as an individual,[16] man appears as a species, animal appears as a genus. Man is seen as a concept and as predicable of Socrates. Animal is seen as an object and as predicable of man. Predicates like species, genus, concept, object, predicable, pertain to the second intention. Intentional being, accordingly, is of two sorts, first and second. The first intention bears directly upon the thing as it is in real being or in the imagination. The second intention bears only upon the thing as it is in intentional being in the intellect.

---

in mind that the common nature is neither directly known in itself as common, nor is it properly universal. The universal is for St Thomas an *unum quid* (*De Ente,* c. III; p. 27.9), while the nature as common or absolutely considered is not *una* (p. 24.11).

[14] *De Ente,* c. III; pp. 24.1 ff.

[15] *Ibid.,* p. 28.1–11. Cf. *De Pot.,* VII, 9c.

[16] See text above, Chapter 4, n. 3.

"Individual," "object," "concept," "species," "genus," and "predicable," then, do not characterize a thing in its real existence. What is in the real world is Socrates. He is, in the same real being, the man and the animal and the substance. Viewed reflexively, however, Socrates has in the knower's intellection one act of intentional being, his specific nature has another act of intentional being, and correspondingly his generic nature has its own separate intentional being.[17] The predications then made are "Socrates is an individual," "Man is a species," "Animal is a genus." The act of judgment, which attains their being, separates them instead of joining them as in the first intention. You say "The individual Socrates is not the species 'man'" and "The species 'man' is not the genus 'animal.'" In the first intention, on the contrary, you say "Socrates is a man." "Man is an animal." Viewed in the first intention, Socrates and man and animal have but the one existential act. Viewed in the second intention, each has its own separate existential act. In real being, they are one. As objects of the second intention, on the other hand, they are diverse in being.

Each object of the second intention is accordingly a distinct "being of reason" (*ens rationis*).[18] For convenience, each may by way of technical shorthand be called a "second intention," instead of "an object of the second intention." Second intentions by which concepts stand in definite relation to one another constitute the object of logic. Correspondingly, objects of the first intention may be called simply "first intentions." They are objects of the sciences that deal with real things.

Structure of Objects. For the logician, the terms that constitute the subject and predicate of propositions are absolutely basic. These are, for instance, Socrates, man, animal, red, cold, running. They are the materials from which the whole structure of human knowledge, as viewed by the logician, is built. They are accepted by him as given, and are not submitted to any deeper analysis. For the metaphysician, however, each such finite term is a composite of essence and being. Socrates, man, animal, living thing, body, substance, accident, are things or natures that when viewed directly in the first intention have in the sensible world real being, distinct from themselves. Further, viewed through reflection, they are seen as having each its own intentional being in one's mind. In either case, in the actual composition, the being is prior to the nature. For the metaphysician, then, neither the nature predicated nor the subject of predication, as they are attained through

[17] See *De Ente*, c. III; p. 28.11–15.
[18] See above, Chapter 2, nn. 18–19.

simple apprehension, is the prior constituent.[19] From the metaphysician's viewpoint the being of the things, whether it is real or intentional, is always prior to the things themselves. The logically "simple object" is structured entitatively.

Concept. By the very act of knowing the really existent thing, the intellect gives it intentional being. By reflection the intellect then knows it through a new act of cognition as an existent in the mind. In this reflection the intellect sees it as a concept, and so can make a predication like "Animality is a generic concept." In seeing it as a concept, the intellect sees it as an intellectual representation through which and in which the really existent thing is known. From that viewpoint it may be called an intelligible similitude[20] or likeness of the external thing. In Scholastic Latin it is called a *species*,[21] in the meaning of "likeness" or "image" that is carried by the Latin term.

---

[19] The opposite view is "One cannot judge that a thing exists . . . unless existence has already (by an analytical priority) been conceived." J. Bobik, "Some Comments . . ." *The New Scholasticism*, XXXIII (1959), 69. Cf. above, Chapter 7, n. 12.

[20] St Thomas describes the similitude as "impressed" on the mind, but, against an Avicennian background, in the sense of a similitude that is not abstracted. See *In II Sent.*, d. 17, q. 1, a. 1, ad 4m (ed. Mandonnet, II, 415); *De Ver.*, VIII, 7c and ad 4m. Cf. *ST*, I, 85, 1, ad 3m. The concept is also called regularly a *verbum*, "word," as "the word of the heart signified by the word of the voice." *ST*, I, 27, 1c. Against an Augustinian background the *verbum* is likewise described as "impressed." See *In I Sent.*, d. 27, q. 2, a. 1, Solut.; I, 654–655. The concept is described by St Thomas as both what is understood and the means of understanding it: "And therefore the conception of the intellect is not only that which is understood, but is also that by which the thing is understood. In this way what is understood can be said to be both the thing itself and the conception of the intellect; and similarly what is said can be said to be both the thing that is said through the word, and the word itself." *De Ver.*, IV, 2, ad 3m. Cf. *Quodl.*, VIII, 4c. In later Scholasticism "objective concept" was used for the thing conceived or object of the concept, and "formal concept" for the similitude in the mind. See Suarez, *Disp. Metaph.*, II, 1, 1; ed. Vivès, XXV, 64–65. Also John of St Thomas, *Log.*, II, 2, 2; ed. Reiser, I, 291a4–25.

A *verbum* is required by both the first (simple apprehension) and the second (judgment) operations of the mind. See St Thomas, *De Ver.*, IV, 2c; *Quodl.*, V, 9c. He describes it as *expressivum* (*ST*, I, 34, 3c), and as something the intellect forms and "can also express by voice" (*De Pot.*, IX, 5c). Cf. *ST*, 85, 2, ad 3m. The development of St Thomas' thought on the topic is sketched by J. de la Vassière, "Le Sens du Mot 'Verbe Mental' dans les Ecrits de Saint Thomas," *Archives de Philosophie*, III, 2 (Paris, 1925), 168–175. See also Gaston Rabeau, *Species. Verbum* (Paris, 1938).

[21] E.g.: "And yet the stone is what is understood, and not the species of the stone, except by the reflection of the intellect upon itself; otherwise the sciences would not be about things, but about intelligible species." St Thomas, *ST*, I, 76, 2, ad 4. For other numerous instances, see Ludwig Schütz, *Thomas-Lexikon* (Paderborn, 1895), s.v., e). *Species intelligibilis* is also used by St Thomas for the form that actuates the intellect in first actuality and is not immediately known except by reflection: "Therefore the intelligible species that is the principle of the intellectual operation necessarily differs

The concept, accordingly, is something that is produced by the activity of intellection, while the thing known in it is not so produced but is presupposed. The concept is produced as a similitude of the thing in order that the thing itself may be known in and through it. Its whole purpose, like the purpose of intentional being in general, is to enable you to know something else. Its knowable content is the same as the thing itself, but it is that content as actuated by intentional being. In this way the intelligible similitude differs from the thing, even though in it the knower is made one with the thing. The thing can have either kind of being. The similitude is the same knowable content considered precisely as in intentional being. The concept, therefore, is the content as it exists in the intellect and not in the thing, in a way that constitutes a distinct object for reflection.

But why is such a concept required? In external sensation, nothing comparable is necessary. The thing is concretely present to the sense, and so can be perceived as there in itself. It is seen and heard and felt in itself, and not in any image. However, for imagination and sense memory, a sensible similitude is indeed required. When you imagine a mountain of gold, your cognition has an object that just is not there to be known in itself. The mountain of gold is of course what is attained by the cognitive act, for it is the mountain of gold that is imagined. Yet it is not attained in itself, but only in an image in the imagination. Imaginitive cognition, accordingly, has to take place in an image that it itself produces. The same holds for sense memory. A thing seen yesterday can be remembered in a sensible image, even though it is not here today to be perceived in itself. The external senses become a thing intentionally without forming an image of the thing. Only by expressing an image of it, on the other hand, can imagination and sense memory intentionally become the thing.

These reasons alone would require that the intellect produce a corresponding similitude, since it too can remember things and think of things that have no real existence. But there is another reason that makes cognition in a similitude necessary for every act of the human intellect. The intellect knows the sensible thing in abstraction. It knows

from the word of the heart that is formed through the operation of the intellect; although the word itself can be called an intelligible species or form, as constituted by the intellect . . ." *Quodl.*, V, 9c. *Species impressa* is used for the species that is the principle of the intellectual operation by Suarez, *Disp. Metaph.*, VI, 5, 7; XXV, 226b. Suarez (*De Angelorum Natura*, II, 27, 25; II, 25) is aware of the phrasing "express one's concept." With John of St Thomas the wording of the contrast as *species impressa* (*medium quo*) and *species expressa* (*medium in quo*) is fullfledged in Scholastic tradition. See *Log.*, II, 22, 2–3; I, 702a44 ff. The study of the processes by which the species are impressed and expressed pertains to natural philosophy.

Socrates as man, as animal, and so on. Those objects of the intellect's first intention are not present in the thing as distinct objects. They cannot be known in themselves in the way a concrete thing is seen with the eye. They have to be made present to the human intellect in a much less material way than in the sensible body.[22] They are represented, consequently, in an intelligible similitude in order to be grasped by the simple apprehension of the intellect. Human intellection is of such a nature that it has to produce an intelligible similitude in which it may know its object. While in external sensation the knower becomes one with the known in direct contact, in imagination and memory and intellection the knower becomes identified with the thing just by means of and in a similitude.

The cognitional similitude or image, however, is not to be conceived in the manner of a material picture or a mirror. The picture on the wall, rather, is seen as the direct object of cognition, and through it Lincoln is remembered. But in the intelligible similitude or concept of Lincoln, Lincoln himself is the direct object of the cognition and the similitude is known only through vague concomitant consciousness. To know it as a concept or similitude, and so to be fully aware of its presence, a new act of reflex cognition has to be focused upon it. Its status can be illustrated only very imperfectly by the illusion you might have for a moment when on ringing at a prison entrance you see the guard appear suddenly in the unsuspected mirror behind the gate, and you believe for the instant that you are looking directly at him.[23] Or, when you are watching a stereoscopic moving picture, you may get the illusion for a while that you yourself are in the roller-coaster and you lose the awareness that you are seeing it on a screen. Just as through illusions the cognitional medium escapes one's vision in those cases, so in actuality the intelligible concept avoids one's direct cognition and has to be known through reflection.

When the actual intellection ceases, the concept in which it took place remains stored in the intellectual memory. It reverts from the order of operation or second actuality to the order of first actuality, the order of being as contrasted with operation. Of the similitude in this order of

[22] ". . . also it understands the thing as separated from the material conditions without which it does not exist in reality . . ." *CG*, I, 53, Ulterius. This means that intellection is a more immaterial way of knowing than is sensation, for cognition is graded according to degree of immateriality; *De Ver.*, XXIII, 1c; *ST*, I, 14, 1c.

[23] In contrast to the intelligible similitude as a *medium in quo formale et intrinsecum,* a mirror in which the image of a man is seen is regarded by John of St Thomas (*Log.*, II, 22, 1; I, 693b42 ff.) as a material and extrinsic *medium in quo.* On the absence of an image in external sensation, see St Thomas, *Quodl.*, V, 9, ad 2m; cf. VIII, 3c, and *ST*, I, 27, 5c & I, 85, 2, ad 3m. The sensible thing, however, "impresses" (*Quodl.*, V, 9, ad 2m; *ST*, I, 85, 1, ad 3m) its form upon the sense.

first actuality, one has no immediate consciousness. One reasons to its presence there through the fact that the form of a thing once known remains in the intellect through memory. One reasons also that whatever the intellect becomes in second actuality, it already has to be in first actuality, since its operation proceeds according to its form. It must therefore possess in first actuality the form of the thing known, before it can become the thing in cognitional activity. It has therefore to be informed in first actuality by the thing known, before it can know the thing in actual cognition. This reason holds for all cognition, including that of the external senses. Even though the external and the first of the internal senses attain their object in itself and not in an image, they have to be informed in first actuality by the thing in order to become it in second actuality. But that informing lasts only as long as the action of the sensible thing upon the sensory organs. The image that is conserved is the image that has been expressed in actual cognition, as in the imagination. As the human intellect always expresses similitudes of the things it knows, it is always able to conserve them.

Résumé. Through sense cognition a man is able to become intentionally one by one the sensible things he encounters in his daily life. He enriches himself with their forms as he perceives each of them in actuality, and conserves the forms in his imagination. But through intellection he is able to transcend the confines of the here and now, and become objects whose extent is unlimited. In knowing a thing under the aspect of universality, he knows it in a way that holds for all possible instances of its common nature, past, present, and future. He is enriched with a form that breaks through individuating conditions and equips him to deal with unlimited occurrences of its nature. Though remaining an individual he is brought by intellection into a life that bursts away from the ghetto of his immediate surroundings and extends as far as do the natures of the things with which he comes in contact, that is, universally.

In knowing sensible things under the aspect of universality, a man likewise transcends the contingence of the singular and acquires knowledge that is necessary. In the intellection he penetrates[24] to the essences

[24] "'Penetration' for St. Thomas is not an operation which pierces a material and accidental crust to feed upon a 'pure essential' or substantial core but is a figure of speech for intellection . . . accidents as well as substances have their *intima*, their intelligibility." R. B. Gehring, "The Knowledge of Material Essences according to St. Thomas Aquinas," *The Modern Schoolman*, XXXIII (1956), 181. On Maritain's notion of "perinoetic" knowledge, see below, Chapter 20, n. 10. Since through being known a thing is made an object, Maritain (*The Degrees of Knowledge*, tr. G. B. Phelan [New York, 1959], pp. 93–94) calls the knower a cisobjective subject,

of things, on both the accidental and substantial levels. Recognizing the necessities of essences, he is able to follow out their implications and reason to things he does not immediately know. Through science he can enrich himself with myriad forms that could never impinge themselves on his immediate cognition. In grasping the being of sensible things through the second operation of the intellect,[25] he has the starting point from which he can reach subsistent being. By intellective reflection he becomes himself intentionally and is himself in a way that enables him to dominate his own activity. Knowing his own actions through reflection he has starting points for the investigation of spiritual nature.

The kinds of things that a man can know through his intellect are consequently unlimited. This aspect under which intellection takes place is the aspect of being, which extends to all things. As long as a man has the sensible or other data from which a thing can in some way be reached, he is able to know it at least as a being. Intellection, therefore, is able to enrich the knower cognitionally with the form of anything

---

and the thing known a transobjective subject. In the use of this terminology care has to be taken to avoid conceiving the "object" as a prior datum through which knower and thing known are attained.

[25] The unicity of the intelligible species in any one judgment is stressed by Frederick D. Wilhelmsen, *Man's Knowledge of Reality* (Englewood Cliffs, N. J., 1956), pp. 109–110. From the nature of the judgment, however, the species is that of the synthesis of subject and predicate, not that of either the subject or the nature predicated. The intellect "understands the proposition simultaneously, not first the subject and afterwards the predicate; because in one species of the whole it knows all the parts." St Thomas, *CG*, I, 55, Intellectus. Cf.: It "understands simultaneously the subject and the predicate . . ." *ST*, I, 58, 2c. "For it does not understand a house by understanding first the foundation and then the wall and then the roof; but it understands all these simultaneously, insofar as a unit arises out of them. Likewise it understands the subject and predicate simultaneously, insofar as a unit arises out of them, namely the affirmation and the negation." *In VI Metaph.*, lect. 4, (ed. Cathala-Spiazzi) no. 1229. The species, accordingly, is that of the affirmation or negation, not that of the nature predicated.

For Wilhelmsen the "intelligibility of the subject is the predicate" (p. 105). The "subject of judgment is, as it were, the finger of the intelligence pointing at a thing" (p. 108), and therefore "the meaning of the subject is *symbolized* meaning" (p. 111). The predicate, of course is formal with regard to the subject, insofar as it qualifies the subject either substantially or accidentally. But from a metaphysical viewpoint the meaning of the subject, as subject, is all its concrete reality, both substantial and accidental, as is illustrated in the last text quoted above from St Thomas. In "The house is roofed," the subject means the totality of foundations, walls, roof, and so on, as one whole. Meaning is not added to it by the predicate. Rather, the meaning of the predicate is known in the subject's concrete richness; cf. above, Chapter 16, n. 11. "A sash is red" has a notably different meaning from "A rose is red" or "A brick is red." The subject, as such, has a distinct meaning in each of these sentences, while the meaning of the predicate remains the same. Further, the reason why you may say "A square is a foursided figure," but not "A circle is a foursided figure," lies in the different meaning of the respective subjects.

whatsoever. Those forms remain with the knower permanently as intelligible similitudes in which the thing may again be actually known at any time. There need be little wonder, then, that Aristotle saw in intellection the supreme happiness and destiny of man, and that according to Christian faith the Beatific Vision is the ultimate goal of human living.

SUGGESTED READINGS AND REFERENCES

Aristotle, *Metaphysics*, Λ 9, 1074b15 ff.

St Thomas Aquinas, *On the Power of God* (*De Potentia*), VIII, 1c, and IX, 5c; tr. English Dominican Fathers (London: Burns Oates & Washbourne Ltd., 1932–1934), III, 70 ff. and 123 ff.

——— *Summa Theologiae*, I, 84–87; tr. English Dominican Fathers (London: Burns Oates & Washbourne Ltd., 1911–1925), IV, 156 ff.

George P. Klubertanz, "St. Thomas and the Knowledge of the Singular," *The New Scholasticism*, XXVI (1952), 135–166.

CHAPTER 17

Knowledge of Truth

Errors. The process of enriching one's personality through intellective acquisition of new being, however, turns out in practice to be far from continuous and unilinear. Quite early in childhood one's judgment that Christmas gifts are put under the tree by a whitebearded Santa Claus is abandoned as false. The conviction that one can rely on a particular neighbor's word is shattered when he fails to keep a promise. The belief that the ice on a pond is thick enough for skating turns out to be wrong when one falls through. In innumerable cases a person discovers upon examination or from sad experience that what he had considered to be knowledge was not genuine knowledge at all but merely deception. Such cognition does not provide any more enrichment than does a counterfeit bill. It has to be cast aside and replaced by other cognition.

After experiences of error one wishes not merely to acquire cognition of things, but to know that each particular instance of cognition is genuine and not of the bogus type so often encountered. This is expressed by saying that one wants to know that one's cognition is true. Not only knowledge, but knowledge of the truth, is required for the cognitional enrichment of the human intellect. The experience of frequent errors leaves a man's natural desire for knowledge unsatisfied until he knows that the knowledge he has is true.

Judgment and Fact. But what is truth? The question of Pilate rings through the centuries, and has received widely varying answers in different philosophies. As already seen,[1] truth is concerned not just with essences but with being. It is found therefore formally not in the act of simple apprehension, but in judgment. The truth to which one swears in a traffic case, for instance, is neither "the light" nor "red," but that "the light was red." This statement and the judg-

[1] Above, Chapter 8, n. 20.

ment it expresses are considered to have the characteristic of truth. They are regarded as true because they both express the actual fact at the time, namely that in reality the light was red. The contrary judgment "the light was green" would be held false, because at the moment the light really was red. Truth, accordingly, pertains to the judgment, and is had when the judgment expresses the being or not-being that is present in the thing.

But how can truth be *known*? The sole means one has of originally knowing a thing's being or not-being is the judgment. Only through a judgment did one know that the light was red. The fact is grasped through the judgment alone. How, then, can the fact be represented apart from the judgment by which it is known? How can the fact be set up as a separate object and used as a means to determine whether or not the judgment is true? The fact is what specifies the judgment and gives the judgment cognitional content. Apart from the fact, the judgment has no cognitional content whatsoever. A judgment's own content, therefore, cannot be immediately the means of determining whether or not it is true. Yet only judgment grasps the being or not-being of the thing. Is a further judgment, then, required? If so, what will its object be? It can hardly consist in a mere repetition of the prior judgment, for the problem would still remain. The prior judgment, though an activity, somehow has to be made into an object and confronted with the fact, as one object with another. But how can this be done? A penetrating and detailed analysis of one's direct and reflex judgments, coupled with an investigation of the way a judgment grasps real being, is quite pointedly demanded by the question.

Analysis of Judgments. For sensible things, being always consists in a composition. In Khrushchev real being, substantial and accidental, composes into a single whole the matter and form and accidents that make up the living Khrushchev at a particular moment of time. In the existential synthesis Khrushchev is grasped by the intellect through its act of direct judgment. The judgment is expressed by saying that Khrushchev is a man, is stocky, is the leader of the U.S.S.R. It cannot be expressed in the simple form of an incomplex concept, or by a noun or verb spoken separately. It has to be expressed by way of an active synthesis. Even in a judgment that states only the existence of the thing, the expression is still by way of active synthesis: "Khrushchev exists." In material things the existential act is always an actually exercised synthesis, and has to be expressed that way.

But the intellect can also reflect upon its act of direct judgment. It apprehends, by a new and reflex judgment, the act of direct judgment as existing in its own cognition. It makes the reflex judgment "I am thinking that Khrushchev is a man." What is synthesized in that reflex judgment is "I am thinking," or "My thought," on the one hand, with "Khrushchev is a man," on the other. It is the new synthesis that is given intentional being in the mind through the reflex act of judgment. The prior combination "Khrushchev is a man" is not at all synthesized anew, but is viewed as an object already complete and static, as it were in a still-life shot.

Reflexive Simple Apprehension. In this way an already elicited judgment appears spread out as it were in flat projection to the simple apprehension focusing upon it. So held before the intellect's reflexive gaze, the judgment as object can readily be analyzed into its components. It has two terms, "Khrushchev" and "man." Each term is given separate intentional being as it is made an object of the mind's analyzing process.[2] Each appears as a concept through which a really existent thing has been known. Similarly the union between the two, expressed by the copula "is," appears as a separate object enjoying its own act of intentional being. It is seen as a link that can be made the subject of predication. You can say: "The 'is' is the copula in this assertion; it represents conceptually the real existential synthesis of the two terms." In the copulative concept "is" the real existence grasped in the direct judgment is statically represented.[3] In the concept, however, it is not making anything exist. It is not actively synthesizing anything. Rather, it itself is made to exist only by another act of intentional being, an act that is given it by the intellect's reflection and that is other than it. It is now an object of simple apprehension. It can be expressed in a simple verb-concept and signified by the one word "is." As object of reflexive analysis it is no longer grasped by way of a complexity. Just as actually exercised existence can be conceptualized under the notion of act, so the "is" in the reflexively considered judgment appears under the general notion of a synthesis, of a union or link between

[2] Cf.: "What are composed and divided by the intellect are by their nature able to be considered separately by it." St Thomas, *CG*, I, 58, Adhuc. ". . . the intelligible species represents the one in such a way that it does not represent the other. Hence in understanding what man is, we do not thereby understand the other things that are in him, but separately in a certain succession." *ST*, I, 14, 14c.

[3] "In the third way, what signifies the truth of the composition in propositions is called being, insofar as 'is' is called the copula; and in this way it is, in regard to its completion, in the composing and dividing intellect, but it is based upon the thing's being, which is the act of the essence." *In I Sent.*, d. 33, q. 1, a. 1, ad 1m; ed. Mandonnet, I, 766.

subject and predicate, though it is not actively effecting any synthesis. It does not represent the real existential synthesis in the immediately corresponding way in which the concept "green" represents the color green. Rather, it represents in still-life what was not originally grasped in still-life fashion. Accordingly the reflexive simple apprehension, while not itself synthesizing the terms, is seeing them as already synthesized in its object, that is, in the act of judgment previously made.

When real existence is conceptualized in the first intention, it is represented first and foremost as actuality, and only secondarily as a synthesis. The notion of synthesis accordingly can be eliminated from it as it is applied to subsistent being. As object of the second intention, in the analysis of the judgment, the notion of synthesis is on the contrary dominant. This occasions difficulty for the logician in explaining judgments in which existence is the only act predicated, as "Khrushchev exists." The being that is signified by the copula interests the logician only insofar as it is a synthesis of subject and predicate. As a logician, he has no means of knowing the real act that the reflexively known synthesis represents, for that act is not exercised in the mental synthesis.[4] "Man" is a common nature that appears essentially the same in both real and intentional being. Existence, on the contrary, loses what is most characteristic of it when it is seen in a flat concept instead of in an actually exercised synthesis. In the second intention it appears merely as a link between two already established concepts.

From the logician's viewpoint, accordingly, the subject and predicate terms are regarded as prior to the synthesis. They are looked upon by him as the given materials, to be joined or separated by a synthesis or division that is subsequent to them. They are viewed as building blocks that are already there to be brought together, as separate parts that are to be put together on the assembly line. The acts of intentional existence that give them being as separate units escape the regard of the logician. He is interested only in the being that is objectified as the synthesis of the two terms and that appears as a still-life bond of union. He has no notion of the actual priority of being to essence. The metaphysician, however, has to keep that priority in view as he analyzes the act of judgment and explains its bearing on the real existential synthesis exercised in the outside world.

Object of Judgment. From the metaphysician's viewpoint, then, a prior synthesizing act of existence makes a thing be either in reality or in cognition. This synthesizing act is apprehended

[4] Cf. Etienne Gilson, *Being and Some Philosophers*, 2nd ed. (Toronto, 1952), pp. 190 ff.

through judgment. It is the object of the judgment. It is an object that is not a still-life relation, which would be an essence, but is rather an existential joining of the essential elements, a joining that is other than any essence. On account of the receptive phase of all cognition, the object here has to be known through a cognitional act that exhibits a corresponding structure. Judgment accordingly is a cognition that has the character of an active synthesis. The cognition proper to judgment, metaphysically considered, is therefore not a further simple apprehension, as though a still-life shot of a relation between subject and predicate terms. It is a direct cognition of their being as that being is exercised, namely as a synthesis. In the one synthesis, the one act of being, Khrushchev is a man, an animal, a living thing, a body, a substance. In accidental being he is stocky, cunning, aggressive, a Communist, a world leader. In intentional being in the mind he is an individual and a subject of predication. Through acts of simple apprehension the intellect knows these characteristics according to their natures, and through judgment it knows them according to their being in the one man Khrushchev. What the judgment attains, then, is real being when it bears upon things in the real world, and intentional being when it bears on things as they are in cognition. When you say "The tree before my eyes in the garden is green," the being that is known is obviously the real being of the tree. You are perceiving that the tree really is green. You are not saying that the tree exists in your intellect, or that it is green in your intellect. The direct object of such a judgment is clearly the being that the tree exercises in the real world.

But how can real existence be a direct object of apprehension in the judgment? To know something means to be it intentionally. How can you at all be the real existence of anything without thereby giving both yourself and the thing real existence? But in knowing the real existence of an external thing you are not thereby making either yourself or it really exist. Is not the very notion of intentionally becoming real existence a contradiction in terms?

The objection would hold if the existence of sensible things were in itself the thing or reality that the intellect became intentionally. If their existence were a finite thing or a finite reality, it would be known through an act of simple apprehension and would not call for a judgment. But it is the synthesizing act of a reality without being a reality in itself. It is other than the finite thing it actuates. In cognition the intellect becomes the finite thing intentionally. Through simple apprehension the intellect becomes it according to its essence. But the essence as absolutely considered cannot be the object of any immediate cognition. To be known it has to be there, in either real or intentional being. To be known, it has to be already actuated by existence. To know it as it is, to become it intentionally as it is, the intellect has to know it according to the existence by which it is actuated. It knows it in this way through the synthesizing act of judgment, and not through another act of simple apprehension. In the case of a really existing thing, what the intellect becomes is a thing synthesized by real existence. The intellect is informed intentionally by the thing's form, but it is not made to exist by the thing's real existence. In knowing through judgment that the thing really exists, the intellect does not become intentionally any real existence, but becomes intentionally a really existent thing. There is no contradiction in the notion of becoming cognitionally a thing that is really existent. The objection arises from an attempt to view the immediate object of cognition as an essence absolutely considered.

In true predication, the objects that constitute the terms differ in first intention, even though if they belong to the same category they both together have but the one real being. In the first intention man and animal are different objects from Khrushchev. Both are much wider than he, for they are found in many other men and many other animals. Yet both these natures belong to Khrushchev in real identity. They are one with him in real being. It is that real synthesizing being that you directly apprehend in your judgment "Khrushchev is a man." The difference from the case of an imaginary man is apparent enough. When you say "Colonel Blimp is a man," you apprehend a different kind of being. It is intentional being, being in the imagination, even though it is the object of a direct judgment. The corresponding reflex judgment would be "I am imagining that Colonel Blimp is a man." In the analysis of the reflex judgments, "man" appears as a predicate of Khrushchev and of Colonel Blimp. It is a concept that is not the concept of Khrushchev and not the concept of Blimp. But it is a predicate of either. The still-life union or nexus of concepts expressed by "predicate of" is evidently enough of a different object from the actual synthesizing in real being that is known through the judgment "Khrushchev is a man," and the actual synthesizing in intentional being that is apprehended in "Colonel Blimp is a man." If the predication is accidental, as "Khrushchev is embracing Gagarin," the synthesizing takes place in accidental being, but the above observations apply in corresponding fashion.

In identical predication the objects do not differ in the first intention, but only in the second. When you say "Khrushchev is Khrushchev," you take the same object of the first intention, Khrushchev, and consider it first as a subject and then as a predicate. The concept of Khrushchev as subject is different from the concept of Khrushchev as predicate. You are not saying that one concept is the other. But you are saying that Khrushchev in real existence is Khrushchev. Your judgment of identity here has real existence as its direct object.[5]

Object of Reflex Judgment. In reflection, you see that a thing like a tree exists also in your intellect. Here the being is likewise a synthesis, and is the immediate object of the reflexive *judgment*. Unlike the reflexive simple apprehension, a reflexive judgment is not a still-life viewing of a previous cognition. It is a grasping of new being, of being that was not present in any other judgment. Further reflexive judgments synthesize with tree notions like concept, subject of predication, and so on, as you see that the tree is an individual, and is the subject of the predicate "green," and is a concept of the first intention, and the like. As a term that is synthesized, "green" is likewise

[5] Cf.: "But our intellect, in apprehending the incomplex, does not yet reach its ultimate perfection because it is still in potency with regard to composition and division; just as in natural things the simple are in potency with regard to the mixed, and the parts in respect to the whole." St Thomas, *CG*, I, 59, Adhuc. "Because our intellect forms different conceptions for knowing subject and accident, and for knowing different accidents . . . to know the inherence of the one in the other, it composes one species with another, and unites them in a way, and so forms enuntiations in itself." *De Ver.*, II, 7c. The view that knowledge consists in perceiving the agreement or disagreement between the mental representations may be seen in Locke: "Since the mind, in all its thoughts and reasonings, hath no other immediate object but its own ideas, which it alone does or can contemplate, it is evident that our knowledge is only conversant about them. Knowledge then seems to me to be nothing but *the perception of the connexion of and agreement, or disagreement and repugnancy of any of our ideas.* In this alone it consists." *An Essay concerning Human Understanding*, IV, 1, 1–2; ed. Fraser (Oxford, 1894), II, 167. Strangely, the fact of identical predication has been used to show that for St Thomas "the judgment is concerned with the composition of concepts and not with human *existere* in its outward reality." L.-M. Régis, *Epistemology* (New York, 1959), p. 324. This confuses the act of judging with the judgment as object of reflexive simple apprehension. The second argument of Fr Régis (*ibid.*) is that "the *est* which signifies the composition made by the mind" is an accident, while real existence as "an act of the substance" is substantial. The argument seeks support in a text of St Thomas meant to show that "It is accidental to anything that something be truly affirmed of it either in the intellect or in speech." *In V Metaph.*, lect. 9 (ed. Cathala-Spiazzi), no. 896. That a knower should give a thing existence in his mind is of course accidental to the thing. But this does not at all imply that the substantial being of the thing is not the immediate and direct object of a judgment. Cf. above, Chapter 3, nn. 20–21. The difficulty here lies in the refusal of Fr Régis to admit that real existence is *apprehended* originally by a judgment, even though he states that the existence of the act itself is so perceived: "The existence of this judicative act is perceived in and by the act of judgment itself." *Epistemology*, p. 413. His third argument (pp. 324–325) is that mediately known existence is known not in itself but in the composition effected by the mind, as seen in the demonstration of God's existence. On this, see above, Chapter 6, n. 6.

known through reflexive judgment to exist in the intellect. It has been given intentional being as a concept. In this intentional being it is an object of simple apprehension. It can accordingly be made the subject of predication in a judgment like "'Green' is the predicate of that tree." Moreover, the existence that synthesizes the terms either really or intentionally can be considered separately from the terms. It is thereby made an object of reflexive simple apprehension and is known to be in the intellect through the corresponding act of judgment. But in every case the object of a reflex *judgment* is a radically new act of being, and never something that belonged to a preceding judgment. Only through reflexive simple apprehension is the content of a previous judgment reviewed. This has been seen in the example "I am judging that Khrushchev is a man."

In probing the truth of a judgment, then, does the intellect compare its object with the object of another and reflexive judgment? Obviously not. The two objects are diverse, for they are diverse acts of being. The one does not reveal anything about the other. Rather, an object of reflexive simple apprehension is compared with the object of a judgment. "The tree is green" or "Khrushchev is a man" is held in still-life projection before the intellect's gaze and compared with what is now judged about Khrushchev or the tree.

Judgment of Truth. Accordingly, the very being of the thing itself is the immediate object of judgment. Here a synthesizing act is known in a synthesizing way. In reflection, however, the direct synthesizing cognition becomes the object of a still-life intellectual gaze. The really exercised act that is synthesizing the tree and its quality in the outside world is apprehended in the direct judgment "The tree before my eyes is green." Reflecting upon its direct judgment, the intellect sees an object that is signified by the copula "is" and that represents the synthesis really exercised in the tree itself. The direct object of the first judgment is making the tree really exist. The immediate object of second and reflex judgment does not actually make the tree or anything else exist. Rather, it is a concept that exists in the mind through an existential act other than itself. Like the act of simple intellectual apprehension, the judgment produces a similitude in which it knows its direct object. As in the case of simple apprehension it knows this similitude only concomitantly. To focus attention on it, the intellect has to make the new act of reflex cognition. In this reflex act it simultaneously perceives the content of the similitude and judges that the similitude exists. Here as elsewhere simple apprehension and judgment accompany each other unavoidably in actual cognition. But in this case the whole content of the direct judgment is the object only of simple apprehension. "Tree," "green," and the nexus signified by the copula "is" are merely observed as they are present in still-life fashion before the mind's reflexive gaze upon it. The two terms are not actually being synthesized by the copula. The accompanying judgment is solely that the similitude and its content exist intentionally in the mind. As an object for comparison with the fact, the whole judgment and each of its three elements are known through reflexive simple apprehension. The comparison is between an object of reflexive simple apprehension on the one hand, and an object of actual judgment on the other.

As in simple apprehension of the intellect, however, so also in judgment the cognitional act and the similitude produced by it, viewed reflexively, have the same knowable content. Hence the similitude produced by the judgment may be called by the same name, a "judgment," somewhat as the act of simple intellectual apprehension and the concept in which it takes place may each be called a "conception." You may speak of the intellect's first act of conception, and likewise of the concept of a stone as a conception in the intellect. Correspondingly you may name the intellect's synthesizing cognition a judgment, and also refer to the expressed enunciation "Chicago is a city" as a judgment. Understood in this sense, the judgment or enunciation is signified verbally by what is called a proposition or statement. But so regarded, the judgment itself is an object of simple apprehension.

A judgment in this sense of an enunciation, and known by reflection, may be compared with the real existential synthesis known by the direct judgment. On leaving home in the early morning of a piping hot spring day, I may have noticed that the buds were starting to break on the tree outside my window, but had not yet made it green. Because of that observation, I may on my return in the evening make the statement "The tree is not yet green." I am told to look and see. Under the heat of the day the buds have sprouted and I see that the tree is green. I confront my judgment of a moment before with what I see, and in a new reflex judgment I see that it does not agree with what I perceive in real existence, and I say that it is wrong or false. I compare my present judgment "The tree is green," with what is existentially synthesized in the real world before my eyes, and I see that they agree.[6] I say "It is true that the tree

[6] On the classical definition of truth as "correspondence of thing and intellect" (*adaequatio rei et intellectus*), a definition traditionally ascribed to the ninth-century writer Isaac the Jew, see G. B. Phelan, "Verum Sequitur Esse Rerum," *Mediaeval Studies*, I (1939), 12–14.

is green," or "My judgment that the tree is green is true." It is accordingly the judgment, not the thing, that is primarily true or false. Truth and falsity, therefore, are properties of judgment. They are often expressed merely by emphasizing the copula, as "The tree *is* green" or "*is not* green."

Judgment About a Judgment. What have I been doing in this reflection? I have been confronting the judgment I see in my mind through a reflex act of simple apprehension, with the really exercised existential synthesis that I see in the outer world through the complex act of direct judgment. Accompanying the reflex act of simple apprehension there is always the reflex judgment that its object exists in my mind. This reflex judgment is still not the judgment of truth or falsity. The judgment of truth or falsity is a further reflex judgment. It is not the judgment that my direct judgment exists in my mind, but the still further judgment that its content agrees or disagrees with the real existential synthesis. The direct judgment that is the object of the reflex act of simple apprehension is compared with the existential synthesis known through that same direct judgment in its role not of object but of synthesizing cognitive act. Seen in this confrontation, the direct judgment is known through the new reflex judgment to be either true or false. The judgment of truth or falsity, accordingly, is a judgment about a judgment. It perceives reflexively the synthesis of a judgment with a judgment's property. It grasps the existence of a judgment's relation to a fact.

Résumé. To know the truth about a thing, then, means to know that your judgment about it agrees with the thing as it actually is.[7] These observations hold correspondingly in regard to the truth about things that exist intentionally in cognition. In all cases the natural desire of man to know tends not only toward knowing things but also toward knowing the truth about them. Human knowledge culminates not just in knowing things according to their essence and their existence, but in knowing that one's judgments about them are true. Knowledge of truth, accordingly, is the perfection of the human intellect.[8] It is the goal toward which the intellect strives.[9] It does not consist formally in original judg-

[7] "And on this account truth is defined through the conformity of intellect and thing. Hence to know this conformity is to know the truth. . . . The intellect can know its conformity to the intelligible thing. . . . when it judges that the thing is so disposed as is the form it apprehends regarding it, then it first knows and expresses truth." St Thomas, *ST*, I, 16, 2c.

[8] "For just as every other thing is called good through its perfection, so is the knowing intellect through its truth." *In VI Metaph.*, lect. 4, (ed. Cathala-Spiazzi) no. 1239. Cf. no. 1234.

[9] *Verum finis ipsius* — St Thomas, *ST*, I, 82, 3, ad 1m.

ments that first apprehend the existence of things, nor in those that apprehend the existence of reflexively known judgments in the intellect's simple apprehension or that apprehend the existence of the truth judgments themselves. Rather, it consists in those that apprehend the conformity of the reflexively considered judgments with the actual existence of things.[10] The conformity is a relation in a judgment when the judgment is perceived reflexively as an object.[11] It is a relation that is attained in its notion by reflexive simple apprehension, and in its being by reflexive judgment.

SUGGESTED READINGS AND REFERENCES

St Thomas Aquinas, *Truth*, I, 1–3; tr. Robert W. Mulligan (Chicago: Henry Regnery, 1952), I, 3–14.

[10] Cf.: "For, since the intellect's truth is the equation of understanding and thing, insofar as the intellect declares that what is is or what is not is not, truth pertains in the intellect to that which the intellect declares, not to the operation by which it declares it." St Thomas, *CG*, I, 59, Cum enim. As an object of reflexive simple apprehension, a judgment, whether affirmative or negative, is always a *composition*. As an act of judging, however, it is composition when affirmative and division when negative. See *In I Periherm.*, lect. 3 (ed. Leonine), no. 4.

Peter H. J. Hoenen, *La Théorie du Jugement d'après St. Thomas d'Aquin* (Rome, 1946), while acknowledging that all judgments have an existential cast, separates judgment from apprehension by a "césure" (p. 346; cf. pp. 21–22; 163), restricting judgment to a "reconnaissance" of being instead of seeing in it the original apprehension of the thing's being. In this view the sole function of judgment seems to be a sort of rubber stamp pronouncement on what is already known through simple apprehension. C. Boyer, "Le Sens d'un Texte de Saint Thomas: 'De Veritate, q. 1, a. 9,'" *Gregorianum*, V (1924), p. 424, in a summary of his own position, thinks "that reflexion, of which there is discussion in the text, is completed in the act of direct judgment itself. Truth, namely, is in the intellect as known, because the intellect in its second operation, which is judgment, reflects on its first operation, which is simple apprehension." In the light of all that has been considered in St Thomas' teaching on being and judgment, this is a patent oversimplification. Both simple apprehension and judgment can be direct, and both can be reflexive. The process is much more involved; see below, Chapter 18, n. 28. As Hoenen (p. 22) notes, "judgment" may be used in the sense that includes a preceding "critical examination." Cf.: ". . . nor through this can there be had a perfect judgment about that to which assent is given." St Thomas, *In Boeth. De Trin.*, III, 1, ad 4m. In this sense *dijudicare* is used as a synonym. But even though the relation of conformity or disagreement has to be sought out laboriously and examined carefully, the truth judgment proper is the perception that this relation does exist in the object under examination.

[11] Knowledge of truth "in represented act" (*in actu signato*) bears upon the relation of conformity set up in itself as an object. Knowledge of truth "in exercised act" (*in actu exercito*) has for its object the judgment as so related. On this late Scholastic distinction, see Cajetan, *In ST*, I, 16, 2, no. vi. It is the same distinction found between fatherhood known in itself as a relation, and fatherhood known in the cognition of a father as a father. The distinction does not offer much positive help in the discussion of the truth judgment.

——— *Summa Theologiae*, I, 16, 1–3; tr. English Dominican Fathers, 2nd ed. (London: Burns Oates & Washbourne Ltd.), I, 224–230.

——— *Commentary on the Metaphysics of Aristotle*, Book V, Lesson 9, nos. 895–896; Book IX, Lesson 11, nos. 1895 ff. Tr. John P. Rowan (Chicago: Henry Regnery, 1961), I, 346–347; II, 699–704.

Charles Boyer, "The Meaning of a Text of St. Thomas: De veritate, Q. 1, A 9," in Henry F. Tiblier's translation of Peter H. J. Hoenen, *Reality and Judgment according to St. Thomas* (Chicago: Henry Regnery, 1952), Appendix, pp. 295–309.

CHAPTER 18

Certitude

Assent. The judgments required to reach even minimal truth seem surprisingly multiple. You have to make a first judgment to know the thing in its own existence, then a second and reflex judgment to know that the cognitional synthesis of the first judgment exists as an object in your mind, and then another reflex judgment to know that the judgment as object agrees with what as an act it now attains in the thing. This process may seem complicated, yet it is only the stripped skeleton of the exuberant mental life that actually is lived in man's striving for truth. There are other necessarily concomitant reflex judgments, for instance that you yourself exist, that you are performing an act of cognition, that you are different from your cognitive act and from the external thing it knows, and that each cognitive act differs from the other. Besides these a host of accidentally connected judgments continually hover about at any moment in one's extremely involved conscious life. Have any of them special importance for the problem of knowledge?

One further reflex judgment that has to be considered in the study of man's quest for truth is the judgment of assent. When you see that your mental synthesis "The tree is green" conforms with the real existential synthesis, you know the truth. Often, however, after having made a true judgment you face the question "Should I have inquired further before making that judgment?" or "Am I certain of it?" In the present instance you see in a new reflex judgment[1] that there is no room for further inquiry. You thereby are determined to your truth judgment as final, and your investigation about it ceases. This judgment expresses your

[1] ". . . in regard to the object, concerning which two acts of reason are in question; first, that it apprehend the truth about something. . . . The other act of reason is when it assents to what it apprehends." St Thomas, *ST*, I–II, 17, 6c. On the dynamic continuity of the movement in the second operation of the intellect from the preceding judgment to the further "reflex and modal judgment that is assent," see L.-M. Régis, *Epistemology* (New York, 1959), pp. 418–419. On the object of assent as "a truth formally apprehended as existing by the intellect, a truth which becomes an object of reflection," see *ibid.*, p. 406.

assent to truth.[2] As your assent here is unconditional, you are **certain**[3] that you know the truth. You now consciously *adhere* — in the sense that you are *determined* by a reflex *intellective* act — to one side of a pair of contradictories, that is, to the side already judged to be *true*. "I am certain of it" is your new judgment.

Erroneous Assent. Man's innate desire for knowledge, accordingly, tends not only toward knowing the truth about things, but likewise toward being certain that he knows it. In the sequence just considered, after the original knowledge of existence, knowledge of truth comes first, and upon it follows certitude. Certitude therefore should presume knowledge of truth. Yet in point of fact men are often certain of judgments about things in regard to which they do not know the truth. A witness at a trial may be unhesitatingly certain about statements to which he is swearing, and yet under severe cross-examination come to see that he has been the victim of illusions. A Nazi youth may have been in unquestioning certainty about Germany's military superiority over her enemies, and then find himself bitterly disillusioned on seeing the outcome of the Second World War. You will not have to review your mental history very thoroughly before finding that in the past you have been as certain of some tenets as a child is that Santa Claus puts the gifts under the tree. Yet you now recognize you were mistaken. Those tenets were erroneous. You continually meet people who are certain of views that you know to be wrong. Error is ubiquitous as a fact, and poses troublesome problems for the epistemologist.[4] If judgment is the apprehension of being, how can the mental similitude in which it

[2] "It is clear from what has been said, that assent is not found in the operation of the intellect by which it forms simple quiddities of things, since no truth or falsity is there; for we are not said to assent to anything except when we adhere to it as true." St Thomas, *De* Ver., XIV, 1c. Accordingly "we can define assent as a determination or adhesion of the intellect to an object as true." F. M. Tyrrell, "Concerning the Nature and Function of the Act of Judgment," *The New Scholasticism*, XXVI (1952), 419.

[3] "And therefore to assent pertains properly to the intellect, because it implies absolute adherence to that to which assent is given." St Thomas, *De Ver.*, XIV, 1, ad 3m. On this assent as coinciding with the present-day notion of certitude, see F. A. Cunningham, "*Certitudo* in St. Thomas Aquinas," *The Modern Schoolman*, XXX (1953), 304; — "our act of certitude, the Thomistic *assensus*" — *ibid.*, p. 302, n. 45. In St Thomas, certitude does not have the psychological meaning of "a state of mind," but in the present connection indicates "a manner of knowing." See Cunningham, pp. 299, n. 28; 303. Accordingly St Thomas (*ST*, II–II, 70, 2c) can speak of "probable certitude." On the type of assent in opinion, see below, Chapter 19, nn. 17–19.

[4] Cf. attacks on epistemological monism, listed by J. A. Ryan, "Two Essays on American Critical Realism," *Revue de l'Université d'Ottawa*, VI (1936), Section Spéciale (V), 109*, n. 22.

takes place ever disagree with the being that is directly known? How can that mental similitude represent what just is not there to be represented? If human cognition is passive in the reception of its object, how can it receive something that was not there to be received? Is the judgment, on the contrary, active in such a way that it can produce the object it knows? But human knowledge is not of itself creative.[5] It can influence production of external things only through guiding the activities of other faculties. If a judgment is a knowing of something it does not produce, how can it ever be erroneous? Why need a person hesitate to accept every truth judgment as irreversible and therefore as certain?

This problem calls for a scrutinizing analysis of erroneous judgment. The collector at your door presents his credentials and letters of recommendation, you judge that he is actually a worker for a charitable cause, and you give him your cash contribution without any hesitation. Later you read that he has been convicted of soliciting money under false pretenses, and that all his credentials were forged. Now you say that you know the truth. The truth is that he was an impostor. This latter judgment is seen to agree with reality. Your former judgment that he was genuine appears as false. Yet when you made it you judged it to be true. You assented to it, for you saw no reason to question it. Your certainty was shown by your donation in hard cash. You were certain of what was not true.

But with what did you confront your judgment "He is genuine"? Certainly not with the reality. In reality he is an impostor. On confrontation with the reality you would have seen that this judgment is in disagreement with what he really is, just as you see it now. But your act of direct judgment is an apprehension of the thing as it is in its real existence. The intelligible similitude in which that judgment was made, and which is the object of your reflexive judgment of truth, cannot be in disagreement with the act itself. The objective content is identical in the two cases. What, then, is the intelligible similitude of the judgment that you actually made at the time? What was it that you apprehended when you made your direct judgment about the man with the credentials at your door? Does the judgment "He is genuine" correspond exactly with what was apprehended in your direct judgment of real existence in this man? Or did you in fact confront it with something else? In a word, what were the two terms that you actually confronted with each other in making the wrong judgment?

[5] Cf. G. B. Phelan, "Verum Sequitur Esse Rerum," *Mediaeval Studies*, I (1939), 22. On the judgment's activity regarding things, see above, Chapter 3, n. 20.

Terms Actually Confronted. What you in fact apprehended in your original judgment of real being was that the man had credentials. That was the direct object of your immediate judgment regarding real existence. The writing of the credentials did not take place before your eyes. You had no immediate judgment whether they were written by the authorized persons or by a clever forger. Yet on their strength you "jumped" to the conclusion that the man was genuine. It was not with the object of your immediate judgment concerning real existence that you compared the false judgment, but with real existence that was "jumped at" over steps you did not take the trouble to discern. You compared your judgment, "He is genuine," with that supposed existence, and you saw that they agreed. If someone had asked you if it is true that the man is collecting for the charitable cause, you would have answered: "Certainly it is true; I saw his credentials; if I had not been sure, I would never have given him the cash." Because of agreement with existence to which you had concluded, you were certain, yet wrongly so.

But what about agreement or disagreement with the object of your immediate direct judgment? You confront your judgment "He is genuine" with his possession of the credentials. Is there agreement or disagreement? Thorough scrutiny fails to reveal either, but shows that either is possible. He could have had the credentials legitimately, or he could have forged or stolen them. The comparison just with the immediate direct judgment leaves wide open the question of agreement or disagreement. You could have made a few phone calls, and secured the necessary information. But from past experience you have formed the habit of judging people with such credentials genuine. Without further thought you make your cognitional jump over all intervening steps from possession of credentials to actual commission by the charitable organization. This commissioning is the direct object of your erroneous judgment, and it is a commissioning that is non-existent in reality. Yet the commissioning is judged to be really existent.

Object of Erroneous Judgment. But if judgment is a cognitive act, how can it know as really existing what is not really existent? Real existence, however, was what you jumped at in your quick reasoning. A reasoning process is from something known to something not yet apparent in the starting points. In the proof for the existence of the first cause, the real existence of sensible things was the starting point. Their existence was the object of a direct judgment. That they existed, however, was seen to involve the existence of their cause, and ultimately the existence of their first cause, subsistent being. The existence of the first cause was not apprehended in itself, but only in the exigencies of existent sensible things. The concluding judgment does not have the existence of the first cause immediately before it to apprehend. It knows this existence in and through the actual synthesizing in which the reasoning process concludes, on the basis of what was directly judged in the sensible things. What is known through the concluding judgment is the real existence, outside the human mind, of the first cause itself. The judgment is not that certain concepts exist within the mind, but that the first cause really exists outside the cognition. The direct object of the concluding judgment is accordingly the real existence of the first cause. The judgment itself can be made the object of a reflex act of simple apprehension, and compared with what it attained as an act. The result, if the demonstration itself is not questioned, is the reflex judgment of truth, that the conclusion "The first cause really exists" is true.

In this example, real existence that is not immediately apprehended is known through a judgment. It is possible therefore for a judgment to be cognitive of existence that it does not attain immediately in a really existent thing. Such judgments are made continually in daily life. From the smell of smoke you know there really is fire that you do not see. In physics you conclude to the real existence of unseen molecules from the observed transference of odors and diffusion of gases. The direct object of the judgments is real existence, even though in them the real existence is not immediately apprehended.

These instances show the capacity of the intellect to know through its acts of judgment real existences that it does not immediately apprehend. On the basis of what it apprehends immediately in a previous judgment, it judges that something else really exists. On the basis of the credentials you concluded to the real commissioning of the man at your door. That was the direct object of your mediate judgment "He is genuine." The credentials, you reasoned, implied the real commissioning. The cognition given in your judgment is that he really was commissioned, and not just that the two concepts go together in your mind. This cognition, when confronted with later known reality, proves illusory. It vanishes before your sight when faced with further evidence. Like the wind-egg in Plato's dialogue,[6] it is not endowed with lifegiving content. It is a cognition, but its content is not genuine. Though accepted as really existent, the content turns out to be a mirage.

How such illusory cognition is possible for the human faculties, and how it takes place, are further questions. For the present, the point de-

[6] *Tht.*, 150B–151E, 210B.

manding clear consideration is that the direct object of these erroneous judgments is real existence, wrongly judged. Presocratics taught that the earth is flat. That erroneous judgment bore on the really existent earth, and not directly upon concepts in their minds. For centuries nearly all astronomers said that the earth was really at the center of the universe. This was not a judgment directly concerned with concepts, but with real things. Skeptics from the time of the ancient Greeks have capitalized on such easily checked fallacies as the assertions that the stick is bent in water and that there are various pigments in the feathers on the pigeon's neck.[7] The Skeptics were not concerned with doubting the way these things appeared in human cognition. What they signalized were judgments that transferred the appearances to the really existent things. Judgments are erroneous because they bear not on existence in the mental synthesis but on the independent existence merely represented by the synthesis as object of reflexive simple apprehension.

Corrections. The fact of frequent erroneous judgments, as not only the Skeptics in different ages have pointed out, is incontestable.[8] Just as obvious, however, is the ability and the tendency to correct one's judgments through further acquaintance with things. This is part of the naturally inspired human striving for knowledge and truth. New knowledge, for instance that the stick is straight when pulled out of the water, makes one question one's former judgment that it was bent. Study of the refraction of light shows that the stick does not bend when placed in the water, and likewise reveals why it appears as bent. Modern physics shows that fire is not a body in itself, but an accident of other bodies under certain conditions. The hasty reasoning of the ancient physicists from distinct appearances to a distinct corresponding substance is shown to be wrong in the case of fire, even though it happened to hit the right conclusion in the case of water. The ingrained conviction that you see things as distant from you is corrected by a study of optics. Revision of judgments is as much a fact as is error.

New judgments of reality, accordingly, may run counter to former ones and initiate a process of correction. Descartes exploited this natural tendency of the human mind by requiring that philosophical thinking begin by deliberately doubting tenet after tenet till one arrived at some-

[7] See Cicero, *Acad.*, II, 25, 79.

[8] Cf.: "For we see that of themselves men can be deceived and err. But in order to know the truth they have to be taught by others. And again, the soul is under deception a longer time than in knowledge of truth; because knowledge of truth is hardly reached after a long time of study." St Thomas, *In III De An.*, lect. 4, (ed. Pirotta), no. 624. Cf. *Quodl.*, VI, 6c.

thing that could not at all be doubted.[9] St Thomas spoke of commencing metaphysics, in the Aristotelian framework, by a universal questioning of truth.[10] But will one ever arrive by this process at judgments that are

---

[9] See Descartes, *Principia Philosophiae*, I, 1–2; A–T, VIII, 5.5–14 (IX, 25). Cf.: ". . . and I will proceed onwards until I come to something certain, or if nothing else until I know this for certain, that nothing is certain." *Meditationes de Prima Philosophia*, II; A–T, VII, 24.7–9 (IX, 19). The initial methodic doubt, accordingly, was never envisaged by Descartes as "universal," though it is so interpreted by Mercier, *Criteriology*, I, 13–15, in *A Manual of Modern Scholastic Philosophy*, tr. Parker (London, 1916), I, 353–355. It was merely to continue until something certain was reached. It was artificial, because, except for ulterior purposes in Descartes' philosophy, it could have stopped at any of the immediately evident common notions (see *Principia*, I, 13; A–T, VIII, 9.14–10.4, or IX, 30–31) just as easily as at the *Cogito*. Cf. H. G. Wolz, "The Double Guarantee of Descartes' Ideas," *The Review of Metaphysics*, III (1950), 473–489. On the "masked" (*Cogitationes Privatae*, A–T, X, 213) character of Descartes' procedure, see Jacques Maritain, *The Dream of Descartes*, tr. Mabelle Louis Andison (New York, 1944), pp. 35–41. For a discussion of the accusation of circularity in Descartes' reasoning, see E. Salmon, "The Cartesian Circle," *The New Scholasticism*, XII (1938), 378–391. On the interpretations of his doubt, see Wolz, "The Universal Doubt in the Light of Descartes's Conception of Truth," *The Modern Schoolman*, XXVII (1950), 253–279.

[10] ". . . universalis dubitatio de veritate," *In III Metaph.*, lect. 1, (ed. Cathala-Spiazzi), no. 343. "Truth" in this context means for St Thomas the reality dealt with by metaphysics, and is not restricted to a property of knowledge; see A. Mansion, " 'Universalis Dubitatio de Veritate,' " *Revue Philosophique de Louvain*, LVII (1959), 513–542. Neither the *aporia* of Aristotle nor the *dubitabile* of St Thomas implied what is meant by the English word "doubt"; see Régis, *Epistemology*, pp. 21–28. No more notion of doubt is involved here than when in answer to the question "Does God Exist?" (St Thomas, *ST*, I, 2, 3), the position "It seems that God does not exist" is first stated. "Doubt," as Régis (p. 27) shows, is not an initial state of mind at all, but is concerned solely with conclusions. Nevertheless Msgr Noel, expressly claiming to represent the "epistemology of the New Scholasticism," wrote: "We assume as a technical starting point universal methodical doubt — *universalem dubitationem* — which appears in Aristotle's *Metaphysics* and in St Thomas' *Commentary*, as a condition of all sound philosophical thinking." *Le Réalisme Immédiat* (Louvain, 1938), p. 270. Joseph Maréchal, *Le Point de Départ de la Métaphysique*, 2e éd. (Brussels & Paris, 1949), V, 84, claims that for St Thomas the doubt is more universal but less serious than for Descartes. Georges Van Riet, *L'Epistémologie Thomiste* (Louvain, 1946), pp. 638–639, wants a universal, positive, real and "lived" initial doubt, but a doubt that is able to keep from becoming a final state. To it are submitted certitudes that will resist it. As is apparent from this last observation, the "universality" of the methodic doubt is taken in the restricted Cartesian sense of proceeding till something that cannot be doubted is encountered. In *Problèmes d'Epistémologie* (Louvain & Paris, 1960) Van Riet, though accepting (p. 107, n. 38) Mansion's exegesis of the Thomistic text, still requires "doubt" as the initial epistemological attitude (p. 168, n. 27).

On the philosophical mentality involved in this question, see Etienne Gilson, *Réalisme Thomiste et Critique de la Connaissance* (Paris, 1939), pp. 50–68. Taken literally, a "universal" doubt would leave nothing upon which any certitude could be built, not even the tenet that nothing is certain. The latter tenet was not exempt from the Skeptical *epoché*; see Diogenes Laertius, *Lives*, IX, 74, and Cicero, *Acad.*, I, 12, 45. Outside the Louvain circle, the doctrine of the initial universal doubt has not gained acceptance among Neoscholastics. Rather, it has generally been combatted.

not subject to correction and so cannot be doubted? The ancient Greek Skeptics maintained that one could reach no such judgments on the philosophical plane.[11] It is a fairly common view today that conclusions in the physical sciences are always open to revision, and that human knowledge strives to approximate but cannot attain truth. Can any judgments be had, then, that after thorough scrutiny show they exclude all possibility of correction? Is certitude ever intellectually justified?

Immediate Judgments. When in the waking state in which you can do metaphysical thinking you see or feel anything, you spontaneously make the judgment that what you see or feel exists. The judgment may take the vague form "Something exists." Upon examination the "something" appears as something corporeal and extended, which is the type of thing that is felt or seen. You know that it exists. Make an attempt to doubt or correct that judgment. Try as you like, you cannot, while you are actually feeling or seeing the thing, shake in any seriousness your knowledge that something—in the sense of an extended or bodily something—exists externally to your cognition.[12] You

---

Mercier, *A Manual of Modern Scholastic Philosophy*, 8th ed., tr. T. L and S. A. Parker (London, 1916), I, 360, had maintained an initial state of certitude in regard to immediate judgments and of doubt in regard to "*mediate* propositions," and interpreted Aristotle and St Thomas in this sense.

[11] See Sextus Empiricus, *Adv. Math.*, IX, 49; Diogenes Laertius, IX, 102–108. Accordingly, universal Skepticism, in the Greek sense, is a possible philosophical position. It need not touch the certitudes of ordinary life, nor those of the arts and crafts and non-philosophic sciences. It does not involve the denial of the principle of contradiction on non-philosophic levels. Its philosophic life, however, as noted by Mario dal Pra, *Lo Scetticismo Greco* (Milan, 1950), p. 217, can be only that of a parasite, nourished entirely by the philosophies it attacks. The Husserlian *epoché*, in quite opposite fashion, suspends the ordinary certitudes of naturally disposed men in regard to existence, and seeks philosophical certitude in a purely eidetic realm.

As an attitude, universal Skepticism is philosophically irrefutable on its own ground, for it admits no certitudes that could be used to argue philosophically against it. On the Skeptical attitude, see V. Cauchy, "The Nature and Genesis of the Skeptic Attitude," *The Modern Schoolman*, XXVII (1950), 203–221; 297–310.

[12] Cf. "Although there is no one not sufficiently convinced that material things exist . . ." Descartes, *Principia*, II, 1; A–T, VIII, 40.5–6 (IX, 63). ". . . for I think nobody can, in earnest, be so sceptical as to be uncertain of the existence of those things which he sees and feels. At least, he that can doubt so far, (whatever he may have with his own thoughts,) will never have any controversy with me; since he can never be sure I say anything contrary to his own opinion." Locke, *An Essay concerning Human Understanding*, IV, 11, 3; ed. Fraser, II, 327. Yet on account of their starting point in the mind's direct cognition of its own ideas, men in the Cartesian tradition had to prove the existence of the external world. On their attempts, ending in Berkeley's denial of a material universe, see E. Gilson, *The Unity of Philosophical Experience* (New York, 1937), pp. 180–216. The argument that the passive and uncontrollable character of sense perceptions requires an external world

cannot of course remember your first external sense perception and your first judgment of existence. With the conclusions of physics and experimental psychology, you can reason that at first you did not see things as distant from you or as specifically distinct from one another in substance, but rather like the markings as it were on the one flat canvas.[13] The only judgment that could then take place would be that something — in the sense of something extended — exists. Today you have still no reason to think that your present vague immediate judgment, just by itself, carries you any further. But as you see and feel something at the present moment, you make at least that spontaneous judgment, even though as a rule you do not reflect on your making it. You know that something corporeal exists, and that try as you like you cannot correct or doubt that judgment.

Why does the real existence of what you are seeing or feeling prove impossible to doubt and impossible to judge otherwise? The reason appears right away in the very existence that you are judging. It excludes its own not-being. The real existence means that it is not non-existent in reality. The existence immediately judged shows of itself that its own non-existence[14] at the moment is impossible. The judgment, accordingly, is not open to doubt or to correction. Existence reveals its own necessity.[15] It itself makes manifest not only that it is there but also why it cannot at the moment be otherwise.

Immediate Reflexive Judgments. When you later reflect in full consciousness upon your thinking, you find it has characteristics that differentiate it from what is directly known. You see clearly that you act differently from and are other than

as their cause (Descartes, *loc. cit.;* Mercier, *Criteriology*, 60, a & b, p. 394) has not been able to stand up under serious criticism, since it in one way or another presupposes what it undertakes to prove. Attempts to justify one's immediate judgment that the external world exists, on the basis of some supposed independent starting point in human thought, go under the name of "Critical Realism." On uses of the expression that are not legitimate, see Gilson, *Réalisme Thomiste et Critique de la Connaissance* (Paris, 1939), pp. 181–182. Neoscholastic critical realisms, mediate and immediate, are criticized by Gilson, *op. cit.*, and *Le Réalisme Méthodique* (Paris, 1936), pp. 18–44. On American critical realism, see J. A. Ryan, *art. cit.*, pp. 102*–128*; 262*–296.* The use of the term "critical realism," however, is defended by Jacques Maritain, *The Degrees of Knowledge*, tr. G. B. Phelan (New York, 1959), pp. 71–73, and Fernand Van Steenberghen, *Epistemology*, tr. M. J. Flynn (New York, 1949), pp. 245–257.

[13] Cf. Robert Edward Brennan, *General Psychology* (New York, 1937), pp. 188–194.

[14] On the therapy required in speaking of existence as existent or non-existent, see St Thomas, *De Ver.*, XXI, 5, ad 8m.

[15] See above, Chapter 8, nn. 7–8.

the corporeal object you first knew. The corporeal something is the object directly known in your first cognition, and only in subsequent reflexion do you know yourself as an object different from the corporeal thing. The process, therefore, is one of differentiating yourself from the corporeal reality whose existence is first directly known, and not in idealistic fashion an attempt to set up something external to a cognition already known in itself.[16] The cognition itself, rather, is known only in function of the external object, that is, as the knowing of the external thing. In this indirect way, however, the thinking subject is immediately known and judged to exist. For the same reason as in the case of the external corporeal thing, it cannot be non-existent while it is actually existing. Its existence, likewise, carries that necessity. While you are knowing in reflection that you exist, you cannot simultaneously be seeing that you do not exist. You see that your judgment of your own existence while you are reflecting cannot be doubted or corrected, and you see the reason for the impossibility. The reason is the existence itself, which involves its own necessity. Of its very self, indeed, it is its own necessity, for it cannot fail at the moment to exclude its non-existence.[17]

First Principle. Existence that is immediately judged, then, whether directly or reflexively, presents itself as necessarily an exclusion of its own non-existence. Without that exclusion it would not be existence. The exclusion is seen as necessarily present with existence wherever existence may be found. It presents itself as universal for existence. It may be expressed in the judgment "It is impossible to be and not to be at the same time."

This necessity of being is communicated to the existent *thing* itself. As far as its essence is concerned, any sensible thing may either exist or not exist. It abstracts in essence from all being, it excludes neither being nor non-being. But when actuated by existential act, whether real or intentional, it excludes its own corresponding non-being. It determines and limits the existential act to its own self. It thereby cannot fail to be *itself*, as far as that existential act is concerned. If it is anything else, it is so by a further act of accidental existence. This may now be expressed in the judgment "A thing cannot be and not be at the same time in the same respects." This is the principle of being or the principle of contradiction. No matter how much you try to deny it in words, you cannot

[16] See above, Chapter 15, n. 13.

[17] Certitude, accordingly, is not to be explained in terms of a subjective state, but in terms of the necessary character of being. On "subjective certitude" in early Neoscholasticism, see Van Riet, *L'Epistémologie Thomiste*, pp. 5–6; 44; 68; 110.

deny it in thought.[18] Any attempt to deny it involves its affirmation, for its denial is accepted as something that cannot be its affirmation. It is admitted in every definite meaning given to the words used in its attempted denial. It is accordingly open to neither doubt nor correction. It is a judgment that expresses universally the being that is immediately known in things perceived through the external senses and in one's own self through consciousness.

In the wording of this principle, the qualification "at the same time" is required on account of the temporal character of every existential synthesis in sensible things. A man may be ignorant at one moment that his car has been stolen, and may know it at the next moment when a witness phones, but he cannot know it and not know it at the same time. The relative nature of many accidental aspects requires the addition of the restriction "in the same respects." The temperature of the television studio may be warm for one speaker and cool for another, according to different conditions of blood in each. But, with these qualifications, all finite being is limited to the essence that specifies it. A thing cannot be what it is not.

Innumerable other immediate judgments may be made on the basis of the transcendental aspects of being and the particular essences of things. A thing is one in itself and is different from other things. A thing is intelligible. A thing is good. These judgments follow upon the unity and otherness and truth and goodness of things. Correspondingly, every particular essence will form the basis for new immediate judgments. In quantity, for instance, two things equal to a third are equal to each other. The third is immediately seen as the measure of each.[19] Since a thing is its essence abstracted without precision, whatever is contained in the definition is immediately seen as predicable of the thing. This is expressed by saying that where the predicate is contained in the definition of the subject, the proposition is immediately evident.[20] A straight line is defined as the shortest distance between two points, in Euclidean geometry. The judgment that a straight line has at least two points is immediate. It is not open to correction, or to doubt, for without the two points you could not have the straight line. All these judgments are but particularizations of the first principle of demonstration. From this point of view they are said to be established by reduction to

[18] See Aristotle, *Metaph.*, Γ 3, 1005b23–32. For the "vegetable" simile, see 4, 1006a15.

[19] The quantity, as quantity, is the *same* or is *one* in all three; cf. above, Chapter 13, nn. 12 & 19. The identity is judged immediately, not inferred.

[20] St Thomas, *ST*, I, 17, 3, ad 2m (text below, n. 25). Cf. I, 2, 1c; *CG* I, 10, Illa enim & Adhuc.

that first principle. If a line did not have at least two points, for instance, it would be a line by definition and yet not a line because it would not be a distance between points. So it would be and not be at the same time in the same respects. This reduction, however, does not in any way preclude the immediate basis for these judgments in the being of particular things. They are merely less universal expressions of the all-embracing principle of being, which is the principle of contradiction and the first principle of demonstration. Correspondingly, every immediate judgment that a new motion or a contingent accident exists, and cannot be nonexistent while it exists, is a particular expression of the principle in contingent matter.

Criterion of Certitude. Has this inquiry brought to light the means of knowing with certitude that a judgment is true? According to the above considerations, the criterion is being. If a thing actually *is* in the way represented by your reflexively known judgment, it absolutely cannot be otherwise at the moment. The other side of the contradictory is therefore excluded. The investigation is closed. You are certain of your truth judgment. There is no "fear of error," in the sense that you have seen there is no possibility of error in the case. Being, consequently, is the criterion of certitude as well as the ground and norm of truth.

To cause certitude, of course, the being of the thing has to be known in its necessitating force as being. This is expressed by saying that it has to be evident to you. It has to be grasped not just as a possibility or a probability, but as existing at the moment. It is so grasped by all persons in immediate judgments. It shows its own necessity to everyone who so grasps it. It requires no philosophical reasoning to justify it in its necessity. Rather, the being that is grasped spontaneously in immediate judgments is what grounds and justifies all philosophical reasoning, no matter how critical the reasoning claims to be.

When "evidence" is called the criterion of certitude, then, it is to be understood in the sense of what is apprehended through judgment, and not in the sense of what is known just through simple apprehension. Even in courtroom procedure, the exhibits themselves cannot function as evidence unless it is shown that they are related to the case. What is apprehended through judgment is the being of the thing. With this being as your criterion, you decide whether or not the previous judgment now held before your reflexive simple apprehension is true and certain. Solely the being of the thing, not your cognitive faculty or philosophical reflection, is the criterion. Why?

Passivity of Immediate Judgments. In all immediate judgments the being of the object, as has been seen, compels the assent of the intellect and leaves it in a state of absolute certitude. With the object clearly before its gaze in these cases, the intellect cannot withhold its judgment of assent. From this viewpoint the assent is said to be caused by the being of the object and to follow in the very functioning of the cognitive faculty.[21] It is not within the power of the human will to refuse the assent. To that extent the immediate judgment, even though it is an active synthesizing, shares the receptive or passive character of all human cognition.

Denial

Why is the immediate judgment passive in this way? Careful analysis of man's cognition shows that all simple natures as found in human cognition have their origin in sensible things.[22] None are created by simple apprehension, but rather all are received. Simple apprehension adds nothing to their objective content. It receives them as they are. No error, accordingly, is possible in simple apprehension. In immediate judgment, correspondingly, the being of things is apprehended as it is there before the knower's gaze, whether direct or reflexive. It comes into the knower's cognition, without anything in between to cause distortion or addition. The sensible thing is being seen or felt in itself and not in any image.[23] The knower through sensation becomes it intentionally in that way, and is passive to the cognitional reception of it as there in its real existence. The judgment actively synthesizes, but in the very synthesizing it is cognitionally receptive of real existence, insofar as it

---

[21] "But sometimes the passive intellect is determined to entire adherence to one side . . . immediately, when the truth of the intelligible propositions at once appears infallibly from the intelligible objects themselves." St Thomas, *De Ver.*, XIV, 1c. As the study of the processes of human cognition in natural philosophy shows, the intellect can be determined to one side of a contradiction by the intelligible object as well as by the will: "But the passive intellect can be moved by only two things; that is, by its proper object, which is an intelligible form, namely what something is, as is said in *De Anima, III*, and by the will, which moves all other powers, as Anselm says." *Ibid.* Cf. *ST*, II–II, 1, 4c.

[22] See above, Chapter 15. Cf. St Thomas, *De Ver.*, X, 6.

[23] ". . . cognition of an external sense is accomplished through the sole immutation of the sense by the sensible thing. Hence sensation takes place through the form that is impressed upon it by the sensible thing. But the external sense does not form for itself any sensible form. The imaginative power does this . . ." St Thomas, *Quodl.*, V, 9, ad 2m. Sensation accordingly can be had only when the sensible thing is present to it in real existence, exercising efficient causality: "But as a sense does not have sensation except in the presence of the sensible thing, the impression that it merely undergoes from what is active in its regard suffices therefore for its perfect operation." *In III Sent.*, d. 14, q. 1, a. 1, Solut. IIc; ed. Moos, III, 436 (no. 35). Cf.: "And in this way the things that are outside the mind . . . are in regard to the external senses as sufficient agents with which the patients do not work but only receive." *Quodl.*, VIII, 3c.

knows that something really exists. The judgment itself produces a similitude, but the similitude here does not change the immediate and passive character of the cognition any more than it does in simple apprehension. From the viewpoint of receptiveness of its object, immediate judgment and simple apprehension are on a par,[24] even though in immediate judgment the object is received through a synthesizing, while in simple apprehension it is received through a still-life gaze, and even though both simple apprehension and immediate judgment produce images on the intellectual level.

The same character of receptivity is seen in immediate judgments based on the necessary connection of essential constituents. In these cases the essence specifies the act of being in such a way that the thing cannot exist either really or intentionally without the feature that is predicated. A line cannot be without at least two points. A Euclidean square cannot be without four right angles. The necessary connection in being is apparent as soon as the two terms are known,[25] the truth judgment following inevitably upon reflection and compelling the assent. Since all the simple natures that are known by man come to the intellect from sensible things through simple apprehension, these immediate judgments of essence are all based upon the way things are in the sensible world.[26]

The receptivity of any immediate judgment in regard to its direct object, therefore, shows why assent follows automatically and why you are unconditionally certain of such a judgment. In the expression of such judgments the tendency is accordingly to use the forms "I know" or "I see" and the like, rather than forms like "I assert" or "I say" or "I declare." You say "I see that two and two are four," "I know that the tree in front of me exists," rather than "I assert that two and two are four." The cognitive rather than the assertive character of judgment is most striking in those that are immediate. Since an immediate judgment is a synthesizing, however, the other forms that emphasize this active feature are also in order.

[24] ". . . the understanding is always right insofar as it is an understanding of principles. About these it is not deceived for the same reason it is not deceived about *what* a thing is." St Thomas, *ST*, I, 17, 3, ad 2m.

[25] "For principles evident in themselves (*per se nota*) are those that at once, on the understanding of the terms, are known by the fact that the predicate is placed in the definition of the subject." *Ibid.* Correspondingly, assent to the immediate contradictories of such principles is impossible for the intellect. See *In II Sent.*, d. 25, q. 1, a. 2, Solut.; ed. Mandonnet, II, 649.

[26] ". . . the understanding of the naturally implanted principles is determined by received sensible things." *In I Sent.*, Prol. q. 1, a. 5, *Solut.*; ed. Mandonnet, I, 17. Cf. *In Boeth. De Trin.*, III, 1, ad 4m. ". . . the composition is therefore found already in the sensible data." Peter H. J. Hoenen, *La Théorie du Jugement d'après St. Thomas d'Aquin* (Rome, 1946), p. 26.

In cases where the being of the thing is not immediately judged, however, the tendency is rather to use expressions of assertion. You would say "I assert that there is life on other planets," or "I maintain that he is an impostor" in expressing these judgments. The active feature of the judgment is now brought to the fore. How can the truth or falsity of such judgments be known, since the real being of their objects is not immediately apprehended? In what way may they claim assent? This is the problem of mediate knowledge.

Résumé. Certitude consists in a reflex judgment by which the intellect sees itself definitely determined to one of a pair of contradictories. Its immediate object is a judgment of truth. Just as the truth judgment is often expressed by emphasizing the copula in the direct judgment, for instance in "Socrates *is* cultured," so the judgment of certitude may be expressed by emphasizing the copula in the truth judgment. At the conclusion of a thorough review of the evidence, one may say "It *is* true that Socrates is cultured." Being, not philosophical criticism, is the full and ultimate justification of certitude.[27] Where the being of a thing is immediately known, it compels reflexive judgments of truth and of assent[28] when the judgment that apprehends it is made the object

[27] Hence the doctrine of St Thomas "makes clear that the judgments of man, in his natural attitude, in his daily life and in his scientific life, prior to any *theory* of knowledge and before any philosophizing, are critically justified." Peter H. J. Hoenen, *Reality and Judgment according to St Thomas*, tr. Henry F. Tiblier (Chicago, 1952), p. 290. Hoenen, pp. xiii–xiv, observes that the texts indicate no essential development nor change in St Thomas' doctrine on this subject during the different periods of his career.

[28] Francis Martin Tyrrell, *The Role of Assent in Judgment* (Washington, D. C., 1948), p. vii, regards assent as the "formal element" of the act of judgment. From this viewpoint, every judgment insofar as it grasps the being of a thing is an assent. Assent is taken in a different meaning from the conscious acceptance of an already made judgment as true or as probable. The meaning is developed in an historical context that distinguishes the *perspicientia nexus* as comparative simple apprehension from judgment. On the history of the controversy on this question, see Tyrrell, pp. 24–73. The controversy proceeds as though there were but one *nexus* to be perceived, and asks whether or not it is perceived by the act of judgment. Actually, there are a number of *nexus* involved, some perceived by simple apprehension, others by judgment. The existential synthesis in the real thing, the intentional existence of subject, predicate, and copula in the mind, the existence of the conformity of understanding and thing, are some of the syntheses originally apprehended by judgment. The relation in which the predicate notion belongs to the subject, and the relation of conformity to the real in the judgment considered as object, are perceived by simple apprehension. The relation with which the truth judgment is concerned, namely the conformity of understanding and thing, is perceived by both simple apprehension and judgment — in its notion by simple apprehension, in its existence by judgment. St Thomas' statements can hardly avoid exhibiting a "strange inconsistency" (Tyrrell, p. 72), if they are forced into either one of the two alternatives conjured up by this later controversy. The *nexus* between predicate notion and sub-

of conscious reflection. The judgments that immediately grasp the being of a thing provide therefore the model for certitude. In their light the problem of certitude in mediate judgments is to be approached.

SUGGESTED READINGS AND REFERENCES

St Thomas Aquinas, *Truth,* XIV, 1c; tr. James V. McGlynn (Chicago: Henry Regnery, 1953), II, 208–211.

John Henry Newman, *A Grammar of Assent,* Part II, Chapters 6–7.

Etienne Gilson, "Vade Mecum of a Young Realist," tr. W. J. Quinn, in *Philosophy of Knowledge,* ed. Roland Houde & Joseph Mullally (Chicago, etc. J. B. Lippincott, 1960), pp. 386–394.

Francis H. Parker, "A Realistic Appraisal of Knowledge," in *Philosophy of Knowledge,* pp. 19–48.

Yves R. Simon, "An Essay on Sensation," in *Philosophy of Knowledge,* pp. 56–95.

ject, as perceived in reflexive simple apprehension, and the existential synthesis in reality, as perceived by direct judgment, plus the relation of conformity both in its notion and in its existence, seem grouped together as the one object of the controverted *perspicientia nexus.*

CHAPTER 19

Mediate Knowledge

Activity of Judgment. Besides grasping the existence of a thing, every immediate judgment reveals itself as both true and certain. As object of reflexive simple apprehension it manifests not only its own conformity with the being that it apprehends in its function as cognitive act, but also its definite determination by the necessity of this being. It thereby grounds the judgment of its own truth and the judgment of absolute assent by the intellect. It leaves the knower not with provisory but with unconditional and intellectually justified certitude. Such certitude is the culmination of a man's natural desire for knowledge and truth in regard to what is immediately known. But the natural desire extends far beyond things immediately present to human cognition. It prompts a man to seek knowledge of the unseen motives of other people's conduct, of the origins of observed meteorological phenomena, of particles required to explain chemical and physical reactions, or of the causes of a disease like cancer. It makes a person want to know the truth about these things also, and with certainty. Yet the unseen causes are not directly before human cognition to inform it passively, as it were. If the intellect is to reach them, it has to proceed actively from what it immediately knows to what it does not as yet know explicitly. Every judgment, of course, is active in the sense that it knows through synthesizing and not through still-life perception. But in the present context "activity" is contrasted with the apprehension of the being that is immediately manifest in anything known through sensation or reflection. It means a synthesis made actively, as it were, by the intellect beyond the syntheses to which the intellect is compelled by the immediate presence of the thing before its cognition.

Extension of Knowledge. How is this extension of human knowledge possible? There is no doubt about the fact that in everyday life one is repeatedly passing from what is already known to still further knowledge of things. This activity is taking place just as inevitably as the stomach is digesting food. The details of the respective processes are known only by experts in fields like logic and biology, but the processes themselves go on spontaneously. What is there, then, in the immediate objects of human knowledge that permits a passage to things as yet unknown?

You may know, for instance, that your next door neighbor is a qualified surgeon. You know this not because you have ever seen him operating or perhaps even heard of any operation he performed, but because you have seen his diploma and have heard him referred to regularly as a surgeon. You know also, from your acquaintance with what is taught in medical schools, that a qualified surgeon knows how to perform an appendectomy. These two judgments have been acquired independently of each other, and each from its own separate source. View them together, and spontaneously you make the third judgment that your neighbor knows how to perform an appendectomy. The two independently acquired judgments "My neighbor is a qualified surgeon" and "A qualified surgeon knows how to perform an appendectomy" issue in the new judgment "My neighbor knows how to perform an appendectomy." Of these judgments the first two are called by logicians the premises, and the third is called the conclusion. In general, all three are called propositions. The whole process is called reasoning. The conclusion undoubtedly gives new knowledge, for you did not know from any other source that your neighbor knew how to remove an appendix, and you did not know it in either of the premises taken separately.

Why does the conclusion issue so spontaneously from the premises? A sensible thing, as has been seen,[1] is objectified in specific and generic aspects when it is known through the simple apprehension of the intellect. In real being, the sensible thing is identified with the specific and generic natures, when these are abstracted without precision.[2] Whatever is known from other sources to belong to the species or genus is united with the individual in real being.[3] The sensible thing really is everything that is contained in its specific or generic nature, and so it is the content that is known independently from the other sources to belong to the species or genus.

---

[1] Above, Chapter 16, nn. 11–17.

[2] See St Thomas, *De Ente et Essentia*, c. II, ed. M.-D. Roland-Gosselin, reprint (Paris, 1948), p. 20.12–19.

[3] "For we may predicate of Socrates everything which belongs to man as man. . . For predication is something accomplished by the intellect's act of combining and dividing, having for its foundation in reality the very unity of those things, one of which is said of the other." St Thomas, *De Ente*, c. III, p. 29.10–16; tr. A. Maurer, *On Being and Essence* (Toronto, 1949), p. 42.

Reasoning, therefore, is based upon the way in which common natures are synthesized with individuals in being. Much can be known about a common nature from sources other than the particular individual before one's eyes. In the example just considered, "qualified surgeon" is synthesized in being with "my next door neighbor" in the judgment "My next door neighbor is a surgeon." "Surgeon" is synthesized from independent sources with the ability to perform an appendectomy. This ability pertains to its content, and its whole content, as a common qualitative nature, is united in being with each of its individuals. Ability to perform the operation is accordingly synthesized already with my neighbor in real being, and the conclusion of my reasoning expresses this union by a synthesizing act of judgment.

In a similar way, all the characteristics known from independent sources to apply to the genera will be united with the species in being. If you know from legal knowledge that persons with moderate incomes are obliged to pay income tax, and you know from statistics that surgeons have moderate incomes, your conclusion is that surgeons are obliged to pay income tax. The obligations belonging to the generic notion "persons with moderate incomes" are synthesized in being with the species "surgeons." The union of the first term "obligation to pay income tax" is seen in the first judgment as synthesized in being with the common generic notion "persons with moderate income," and that common generic notion is seen in the second judgment as synthesized in being with the species "surgeons." Surgeons, accordingly, are seen in this confrontation as synthesized with the obligation to pay income tax, and the synthesis is expressed in the concluding judgment. The three terms have the one being. X is Y, and Y is Z, so X is Z. Logic shows how the common or middle term Y has to be distributed to assure a valid sequence. Under that distribution the unity of the terms in being is made manifest.

Extension of human knowledge through reasoning, then, is grounded upon common natures and their multiple acts of being. Since it abstracts from all being, the whole content of a common nature is united in being with each of its actual subjects. Whatever is known from any of its subjects to belong to the common nature is accordingly united in being with every other subject that shares the nature. When the synthesis of a subject with a common nature is grasped through one judgment, and the synthesis of that common nature with other characteristics in being is known through other judgments, the union of each of these further characteristics with the subject is seen through new acts of judgment. In this way human knowledge of any subject is extended more and more, through the activity of judgment, even though all the characteristics are attained passively through simple apprehension, and the original being from which the first reasoning has to commence is attained in each instance through the receptivity of immediate judgments.

In the conclusion, however, the intellect grasps an existential synthesis that is not immediately before its gaze. If you had watched your neighbor perform an appendectomy, you would have seen in act his knowledge of that operation. You would have become intentionally, according to its real existence, what was going on before your eyes. In it you would have immediately judged that your neighbor knew how to perform the operation. Your judgment would have had that real ability, viewed in act, as its direct object. Not having seen the operation, though, you make the judgment as a conclusion from your premises. The judgment now has the same direct object as if it had been made immediately. It still is that your neighbor knows how to perform an appendectomy. Through it you know the existential synthesis in reality of the man and the knowledge of the operation.

Synthesis in Being. The judgment in the conclusion, therefore, is a cognitive act. It is knowledge of something. In that respect it is like the judgments in the premises. Through the conclusion real being is known, for instance that the man *is* able to perform an appendectomy. Being that was known in the premises provides the way to knowledge of an existential synthesis not explicitly known before the conclusion was drawn. The being that was grasped separately in the first premise is known again in the final judgment. This time, however, the synthesis is richer. In a first premise "qualified surgeon" is seen as synthesized in the real accidental being of one's neighbor. This judgment is confronted with a second premise, in which "qualified surgeon" is further seen as synthesized in specific being with "able to perform an appendectomy." The synthesis in specific being makes the ability to perform an appendectomy pertain to "qualified surgeon" in its every existence. It assures the proper distribution of "qualified surgeon" as a middle term. In confrontation with the first premise it requires that "able to perform an appendectomy" be synthesized in the real being of the individual who is a qualified surgeon.

The original accidental being that was grasped in the first premise follows through, accordingly, in the conclusion "He is able to perform an appendectomy." The concluding judgment thus creates no new being, but sees the being that was known in the first premise as now synthesizing a further predicate. The inclusion of this predicate in its synthesizing was not made known to the intellect in either of the first two judgments. It was not received passively from the object by means of them. The second judgment, rather, synthesized the common qualitative nature "surgeon" with a definite ability. But the common nature was already seen actualized by a particular real existence. A common nature, abstracting from all being without precision[4] can be actualized by any one of its existences. Seen now as synthesized with a real existential act in an individual thing, it requires that its own necessary predicates be also synthesized in the same existence. This synthesis, by which the third term of the reasoning is seen existing in the being of the first subject, is expressed in the conclusion. The concluding synthesis, accordingly, is not passively impressed upon the intellect in the way existence is impressed upon it by the object in immediate judgments, but is reached through further activity on the part of the intellect itself.

Erroneous Conclusions. In this active process, however, faulty reasoning often, as a matter of fact, takes place. Upon examination the conclusion may be found in disagreement with the reality. From the credentials, for instance, you reasoned that the man at your door was a genuine agent. Later you found out that he was not. Yet your first conclusion maintained that he was really genuine. It had real existence as its object. It expressed a real existence that it did not apprehend in the object, but merely, in a trite metaphor, "jumped at." How is such a procedure possible? How can the intellect grasp as real what is not there to be apprehended in the object itself?

The answer lies in the functioning of the middle term. For the conclusion to be correctly drawn, the middle term has to be properly distributed. If it is not so distributed, the being of the first subject need not follow through to the final synthesis. A hiatus may occur, causing discontinuity. If the second premise were "Qualified surgeons are able to perform some operations," you would have no means of knowing from it that appendectomies are included in the operations. On confrontation of the premises you now see synthesized in the being of the first subject the generic notion of performing some operations, not the specific one of performing appendectomies. If through haste and inadvertence you substitute the specific notion for the generic, you are predicating of the original subject an aspect that you did not see joined in specific being through the second premise. You are indeed retaining in the object of your concluding judgment the being of the original subject, but you are extending its synthesizing grasp to something that you did not see synthesized in its continuation into the second premise.

[4] *De Ente*, c. III, p. 26.8–10.

Even in the case of a true conclusion, the final synthesis is not impressed upon the intellect immediately by the object. The intellect is functioning actively. There need be little wonder, then, that it is able to go beyond the strict exigencies of the thing known, since it may be substituting a fourth for the middle term in its reasoning. If the particular surgeon did not happen to know how to perform an appendectomy, the conclusion just considered would be false. It would indeed be grasping an existential act that was there in reality, namely the accidental being that synthesizes a man with the habit of surgical art. It would not be manufacturing this act, for it would have it from the first premise. But it would be forcing the existential act to synthesize with the subject what the act was not synthesizing with him in reality. It would be an act of intellection, and so an act of cognition, but cognition that was not in accord with its object, the particular surgeon. The erroneous synthesis is a cognitional synthesis, for it is not a spatial mixing or linking together in the way signified by the original meaning of "synthesis." It is a uniting or a synthesis in the sense of a cognition that one thing is the other, for instance that the charity collector is genuine. If it disagrees with the way the thing itself is, it is false.

Causality of Object. Where the object is the cause of the cognition, as in sensation, simple apprehension, and immediate judgment, the knower is receptive in regard to what is known. In the receptive cognition, all that is known comes from the object to the knower, without any change resulting from the cognitive process in the thing known. Here no error is possible. If an erroneous judgment were received passively from the object, it would give rise to a self-contradictory situation. The cognitional act would at the same time have the object as its form and not have it as its form. In immediate cognition the things known remain unchanged. The same things, accordingly, can be known by many different men, in common natures through simple apprehension and in the same real existential acts through immediate judgments. The basis for common enduring knowledge of the same things and for communication of knowledge from one man to another is thereby established.[5] Different men know and talk about basically the same things.

[5] The requirement of a common external object to ground intellectual communication among men was recognized by the Greek Sophists and its difficulties were tellingly exploited by them. See Gorgias, in *On Melissus, Xenophanes, and Gorgias*, 6, 980b1–17 (Bekker Aristotle) and in Sextus Empiricus, *Adv. Math.*, VII, 83–86. Plato met the requirement by his doctrine of the Ideas, *Prm.*, 135BC. For St Augustine (*De Magistro*, XII, 40; *PL* XXXII, 1217) the things themselves, spread out interiorly through the divine illumination in each person's own thought, make intellectual communication possible. For St Thomas, as has already been seen (above,

In mediate knowledge, however, the active character of judgment becomes prominent. The original simple natures remain known, along with the existential acts grasped through immediate judgment. But in the authentically known existential acts further natures, known originally from other objects, may be actively synthesized in conclusions in ways that do not correspond with the reality. In that case you have a false conclusion, a bubble that will burst at the prick of reality, a mirage that will vanish upon closer contact. As the receptivity of human cognition grounds common knowledge and communication among men, so this activity of human cognition establishes the possibility of the myriad variations and discrepancies in knowledge from man to man, and the occasion of widespread error. It permits the intellect to compound syntheses that are not taking place in real being, even though all the elements, including the original being, are taken from what is immediately and passively known.

Causality of the Will. Since no existential synthesis in the object is the cause of the false cognition, where is the cause to be sought? Natural philosophy shows that a cognitive faculty can be acted upon only by its object and by the appetite that commands it. The appetite that commands the activity of the intellect is the will. Since the object does not prompt the act of false cognition, then, the cause has to be the human will.[6] A bit of introspection will confirm this conclusion beyond reasonable doubt. The reason why you jump at a conclusion is because you *wish* to know something in a hurry. You rush to the conclusion that the charity collector is genuine because you want to get the matter settled at once and get back to your work or your television program.

But the same will that commands the intellect to proceed to a conclusion not caused by the object, can likewise command the intellect to reflect on its processes and discover where the causality of the object ceased. In distinction to the synthetic or inventive process by which the conclusion was built up, this is called analytic or judicative.[7] It analyzes

Chapter 9, n. 12), the common nature is the ground of the object both as it exists externally in the individual thing and as it exists in every human intellect that knows it.

[6] See St Thomas, *De Ver.*, XIV, 1c (text above, Chapter 18, n. 21); *ST*, II–II, 1, 4c.

[7] ". . . nor would the process of reasoning arrive at anything certain, unless the examination of what was found out by the process be carried to the first principles, into which reasoning makes its analysis; so that understanding is found to be the source of reasoning as regards the way of finding out (*viam inveniendi*) but its terminus as regards the way of judging (*viam judicandi*)." *De Ver.*, XV, 1c. Cf.: ". . . all the certitude of science arises from the certitude of the principles; for then are the

the reasoning into its various steps and passes judgment on the soundness of each. By making sure that each separate synthesis in the reasoning corresponds with the synthesis in reality, it can finally know the truth of the conclusion. In this manner certainty in regard to mediate knowledge is attained. The assent is caused by the object, as in immediate judgments, and cannot be withheld by the intellect when the truth of the conclusion as a conclusion is actually being known. The concluding judgment, of course, is stored in the memory and can be recalled. Known separately, however, it is just remembered as true and as having received assent, and so can be used without hesitation, as in the case of previously demonstrated theorems of geometry.[8] But as memorized, the object is not causing the assent. Rather, the will is the cause, and a flaw in memory can make it an erroneous premise for any new reasoning. In general, assent to any erroneous premise and certitude regarding it is caused by the will.

Demonstration. The truth of a conclusion, then, is known when the truth of each of the immediate judgments is seen together with the logically required distribution of the terms. This is called

conclusions known with certitude, when they are analyzed (*resolvuntur*) into the principles." *Ibid.*, XI, 1, ad 13m. This means bringing the conclusions back to sense cognition: ". . . the cognition of the conclusions has its origin in the principles, hence a correct judgment about the conclusion cannot be had except by analyzing back to the principles. Therefore, since all cognition of our intellect arises from sensation, there cannot be a correct judgment unless it be brought back to sensation." *In IV Sent.*, d. 9, a. 4, Resp. ad q. 1m; ed. Moos, IV, 386 (no. 142). In this context, as can be seen from the last quotation, "judgment" has the meaning of a decision made after an examination. It is a "judgment *about* the conclusion." Cf.: "Things about which a judgment is made are examined with reference to some source of cognition, as we judge about the conclusions by analyzing them into the principles." *De Ver.*, XII, 3, ad 2m. ". . . by way of inquiry or of finding out, human reasoning proceeds from things understood in a simple way. These are the first principles. And again by way of judgment it returns by analysis to the first principles, and in reference to them it examines what it has found out." *ST*, I, 79, 8c. The two ways are contrasted as synthesis (*viam compositionis vel inventionis*) and analysis (*viam resolutionis*) at *In Boeth. de Trin.*, VI, 1; ed. P. Wyser (Fribourg & Louvain, 1948), 60.13–15. On the historical background of these two ways and the philosophical method involved in them, see L.-M. Régis, "Analyse et Synthèse dans l'Oeuvre de Saint Thomas," in *Studia Mediaevalia*, in honorem Raymundi Josephi Martin (Bruges, 1948), pp. 303–330. Cf. B. Lonergan, "The Concept of *Verbum*," *Theological Studies*, VIII (1947), 48–52.

[8] The stability of natures or essence provides the ground that a conclusion once demonstrated continues to hold good. In Descartes' philosophy, where stability from the side of essence is lacking, the further guarantee of divine veracity is required for truths accepted through memory; see H. G. Wolz, "The Double Guarantee of Descartes' Ideas," *The Review of Metaphysics*, III (1950), 487; E. Gilson, *Etudes sur le Rôle de la Pensée Médiévale dans la Formation du Système Cartésien* (Paris, 1930), pp. 236–238; 243.

the reduction of the conclusion to first principles. A reasoning process from first principles in correct logical sequence is called a **demonstration.**[9]

The easiest type of example in which demonstration may be seen at work is the mathematical. When you look at the vertically opposite angles made by two intersecting straight lines, you do not see immediately that they have to be equal. Yet you do see immediately that each of the two angles lies along a straight line with another and common angle, totaling in each case the sum of 180 degrees. Take away the common third angle, and the difference from the 180 degrees, you see immediately, will be in each case the same. You know then, mediately, that the two vertically opposite angles have to be equal, no matter what particular instance of this drawing you may happen to have in Euclidean plane geometry. In the first premise you synthesize, in being, each of the angles as subject with the "equal to" the same predicate: "Each of the two angles *is* the equal of one hundred and eighty degrees less the third angle." The more common notion of "equal thing" is substituted for "equal angle" in the second of the premises: "Things equal to a third thing are equal to each other." The common notion "thing," able to have being in any one of its particular instances, is then seen in the conclusion as having being in the subject of the first premise, just as any common nature can have being in any one of its subjects. The synthesizing existential act of the first subject is now seen as synthesizing also the predicate of the second premise: "Each of the two angles is equal to the other." The being that was grasped in the first premise as synthesizing one predicate with the subject is now grasped as synthesizing a second predicate with the same thing. These considerations hold for the much longer and more complicated geometrical demonstrations.

Demonstration of Efficient Cause. You may say that the further synthesis in the being of the first subject is seen easily enough where the sequence is based upon formal causality, as in geometry. All the natures that are involved can be actuated by the same being. But how can this take place in reasoning that concludes from immediately known things to their efficient cause, that is, to something actuated by another and diverse act of being?

From the fingerprints on a murder weapon, the expert concludes to the identity of the man who made them. He did not see the accused place the fingerprints on the gun, but, as far as efficient causality can be observed, he did see him cause the fingerprints that he took in the

[9] See Aristotle, *APo.*, I 2, 71b17–72b4.

laboratory. The two sets have exactly the same formation. He concludes, then, that the accused put the fingerprints on the gun. Here there is no question of the being in the first premise serving as the synthesizing act in the conclusion. The first premise is "The accused made the fingerprints in the lab." The conclusion is "The accused made the fingerprints on the gun." In the objects of these judgments there are two separate existential syntheses, effected at markedly different times.

The second premise in the reasoning is that all fingerprints of the same formation are made by the same person. How is this premise known? It is acquired by inductive experience. It has been found to be the case in all the hundreds of thousands of instances studied by the experts. On this ground it is accepted for the reasoning. There is no other way for men to know it. If an instance of two different persons making exactly the same kind of fingerprints should ever be discovered, the premise would have to be revised to meet the newly discovered facts. As it stands, it includes the efficient cause as already known through experience: "Identical fingerprints are caused by the same person." It does not conclude that there is an efficient cause of the fingerprints. It assumes that there is such a cause, and merely identifies the individual instance. In practical spheres nobody questions the assumption that human fingerprints are caused by men.

In the metaphysical demonstration that every finite thing has an efficient cause, however, the reasoning does conclude to the existence of something else. In this unique case, the subject of the first premise is the existential synthesis itself, and not the thing that the synthesis makes exist.[10] Because the existential act is accidental and prior, it depends as accident upon something other than what it actuates. Its dependence as accident involves something from which it proceeds as well as a subject in which it inheres. Its dependence on the other thing is not by way of formal sequence but by way of efficient causality, which is an operation. To operate, the other thing has to exist. The concluding synthesis here is indeed a different one from the synthesis that was the original starting point. A change of subject takes place during the course of the reasoning. But it is a change that is made necessary by what is involved by the original subject. The original subject is the synthesizing act itself. In the conclusion that it is dependent as accident upon something other than what it synthesizes, it still functions in its role of subject. It shows that it involves a "something else." The question then arises about the existence of this other thing. The other thing now becomes the subject

[10] On the therapy required in representing a sensible thing's existence as a subject, see St Thomas, *De Ver.*, XXI, 5, ad 8m.

of the reasoning, and is seen as synthesized existentially with its operation, and so as existing. The change of subject is possible only because the existential synthesis, alone among accidents, involves dependence through efficient causality instead of through formal causality. It involves not only the being of the subject that it synthesizes, but also the being of the agent that produces it. Another act of real existence, accordingly, is implicit from the start in what the existence of any sensible thing reveals of itself, and so is able to be known explicitly through the final conclusion.

Demonstration *Propter Quid*. In demonstration, the middle term is the reason offered for the conclusion. It can readily be expressed with the conjunction "because." When you say "He is genuine because he has his credentials," you are giving the credentials as the cause or reason of your conclusion. Any syllogism may be expressed in one sentence with the middle term in a clause introduced by this conjunction. The syllogism "Angles opposite equal sides in a triangle are equal, but all angles in an equilateral triangle are opposite equal sides, therefore all the angles in an equilateral triangle are equal," may be worded more simply "The angles in an equilateral triangle are equal *because* they are opposite equal sides." Similarly three times four equals twice six *because* both are equal to the same number twelve.

In these last two examples the reason given is the immediate cause of what is concluded. The angles in a triangle are caused by the lines diverging from common points. You can have lines without angles, but you cannot have angles without lines. The lines are prior to the angles in the order of formal causality. Because the divergence of the lines for each of the angles is equal in distance at corresponding points, that is, because the lines opposite the angles are equal, the angles themselves are equal. The immediate cause, the true and exactly fitting cause, is given. It shows not only *that* the conclusion is true, but also *why* it is true and cannot be otherwise. In its own order, that of formal causality, it is the fully adequate reason for what is concluded. It requires no supplementary feature in its own order of causality to account for the equality of the angles. Correspondingly, the equality of each of the two products to twelve units is the immediate and fully adequate reason why three times four is equal to twice six. Each group is constituted respectively by twelve units.

This kind of demonstration is known in Scholastic terminology as *propter quid* demonstration.[11] It proceeds always from cause to effect,

[11] Aristotle, *APo.*, I 13, 78a22–40, named it demonstration of the *dioti*, and characterized in the same way the scientific knowledge to which it gives rise.

and never vice versa. It always explains through the proximate, that is, the immediate cause, and not through a remote cause. Because its explanation is fully adequate in its own order of causality, it is completely demonstrative. It is the model type of demonstration.[12]

Demonstration *Quia*. Something may be demonstrated, however, by an effect, or, in negative reasoning, by a remote cause. If from the sight of smoke you reason to the presence of fire, you are reasoning from effect to cause. If in the course of a more complicated geometrical theorem, you learn that a triangle you encounter has three equal angles, you can conclude that it is equilateral. In this case the equal angles are the effect of the equal sides, not the cause. Your conclusion is demonstrative. It establishes the fact that the three sides are equal, but it does not give the cause of that equality.

In positive demonstration, you cannot argue from a remote cause to the effect. You cannot conclude that three times four equals twice six because they both have a relation to twelve. The aspect of relation is only a remote, generic cause. It has to be specified to the relation of equality, the proximate cause. Three and four are both related to twelve, but the relation is that of divisor, not of equal. In negative demonstration, however, the remote cause can establish the *fact* of the conclusion. Anything that had no relation to twelve, for instance the abstract quality redness, could not be the equal of three times four. A triangle is shown not to be a square because it does not have four sides. The fact is thereby established. Yet having just four sides is not the adequate cause of a square. It is the proximate cause of a quadrilateral, but only a remote cause of a square. A blood test, accordingly, may be sufficient to rule out paternity, but not to establish it positively.

Demonstration by means of an effect or of a remote cause is named in traditional Scholastic terminology *quia* demonstration.[13] It is sufficient to establish the fact that the conclusion is true, but does not adequately explain the predicate that is synthesized with the subject in the conclusion.

Doubt. The conclusion of a demonstration, known as such, naturally compels the assent of the knower. It is an object that causes assent and certitude. If the reflexive analysis of a reasoning process, however, fails to show that it is demonstrative, the conclusion does not com-

[12] Aristotle, *APo.*, I 14, 79a17–24.

[13] This translates the demonstration of the *hoti*, Aristotle, *APo.*, I 13, 78b7–14. Like the Latin *quia*, the Greek *hoti* as used here indicates that the "fact" provides a reason for the assertion. The notion of a cause, however, is expressed much more strongly in *dioti* and *propter quid*.

pel assent. If the object does not move the intellect in either direction, the result is called **doubt.** A doubt is properly the result of a reasoning process. After considering the reasons available, you find that no assent is caused by the object, and you conclude that you do not wish to accept either alternative. If no reasons are inclining you either way, you have a **negative doubt,** as for instance when you see something moving through the trees but cannot discern anything that would show whether it is game or another hunter. You decide it is too doubtful for a shot. On the other hand, reasons for each alternative may balance. You may find that fluoridation is desirable because of the teeth, but undesirable because of the risk to general health. You remain doubtful about it, this time with a **positive doubt.**[14]

Doubt, accordingly, is to be distinguished from the initial attitude of inquiry that sets a reasoning process afoot. Doubt, when present, comes at the end, and not the beginning, of a reasoning process. Philosophical thinking, accordingly, cannot begin with doubt,[15] even though it does begin with wonder and questioning. It begins, even for Descartes,[16] with certitude regarding immediate judgments.

Opinion. If at the conclusion of the reflexive analysis the object itself does not cause assent but inclines toward one of the two opposite alternatives, the knower may by his own will give assent to that alternative, while acknowledging the possibility that it may be wrong.[17]

---

[14] "Thus, therefore, our possible intellect is disposed in different ways with regard to the sides of a contradiction. For sometimes it is not inclined to one side more than to the other, either on account of lack of motives, as in those problems in which we do not have reasons, or on account of the apparent equality of those that impel to each of the sides; and this is the disposition of one in doubt." St Thomas, *De Ver.*, XIV, 1c.

[15] See supra, Chapter 18, nn. 10–11.

[16] See supra, Chapter 18, n. 9.

[17] "In the other way, the intellect assents to something not because it is sufficiently moved by its proper object, but through a choice inclining voluntarily to one side rather than to the other. And if this is with doubt about and fear of the other side, it will be opinion . . ." St Thomas, *ST*, II–II, 1, 4c. Though called "assent" in this article of the *Summa*, the acceptance of one side of a contradiction with doubt about the other was denied the status of assent in an earlier work: ". . . hence it indeed accepts one side, yet always doubts about the opposite; and this is the disposition of a person with opinion, who accepts one side of a contradiction with fear of the other . . . a person in doubt does not have assent, since he does not adhere to one side rather than to the other; nor likewise has a person with opinion, since his acceptation in regard to an alternative is not made firm." *De Ver.*, XIV, 1c. The latter passage distinguishes "acceptance" from "assent," and requires *firm* acceptance for assent. This restriction of the term "assent" seems a concession to the derivation of "assent" from "sententia," understood, against a background in Isaac Israeli and Avicenna, as "a distinct and most certain conception" (*ibid.*). Isaac had defined "sententia" as "credulitas vel firmitudo rei alicuius." *Liber de Definitionibus,* I; ed.

This consent has been called **probable assent**[18] and the judgment to which the contingent assent is given is an opinion. The probability admits a wide range of degrees, from the near certain to the flimsy and tentative kind that is known as suspicion or conjecture. In everyday life the great preponderance of human cognition is opinion. For practical purposes the knower has to use opinions as the basis of conduct and action. Hence he is willing to give his probable assent to them, rather than remain inactive.[19] It is an assent caused by the will.

Faith. A further type of mediate cognition is faith. If the mechanic who services your car tells you the valves need grinding, you assent to that judgment even though you yourself know nothing about the needs of valves. In this case there is nothing in the object to move you to assent, even to the probable assent of opinion. The assent is all the more caused by your will.[20] You give the assent, because you have concluded that the mechanic understands valves and wants you to know the truth about the ones in your car, and that it is to your own advantage to accept his information. Assenting to a judgment on the word of another is called faith or belief. It requires acquaintance with the reliability of your informant, that is, that he has the requisite knowledge and that he is not intending to deceive you. Both these points are conclusions of your own. In accepting his capacity to give the information reliably,

---

J. T. Muckle, in *Archives d'Histoire Doctrinale et Littéraire du Moyen Age*, XII–XIII (1938), 321.7–8. When speaking untrammeled by this background, St Thomas in the *Summa Theologiae* passage does not hesitate to call the acceptance of an opinion an assent. On the same problem in *In III Sent*., d. 23, q. 2, a. 2, Solut. 1 (ed. Moos, III, 724–725, nos. 137 and 141), and on the other relevant texts, see A. Gardeil, La 'Certitude Probable,'" *Revue des Sciences Philosophiques et Théologiques,* V (1911), 449–453. For opposite interpretation, see F. A. Cunningham, "*Certitudo* in St. Thomas Aquinas," *The Modern Schoolman*, XXX (1953), 304, n. 54.

[18] L.-M. Régis, *Epistemology* (New York, 1959), p. 414. On the historical background of St Thomas' use of the term "probable," see T. Deman, "*Probabilis,*" *Revue des Sciences Philosophiques et Théologiques*, XXII (1933), 260–290. Gardeil, *art. cit*., p. 453, concludes that for St Thomas opinion is a "contingent assent." St Thomas (*ST*, II–II, 1, 4c) calls it assent *cum dubitatione et formidine*.

[19] Similarly, "our intellectual life would be singularly sterile, if we withheld our judgments until they were compelled by clear and convincing evidence." F. M. Tyrrell, "Concerning the Nature and Function of the Act of Judgment," *The New Scholasticism*, XXVI (1952), 412. In opinion, there is assent to only one side of the contradictory, and doubt in regard to the other. See Gardeil, *art. cit*., p. 452. The "fear" that the other side may be true is essentially the intellectual recognition of the possibility: "It is of the nature of opinion that what is opined is considered possible to be otherwise." St Thomas, *ST*, II–II, 1, 5, ad 4m. Though "fear" in an affective sense is not essential to opinion, it is a frequent and normal consequence; see Gardeil, pp. 469–470.

[20] "Believing . . . has assent only from the command of the will." St Thomas, *De Ver*., XIV, 3c. Cf. 2c.

you accept his authority. In human authority there is always the possibility that your informant is mistaken or that he is deceiving you. Faith in human authority, therefore, can never be absolute. There is always the possibility that a judgment accepted solely on human authority may be wrong.

In events immediately perceived by the informants, the reliability can be very high. It is on such testimony of witnesses that the gravest issues are decided in the lawcourts. In doctrinal matters, on the other hand, the authority of the informant is no greater than the reasons he can give. In this sphere human authority is the weakest of arguments.[21] Since authority does not manifest the intrinsic truth of a judgment but only its credibility, it is not a source of philosophical reasoning. At best it can be a confirmation of probable conclusions, or a motive for selecting a philosopher as one's guide in the search for truth. In everyday life, however, much of one's information comes from authority. The news that you get from the daily telecast and daily paper, your knowledge of countries and cities that you have not visited, your knowledge of history, all that you know from reading of books, constitute a sizable portion of your cognition. Yet it is all accepted on faith. Faith, accordingly, is an extremely important means of widening human cognition.

Common sense is a conglomerate of knowledge, opinions, and beliefs held by people in general at any given time.[22] In moral matters it is worthy of consideration, but in theoretical sciences it cannot be admitted as a source. It is the acceptance of judgments on the authority of the people in general. Like anything accepted on human authority, its intrinsic truth is not made manifest, and so it cannot serve as a source for philosophical reasoning. Since in doctrinal matters authority is no stronger than the reasons on which it is based, and in common sense the doctrinal reasons are lacking, common sense has no role to play whatsoever on the level of speculative philosophy.

---

[21] St Thomas, *ST*, I, 1, 8, arg. 2. With supernatural faith, on the other hand, the assent is absolute because of the divine authority and the infusion of grace in the soul, for supernatural faith "holds from infused light things that naturally exceed cognition." *De Ver.*, XIV, 2c.

[22] On the meaning and history of "common sense," and its unwarranted acceptance as a criterion in philosophy through the influence of Fenelon, Buffier, and Thomas Reid, see Etienne Gilson, *Réalisme Thomiste et Critique de la Connaissance* (Paris, 1939), pp. 14–35. Likewise based on authority are the various forms of traditionalism current in France during the first half of the nineteenth century, in the aftermath of the French Revolution, for instance in De Bonald, De Maistre, and Lamennais, and in the fideism of Bautain. These doctrines attempted to base philosophical thinking upon what was established through traditions of the human race. On their meaning and history see Louis Foucher, *La Philosophie Catholique en France au XIXe Siècle* (Paris, 1955), pp. 11–98.

Enrichment Through Mediate Knowledge. Mediate knowledge, in the conclusions of demonstrations as well as in opinions and beliefs, keeps extending human cognition further and further. By its means, a man becomes in intentional being a vast number of things that he does not reach through immediate knowledge. Through human testimony he accumulates riches of historical lore and of findings by investigators in fields where he has no competence of his own. Only through demonstration, however, does he know with full and evident certainty the truth about things not immediately present to his cognition. It is through demonstration, therefore, that the perfection of his mediate knowledge is attained. But there are various levels in the starting points from which demonstration can be initiated. These different starting points open the way to the various human sciences. Through the sciences, on account of their demonstrative processes, human knowledge blossoms into its greatest achievements. With the investigation of the sciences, accordingly, the study of human knowledge will round itself out to its overall completion.

Résumé. The active character of judgment, the second operation of the human intellect, makes possible the extension of knowledge by synthesizing further predicates in being that has previously been known. In demonstration the concluding synthesis is necessitated by the objects as cogently as in immediate judgments.[23] In erroneous conclusions, opinions, and beliefs, on the other hand, the assent is ultimately caused by the human will. Even though the opinion, the belief, or the erroneously drawn conclusion should happen to be true, the assent to it is caused by the will and not by the object.[24] Correction or justification of mediate judgments is based ultimately on being that is immediately known, and not upon a study of cognitive processes. The study of the way the human intellect functions shows how error occurs,

[23] "But the assent of scientific knowledge is not subject to free will, because he who has scientific knowledge is compelled to assent by the efficacy of the demonstration." St Thomas, *ST*, II–II, 2, 9, ad 2m. Cf. I, 82, 2c; I–II, 10, 2, ad 3m.

[24] In contrast to nescience, which is a mere negation of knowledge, and ignorance, which is a lack of knowledge in a person capable of it, error "superadds a certain act to ignorance. . . . But when he makes a false judgment about what he does not know, then he is said properly to err." St Thomas, *De Malo*, III, 7c. The erroneous judgment, accordingly, is about what one does not know. That means that there is nothing on the side of the object that could compel assent. The term "knowledge" is in this way reserved for cognition that is true. But a "false opinion" is a positive intellectual act, compared by St Thomas (*De Ver.*, XVIII, 6c) to a monstrous birth that takes place in a way opposed to the normal workings of the first principles in cognition. St Thomas (*ibid.*, arg. 9) seems to have no objection to the term "fallacious (*fallax*) cognition."

but contributes nothing to the certitude or intellectual justification of mediate knowledge. The criterion from start to finish is the being of the things known.

SUGGESTED READINGS AND REFERENCES

St Thomas Aquinas, *Truth*, XIV, 1; tr. James V. McGlynn (Chicago: Henry Regnery, 1953), II, 207–213.

Daniel Sommer Robinson, *An Anthology of Modern Philosophy* (New York: Thomas Y. Crowell, 1931), pp. 160–174 (Descartes); pp. 327–333 (Locke); pp. 392–400 (Hume); pp. 413–426 (Reid).

Reginald F. O'Neill, *Readings in Epistemology* (Englewood Cliffs, N. J.: Prentice-Hall, Inc., 1962), pp. 22–39 (Aristotle); pp. 93–111 (Spinoza); pp. 113–122 (Leibniz); pp. 176–198 (Kant).

CHAPTER 20

The Sciences

Quest for Causes. The beginnings and development of the sciences, as Aristotle[1] long ago noted, are occasioned by the innate human desire to know the causes of things. Wonder about causes is usually aroused when something functions differently from its expected way. The regular manner of acting can be taken for granted. An unexpected way, however, especially if it seems directly opposite to the accustomed way, arouses human curiosity and sparks inquiry into the reason for the apparently strange behavior. As examples Aristotle mentioned the performance of puppets and the incommensurability of a triangle's hypotenuse with its side. Wooden figures are expected to stay still. When puppets are seen dancing and gesticulating like living things, they prompt a desire to know and understand the unseen cause. Likewise, any two lines would at first sight be expected to have a common integral divisor. When none is found for the hypotenuse and side, a desire to know the mathematical reason naturally arises.

A later example would be the phenomena of suction. The suction of water through a straw or by an ordinary pump could be taken for granted from experience. It could be vaguely accounted for by saying that nature abhors a vacuum. When the pump failed to function for a height greater than 28 ft., nature's abhorrence of a vacuum could hardly be accepted as extending just that far. A different cause had to be sought. It was found in the pressure of air on the water's surface. On calculating the weight of air at sea level, you know why even a perfect suction pump could not raise the water above 34 ft. You have now scientific knowledge of the phenomena, in contrast to ordinary knowledge.

In this way knowledge of the cause is equated with universally valid knowledge.[2] Until the cause was discovered, men knew only that a pump functioned in a certain way for heights under 28 ft., and then found it

[1] *Metaph.*, A 2, 983a12–20.
[2] *Ibid.*, 1, 981a5–b6.

did not function in that way for greater heights. The one true cause provided the reason in each of the cases. Knowledge of it could be used for the construction of force pumps and compression pumps that would apply increased weight of air and make the water rise higher. In a corresponding way knowledge of the causes of disease has brought about the application of the correct remedies to each case, instead of the hit and miss technique of using a remedy that was successful in one case with the hope that it will work in the next. Discovery of the cause of cancer, for instance, will it is hoped lead to a cure for the different cases of the disease, just as the discovery of the causes of tuberculosis and of diabetes led to the means of curing or controlling those diseases in each individual case that had not gone too far.

The reason for this equation of knowledge through cause and universal knowledge is that the form of a thing is a principle of universality in every singular. The form of a triangle is the principle in any individual triangle that makes the geometrical truths seen in one triangle, just on account of its triangular shape, hold for all other triangles. The form is the cause of the specific unity of all the individuals sharing that form. Whatever follows from the form just as form, then, will hold for every individual of the species, even though it has been actually seen in only one individual. Since the form is one of the thing's causes, knowledge through form is knowledge through a cause. An efficient cause, moreover, acts according to its form, and as final cause an object attracts or repels in one way or another according to its form, while the material cause is knowable only through its form. Exemplar and object function as formal causes.[3] Knowledge through cause, accordingly, is in each case universal knowledge, insofar as the cause is conditioned by form. Science, then, is of the universal.[4]

Theoretical Science. As will appear from the above examples, scientific knowledge can be concerned merely with knowing, as in the case of the geometrical study of the triangle or the study of atmospheric pressure in physics. In these sciences the mind is content when it knows the truth with certainty. Their findings are taken by the engineer and used for other purposes, quite as the discoveries of biology are taken over by the medical practitioner and are used in the cure of disease. But just in themselves, sciences like geometry, physics, and biology are concerned only with the discovery of the truth in their respective fields. Their operation consists in a beholding of what is there

[3] On these extrinsic formal causes, cf. above, Chapter 15, n. 14.
[4] See above, Chapter 16, nn. 5–11.

and what is true. It is a contemplating of things in the light of their causes. Sciences of this type, accordingly, are called in the Aristotelian and Scholastic traditions theoretical or speculative sciences, from the Greek and Latin words respectively for "contemplative." Against the historical background, "theoretical" in this context does not imply any divorce from reality whatsoever, but rather a direct concern with reality itself; and "speculative" does not imply any uncertainty or hazarding, but on the contrary the firmness of assent or the certainty that goes with examined knowledge of truth.

Since a theoretical science is concerned solely with the object that is known, the principles from which it proceeds in its demonstrations will have to be found in the object itself. Its object is something given for it to contemplate, and not something that it is going to produce. Its object is therefore something that already has being, although theoretical science, on account of its knowledge through form, is able to predict how a thing will act in the future. As universal, the knowledge holds for past, present, and future, and therefore is able to ground prediction.

Productive and Practical Science. The examples considered, however, show that scientific knowledge can be concerned not only with the contemplation of truth, but also with the production of things. The engineer knows how to apply scientifically the findings of mathematics and physics to the construction of bridges and machines. The psychiatrist knows how to apply the findings of biology and psychology to the cure of mental patients. Engineering and psychiatry are rightly considered sciences, because they proceed not in a haphazard way but in function of knowledge of the causes that are at work in physical and psychic spheres. Guided by knowledge of these causes they are able to manipulate them in such a way that they will produce the desired effect, for instance the machine or mental health. They differ from the theoretical sciences in having as their object not just knowledge but a product outside the knowledge. They differ also in seeing their principles not in their object, but in a formal cause within the knower, that is, in the design or plan or blueprint that he has elaborated or from which he works. They are accordingly dealing with objects that are not as yet made but come into existence as a result of their work. A productive science may also be called an art or a craft.

Science is called practical when its object is not a product but the guiding of human activity itself. Moral and political sciences come under this type. As in productive science, something more than just contemplation of truth is envisaged. But instead of a product, the object is now human conduct itself. The principles are found in the knower, but not in a fixed design or blueprint. They are found in the deliberation of a free agent.[5] Like productive science, then, practical science bears on something that does not yet exist but is to be done. That object, however, is not a product to be made, but conduct that is to be guided.

Subject, Essence, and Property. The perfect type of mediate knowledge sought by the human mind is obtained through *propter quid* demonstration. In *propter quid* demonstration the proximate or fully adequate cause is known. Through that knowledge the effect is seen to follow necessarily wherever the cause is present. Equality of its interior angles to two right angles, for instance, follows necessarily wherever a Euclidean plane triangle is found. The fully adequate and necessitating cause is the very nature or essence of the triangle. The essence of the plane triangle is such that its three lines enclose angles equal to the angles lying along a straight line. The equality of those angles to two right angles is a property that follows from the triangle's essence. In knowing the essence you know its adequate cause. Through the essence you can demonstrate it of any individual triangle you draw. The essence is common to all Euclidean plane triangles whatsoever. The individual triangle is the subject of the demonstration, and the common essence serves as the middle term. The perfect type of science, these considerations indicate, consists in demonstrating a property of a subject by means of the subject's essence. There may be a number of links in the demonstration, but if the essence is shown to be the necessitating cause of the conclusion by reason of being such an essence, the knowledge gained is scientific in the full sense of *propter quid*.

Why this is so should not be difficult to see. The basic principle of specification in any being is its essence. If the properties are understood through the essence, they are understood in the most penetrating and fundamental of ways, insofar as their nature as properties is concerned. The natural desire of the human mind for knowledge, consequently, urges it toward *propter quid* knowledge of things.

Knowledge of Essence. For the essence to serve as a middle term in demonstration, however, it has first to be known. But what essences are knowable by the human mind? The original object of human cognition is the sensible world. This is known immediately as it is in contact with the external senses. No differentiation of substances is directly intuited, but just spatial and qualitative differences.

[5] See Aristotle, *Metaph.*, E 1, 1025b23–24.

The immediate knowledge is only of "something extended." Even that general essence does not immediately make its constitution manifest on the level of substance. Only by a reasoning process from effect to cause does it reveal its substantial principles, matter and form, in the science of natural philosophy. Nor does it immediately explain itself on the level of being. Reasoning from effect to cause is necessary in order to arrive at the nature of being and acquire knowledge of the thing's entitative principles. Nor do the sensible qualities immediately manifest their own essence or the essence of the substance in which they inhere. Incandescence, for instance, does not at once reveal what it is. It was long mistaken for a substance, fire.

One type of essence, however, does reveal itself immediately in knowledge of the sensible world. It is quantitative essence. Even though the differentiations in the immediate vision of the external world appear like surface markings, one is immediately seen as distinct from the other. Their sum, two, is immediately seen as constituted by two units. That is all two means. That is its whole essence in its own order, the order of quantity. It is completely intelligible as quantitative. The same holds correspondingly for all quantitative essences.

Through reflection, one knows one's self, but only in what one knows of corporeal essence and not immediately in one's own essence. One has to reason to the principles of one's own nature. The logical essences, similarly, are difficult to grasp, and have to be attained through reflexive reasoning about sensible things.

Mathematics. Among the things directly knowable to man, then, only quantities immediately reveal their essence. This holds for continuous as well as for discrete quantity. The essence of a straight line, on a Euclidean surface, is to be the shortest distance between two points. That is its whole essence as a quantity. As a quantity it is completely transparent to the human mind. The intellect's simple apprehension penetrates it through and through in the quantitative order. The same holds for what a square is, what a triangle is, what a geometric sphere is, and what the number one hundred and forty-four is. These quantitative essences are considered by the mind apart from the sensible qualities in which all quantities are seen in the real world. This way of considering the quantitative essences is called abstraction.[6] Since substance enters into the definition of every accident, quantity, because it

[6] See Aristotle, *Metaph.*, K 3, 1061a28–b3. Cf. Hippocrates George Apostle, *Aristotle's Philosophy of Mathematics* (Chicago, 1952), pp. 14–16.

is an accident, can never abstract from substance.[7] In the mathematical abstraction, therefore, the quantitative essences do not abstract from substance as such, but only from substance as sensible.[8]

Because the mathematical essences are so immediately knowable, pedagogically mathematics furnishes the model for demonstrating properties of a subject through the essence as middle term. It is accordingly the model in the pedagogical order for *propter quid* science. It was the first to reach scientific status among the theoretical sciences in human history, and it is still the first theoretical science taught as a science to children, in first grade arithmetic. Its very name was meant to identify it with learning, and even today its obvious scientific character makes it seem to many of its devotees to be the quintessence of education. It is divided into different branches according to successive degrees of quantitative complication. The more complicated use the less complicated branches, as for instance algebra and geometry use arithmetic.

Experimental Science. Through groupings of observable qualities, and of motions in the sensible world that are beyond his conscious control, the knower distinguishes myriad things in the universe before him. These things are grouped into various kingdoms and classes through likenesses in their qualities and their observable activities. The cataloguing gives rise to sciences like botany, zoology, and astronomy. At first their procedure was only on a qualitative basis, and could result merely in *quia* science. The qualities do not make manifest either their own essences or the essence of the substance in which they inhere. The blue and yellow of pigments, for instance, do not show why they are blue or why they are yellow. They merely reveal the fact that they are of the particular color. Mixed together, as a matter of fact they become green. You know the fact from experience, but why they should turn green you will never learn by scrutinizing the two qualities. You know the fact, the *quia*, but not the *propter quid*. From the effect, the producing of green, you reason that they are the causes. But you cannot discover the effect by probing the causes, as you could discover why seven and five make twelve by considering what seven and five are, namely twelve units. Qualitative procedures, accordingly, are unable to give perfect scientific knowledge of the sensible world.

All observable qualities, however, are imbedded in quantity. They are extended in space and continue in time. On account of their quantitative substructure they are measurable. They are subject to mathematical

[7] See above, Chapter 12, n. 7. Cf. St Thomas, *In VII Metaph.*, lect. 1, (ed. Cathala-Spiazzi) no. 1258.

[8] St Thomas, *ST*, I, 85, 1, ad 2m. Cf. Apostle, *op. cit.*, pp. 50–52.

treatment. Astronomy, optics, harmonics, and mechanics[9] were already mathematicized sciences among the ancient Greeks. In modern times all the experimental sciences have become mathematicized, and thereby have made marvelous progress. Chemistry and physics are the outstanding examples. But even highly descriptive sciences, like botany and child psychology and sociology, today are mathematicized in their graphs and charts and statistics and samplings. Taking as basic quantitative principles certain observable measures, they are able to explain their sensible objects with all the *propter quid* penetration of mathematics. They give perfect science of the things in the sensible world.[10] Any convenient observable unit could serve as a basic principle. Today the accepted unit of length is the distance between two lines on a bar of platinum-iridium, kept at the International Bureau of Weights and Measures, near Paris. The standard unit of mass, the kilogram, is a cylinder of platinum-iridium kept at the same place, and the second is the standard unit of time. In practice, the centimeter, the gram, and the second are the three basic units of measurement. With those basic units as principles, the scientific knowledge of man has penetrated into the inner recesses of the atom and into the outer galaxies of the cosmos. It has already brought men into the early stages of the atomic age and the cosmonautic age. Its achievements are astounding, and so far its progress is continually accelerating. It proceeds by patient observation, controlled and intensified experiment, and exact measurement. In the light of the measurements it is able to give its completely scientific explanation of the phenomena. It has the superb advantage of being able to verify experimentally what it deduces, at least in principle, as Pascal's law of the transmission of pressure by liquids has been verified in hydraulic presses and Einstein's theory of relativity was verified by the bending of light rays during the solar eclipse.

Experimental science has always been divided into various branches on the basis of difference in its objects. The stars gave rise to astronomy, plants to botany, animals to zoology, mental states to psychology. The

[9] These are the examples used by Aristotle to show that *quia* natural sciences become *propter quid* sciences by being mathematicized. *APo.*, I 13, 78b32–79a16.

[10] Jacques Maritain, *The Degrees of Knowledge*, tr. G. B. Phelan (New York, 1959), p. 55, regards the physico-mathematical sciences as substituting "a mathematics *quid est*" for the sensible thing's substantial essence, and therefore giving "perinoetic" and not "dianoetic" understanding of the thing. — This "perinoetic" knowledge, however, is undoubtedly *propter quid*. As long as it remains within its own order it does not substitute for anything else, but is its honest self. It has no need to pretend to any penetration into substantial essence. Maritain (*ibid.*, p. 209) also expresses the contrast by "empiriological" versus "ontological." Cf. *The Range of Reason* (New York, 1952), p. 8.

tendency has been to keep dividing into narrower and narrower specialties as knowledge increases and further penetration requires concentration on a smaller area of research. Yet the common quantitative basis in all these branches of experimental science keeps operative a tendency toward unity and cooperation, so that "the very sciences which tend to divide and multiply *also* tend of their own interior dynamism to amalgamate and unify."[11] Their divisions and amalgamations, accordingly, cannot be dictated apriori, but have to be left to the convenience of the workers in the field.

Nevertheless a philosophical discipline that has attained great popularity today is called the philosophy of science.[12] It aims to establish critically the basic presuppositions and categories that the experimental scientist takes for granted. It is as yet in a quite fluid state. Its projected work can be done quite well, as far as it needs to be done, by metaphysics and natural philosophy and logic, as these are understood in the Aristotelian and Scholastic traditions. There is no question of supplying the experimental scientist with his object. He has it already. From it and from no other source does he get his methods. His proven success is amply sufficient to protect him from any skepticism regarding his procedure. He is doing his own genuine work, and is doing it well. He is not trying to substitute an abstract mathematical essence for a real essence, but is explaining sensible things according to their real quantitative measurements. Besides enormous practical value, his explanations have the full status of theoretical *propter quid* science, even though he himself, as scientist,[13] would show no interest in that designation.

Philosophy of Nature. Extended substance, known in one's immediate cognition of the sensible world, requires two substantial principles. As something quantitative, it has to remain the same thing while extended through different parts. One substantial principle is required to account for the sameness, the other for the difference. The sameness is what is directly intelligible in the simple apprehension

[11] J. T. Clark, "Comment on Dr. Maritain's Paper," *Proceedings of the American Catholic Philosophical Society*, XXVII (1953), 55.

[12] E.g., Henri Poincaré, *The Foundations of Science*, tr. George Bruce Halsted (Lancaster, Pa., 1946); Stephen Edelston Toulmin, *The Philosophy of Science* (New York, 1953); Norwood Russell Hanson, *Patterns of Discovery* (Cambridge, Eng., 1958).

[13] The term "scientist" originated around the year 1840, and in its use is restricted to the experimental and physico-mathematical or statistical areas. The same restriction, however, need not be imposed upon the terms "science" or "scientific." See above, **Chapter 1, n. 6.**

of the thing, and accordingly is form. The other principle does not of itself add any intelligibility to the thing, but explains how the same form is extended through additional parts outside parts without any formal addition whatsoever. The second principle, accordingly, is of itself entirely formless, and is called matter.

These two principles are reached from their effect, the extended thing. They are known, therefore, by *quia* demonstration. They are not immediately intuited, as are the mathematical principles. Once they are known by *quia* demonstration, however, they can furnish *propter quid* knowledge. As the substantial principles or causes of extended reality, they give rise to a *propter quid* science, even in regard to the effects from which they were first known.[14] They make manifest the general essence of body or extended substance, and allow that essence to be used as a middle term in demonstration. In this way they make possible a deeper science of nature than the experimental sciences, because it is a science that demonstrates through a more profound essence than the quantitative. It demonstrates through the substantial essence of the thing, and is called natural philosophy.

The penetration of human knowledge into the essence of corporeal substance, however, does not proceed any further than the generic grade of body. The specific differentiae remain impenetrable to the human intellect's gaze.[15] The specific essences of bodies, accordingly, are not known by man in such a way that they could form the starting points for *propter quid* knowledge of things. The general effect of quantity manifests its nature to the intellect and permits reasoning to the nature of the substance that can have that effect. The general essence of body is therefore knowable to man. But the qualities and groupings of qualities and activities do not reveal their special essences, and so provide no means of reasoning to the special substantial natures underlying them. These have to be distinguished on the basis of their superficially observed qualities and activities, or, far more preferably, according to the findings of the experimental sciences. But just as superficial observation is corrected by the experimental sciences, so the findings of these sciences, on account of the inductive origin of the qualitative knowledge submitted to their mathematical treatment, remain always provisory and subject to later revision. Natural philosophy can judge and explain these

[14] "And besides, the sensible effects from which natural demonstrations proceed are in the beginning better known for us. But when through them we reach the cognition of the first causes, we will know from them the *propter quid* of those effects upon which the *quia* demonstrations are based." St Thomas, *In Boeth. de Trin.*, V, 1, ad 9m; ed. Wyser, p. 31.20–23.

[15] See above, Chapters 5, n. 3, and 15, n. 4.

findings in the light of its own principles, substantial matter and form, but it has no means to make new or independent discoveries in the realm of particular essences. It has no means, for instance, of determining whether the natural species are evolving or fixed, or whether life is entirely lacking in things of the mineral kingdom or of the outer galaxies. It may sometimes be able to offer highly probably arguments, but these are always dialectical and do not belong to its strictly scientific procedure.

In one case, however, natural philosophy is able to establish diversity of substance, even though here it does not penetrate the specific differentia.[16] A man is conscious of himself as an individual agent, and as the substantial source of actions characterized as rational. He sees actions of the same character in other groupings of phenomena, and can reason that they have a corresponding substantial source. Through internal sensation he is conscious that he is the substantial source of bodily as well as of rational activity, and he can reason to the unicity of substantial form in any one body. In this way he can establish himself as a different corporeal substance from others. The observed changes that take place in nutrition and in death furnish accordingly another way of establishing substantial change and the two principles, matter and form, that make substantial change possible.

On the basis of substantial principles, natural philosophy investigates the causes, act and potency, movement, time, place, the continuum, and many other such problems. The knowledge that it reaches is always theoretical, and remains so. It enriches human understanding of the corporeal world, but furnishes no information that can be applied for controlling natural forces. From that viewpoint it is of no use, but rather is above use. It is an end, and not a means, as far as bodily interests are concerned. Action and reaction between bodies in the corporeal world take place according to their specific differences, and not according to their generic nature as bodies. Nor are the experimental sciences in any way subalternate to natural philosophy. On the contrary, they are subalternate only to mathematics.[17] The experimental sciences, therefore, cannot in any way be viewed as a continuation of natural philosophy. The two disciplines proceed from different sources, in the one case from accidental essences, in the other case from substantial

[16] As a substantial differentia for man, "rational," like the other specific differentiae, is known only through proper accidents. See St Thomas, *De Ver.*, X, 1, ad 6m; *De Spir. Creat.*, a. 11, ad 3m.

[17] They are called "intermediate sciences" (*scientiae mediae*) by St Thomas, *In Boeth. de Trin.*, V, 3, ad 6m & 7m, because they apply mathematical principles to natural things. The mathematical side is formal in them, because it provides the means of demonstration (ad 6m). They are in consequence "formally mathematical" — J. Maritain, *The Degrees of Knowledge*, p. 138.

essence. They are radically distinguished by the principles from which they proceed. There is no continuity between human knowledge of corporeal essence, and human knowledge of specific qualities and activities.

Metaphysics. The entitative principles of sensible things are being and the corresponding potency, essence. Those have been serving as the principles for the present study. Like form and matter in natural philosophy, they are reached as the conclusion of *quia* demonstration from effects. Once they are known, however, they are able to function as the source of *propter quid* knowledge. Though the concrete notion of "a being" does not have its origin entirely through simple apprehension, but through simple apprehension combined with judgment, it has proved able to fill the role played by essence in other sciences in serving as middle term. The characteristics that follow in anything upon being are demonstrated through their fully adequate and necessitating cause.[18]

Because being extends to everything, metaphysics may on account of its object be called a general science. But insofar as it proceeds from one set of principles distinct from the sets that give rise to other sciences, it is a special science among other special sciences. As a science it is not a genus that embraces the others as species.[19] The others all have their own independent starting points. These cannot be found in the object of metaphysics in a way that would allow them to function as the principles of their own sciences.[20] Other sciences are said to "borrow" or "derive" their principles from metaphysics only insofar as metaphysics shows that the link of being that binds subject with predicate in a judgment remain stable throughout any reasoning process and so makes demonstration possible.[21] This, however, gives metaphysics no means of even entering into the fields of the other sciences. It can judge their objects and procedures and results in terms of being, but it cannot do any of their work or guide or direct or rule any of their activities. Accordingly it can exercise no imperialism over other sciences.

Logic. The second intention relations that are necessarily present between human concepts of things, relations like those of genus, species, and individual, are the principles of a distinct science called

[18] E.g., the transcendentals, above, Chapter 8.

[19] See St Thomas, *In Boeth. de Trin.*, V, 1, ad 6m.

[20] I.e., from the common principles of a being insofar as it is a being, no particularized being is understood as sufficiently caused. See St Thomas, *In IV Metaph.*, lect. 2, (ed. Cathala-Spiazzi) no. 559. Text below, Epilogue, n. 6.

[21] See St Thomas, *In Boeth. de Trin.*, VI, 1(3)c; ed. Wyser, p. 61.1–3.

logic.[22] Just as the different numbers and the different figures are the principles of mathematical science, so the different second intentions make possible a science of the reasoning processes. Since human reasoning processes extend to all things, logic on account of its object is like metaphysics a general science,[23] while remaining a special science in its procedure from a distinct set of principles.

Because it bore upon an object as in the human mind and not as in real being, logic was not given the status of a science by the Peripatetics but was regarded merely as an instrument for the sciences. It had to be learned before any theoretical science could be approached.[24] Among the Scholastics, however, logic was given full scientific status. In the order of teaching it is placed at the beginning of a philosophy course. It is helpful in familiarizing the student with the predicaments and the predicables and the other notions that are used throughout the various branches of philosophy. Yet its remoteness, in the second intention, from the direct objects of human cognition has occasioned doubts in Neoscholastic circles regarding the wisdom of making logic the student's introduction to philosophy.[25]

Mathematical or symbolic logic submits the object of logic to thorough mathematicizing treatment.[26] So developed, this modern logic be-

---

[22] " 'A being of reason' is properly applied to those intentions that reason devises in the things considered, as the intention of genus, species, and the like, which are not found in the real world but are consequent upon the consideration of reason. And such, namely being of reason, is properly the subject of logic." St Thomas, *In IV Metaph.*, lect. 4, (ed. Cathala-Spiazzi) no. 574. Cf. *In Boeth. de Trin.*, VI, 1 (2), ad 3m; ed. Wyser, p. 59.18. *In I Post. Anal.*, lect. 1, (ed. Leonine) nos. 1–7, explains the extension of logic to the sphere of the probable in dialectic, rhetoric, and poetics.

[23] *In IV Metaph., ibid. In Boeth. de Trin.*, VI, 1(1)c; p. 56.8–10.

[24] Aristotle, *Metaph.*, Γ 3, 1005b2–5. Cf.: "All logical treatment is about second notions. But these are our own work, and can be and not be at our will. Therefore they are not necessary but contingent things, and so do not fall under science, since science is only about necessary things, as has been said." Jacobus Zabarella, *De Natura Logicae*, I, 3; in *Opera Logica* (Basle, 1594), col. 7DE. Cf. *Ibid.*, col. 5E. In regard to Aristotle's occasional concession that logic is a science, Zabarella (I, 5; col. 10F) maintains that though per se logic is not a science, it gives rise to science remotely through its application in other spheres.

[25] E.g.: "On the other hand, sound pedagogical results are obtainable if logic is taken after the philosophy of mental life when the viewpoint of logic is much better understood, as well as more thoroughly entered into." Virgil Michel, "Reflections on a Scholastic Synthesis," *The New Scholasticism*, II (1928), 13. St Thomas (*In Boeth. de Trin.*, VI, 1(2), ad 3m; ed. Wyser, p. 59.13–21), while acknowledging that logic presents the greatest difficulty, places it first in pedagogical order.

[26] "Pure logic, and pure mathematics (which is the same thing) . . . There is a certain lordliness which the logician should preserve: he must not condescend to derive arguments from the things he sees about him." Bertrand Russell, *Introduction to Mathematical Philosophy*, 2nd ed. (London & New York, 1920), p. 192.

comes a branch of mathematics without relevance to sciences that are not subalternate to mathematics.[27] Aristotelian and Scholastic logic, on the contrary, retains an object distinct from any mathematical object. Mathematical logic, accordingly, is not continuous with Scholastic logic.

Productive Sciences. In a productive science, the knower has not only to become a thing intentionally, but has to be trained in such a way as to be able to produce it. The surgeon not only knows the anatomy and physiology of the area in which he operates, but also is habituated in using the scalpel. Productive knowledge, accordingly, is imbedded in the powers of acting and doing things. The carpenter's technical knowledge stamps his activities in building a house, and is located in the habitual power of building. The total immersion in such habituation is what distinguishes productive science from theoretical science. It makes the difference between the engineer and the physicist, between the medical doctor and the biologist.

Productive sciences may borrow any theoretical knowledge they need from the competent speculative sciences. The knowledge of the experimental sciences is in this way put to use in the production of the automobile, the airplane, the dial telephone, the television set, the radar equipment, and the fission or fusion of the atom in nuclear explosions. Through productive science the experimental sciences have profoundly changed human ways of living during the past century.

Practical Sciences. Ethics and political philosophy find their principles in habituation, as in the case of productive science. Here, however, the habituation is not toward working a fixed form or design or blueprint into materials, but toward correct conduct amidst the circumstances of the moment. This habituation is largely developed by culture and education. As cultural and educational standards differ, people in all sincerity make widely differing judgments on moral, political, and religious matters. The difficulties in arriving at correct universals in the sphere of practical science is accordingly greater than in any of the other kinds.

Other Sciences. The sciences considered so far manifest clearly enough the traditional Aristotelian framework for the classifi-

[27] "That symbolic logic, in its techniques, concepts, or specific propositions, can aid in the solution of any philosophical problem, is seriously doubted." M. Weitz, "Oxford Philosophy," *Philosophical Review*, LXII (1953), 221. Attempts have been made to apply the techniques of symbolic logic to Scholastic metaphysical problems, but without obtaining any very wide vogue. E.g., J. Salamucha, "The Proof 'Ex Motu' for the Existence of God: Logical Analysis of St. Thomas' Arguments," *The New Scholasticism*, XXXII (1958), 334–372.

cation and grading of the various kinds of scientific knowledge. There are other acknowledged sciences that do not fit neatly into this framework. The philosophy of man, or philosophical anthropology, is an intensely cultivated science today. It has man as its specific object. It arose as a search for the answer to the last of four questions proposed by Kant,[28] and has been developed in the orbit of existentialist and personalist philosophies. Around the topic man it assembles and investigates problems from the realms of natural philosophy, metaphysics, religion, and practical science. Kant's question was "What is man?" Since the specific essence of man, namely what man is, remains impervious to human cognition, it cannot serve as the middle term for *propter quid* demonstration. From the Aristotelian viewpoint, therefore, it cannot specify a human science. It does not provide a new scientific viewpoint. For convenience in treatment, it can group its problems around the one topic man and in that unity give them interesting and inspiring development.

Esthetics likewise combines theoretical and non-theoretical treatment in the study of the beautiful and of its production through the fine arts. Philosophy of values[29] investigates the objects that move the human will, and so combines topics from the realms of metaphysics and productive and practical science. Natural theology separates from general metaphysics the problems concerned with subsistent being, and cosmology separates from natural philosophy the problems concerning inanimate things or even non-rational animals. Rational psychology combines from natural philosophy and metaphysics the questions regarding the human soul, while epistemology, in a range that is still quite fluid, brings together problems concerning knowledge from metaphysics, logic, and natural philosophy.

Order of the Sciences. There is a traditional saying that to place things in order pertains to the wise man.[30] Every science is specified by its proper object. The order of the objects, therefore, determines the order of the corresponding sciences. Metaphysics, because it treats of things from the most universal viewpoint of being, is able to view them according to their basic order. As accidents, substances, and subsistent being it sees them on their respective entitative levels. It discerns, accordingly, mathematics as dealing with a single accidental category in abstraction from the richness of concrete reality. On

[28] *Logik*, Einleitung, III; in *Werke* (Berlin & Leipzig, 1923), IX, 25. Cf. *K. R. V.*, B 866–867.

[29] E.g., Ralph Barton Perry, *General Theory of Value* (New York, 1926), p. 4.

[30] St Thomas, *In Metaph.*, Proem.

a higher level is mathematicized experimental science that gives *propter quid* knowledge of real sensible things, though on the basis of accidental principles. Still higher is knowledge of things through substantial principles, matter and form, as given in natural philosophy. Higher still is knowledge through their entitative principles, being and essence. All these sciences deal with objects of the first intention. The necessary relations in the second intention form the object of logic. Though general in its scope, logic deals with things as they are in intentional being, a type of being that is secondary to real being. While logic deals with science in general, it deals with it only on the one level, that of human reasoning. It has not the means to determine the levels on which the different sciences function. The order of the theoretical sciences, then, has to be determined by metaphysics. Mathematics occupies the lowest level of *propter quid* science, then comes mathematicized experimental science, then natural philosophy, and finally metaphysics as the highest. These all deal with real beings. Dealing with a lesser type, namely, with second intentions, is logic.

The practical and productive sciences stand on a different footing. They are specified not by what is, but by what is going to be. Their hierarchy is very complicated, and is determined by the way in which one guides the other, as the engineer directs the technician and the business executive directs the engineer in the production of machinery. Higher still is political direction, and supreme is morality.[31] The gradation of these sciences, accordingly, cannot be made to fit in with the grading of the theoretical sciences.[32] In the theoretical order, metaphysics is supreme, for it judges moral science from the viewpoint of the latter's being. In the practical order, ethics is supreme, for it determines the extent metaphysics is to be engaged in by men.

The order of the sciences as determined by metaphysics, therefore, is solely theoretical. Metaphysics does not impose the order upon them, as would a practical science, but sees it there and explains it. In this way it determines its own limitations as well as those of the other sciences,[33] and fulfills its task of manifesting the order and gradations

[31] See Aristotle, *E N*, I 1–2, 1094a1 ff.

[32] Some Neoscholastics, however, do attempt this subordination. E.g., Fernand Van Steenberghen, *Epistemology*, tr. M. J. Flynn (New York, 1949), pp. 290 & 295, defends a "metaphysics of behavior or moral action," and Joseph Gredt, *Elementa Philosophiae Aristotelico-Thomisticae*, ed. 7a (Freiburg i. Breisgau, 1937), II, 303 (no. 879), sees ethics subalternated to the third part of natural philosophy.

[33] "For the theory of knowledge is part of metaphysics, and it is wisdom's privilege reflexively or critically to elucidate and defend its own principles as well as the principles of the other spheres of knowledge and the various sciences, thus making them aware of their own genuine truth and competence and their own genuine

of the sciences, just as it makes manifest the order and gradations of beings.

Résumé. The quest for causes gives rise to the various human sciences. The causes may be of existent things, or of human conduct, or of things to be produced by man. Accordingly the basic division of the sciences is into theoretical, practical, and productive. Since the division is grounded upon causes, it is investigated and determined by the science that treats of causes under their widest aspect, the aspect of being. The task of making manifest the order, rank, and interrelation of the sciences in general pertains therefore solely to metaphysics.

SUGGESTED READINGS AND REFERENCES

St Thomas Aquinas, *The Divisions and Methods of the Sciences* (*In Boeth. De Trin.*, V–VI), tr. Armand Maurer, 2nd ed. (Toronto: Pontifical Institute of Mediaeval Studies, 1958).

Jacques Maritain, "Philosophy and the Unity of the Sciences," *Proceedings of the American Catholic Philosophical Association*, XXVII (1953), 34–54.

Joseph Owens, "Our Knowledge of Nature," *Proceedings of the American Catholic Philosophical Association*, XXIX (1955), 63–86.

——— "St. Thomas and Elucidation," *The New Scholasticism*, XXXV (1961), 421–444.

Edward D. Simmons, "The Thomistic Doctrine of the Three Degrees of Formal Abstraction," *The Thomist*, XXII (1959), 37–67.

Emil L. Fackenheim, *Metaphysics and Historicity* (Milwaukee: Marquette University Press, 1961).

frontiers." J. Maritain, "Philosophy and the Unity of the Sciences," *Proceedings of the American Catholic Philosophical Association*, XXVII (1953), pp. 40–41.

PART FOUR . . . SPIRIT

CHAPTER 21

Spiritual Soul

Goal of Metaphysics. As the term itself indicates, metaphysics is a study of what is beyond the physical order, in the sense of what is beyond sensible nature. In the course of its procedure it has shown that being is an act beyond or outside all sensible natures, and that remains other than any finite nature it actuates, either in the real or in the cognitional world. To establish the conclusion that being is other than finite nature, it had to demonstrate that being itself is a real nature. In so doing, it showed that there is at least one substance that exists beyond the sensible world. It arrived at a supersensible substance.[1] Instead of dealing just with an act that is beyond sensible natures but inhering nevertheless in sensible things, it has brought into the focus of its demonstrative cognition a substance that is beyond the physical order. It has made clear that substances are not necessarily sensible or extended things, but include in their number at least one thing that is not extended. Can other supersensible substances be reached in any way by metaphysics? Can more be known about subsistent being than what the transcendental notions reveal? These questions about supersensible substances still face the present investigation. As they are con-

---

[1] The tenet that all being is necessarily quantitative has deep roots in Western philosophical thought. It is common among the Presocratics, e.g., Zeno of Elea, Fr. 2 (DK). Combatted by Platonic and Aristotelian teachings, it continued in the Stoic and Epicurean traditions and is widely spread in modern materialistic and positivistic conceptions of reality. The opposite extreme denies the existence of any material beings, e.g., George Berkeley (1685–1753). In Berkeley the denial of a material universe appears as a consequence of the Cartesian doctrine that what the human mind directly knows are its own ideas. For St Thomas, in the Aristotelian tradition that all human cognition originates in sensible things (*De Ver.*, X, 6; see above, Chapter 1, nn. 3–4), the human intellect "indeed understands immaterial things, but beholds them in something material" (*CG*, II, 73; ed. Leonine, XIII, 462a54–55). Accordingly the notions of immaterial things are constructed by the human mind in terms of what is found in the material universe, from which it receives its forms; cf. above, Chapter 15, n. 12.

cerned with what is supersensible in itself, and in this sense metaphysical[2] in itself instead of just a transcendental aspect shared by sensible things, the ultimate goal of metaphysics as a science will be to provide knowledge of supersensible substances.[3]

Sources. Since human cognition has no other origin than sensible experience, the path to any knowledge about supersensible things will have to start from the sensible world. The being of sensible things provided a starting point from which something supersensible, namely subsistent being, may be reached. Have further topics in the ensuing course of the study revealed aspects that can lead to other supersensible substances and to richer knowledge of subsistent being? The universal and necessary character found in the object of simple apprehension implies cognitive activity that is functioning in a manner superior to the conditions of the sensible world, the world in which things are singular and ever changing with the course of time. The way in which the human intellect has been able to study reflexively its own cognitive processes seems to indicate a self-objectivization and a self-penetration that defy explanation in terms of merely physical or sensory activities. Man's free direction of his own conduct is an anomaly in the physical world, and would appear to involve a supersensible cause. *Prima facie* indications like these merit investigation, in order to determine whether or not, and if so, how far, they lead metaphysical inquiry to scientific knowledge of supersensible substances.

The purpose of examining the cognitional and volitional operations of the human person, then, will be to find out if they really take place in a way that exceeds the capacity of entirely material things. If these activities are found to be above the power of merely material substances, they will be shown to proceed from a principle that is not limited to the conditions of purely material being. All activities proceed ultimately from a substance. Though specified by their objects, they are also deter-

---

[2] This use of the term "metaphysical," though hardly to be recommended, is not without some sanction in Scholastic tradition. E.g.: "Therefore that simple essence existing above the nature of mobile things, is a thing of metaphysical kind." *De Natura Generis*, c. V; in *S. Thomae Opusc. Spuria*, ed. Mandonnet (Paris, 1927), V, 229. ". . . the angels, who are incorruptible and metaphysical substances." J. M. Ramirez, "De Analogia secundum Doctrinam Aristotelico-Thomisticam," *La Ciencia Tomista*, XXIV (1921), 349, n. 2.

[3] ". . . and first philosophy itself is wholly directed to the cognition of God as to its ultimate end; hence it is also named divine science." St Thomas, *CG*, III, 25, Item, *Quod est*. Cf. *In Boeth. De Trin.*, V, 4; *In Metaph.*, Prooem.

mined according to the form of the substance from which they proceed.[4] Human actions are human because the substance from which they proceed is specified by a human form. If some human actions are performed in a certain independence of material conditions, their substantial principle will require a corresponding independence of matter.

Universal Cognition. In the sensible world activities are concerned only with singular things. An individual ball hits an individual wall. There could be no question of one universal hitting another universal, except as they are imbedded in singular things. The actions and reactions in the material universe take place under the conditions of singularity. Each is performed in a particular place and has as its object a singular thing. Sensation and imagination are no exceptions. You see and touch and imagine an individual orange or apple. Sensation and imagination, accordingly, attain their objects under individual conditions. The reason, as natural philosophy shows, is that matter in the real world limits a material form to being under designated quantitative dimensions of length, breadth, and thickness. The action of the material thing, which is the action of the composite of matter and form, is correspondingly limited to designated quantitative dimensions. In transient action, consequently, it is limited to an individual effect. One throw with the shovel removes only one shovelful of earth. In immanent operations, the same restriction to individuating conditions holds, even in regard to the object.[5] The composite's immanent action can attain the object only as limited to definite dimensions. To break out beyond those dimensions would be to break away from the limitation of form by matter. It would be to act in a way that was to that extent independent of matter.

The simple apprehension of the human intellect, however, attains things as universal. It knows a sensible nature not as something restricted to the singular thing before its gaze, but as applicable to all individuals of the species. It knows it in a way that breaks through the individuating conditions of matter. It knows it in a way that is not possible for a merely material knower. The universal way in which the human intel-

---

[4] "For the operation of everything whatsoever is according to the mode of its substance." St Thomas, *ST*, I, 50, 2c. Cf. *CG*, III, 84, Adhuc, Propria. See also *ST*, I, 89, 1c.

[5] "To understand cannot be the act of a body, nor of any bodily power; for every body is determined to the here and now." *ST*, I, 50, 1c. "For if the intellective soul were composed of matter and form, the forms of things would be received into it as individual, and so it would know only the singular, as happens in the sense powers, which receive the forms of things in a corporeal organ." I, 75, 5c.

lect knows things, therefore, marks it as a cognitive principle that is to a certain extent functioning independently of matter.

Necessary Cognition. A similar breaking away from the conditions of time may be seen in the object of intellection. The individual sensible thing is continually changing from moment to moment. As perceived by the senses, it is attained under these changing conditions. A leaf is seen as swaying in the wind, as green in summer, as multicolored in autumn, as decaying and falling in the frosty weather. Under the universal aspect of leaf, however, it is known by the intellect in a way that transcends time. It is known under an aspect that can be applied to any leaf at any time, an aspect that does not undergo any changes with the passage of time. Since matter is the principle of mobility in sensible things, anything that eludes mobility and the time aspect that follows on mobility, is thereby acting in a way that is independent of matter. In attaining its object as immune to the changes of time, the intellect is operating in a way that cannot have as its substantial source a principle composed of matter and form.

The cognition of objects immune to change was the reason that led to the first clear philosophical distinction between intellection and sensation. It led Plato to see that the knowledge of unchangeable objects could not take place through any sensory organ.[6] The senses functioned in an order of continual change, and so could not attain an object as eternally unchangeable. Yet such is the character of the objects of human intellection. With Plato there was as yet no philosophically precise notion of material cause. The difference between intellection and sensation could not be explained in terms of the causality of matter. Plato did not have the means of controlling the extremely important distinction he had established. He could only separate quite drastically the intelligible and sensible orders, in regarding the soul and the body as two different things. But he had discerned clearly enough that cognition of the timeless objects of intellection required a principle outside the conditions of sensible reality.

Reasoning and Science. The freedom from limitations to a particular space and a particular time makes possible the astounding progress of human knowledge through the arts and sciences. Knowledge gained in one piece of research or one experiment is communicated to thousands of other minds and is handed down to succeeding generations. The scientific reasoning of one man becomes the common property of all who pursue the science from one generation to the other.

[6] *Phd.*, 65A–66A; *Tht.*, 185CE.

The enormous body of knowledge is not lost with the death of the individuals who so far have been bringing it into being. It is not limited to the conditions of individuation and change, conditions inevitably imposed by matter. Scientific progress, accordingly, requires that the intellects through which it takes place function in a way that is independent of the strictly material principle in the knowing subjects.

Even the very process of reasoning itself could not take place without this independence from material limitation. The universality that allows the major notion to include the middle one, and the middle to include the minor, would be impossible for any operation that was determined to individual conditions. The inclusion of one term in the other, moreover, is an inclusion in being; for instance "A man is an animal." If the object "animal" were individuated, it could not share the one being any more than Khrushchev could be Kennedy. Likewise, in passing from one judgment to another in the process of reasoning, the notions have to remain the same. If they were liable to change, demonstration would be impossible. What was established in the predicate of one judgment could be changed when carried over to function as subject in the next combination. Communication in speech, further, is based upon this same immunity to change and transcendence of individuating dimensions in the intelligible objects.[7] Culture and civilization, accordingly, provide ample evidence of the human intellect's functioning in ways that break through the limitations of matter.

Knowledge of Essence. The object of human intellection may on account of its universality lack the vividness and richness of a concrete singular thing.[8] It might look at first sight as though gain in extent was compensated in exactly inverse ratio by loss in content. However, the universal cognition of the intellect differs from sensation more than in terms of extent and content. It differs also in degree of penetration into the content. In knowing the sensible thing according to its universal nature, it knows the thing according to its essence. It knows *what* the thing is. It does not consist in becoming intentionally a thing in the way a tree is seen or a stone is felt, but in knowing each of these things as an extended substance. The mathematical essences can be known and penetrated in ways that defy sensible existence, for instance in the fifth and subsequent dimensions and in square roots like

[7] See Plato, *Prm.*, 135AC.

[8] Cf. Hume's teaching that "all ideas are derived from impressions, and are nothing but copies and representations of them. . . . Impressions and ideas differ only in their strength and vivacity. . . . An idea is a weaker impression . . ." *A Treatise of Human Nature*, I, 1, 7; ed. Selby-Bigge (Oxford, 1896), p. 19.

that of two. In such mathematical reasoning the intellect functions in a way that eludes the conditions of real matter. Through knowing the essence or notion of relations, the intellect can not only know related things, but can relate them in ways meant to serve its own purposes. Language is an outstanding example of this. Words are conventionally related to things and serve to communicate thought. Without understanding the notion of relation, language and other artificial symbolism would be impossible. In understanding things according to essence, also, the intellect is able to distinguish them from their being and proceed to a knowledge of things under the aspect of being. It knows them under an aspect that extends beyond the sensible order and even beyond the finite order. It penetrates through the barriers set up by limiting essence as well as by concretizing matter.

Knowledge of essence, therefore, is a way of knowing that is not conditioned by sensible concretion. It is an operation that functions in a manner impossible to a merely material agent. Corresponding to knowledge of essence as essence is knowledge of being as being, with the consequent cognition of the true, the good, and the beautiful. This is all above sense cognition.

Reflection. Since a man knows sensible things universally according to their natures, he is thereby able to know himself. He is a composite of matter and form, as natural philosophy shows. With these as his substantial principles, he also is a sensible thing. As an object he comes under the range of the universal abstracted from any sensible thing. Knowing the essence of sensible body, he knows to the same extent his own essence. This self-knowledge would not be possible if the operation by which it takes place were on the corporeal plane. The individuating conditions under which corporeal activities are carried out oppose the agent to the object as singular to singular. An act of seeing or of any other external sense is always different from the thing it perceives. It cannot perceive itself. The imagination represents other sensible things and sensible activities, but it cannot represent itself. These external and internal sense operations function under the individuating conditions imposed by real matter. A body that can know all bodies including itself, then, is functioning according to a principle that operates independently of matter.[9]

Men experience this self-knowledge through reflection. The reflection is complete. It is not a case of one sense perceiving the operations of another sense, as an internal sense attains the workings of the external

[9] See St Thomas, *ST*, I, 75, 2c.

senses. It is a case of the intellect making itself and its own activities the object of its full reflexive gaze. It is much more than the concomitant consciousness that goes with every cognitive act. It is a complete bending back to view its own self. Any material thing can bend back at most so that half its surface covers the other half. The spatial dimensions that condition its action do not allow it completely to cover itself. Yet in complete reflection the intellect is entirely facing itself. It is operating, therefore, in a way that requires something more than a merely material source,[10] as a man sees himself thinking, enjoying, attracted to or recoiling from things, planning and making decisions.

Free-Will. Reflexive consciousness, accordingly, makes a man aware that he is a free agent.[11] He can choose his own course of action. Moral and political and social life is based upon free choice as a fact. Yet free choice cannot be explained as proceeding from a material source. Matter is determined by substantial form to be of a certain kind. The operations of the composite substance are accordingly determined. Where there is no principle that acts independently of this restriction, there can be no free choice. The agent will act as determined by the physical form. Even where the action of animals is determined by forms received intentionally through sensation, it is still not free. It is determined by forms limited to the individuating conditions of matter, and follows according to the animals' instincts. A man, however, knows a thing under the aspect of being, and so under the transcendental character of good. This aspect is infinite in scope, like being. No finite good, and so no good immediately known to man, can fill it. Every thing that man encounters through the senses, therefore, can be seen as partially good and partially not good. It cannot determine him to action. No matter how strong his instincts toward it are, he knows he can turn away

[10] Self-knowledge as a sign of the separate or immaterial nature of mind is dwelt upon by Aristotle, *De An.*, III 4, 429b9–430a9. The argument was given its development by Proclus, *The Elements of Theology*, Props. 15–17; tr. E. R. Dodds (Oxford, 1933), pp. 17–21. It is used by St Thomas, *CG*, II, 49, Item, Nullius; cf. 66, Item. The *Liber de Causis* is mentioned as its source by St Thomas, *In II Sent.*, d. 19, q. 1, a. 1, Solut; ed. Mandonnet, II, 482.

[11] See St Thomas, *De Ver.*, XXIV, 1–2; cf. *In III Eth.*, lect. 11 (ed. Pirotta), nos. 496–506; *De Malo*, VI; *ST*, I, 59, 3; 83, 1. ". . . the introspective datum that we deliberate about future actions provides adequate evidence for believing that some of our actions are in our power, that is, that we can choose to perform the action and also that we can choose not to perform the action, and in this sense we have adequate evidence that we have free will." Keith Lehrer, "Can We Know that We Have Free Will by Introspection?" *Journal of Philosophy*, LVII (1960), 156. The "inward look" of consciousness is denied by Bernard J. F. Lonergan in favor of "self-affirmation," *Insight* (New York, 1956), p. 320, with consciousness itself regarded as "a quality of cognitional acts" (p. 326).

from it. He is conscious of the power to choose. This power cannot come to him from anything corporeal, for what is corporeal is already determined to a definite way of acting. Free choice is an activity that functions beyond the limiting conditions of matter, and cannot proceed from a principle that is corporeal.[12]

Immaterial Principle. The activities of the human mind that in one way or another are carried on independently of material restrictions are accordingly numerous and manifest. They are the activities that sharply distinguish man from other animals, no matter how gradual the approach through the primates is in bodily shape. Intellection and free choice are actions of a different kind than those that proceed from a principle composed of matter and form. In man, then, they cannot have as their source a faculty of the composite nature. The nature in that case would be acting in dependence on matter, and would not in any way be able to get outside the dependence. Its object would be restricted to things as individually determined in space and time. Operations carried on in a certain independence of matter have to proceed through faculties that are correspondingly independent of matter, for the faculties are specified by their objects. Intellect and will, accordingly, have to be faculties that are in their own constitution independent of matter to the same extent their activities are free from the restrictions of time and place.

So far the reasoning has been that the objects of intellection and free choice show a clear independence of material restriction to the conditions of individuation. The actions specified by those objects will therefore be to the same extent independent of matter. Likewise the faculties specified by those objects and acts will have corresponding independence. The substantial principle of such actions, further, will be informed by the faculties in independence of matter. If the faculties informed the composite nature, they would have their being through a material as well as a formal principle. They would thereby be material faculties, and would be restricted in their activities and objects to the individuating conditions of matter.

The substantial principle of intellection and free choice, therefore, sustains the intellective faculties in being without any concomitant sub-

[12] "Secondly, the will is undetermined in regard to its act, because it can make use of or not make use of its act when it wishes concerning a determined object; for it can go into or not go into its act of willing in regard to anything whatsoever, which is not the case in natural things." St Thomas, *De Ver.*, XXII, 6c.

stantial causality of matter. In sense cognition and sense appetition, the actions attain their objects as individual and the sense faculties are specified by accidents that inhere in the composite nature. The composite of matter and form is the substance in which they have being. The matter exercises its substantial causality in their regard. It does not, however, constitute any part of the substantial principle in which the intellective faculties inhere. The principle, consequently, is in this respect immaterial.

What is the substantial principle, though, in which the intellective faculties inhere? The traditional Platonic answer that intellection is the activity of one substance, the soul, while corporeal activities are the operations of another substance, the body, is too hasty. The conclusion that the substantial principle of intellection is in some way immaterial need not prevent it from informing matter. The situation is considerably more complicated than the facile Platonic view admits. The reflexive consciousness that shows intellection as functioning in a certain independence of individuating conditions also shows the identity of the subject of intellection with the subject of sensation. The person that is seeing and hearing and feeling is the person that is thinking. The one agent is acting through sensation and other corporeal faculties in a way restricted by individuation, and through intellection and free choice in a way that is not restricted by the conditions of matter. The intellectual reflection that establishes the immaterial scope of these activities is fully as clear and fully as certain in manifesting also the identity of agent in the intellectual and corporeal activity of a man.

Soul and Body. The one substance that is constituted by matter and form, then, will have to be the agent for both corporeal and intellectual operations in a man. The difference will be that in corporeal actions both the matter and the form constitute together the substantial principle of the activity. In intellection, the matter is excluded from this role. Yet it is the same substance that continues in operation. This means, then, that it is now grounding the action through its form alone, and not through its matter. The form alone is the substantial principle of the intellection, whereas the composite of matter and form is the substantial principle of the corporeal actions. In man, as in any other living thing, the form is called the soul, and the composite of matter and form is called the body. There is a real distinction between soul and matter, just as form and matter in general are really distinguished. But in strict Aristotelian terminology, there is no real distinction between soul and body, except as part from whole.[13] The body is the composite of soul and matter, and so includes the soul.[14] When soul and body are contrasted with each other as though they were two separate things, the contrast is between two products of an abstraction.[15] The body is the human agent considered as a substance capable of extension in the three dimensions, or even as living and as sensitive, while the soul is taken as the same agent insofar as able to act intellectually. The one real form, however, has to function as substantial principle for both the corporeal and the intellectual activities. It has accordingly a twofold way of being a substantial principle. In conjunction with matter it is the partial substantial principle of the body and of corporeal actions, in itself it is the substantial principle of intellective operations.

In both cases, however, there is but the one substance that is operating. In the one instance, the substance is using both its principles, soul and matter, as a composite from which corporeal activity originates. In the other case, it is using only one of its principles, the soul, as the complete substantial source of intellection and free choice.

Subsistence of the Human Soul. Since the human soul can be a substantial principle just in itself, it can therefore be in itself, for substance is a potency to being. Indeed, it is primarily a potency to being, and only secondarily a mediated potency to operation. If it can operate in any way independently of matter, it

[13] See Aristotle, *De An.*, II 1, 412a15–b9. This conception of soul and primary matter as the intrinsic substantial constituents of the one body, radically excludes the Platonic (*Phd.*, 82DE; cf. *Alc. I*, 129E–130A) notion of the body as a sort of external receptacle and instrument of the soul, and the Cartesian doctrine satirized by Gilbert Ryle as "the dogma of the Ghost in the Machine," *The Concept of Mind* (New York, 1949), pp. 15–16. The independent existence of some "part" of the soul is broached by Aristotle (*De An.*, II 1, 413a5–9; 2, 413b24–29; III 5, 430a10–25) and apparently admitted by him. The crucial difficulty in making soul the form of body and at the same time the principle of intellection, an activity independent of matter, was noted by Plotinus, *En.*, IV, 7, 8⁵.15–16. On the encounter of St Thomas with this difficulty, see A. C. Pegis, "St. Thomas and the Unity of Man," in *Progress in Philosophy*, ed. James A. McWilliams (Milwaukee, 1955), pp. 153–173; "Some Reflections on *Summa Contra Gentiles II, 56*" in *An Etienne Gilson Tribute*, ed. Charles J. O'Neil (Milwaukee, 1959), pp. 169–188. For St Thomas, the ever present distinction between its essence and its being allows the human soul to remain by nature the form of a body while having operations and being of its own. E.g., *De Unitate Intellectus*, III, 84; ed. Leo W. Keeler (Rome, 1936), p. 53. In the strict Aristotelian equation of act with finite form, on the other hand, the form and being of a thing should have exactly the same exigencies — if the nature of a soul is to inform matter, its being should be confined to being in matter.

[14] For Plotinus, on the contrary, body is contained in soul (*En.*, IV, 3, 9.36–38) as something produced by contemplation (III, 8, 3.20–22).

[15] St Thomas, *De Ente*, c. II; ed. Roland-Gosselin, reprint (Paris, 1948), pp. 12.5–16.1.

can all the more exist in a corresponding independence of matter. The human soul, accordingly, is in some way subsistent. It is able to receive existence immediately in itself, and not as one part of a composite that immediately receives the existence as a composite.

From an absolute viewpoint, then, the human soul is able to exist in itself, apart from matter. That is what is meant by saying that it is subsistent. Yet it remains a soul, and so of its nature it is always a form of matter. It is not a complete substance, but only the formal principle of a complete substance. For this reason it cannot be called a supposit, as a supposit means a complete substance. Just by itself, therefore, the human soul is not a person. The person is the composite of soul and matter, in the case of a man. Yet of itself the soul is a spirit. A spirit is something that has substantial existence apart from matter. As an incomplete substance, the human soul has such existence. But its relation to matter remains. It is always the form of a body. It is accordingly not a pure spirit, but a spirit that naturally requires union with matter in order to operate and fulfill its destiny.

Résumé. Operations like universal and necessary cognition, knowledge in terms of essence and being, complete reflection, and free will, transcend the limits of the merely material. To the extent in which they are independent of matter, they require a principle independent of matter, in the sense of a substantial principle that acts beyond the restrictions of matter. Through its operations the nature of this principle can be known.[16] The operations show sufficiently that they proceed from a substantial source that has activities in independence of matter. The substantial form by which this agent acts independently of matter will in consequence have its being independently of matter. But the substantial form of a man is his soul. The human soul, accordingly, is a subsistent form.

SUGGESTED READINGS AND REFERENCES

Aristotle, *De Anima*, III, 4–5, 429a10–430a25.

St Augustine, *The Greatness of the Soul*, tr. Joseph M. Colleran (Westminster, Md: Newman Press, 1950).

[16] Since the nature of the soul is known only mediately by reasoning from operations, it is grasped with difficulty and laborious investigation: ". . . diligent and acute examination is required. Hence many do not know the nature of the soul, and also many have erred regarding the nature of the soul." St Thomas, *ST*, I, 87, 1c. Cf. *De Ver.*, X, 8, ad 8 in contr. On the complete lack of historical antecedents for the Thomistic doctrine of man, see Pegis, "Some Reflections on *Summa Contra Gentiles II*, 56," p. 183; E. Gilson, "Autour de Pomponazzi," *Archives d'Histoire Doctrinale et Littéraire du Moyen Age*, XXVIII (1961), 276.

St Thomas Aquinas, *Summa Theologiae*, I, 75, 1–5; tr. English Dominican Fathers (London: Burns Oates & Washbourne Ltd., 1911–1925), IV, 3–16.
Anton C. Pegis, "St. Thomas and the Unity of Man," in *Progress in Philosophy*, ed. James A. McWilliams (Milwaukee: Bruce, 1955), pp. 153–173.
——— "Some Reflections on *Summa Contra Gentiles* II, 56," in *An Etienne Gilson Tribute*, ed. Charles J. O'Neil (Milwaukee: Marquette University Press, 1959), pp. 169–188.
Richard J. Blackwell, "Christian Wolff's Doctrine of the Soul," *Journal of the History of Ideas*, XXII (1961), 339–354.

CHAPTER 22

Spiritual Being

Necessary Character. A subsistent form has being in itself, and not just in a composite essence of which it is the formal principle. Things that have no activities beyond those of the composite give no reason for concluding to any being that would belong to their essence otherwise than as the actuation of the composite. Since the act of being is determined by the essence, the existential act of a material thing will be material being. It is specified by a material essence, for the matter in the composite essence renders the essence something material. As such the essence receives the existential act and determines it to material being. Where the form is subsistent, on the other hand, it receives the existential act into itself alone. The form as in itself, and not as the actuation of the composite, determines the character of the existential act. It determines the act independently of the material principle, and so renders it immaterial or spiritual being. In man the subsistent form is at the same time the form of matter, and as actuated by being it informs the matter and makes the matter be. In man therefore the act of being comes to the matter and the composite not directly but because they are actuated by an existent form.[1] A non-subsistent form, on the contrary, is not directly actuated by being. The composite essence, of which it is the formal principle, is directly made to be. The composite essence receives the existential act, in the sense that it is directly actuated, even though in the order of formal causality it is receiving it through the form. The form cannot receive its existential act in this case except as actually informing matter.[2]

---

[1] "There is a form whose act of existing does not depend on matter, for instance, the intellectual soul. Matter, on the other hand, exists only through form." St Thomas, *De Ente*, c. VI (ed. Roland-Gosselin), pp. 44.17–45.2; tr. A. Maurer (Toronto, 1949), p. 56.

[2] See *De Ente*, c. II, p. 10.2–7. This is considerably different from the Aristotelian notion of being. For Aristotle the form is "the primary entity" (*Metaph.*, Z 7, 1032b1–14; 11, 1037a28), that is, the primary instance of being in the composite thing, and in this way the "cause of being" (*Metaph.*, Z 17, 1041b26–28; H 2, 1043a2–4) without requiring any further actuation by a more primal act.

Since matter as the substantial principle of mobility is able to change to another form, it is the reason why a composite essence can perish, or lose its being. The being actuates the composite. When the composite perishes, the being that it had is gone. The actuation depended upon the inherence of the form in the matter. When that inherence ceases, the actuation ceases. With a subsistent form, however, the existential actuation does not depend upon the matter. Directly, it makes only the form be. In the form itself there is no principle of change. The only tendency it has is toward being. There is nothing in it that could make it lose its being.[3] Its character is to be actual, and it is actual through its being. Of itself it is an act, and yet it is in act only by its being. Of itself therefore it requires being, it necessitates being. It is an act, yet cannot be an act without being. The necessary concomitance of formal and existential act in any finite reality becomes emphasized in this situation. Being and essence are not two realities in a creature, but constitute one and the same reality. Where that reality is perishable, the being can be lost, if it is the being of the composite. If on the other hand it is the being of the form, it actuates directly a subject that is not composed of matter and form and that therefore has no intrinsic principle of substantial change. It actuates something whose whole tendency is to be actual. It actuates something that is an act, yet cannot be in act without its being. The form cannot be itself without existing. Existence belongs to it in its very character of act. Once it exists, then, it could not be separated from its existence any more than it could be separated from itself.[4] Existence goes with a subsistent form to the same extent that its very nature goes with it.

This means that there is no process in the whole of nature or of spirit by which a subsistent soul could lose its substantial being. Once it has that existence, it has it with all the tenacity with which it is itself. The only conceivable way it could lose its substantial existence, would be through withdrawal of conservation by the first cause of being. But the giving and withdrawal of conservation takes place according to the exigencies of a thing's nature. Where the nature does not permit the withdrawal, as in the case of a subsistent form, the conservation continues.[5]

---

[3] See above, Chapter 10, n. 10.

[4] St Thomas, *ST*, I, 75, 6c. Cf. *Q. de An.*, 14c. On Cajetan's unwillingness to accept the demonstrative force of this reasoning, see Etienne Gilson, *Elements of Christian Philosophy* (New York, 1960), pp. 217–219. On a more recent criticism, see G. St. Hilaire, "Does St. Thomas Really Prove the Soul's Immortality?" *The New Scholasticism*, XXXIV (1960), 340–356. In *De Pot.*, V, 3c (text below, n. 6), the force of the argument lies in the impossibility of separating being from itself.

[5] See St Thomas, *ST*, I, 104, 4c. Cf. *De Pot.*, V, 4c.

Every human soul, then, is imperishable. Once it has existence, it will retain that existence forever. It is incorruptible in itself, because it is not a composite that contains matter. It is not corruptible in accidental fashion, as other material forms are corruptible, because it receives being directly in itself and not just as a principle of a composite that is subject to corruption. The composite that it actuates, the human body, is perishable. The human body contains matter as one of its substantial principles. That matter is open to other forms, and so is the principle of the tendency to dissolution and death for the body. At death the matter takes on other forms, but the human soul, unlike brute and plant souls and the non-vital forms, does not lose existence because the composite perishes. Its existence does not depend upon the material composite, but upon itself. The loss of the matter and the death of the body do not entail even in accidental fashion its destruction. It has its existence directly and independently of the matter. Every human soul, accordingly, is a necessary being.[6]

Creation of Soul. As the human soul is not subject to corruption, by the same token it is not subject to generation. Properly, only a composite is generated, just as properly only a composite undergoes corruption with the separation of its parts. The soul itself is not a composite of matter and form, and so cannot be generated by a uniting of those two substantial principles. Material forms, however, are said to be generated in accidental fashion, as they come into being by the fact that the composite of which they are part receives being. But the human soul is subsistent. It does not share in being that is given directly to the composite. Its being pertains to it directly, and not through the composite. The human soul, therefore, is ingenerable. Its being comes to it directly in itself, and not just as it is part of the body. It has to receive its being directly in itself, and not as an evolution or change of a material substrate. Accordingly it is not made out of matter. It does not presuppose any subject out of which to be produced.[7] But

[6] "Where the form itself subsists in its being, in no way will it be able not to be, just as being cannot be separated from itself. . . . Therefore only those things in which there is matter subject to contrariety have a possibility of not being. Other things have in their own nature the necessity to be . . . Nor does this do away with their having from God the necessity of being since one necessity may cause another . . ." *De Pot.*, V, 3c; cf. ad 7m.

[7] *ST*, I, 90, 2, ad 1m. Cf. I, 118, 2c; *In II Sent.*, d. 1, q. 1, a. 4, Solut. (ed. Mandonnet, II, 25); d. 18, q. 2, a. 1, Solut. (II, 459–460); *Quodl.*, IX, 11; XI, 5, ad 1m and 4m; XII, 10; *De Ver.*, XXVII, 3, ad 9m; *CG*, II, 83–87; *De Pot.*, III, 9; *Comp. Theol.*, I, 93; *In Epist. ad Rom.*, V, 3. St Augustine was definite in maintaining that the soul was not a body (*De Gen. ad Litt.*, X, 24, 40; *PL*, XXXIV, 426–427), but was made by God in its entirety, and not in any way produced from

to be produced out of nothing is to be created. Each new human soul, consequently, can come into being only through a new act of creation.

This origin of the soul through special creation, however, in no way prevents it from receiving existence as the act of a particular body. Indeed, its nature is to inform matter. Its nature therefore requires that it be produced as the form of a particular matter. It is thereby individuated, as any form is individuated by the matter into whose designated dimensions it is plunged. If by the absolute power of the first cause it were created, against its nature, in separation from matter, it would still be related to a particular matter in designated dimensions, as its nature requires.[8] But in the ordinate power of the first cause, and so in actual creation, pre-existence of soul to body is impossible.[9] Similarly, the individuation of each soul by its designated matter prevents any transmigration of souls.[10]

Separate Soul. Because it is a subsistent form, the human soul continues to exist after the death and dissolution of the body. It retains its intellectual and volitional faculties, since these are its own faculties rather than faculties of the composite nature. But in order to use them, is it not dependent upon union with the body? As the form

the divine substance (*ibid.*, VII, 2, 3; col. 357) nor from anything else (*Retract.*, I, 1, 3; *PL* XXXII, 587). Yet he remained undecided (*ibid.*) whether souls are in some way derived through the parents from one original soul (traducianism), or whether each soul is created individually as it is placed in the body of each individual man. His reason for allowing the possibility of this spiritual traducianism seems to have been wholly theological, namely the explanation it offered for the transmission of original sin. The texts of St Augustine on the question are assembled in Andrea Martin, *Sancti Augustini Philosophia* (Paris, 1863), 412–457.

[8] "If human souls had been created outside bodies, they would have to be different in species, on account of the removal of the material principle of distinction, just as all the separate substances are posited by the philosophers as differing in species . . . the rational soul cannot be created in the manner appropriate to its nature except in a body, without prejudice nevertheless to the divine power." *De Pot.*, III, 10c.

[9] See St Thomas, *ST*, I, 90. 4, Cf. I, 91, 4, ad 3m; *In II Sent.*, d. 17, q. 2, a. 2 (ed. Mandonnet, II, 430–434); *De Pot.*, III, 10; *CG*, II, 83–84.

[10] The soul "has an essential relation to the body, inasmuch as a soul that gives being to one body cannot perfect another." *In II Sent.*, d. 17, q. 2, a. 2, Solut.; ed. Mandonnet, II, 432. The individuation in regard to the same body always remains with the soul: "Although the soul's individuation depends on the body for the occasion of its beginning, since it comes into possession of its individuated act of existing only in the body of which it is the act, it is not necessary that the individuation come to an end when the body is removed. Since its act of existing is independent, once it has acquired an individuated act of existing from its being made the form of this particular body, that act of existing always remains individuated." *De Ente*, c. V (ed. Roland-Gosselin, p. 39.17–24); tr. A. Maurer, p. 52. The doctrine of metempsychosis seems to have been taken over from religious traditions into the Pythagorean and Platonic currents of thought. Cf. Plato, *Phd.*, 70C, 81D–82B; *Ti.*, 90A–92C. St Thomas, *De Pot.*, III, 10c, terms it *transcorporatio*.

of a body it is adapted to act in conjunction with the senses. It is naturally dependent upon phantasms in which to understand its intelligible object, the quiddity of material things. How then can it perform any act of intellection in separation from the body? If it cannot attain anything intellectually, it will not be able to will anything, for an act of the will presupposes that its object is known. Even if the soul continues to exist after death, how can it continue to live? Would its status after death be like existence in the Greek Hadys or the Hebrew Sheol, a shadowy continuance in being without any of the rich fullness of life?

In the Platonic conception of the soul as a complete substance and nature in itself, no such problem arises. Separated from conjunction with the body, the soul would be freed from a hindrance to its full operation and would at once commence the life it was naturally meant to lead. As a form existing in itself, it would be immediately intelligible to itself, like an Aristotelian separate substance.[11] The object directly confronting it would be spiritual substance, in a richness and brilliance far beyond the comprehension of knowledge based upon sensible things. Such direct knowledge of spiritual substance would be the basis for a life of unfathomable goodness, beauty, and truth.

Unfortunately for so facile a solution to the problem actually involved, the knowledge that the human soul is by nature the substantial form of matter cannot allow separation from the body to be naturally a better state for the soul. If the soul were such that it could naturally have much more perfect knowledge in separation from matter, union with the body would be rather a hindrance and a punishment. By nature the soul would tend toward that higher way of knowledge, and not toward knowledge through the senses. On the contrary, however, it is directly the nature of the human soul to inform matter, and to work out its destiny through activity in and with the body. As far as its nature is concerned, the type of knowledge that belongs to the soul after death cannot be of a kind superior to what it has through the body. If the soul is naturally meant to have knowledge when separated from the sense channels, it would in that event have a less perfect way of knowing in separation than in union.

Is a less perfect way of knowing possible for the soul after death, as far as its nature is concerned? The soul has being and activity inde-

---

[11] See St Thomas, *ST*, I, 89, 1c. The difference in the *nature* of human souls from pure spirits, however, does not allow them naturally the perfect type of cognition proper to separate substances: "If therefore human souls were so instituted by God that they should understand in the way that pertains to separate substances, they would not have a perfect cognition, but one confused and in common." *Ibid.*

pendently of matter. The difficulty is that the object of its independent activity is immediately contacted only through phantasms. In separation from the corporeal faculties of sensation and imagination, no phantasms are available to it. The way of cognition adapted to it then would have to be through objects that are intelligible only, and not sensible. This way of knowing would be beyond its natural tendency, for by nature it is intended to know through phantasms. Yet such cognition can hardly be said to go against its nature, any more than separation from matter is against its nature. Its nature makes it the form of matter, yet allows it to exist without matter. Correspondingly, its nature allows it to know itself without material help, for in allowing it to have itself as a form without matter it allows the soul to possess itself intentionally, that is, to know itself. This, however, is a potential knowledge, and has to be brought into operation. It is not like the knowledge of an Aristotelian separate substance, in which the separate form is itself the actual knowledge and is limited to itself as object. The knowledge that the separate soul has of its own self could not be actualized in the clear and definite way of self-knowledge proper to a spirit that is by nature separate from matter. It will have to be a vague knowledge, just as the soul's knowledge through universals is vague. In a correspondingly vague way it will be able to receive intelligible similitudes of other things, similitudes imprinted upon its intellect by the first cause of all things. What these similitudes are, and to what extent they are impressed upon the separate soul's intellect by the first cause, metaphysics has no means of knowing. Metaphysics can only show that knowledge after death is beyond though not opposed to the unaided nature of the soul, and that the knowledge, whatever it is, is naturally less perfect than the knowledge obtained through the aid of the bodily faculties. At the same time, these conclusions leave the way open for the much higher kind of knowledge assured to the separate soul by the teachings of Christian revelation.

Résumé. Spiritual being is being that does not depend upon a material substrate. In the substantial order it is necessary being, for matter is the principle of contingence in substances. A substance whose being is spiritual is therefore imperishable, and can be produced only by creation. The human soul, because its being is spiritual, survives the death of the body. Yet, because its operations naturally depend upon the activity of the body for their perfection, they will just of themselves be less perfect when the soul is separated from matter.

SUGGESTED READINGS AND REFERENCES

Plato, *Phaedo*, 64C–107D.

St Augustine, *On the Immortality of the Soul*, tr. George G. Leckie (New York: Appleton-Century-Crofts, 1938).

St Thomas Aquinas, "Knowledge of the Soul after Death," in *Truth*, XIX, 1–2; tr. James V. McGlynn (Chicago: Henry Regnery, 1953), II, 383–395.

——— *Summa Contra Gentiles*, II, 78–87; tr. James F. Anderson, *On the Truth of the Catholic Faith*, Book Two, Creation (New York: Image Books, 1956), pp. 249–295.

——— *On the Power of God*, III, 9–10; tr. English Dominican Fathers (London: Burns Oates & Washbourne Ltd., 1932–1934), I, 145–169.

——— *The Soul*, 14–20, tr. John Patrick Rowan (St. Louis: B. Herder, 1949), pp. 176–268.

Anton Charles Pegis, *St. Thomas and the Problem of the Soul in the Thirteenth Century* (Toronto: St. Michael's College, 1934).

Victor Edmund Sleva, *The Separated Soul in the Philosophy of St. Thomas Aquinas* (Washington, D. C.: Catholic University of America Press, 1940).

CHAPTER 23

Pure Spirits

Possibility of Pure Spirits. The subsistence of the human soul shows that a finite form can exist in separation from matter. It proves that finite existence is not reserved to material things only. Yet the human soul is by nature the form of a body. It is not a pure spirit, but a spirit meant to inform matter. Are there any finite spirits that are not forms of matter? They would be purely spiritual forms. The gradual ascent in perfection from the inanimate to the vegetative and animal kingdoms and then to the mixture of animal and spiritual in man, would suggest that the gradation be completed by a realm of pure spirits before culminating in subsistent being. Has metaphysical science any means of showing that this is the case?

All human knowledge, metaphysical included, comes ultimately from sensible things as long as the soul is united with the body. Only sensible effects can provide the means of reaching spiritual causes. From sensible effects metaphysics reasons to subsistent being, and from human knowledge, actuated in the sensible phantasms, it reasons to the spiritual character of the human soul. Are there any natural effects in the sensible world from which it could reason to the existence of pure spirits?

Here the answer has to be no. In the ordinary course of natural events, no effects are observed that require the intervention of pure spirits for their explanation.[1] The possibility and nature of pure spirits would be an

---

[1] Spiritist phenomena have been observed by comparatively few persons, and what is accepted on the testimony of those persons is hardly traceable with certainty to the intervention of angels. Apparitions of angels, accepted on religious faith, and help attributed to them by personal belief, cannot serve as philosophical starting points. The argument that the hierarchy of natures in the universe requires pure finite spirits to fill out its perfection (e.g., St Thomas, *ST*, I, 50, 1c) has exceptionally strong probability. But it is not strictly demonstrative, since the first cause is not in Leibnizian fashion obliged to produce the best possible universe nor in any way necessitated to make the present universe as perfect as its cadres allow. These reflections may be kept in mind when reading statements like "Angels are creatures whose existence can be demonstrated. In certain exceptional cases they have even been seen." Etienne Gilson,

idle question for metaphysics, were it not that Christian revelation teaches the existence of these spirits under the name of angels. Assured of their existence on non-philosophical grounds, the human mind naturally wishes to know what it can about their natures, and looks to a Christian metaphysics for the principles through which the angelic essences may be probed.

Persons. First of all, an angelic nature will be intelligent. As a pure form existing without matter, it will possess itself immaterially and so will be the substantial cognition of itself. As a finite substance, however, the angelic nature will not be immediately operative. It will have to be brought into second act to know itself. In this way it differs from an Aristotelian separate substance. It is subject to the concurring action of the first cause in being brought from first act to second act. It is also subject to the action of the first cause in the impression of intelligible similitudes by which it may know things other than itself, for the first cause possesses the ideas of all things and can imprint them upon any intellect. Again the angelic intelligence differs from the Aristotelian separate substance, in being able to know things other than itself. Upon intelligence free will naturally follows. Angels therefore are complete substances of intelligible nature, and so, are persons.

The natural sequence of free will upon intelligence is not difficult to show. As cognition, intelligence consists in having the forms of things as other than one's self, and other than one's subjective modifications.[2] Upon these forms will follow inclinations in regard to the things in real being. Every finite form is a potency to being, and accordingly of its nature grounds an inclination to being, ultimately to subsistent being.[3] A finite form, in a word, cannot be its own final cause, for it is meant for being. It has to give rise to a tendency to being, a tendency that reaches out to real being and finally to infinite being. When this tendency follows upon a form in the intelligence it is known as will.[4] Since

The Christian Philosophy of St. Thomas Aquinas, tr. L. K. Shook (New York, 1956), p. 160. Once the existence of angels is known with certainty through revelation, however, there need be no hesitation in agreeing that "it is difficult to omit the consideration of one whole order of creatures without upsetting the equilibrium" (*ibid.*) of a metaphysical investigation of the universe. Theological treatises on the angels, for instance in Suarez or the Salmanticenses, extend to huge proportions.

[2] See above, Chapter 15, nn. 2 and 3.

[3] Cf. St Thomas, *De Ver.*, XXI, 5c; *ST*, I, 6, 4c.

[4] ". . . all things are inclined in their own way by appetite to the good, but differently. . . . Some tend to the good with a cognition by which they know the notion itself of good. This is proper to intellect. . . . And this inclination is called the will. Therefore, since angels through intellect know the universal notion itself of good, it is clear that in them there is will." St Thomas, *ST*, I, 59, 1c.

intelligence grasps its object under the universal aspect of being[5] and of goodness, it cannot give rise to volition that is necessitated by any finite good, nor even by subsistent being when known under limiting terms. But the immediate object of angelic cognition is the angel. In terms of itself it has its natural cognition of infinite being, just as the human intellect does in terms of material things. No external object, therefore, can naturally determine the will of an angel. The angel has to determine itself to act. It is accordingly endowed with free will.[6]

Since an angel, lacking sensitive nature, does not make decisions on the basis of passion, it has no possibility of revising its decision as passion changes. Since it lacks rational nature, which is proper to man, it does not reason, but grasps each object with all the clarity and unchangeableness with which the human intellect grasps the immediately known first principles. For the angelic intelligence, consequently, no error regarding the natural conditions of things is possible,[7] and so no change of decision on account of previous error. The will of an angel, therefore, adheres unchangeably to any decision it makes.[8]

Individuation of Pure Spirits. In material things, forms specifically the same actuate many different individuals. Humanity, for instance, is found in millions of individual men. The reason why there can be individual difference without formal difference in a species is matter. Without relation to matter under designated dimensions, a specific form would have no principle by which it could be multiplied. If the human form were not the form of matter, there could be only one instance of humanity.

In the angelic forms, however, there is no matter. Nor have they any

[5] "But the intellect regards its object under the common aspect of being . . ." *ST*, I, 79, 7c. "Hence being is the proper object of intellect . . ." I, 5, 2c. Cf. above, Chapter 16, n. 1.

[6] "But only that which has intellect can act with a free judgment, insofar as it knows the universal notion of good, by which it can judge that this or that is good. Hence wherever there is intellect there is free will." *ST*, I, 59, 3c. Cf. *CG*, II, 47–48.

[7] On the exclusion of the possibility of error in immediate judgments, see above, Chapter 18, nn. 24–26.

[8] ". . . an angel apprehends unchangeably by its intellect, just as we apprehend the first principles unchangeably. . . . Hence . . . the will of the angel adheres fixedly and unchangeably. And therefore, if it is considered before the adherence, it can freely adhere to this particular and to the opposite, that is, in the things it does not will by nature. But after it has once adhered to a thing, it adheres unchangeably." St Thomas, *ST*, I, 64, 2c. The angel is of such a nature that its estimate of a situation "is accepted irreversibly." *De Ver.*, XXIV, 10c. On the possibility of error in regard to supernatural things, see *ST*, I, 58, 5c. In this case also, however, the decision once made is immutable, in accordance with the angelic nature; see *De Malo*, XVI, 5c. An angel will never change its mind, no matter what the consequences.

natural relation to matter. There is no way, then, in which they could be individuated by matter. Yet each angel is a person, and according to the traditional Boethian definition of person[9] has to be regarded as an individual. Since form is the angel's only substantial principle, it will have to do the individuating. But form is the unifying principle in a species, and not a multiplying principle. It will unite all the perfection of the species in the one individual, if left by itself. That is indeed the case with each angel. Each angel, then, exhausts all the perfection of its own species. There can be only one angel in each species. In a word, in the angels species and individual completely coincide.[10]

Since an angel has no natural relation to matter, it is of its own nature not in place. It is wrong even to conceive the indivisibility of angel in the manner of the indivisibility of a point. A point has position, an angel has not. The categories of quantity and place do not apply to an angel.[11] A spirit, however, can act on matter, as is clear in the case of the human soul. There is no apparent reason, then, why an angel should not be able to act on corporeal things. In that case, the activity of the angel would in a way locate it in regard to the bodies it controls. Yet it would not be contained by the place, but would rather actively contain the body through its control.[12]

The lack of any necessary relation to matter, however, does not prevent an angel from knowing individual material things and events. Knowing itself directly, it knows itself as created by the first cause and as mirroring in its own limited way the perfection of its maker.[13] But like the human intellect, it is able to receive further the species of finite

---

[9] Above, Chapter 10, n. 16.

[10] See St Thomas, *ST*, I, 50, 4c. Cf. *In II Sent.*, d. 3, q. 1, a. 4–5 (ed. Mandonnet, II, 96–101); d. 32, q. 2, a. 3, Solut. (II, 839); *De Ente*, c. IV (ed. Roland-Gosselin, pp. 30.1–34.3); c. V (p. 39.14–16); *CG*, II, 93–95; *De Spir. Creat.*, a. 8. St Thomas' conception of a subsistent form, even though the form is the specific nature, is modeled upon the Aristotelian notion of individual form in act, and not at all in the fashion of a substantized universal: "And on this account there are as many species in the angels as individuals; because, since they are subsistent forms or quiddities, they have by themselves their being in act and their distinction." *In V Sent.*, d. 12, q. 1, a. 1, q. 3, ad 3m; ed. Moos, IV, 503 (no. 49). On the Aristotelian background, see J. Owens, "The Reality of the Aristotelian Separate Movers," *The Review of Metaphysics*, III (1950), 319–337. On the mediaeval reactions against this position, which was entirely new in Christian tradition, see Etienne Gilson, *History of Christian Philosophy in the Middle Ages* (New York, 1955), pp. 413–415.

[11] St Thomas, *ST*, I, 52, 2c.

[12] *ST*, I, 52, 1c. The capacity of finite spiritual power to act on matter is established by what is known of human activity, and in particular by the illumination of the phantasms by the agent intellect. See St Thomas, *ST*, I, 79, 4; *De Spir. Creat.*, a. 10; *Q. de An.*, a. 4–5.

[13] St Thomas, *ST*, I, 56, 3c.

things other than itself. These it can receive directly from the activity of the first cause, which can give individual things being not only in themselves but also in a creature's cognition.[14] In this way the angel can know singulars as singulars, insofar as each is represented down to the last detail in the unique and simple essence of the first cause and contained in the intelligible species produced in the angel's mind.[15] The angel's intellectual acts, though successive, do not give rise to time.[16]

Résumé. Pure spirits occupy the place in the hierarchy of the universe between spiritual souls and subsistent being. As subsistent finite forms without any essential relation to matter, they are by nature intelligences in which individual coincides with specific essence. With free will consequent upon intelligence, they are persons who dominate their own activity. Since they are subject neither to passion nor, on the natural level, to error, their estimate of anything to be done is final, and accordingly their decision, once made, is naturally unchangeable. Their knowledge originates in each with its own self, and extends to the first cause, and to all other things and events insofar as these are represented in intelligible species derived immediately from the first cause.

SUGGESTED READINGS AND REFERENCES

Aristotle, *Metaphysics*, Λ 6–9, 1071b3–1075a10.

St Thomas Aquinas, *Treatise on Separate Substances*, tr. Francis J. Lescoe (West Hartford: Saint Joseph College, 1959).

Etienne Gilson, "The Angels," in *The Christian Philosophy of St. Thomas Aquinas*, tr. Lawrence K. Shook (New York: Random House, 1956), pp. 160–173.

[14] ". . . as things flow forth from God so as to subsist in their own natures, thus also do they flow forth so as to be in the angelic cognition." *ST*, I, 57, 2c. Cf. *Quodl.*, VIII, 1c (text above, Chapter 9, n. 12).

[15] "Thus through species conferred by God the angels know things not only in regard to universal natures, but also as regards singularity, insofar as they are certain plurified representations of that unique and simple essence." *ST*, I, 57, 2c.

[16] "There is therefore in the intellect of a separate substance a certain succession of intellections, though there is no motion properly speaking, since there is not succession of act to potency, but of act to act." *CG*, II, 101. See *Treatise on Separate Substances*, XIX, 113; tr. F. J. Lescoe (West Hartford, 1959), pp. 118–119.

CHAPTER 24

Existence and God

The word "God" is a bona fide philosophical term. It is used regularly in philosophical writings by pagans like Aristotle and Plato who had no notion of Christian revelation, and by moderns like Whitehead and Weiss who can hardly by any stretch of the designation be called sacred theologians.[1] But in this context the question arises whether the God of the philosophers is the "God of Abraham, the God of Isaac, the God of Jacob," and a negative answer was poignantly urged by Pascal.[2] Today, especially in some circles of existentialist thinkers[3] and Scripture scholars,[4] there is a strange revulsion against considering the God of Christian worship in terms of metaphysical conclusions, a revulsion never experienced in the least by the healthier-minded theologians of the middle ages.[5] A Christian metaphysician, accordingly, has today the task of establishing the identity of subsistent being with the God in which he believes through his faith.

Supreme Being. Even in the popular Christian vocabulary, God is regularly called the Supreme Being. This is understood to mean that God is the greatest of all beings, not only in the

---

[1] See Alfred North Whitehead, *Process and Reality* (New York, 1929), p. 519 ff.; Paul Weiss, *Modes of Being* (Carbondale, 1958), p. 277 ff.

[2] "Dieu d'Abraham, Dieu d'Isaac, Dieu de Jacob, non des philosophes et des savants," *Le Mémorial.*

[3] ". . . cogitative truth means making the absolute into an object from which all other objects must be derived." Martin Buber, *Eclipse of God* (New York, 1952), p. 44. Similarly Paul Tillich, *The Courage to Be* (New Haven, 1952), pp. 181–185. Cf. below, nn. 15–17.

[4] E.g.: "And here is God as he is, not an abstract Prime Mover or a First Cause, but a God who is interested in men of flesh and blood, a father who bends down to appeal to his wayward children." H. J. Richards, "The Word of God Incarnate," *The Life of the Spirit*, XIII (1958), 98, quoted by Frederick L. Moriarty, *Introducing the Old Testament* (Milwaukee, 1960), p. 56. See also John L. McKenzie, *The Two-Edged Sword* (Milwaukee, 1956), p. 20.

[5] E.g., St Thomas, *In XII Metaph.*, lect. 12 (ed. Cathala-Spiazzi), no. 2663.

sense of occupying the highest rank in honor, but of exercising supreme control over all other beings. St. Anselm could capitalize on this conception in locating the ordinary Christian's idea of God as something greater than which nothing can be thought, in the sense of a really existing something.[6] The Old Testament answer of God to Moses, "I am who am," has lent itself readily in Christian tradition to the interpretation that the nature of God is to be.[7]

The philosophical conception of God reached by metaphysical demonstration coincides unmistakably with the Christian conception of God as the Supreme Being. Subsistent being is the highest of all beings, for everything else is only a secondary instance of being. As pure act in an existential sense, it includes all perfections in the highest degree, and so is "that greater than which nothing can be thought." Because all other being, including that of the operations of finite things, is freely imparted by it, it exercises supreme control over all other things. In it accordingly men live and move and have their being. Lacking all limitation, both by matter and by essence, it coincides to this extent with the infinite spirit that is the object of adoration in Christian tradition. It is supremely unique. It cannot leave room for any other supreme being. It is identical therefore with the one God of scriptural revelation, insofar as he is being.

Creator. The God professed in the traditional creed is the creator of heaven and earth. Unlike the Platonic demiurge that merely brought order into a pre-existent chaos, or a source of emanation that overflowed into the universe,[8] the God believed in by Christian tradition made all other things out of nothing. A metaphysics based upon existence maintains the same tenet about the production of things by the first cause. This creative power, metaphysics shows, can belong only to subsistent being. From the viewpoint of creation, accordingly, the first cause is identical with the scriptural creator of heaven and earth. Similarly the first cause that conserves everything created, and concurs in the activities of every creature, is readily seen to coincide in that regard with the God whose consent is necessary for the fall of every sparrow

[6] *Proslogion*, c. II.

[7] See St Augustine, *Sermons*, VI, 3–4, 4–5; *PL*, XXXVIII, 61. St Thomas Aquinas, *ST*, I, 2, 3, Sed contra. For other instances, see Cornelia J. De Vogel, "'Ego sum qui sum' et sa Signification pour une Philosophie Chrétienne," *Revue des Sciences Religieuses*, XXXV (1961), 346–354. On the difficulty of finding this meaning in the Hebrew text, see Gerhard Kittel, *Bible Key Words*, tr. J. R. Coates and H. P. Kingdon (New York, 1958), II, 63, n. 4. On other interpretations, see M. M. Bourke, "Yahweh, The Divine Name," *The Bridge*, v. III (Newark, 1958), pp. 271–287.

[8] Plato, *Ti.*, 30A; Plotinus, *En.*, V, 2, 1.7–21.

to the ground and for each single hair on a person's head,[9] and who inclines the heart of an earthly ruler in whatever direction he pleases.[10]

Ultimate Goal. The God of scriptural revelation has made all things for himself, and does all things for himself.[11] Correspondingly, metaphysics shows that subsistent being is the supreme good and ultimate end of all things. It is the good that finalizes every action, and in virtue of it lesser goods are ends. It coincides, therefore, with the goal of human life as taught by the Christian faith. Intellectual creatures are able to know and will this ultimate end. Accordingly, metaphysics proves, intellectual creatures are related immediately to the ultimate end of all things. They do not attain it mediately, through other creatures, as is the case with brute and vegetative and inanimate creation. Hence arises the dignity of intellectual creatures as persons. The ultimate goal to which they are directed through their own activities is identical with the God that men were created to know and love. The Christian faith teaches that man was created to see God. Metaphysics, of course, cannot establish the possibility of a direct vision of God, for that is something beyond the forces that human nature has of itself.[12] The possibility and the fact can be known only through revelation. Metaphysics, however, can show that the human intellect knows things under the aspect of being, and that no arguments can establish a contradiction in the doctrine of the intellect's receiving supernaturally the elevation necessary to see God face to face.[13]

From all these viewpoints, then, subsistent being as established by metaphysics proves to be identical with the God of Christian tradition. One does not need to be a theologian to see this identity. The metaphysician who is an ordinary Christian cannot help seeing that what he has demonstrated in his science is the God he serves in the daily practice of his faith.

Demonstration of God's Existence. The metaphysical proof for the existence of the first cause, as outlined earlier in the present work,[14] is based upon the being of sensible

[9] *N.T., Mt.*, X, 29–31. [10] *O.T., Prov.*, XXI, 1. [11] *O.T., Prov.*, XVI, 4.

[12] "The nature of man is naturally endless. Since, in fact, no created good can terminate his intellectual desire, short of the vision of the divine essence there can be no termination of man's desire." A. C. Pegis, "Nature and Spirit: Some Reflections on the Problem of the End of Man," *Proceedings of the American Catholic Philosophical Association*, XXIII (1949), 73. Cf. G. Smith, "The Natural End of Man," *ibid.*, pp. 47–61; "Philosophy and the Unity of Man's Ultimate End," *Proceedings*, XXVII (1953), 81.

[13] Cf. Pegis, *art. cit.*, pp. 74–79.

[14] See Chapter 6, n. 1.

things. This is the only form of the proof given by St Thomas in the one treatise in which he is professedly dealing with things from the viewpoint of their being. In his theological works, he multiplies the ways by which the existence of God may be demonstrated. In general, against a Christian background, metaphysicians and apologists usually refer in the plural to the proofs or arguments for the existence of God. These arguments have become notorious. For some, they represent Western thought at its lowest point of deterioration.[15] For others, they appear unconvincing and useless for the unbeliever, and entirely superfluous for the believer.[16] On the popular level they are widely regarded as having been neatly disposed of once for all by Kant, and so as outdated and as utterly irrelevant to the acceptance of God in modern civilization.[17] The arguments, accordingly, invite close metaphysical scrutiny. Since they offer themselves as demonstrations, they will use as middle term either an essence of some subject or a notion that will function in lieu of such an essence.[18] The identification of the middle term should determine the character of the proof.

---

[15] E.g., Nietzsche, "'Reason' in Philosophy," no. 4, *Twilight of the Idols*, tr. Walter Kaufmann, in *The Portable Nietzsche* (New York, 1954), pp. 481–482.

[16] Gabriel Marcel, *The Mystery of Being*, II Faith and Reality (London: 1951), p. 176. The approach to Aristotelian and Scholastic metaphysical arguments, in Marcel's view, overpowers one with "a feeling of fatigue and oppression, I should even say, unhappily, of boredom." *Ibid.*, p. 4.

[17] E.g.: "Ever since Kant critically examined the various 'proofs' of the existence of God, no thoughtful believer has found it possible to give irrefutable rational proof of God's existence." Reinhold Niebuhr, "The Religious Traditions of Our Nation," *The Saturday Evening Post*, July 23, 1960, p. 26. God seems regarded as above existence: "Indeed, can we properly speak of the *existence* of one whom faith regards as the mysterious beginning and end of all existence?" *Ibid.* See also Karl Jaspers, *Way to Wisdom*, tr. Ralph Manheim (London, 1951), p. 42. Cf. below, nn. 25 and 52.

[18] ". . . demonstrative knowledge must be knowledge of a necessary nexus, and therefore must clearly be obtained through a necessary middle term . . ." Aristotle, *APo.*, I 6, 75a12–14; Oxford tr. The middle term, understood in the sense of the overall means of demonstration where the proof is complicated, should normally be the essence of the subject whose attributes are being demonstrated. The essence is expressed in the subject's definition. In approaching the question of God's existence against the background of Christian culture, many notions of God, like Creator, Lord, Providence, are at hand. But they are names taken from effects, and yield only nominal definitions: "But the names of God are imposed from effects, as will be shown later. Hence, in demonstrating through an effect that God exists, we can take as a means what the name 'God' signifies." St Thomas, *ST*, I, 2, 2, ad 2m. Cf. *CG*, I, 12, In rationibus. On the problem of the nominal definition of God, see Fernand Van Steenberghen, *Dieu Caché* (Louvain and Paris, 1961), pp. 27–44; Thomas C. O'Brien, *Metaphysics and the Existence of God* (Washington, D. C., 1960), pp. 190–207. Even a nominal definition in terms merely of being, as in "I am who am," is imposed from effects, in the way St Thomas regards a name applied through "the removal of the divine effects" (*CG, loc. cit.*).

In some of the proofs traditionally offered by apologists, the middle term has no metaphysical character at all. It may be merely human belief, as in the argument from universal consent. The middle term is the general belief of mankind. Aside from the difficulty or even impossibility of establishing the fact of this belief, it is an argument that pertains to human faith and not to metaphysics. The same holds for the popular argument that great men believe in God. Legitimate as these ways may be as approaches to God, they are not scientific arguments.

Arguments From Quidditative Perfection. The attempt to reason to the existence of God from what is known of him in terms of essence was introduced by St Anselm,[19] colored by Duns Scotus,[20] revived by Descartes,[21] and continued by Spinoza[22] and Leibniz.[23] Though incisively criticized and rejected by St Thomas Aquinas on the ground that the notion of a thing does not establish the way it is placed in existence,[24] and by Kant as "ontological"

[19] *Proslogion*, c. *II*. On the background and meaning of the argument in St Anselm, see Gerald B. Phelan, *The Wisdom of Saint Anselm* (Latrobe, Pa., 1960), pp. 34–40. The Anselmian proof is erroneously called "ontological" in the wake of Kant's critique (p. 6). Neither historically nor philosophically is it connected with the abstract or ontological notion of being that was made current by Christian Wolff. However, in the general sense of proceeding from the notion of greatest being to real existence, it is regularly classed today among the proofs called "ontological," even though it presupposes the real existence of God and seeks to make manifest the necessary reason for that existence.

[20] *Ordinatio*, I, 2, 1–2, nos. 137–139; ed. Carolus Balić (Vatican City, 1950—), II, 208.16–211.1. With Scotus the proof, because it starts from what is experienced, is clearly not "ontological"; see A. B. Wolter, "Duns Scotus and the Existence and Nature of God," *Proceedings of the American Catholic Philosophical Association*, XXVIII (1954), 96–98.

[21] The mind "from the sole fact that it perceives that necessary and eternal existence is contained in the idea of a most perfect being, must unhesitatingly conclude that a most perfect being exists." Descartes, *Principia Philosophica*, I, 14; A-T, VIII, 10.15–18 (IX, 31). Descartes' criterion was that whatever is contained in the clear and distinct idea of a thing may be affirmed of the thing itself.

[22] ". . . conceive, if possible, that God does not exist. Therefore (by axiom 7) his essence does not involve existence. But this (by prop. 7) is absurd. Therefore God necessarily exists." *Ethica*, I, Prop. XI. In the following scholion the argument is called apriori, in the sense that the nature of God is conceived as prior, with the divine existence following from the nature.

[23] "And as nothing can prevent the possibility of that which includes no bounds . . . that alone suffices to know the existence of God *a priori*." *Monadology*, no. 45. Leibniz takes the argument from Descartes, but, like Scotus, requires that the real possibility of God be shown, on the basis of real and not just nominal definitions; see *Thoughts on Knowledge, Truth, and Ideas* (Nov., 1684). On the problem, see F. Crahay, "L'Argument Ontologique chez Descartes et Leibniz et la Critique Kantienne," *Revue Philosophique de Louvain*, XLVII (1949), 458–468.

[24] For St Thomas an essence posited in intentional existence provides of itself no basis for arguing to its real existence: "For the thing and the notion expressed by the

because it abstracts from experience in introducing the concept of existence,[25] it still has not lost its fascination.[26] In various ways it takes an essence as its starting point and argues to real existence. For St Anselm the essence was something greater than which nothing could be thought. If this object were said to lack real existence, a greater, namely the object with real existence, would be the original notion. For Scotus the essence was material quiddity known through sensible experience. Though attained as really existent, it was considered in the argument solely according to its possibility. Its existence was disregarded as contingent and so not the suitable means for a strict demonstration. Its real possibility, however, established for Scotus the real possibility of a first efficient cause, an ultimate final cause, and a supreme being. These, if they did not exist, would not be really possible. So proven

---

name have to be posited in the same way. From the fact that what is expressed by the name 'God' is conceived by the mind, it does not follow that God exists except in the intellect." *CG*, I, 11, Nec oportet. St Thomas, however, recognizes that the argument in St. Anselm proceeds from the supposition that God really exists, and on that supposition shows that he cannot be thought of as non-existent. *In I Sent.*, d. 3, q. 1, a. 2, ad 4m; ed. Mandonnet, II, 95. Cf. *De Ver.*, X, 12, ad 2m; *ST*, I, 2, 1, ad 2m.

[25] ". . . they abstract from all experience and conclude entirely a *priori* from mere concepts to the existence of a highest cause." *Critique of Pure Reason*, B 618. ". . . when you introduced, under whatever disguised name, the concept of its existence into the concept of a thing you wished to think of solely in regard to its possibility." *Ibid.*, B 625. Kant, in accord with the exigencies of his philosophical procedure, reduces the other theoretical arguments to the ontological (*ibid.*, B 631–657). Having shown that theoretical reason cannot demonstrate either the existence or non-existence of God, he establishes God's existence in the *Critique of Practical Reason* (Book II, 2, 5) as a postulate required for moral action. Accordingly "it is morally necessary to accept the existence of God" (*ibid.*). The moral argument is pressed home very tellingly by John Henry Newman, *A Grammar of Assent*, I, 5, 1. On the whole procedure as "an extraordinarily beautiful begging of the question," see W. Barden, "The Moral Fact and the Existence of God," *Irish Ecclesiastical Record*, LIII (1939), 193. On the moral argument in recent times, see John-Henry Walgrave, "La Preuve de l'Existence de Dieu par la Conscience Morale et l'Expérience des Valeurs," in *L'Existence de Dieu*, ed. Collège Dominicain à La Sarte-Huy (Tournai, 1961), pp. 109–132.

[26] The "sixth argument" offered by Joseph Gredt, *Elementa Philosophiae Aristotelico-Thomisticae*, 7th ed. (Freiburg i. Breisgau, 1937), II, 199–200 (no. 790), "from the non-contradiction (*non-repugnantia*) of God . . . proved positively a *posteriori* . . . . draws the conclusion of his existence" (p. 200). The argument is only too evidently from essence to existence, though unlike Leibniz (and Scotus) it does not use the term "possible" of God (*ibid.*, n. 2). For a contemporary discussion, see R. E. Allen, "The Ontological Argument," *The Philosophical Review*, LXX (1961), 56–66. Gaston Rabeau, *Le Jugement d'Existence* (Paris, 1938), p. 80, notes how the nineteenth-century doctrine known as "ontologism," in which both psychologically and ontologically the mind's first idea is that of God, is a "natural and necessary evolution" of Kant's denial that existence is a predicate.

to exist, they are then shown to coincide in the one infinite being.[27]

In a metaphysics that understands essence as in itself wholly devoid of being, the fallacy in the above ways of arguing is readily apparent. Essence, in the sense of what is known through simple apprehension of the intellect, is of its nature a limitation of being. No matter how far it is considered extended, even *ad infinitum*, it does not include any being. Being, whether real or intentional, is originally known through judgment. Only the being that is judged in sensible things, therefore, can serve as a means to demonstrate subsistent being. Do the other traditional arguments for the existence of God meet this requirement?

The "Five Ways." In current Scholastic manuals and monographs the accepted philosophical arguments for the existence of God are regularly drawn up according to the "Five Ways" sketched in the first part of the *Summa Theologiae*[28] by St Thomas Aquinas. There they are outlined very concisely, and without the detailed treatment that is necessary to make each link in their reasoning cogent. The extensively detailed development that lies back of the "First Way," or argument from motion, may be seen in the *Contra Gentiles* and in the explanation of its principles as given in St Thomas' commentaries on the Aristotelian *Physics* and *Metaphysics*.[29] The other four "Ways" are similarly presented in so sketchy a fashion that a correspondingly deep and complicated background in the other works of St Thomas may be presumed. The arrangement in "five ways" is not repeated or referred to elsewhere in the works of St Thomas, even in those written later than the first part of the *Summa Theologiae*. The arguments are divided

[27] On the Scotistic argument, see A. B. Wolter, *art. cit.*; J. Owens, "The Special Characteristic of the Scotistic Proof that God Exists," *Analecta Gregoriana*, LXVII (1954), 311–327. It is in the general lines established by Duns Scotus that Cajetan (*In ST*, I, 2, 3, no. III) interprets the "five ways" of St Thomas. The "ways," according to Cajetan, lead to five predicates, which, though they do not immediately appear so, are in fact proper to God — as in Scotus the initial arguments lead to relative properties of infinite being. From the predicates one concludes *quasi per accidens* that God exists — somewhat as in Scotus (*Quaest. Metaph.*, I, 1, 49; ed. Vivès, VII, 37a) the highest metaphysical notion of God is only *per accidens*. Along similar lines Fernand Van Steenberghen, *Dieu Caché*, pp. 216–220, bases the demonstration on the *essential* perfectibility of finite beings, and maintains (p. 187) that the first and second "ways" of St Thomas have to be "prolonged."

[28] *ST*, I, 2, 3c.

[29] *CG*, I, 13; *In VII Phys.*, lect. 1–2; *In VIII Phys.*, lect. 1–13; *In XII Metaph.*, lect. 5–9. Cf. J. Owens, "The Conclusion of the *Prima Via*," *The Modern Schoolman*, XXX (1952–1953), 33–53, 109–121, 203–215.

differently in his different writings.[30] *Prima facie* it appears that the division into "five ways" had no special significance for St Thomas. The division has the earmarks of an apologetic arrangement that could be altered freely to suit the purposes of the moment.

The arrangement under the "Five Ways," however, is still the mold in which the arguments considered valid by modern Scholastic writers are usually cast, with the occasional addition of some sixth "way" that a particular author considers acceptable.[31] The "Five Ways," therefore, demand careful consideration from a metaphysical viewpoint. By most commentators they are looked upon as five separate demonstrations.[32] By others they are regarded in various ways as just one demonstration based upon existence,[33] but presented in five different contexts. In still another view, they are not to be considered a genuine expression of St Thomas' own thinking.[34] Accordingly, they invite critical study.

[30] *In I Sent.*, d. 3, div. text. (ed. Mandonnet, I, 88–89), following the Pseudo-Areopagite, divides them into three ways, the way of causality, the way of removal, and the way of eminence; for all three it gives as the probative reason "the being of a creature is from another" (p. 88); and it includes potentiality and mobility (cf. *prima via* of the *Summa Theologiae*) in the starting points of the first and second ways. *Contra Gentiles*, I, 13, divides the argument from motion into two ways; then adds the way of efficient causality and the arguments from the grades of being and the governing of things; it omits the third way of the *Summa Theologiae*, but uses it in a following article (*CG*, I, 15, Amplius; cf. II, 15, Praeterea) to prove that God is eternal; and it synopsizes the argument from motion, quite as in the *Summa Theologiae*, in the next article (*CG*, I, 16, Item Videmus). *De Potentia* (III, 5c) divides the arguments under three reasons; the first, allegedly that of Plato, shows that being, because common to all, has to come from one cause; the second, that of Aristotle, is that there is an immobile and most perfect being, from which all other things receive being; the third, that of Avicenna, proves that things participating being receive their being from pure act, which is being itself. In the *Compendium Theologiae* (I, 3), the one argument directly used to prove that God exists is from motion. However, for the opposite view that "One cannot be reduced to another, nor the five to a single proof that would contain them all," see Louis Charlier, "Les Cinq Voies de Saint Thomas," in *L'Existence de Dieu* (Tournai, 1961), p. 189.

[31] E.g., Gredt, see above, n. 26; Jacques Maritain, *Approaches to God*, tr. Peter O'Reilly (New York, 1955), pp. 58–67. The probative force of Maritain's sixth way is the causing of existence: "Everything which begins existed before itself in a certain way, to wit, in its causes." *Ibid.*, p. 63.

[32] E.g., Cajetan, *In ST*, I, 2, 3; J. Maritain, *op. cit.*, pp. 18–19.

[33] E.g., Norbert Del Prado, *De Veritate Fundamentali Philosophiae Christianae* (Fribourg, Switzerland, 1911), pp. xlii–xliii; "Utrum Deus Sit," *Jahrbuch für Philosophie und Spekulative Theologie*, XXIV (1910), 137–138; Gerard Smith, *Natural Theology* (New York, 1951), pp. 86–88. M. J. Adler, "The Demonstration of God's Existence," *The Thomist*, V (1943), 193, calls attention to the reason why there can be only one demonstration, according to the statement of St Thomas: ". . . in speculative matters the means of demonstration, which perfectly demonstrates the conclusion, is one only . . ." *ST*, I, 47, 1, ad 3m.

[34] ". . . the Five Ways . . . do not seem to me to express the real nature of St. Thomas's own thought." Eric Lionel Mascall, *Existence and Analogy* (London, etc.,

Argument From Motion. The framework for the first of the "Five Ways" in the *Summa Theologiae* is taken from Aristotle. As the argument is gradually developed by St Thomas throughout his own works, the operative notion in it is even from the very start found deliberately changed from the eternity of motion to the being of motion.[35] This new casting of the argument in the context of existence is crucial for its interpretation as it is given in the *Summa*. Its starting point is located in sensible things, and its middle term is their observed movements:

> The first and more manifest way is that which is taken from the side of movement. For it is certain, and evident through sensation, that some things are being moved in this world.

The movements meant are clearly enough the accidental changes of sensible things. They are the changes that are immediately apparent to the senses. This is confirmed by the examples used in the course of the argument. One is of qualitative change, from cold to hot. The other is local motion, where a cane is being moved from one place to another by the hand. With this starting point laid down as its first premise, the argument establishes as its second premise the requirement of a movent other than the thing that is being moved:

> But everything that is being moved is being moved by another. For nothing is being moved, except insofar as it is in potency to that towards which it is being moved; while a thing imparts motion insofar as it is in act. For to impart motion is nothing else than to bring something from potency to act. But a thing cannot be brought from potency to act, except through some being that is in act, just as what is hot in act, as fire, makes wood,

1949), p. 176; cf. p. 79. Van Steenberghen, *Dieu Caché*, p. 174, notes that St Thomas in the five ways brings together what he considers best in tradition. The sources for the five ways are collected in René Arnou, *De Quinque Viis Sancti Thomae* (Rome, 1932). That St Thomas in a theological work is expressing himself through traditionally known arguments, however, need in no way preclude his transforming them into the one demonstration of the *De Ente et Essentia*, just as his use of Aristotelian and Augustinian and Avicennian texts to express his own doctrine does not at all bind him to their original meaning. In all five ways the probative force lies in a finite being's "radical inability to account for its own existence" (Mascall, p. 71). The starting point in each case is something (a movement, a substance, a directing to a goal) that is made to exist through an efficient cause.

[35] See above, nn. 29–30. Cf.: ". . . since nothing brings itself out of potency into act, or from non-being to being." St Thomas, *CG*, I, 13, Quorum primum est. "For every act which is in regard to the ultimate, is in potency to the ultimate act. But the ultimate act is being itself. For, since every motion is a process from potency into act, that act to which all motion tends must be the ultimate." *Comp. Theol.*, I, 11. Cf. below, n. 50.

> which is hot in potency, be actually hot, and in this way moves it and alters it. But it is not possible for the same thing to be simultaneously in act and potency in the same respect, but only in different respects; for what is hot in act cannot simultaneously be hot in potency, but is simultaneously cold in potency. It is therefore impossible for anything to be in the same respect and the same way movent and moved, or to move itself. Therefore everything that is being moved has to be moved by another.

This second premise is not accepted as immediately evident, but is demonstrated. The notion of movement is analyzed as in the Aristotelian *Physics*[36] in terms of act and potency. The potential state of the thing that is being moved is clear on Aristotelian grounds. The doctrine that "a thing imparts motion insofar as it is in act," however, carries for St Thomas a meaning considerably different from its Aristotelian sense. For Aristotle a form was of itself actual to the full extent allowed by its nature. As long as something else was not impeding it, it was exercising its activity. But for St Thomas, "being is the actuality of every form or nature; for goodness, or humanity, is not signified in act except insofar as we signify it to be."[37] To be in act means for the thing to exist. Only through something already in act can movement and its term be brought into being. Why? No reason is given in the text of the argument. Only an example is offered. Something that is actually hot, like fire, makes wood *be* actually hot. To make wood be in that accidental way is to move it and alter it. Movement is accordingly explained in terms of the imparting of accidental being. That is what it meant for St Thomas. The explanation that the same motion and the same heat are transferred from one body to another had not yet been evolved by quantitative physics. Even if it had been known to him, it would not have affected the strength of his reasoning. The reasoning here is not concerned with sameness in quantity, but with the fact that new accidental being is brought about in the changing thing. Movement in sensible things means that they are made to be, accidentally, in some other way. But being can be caused only by something that already exists, as the reasoning in the *De Ente et Essentia*[38] had made clear. In this light the cogency of the assertion that nothing can be reduced to act except through a being that is in act becomes readily apparent and needs only to be illustrated by an example.

The argument continues with the familiar denial of an infinite series of movents that are being moved in imparting their motion:

[36] *Ph.*, III 1, 201a10–11.

[37] *ST*, I, 3, 4c. Cf. *De Pot.*, VII, 2, ad 9m.

[38] *De Ente*, c. IV; ed. Roland-Gosselin, p. 35,6–10. Cf. *CG*, I, 22, *Amplius Si.*

> If therefore that by which it is being moved is itself being moved, it also, necessarily, is being moved by another, and this by another. But here one cannot proceed to infinity, because thus there would not be any first movent, nor in consequence, any other movent, because secondary movents do not impart motion except insofar as they are moved by the first movent, just as the cane does not impart motion except through being moved by the hand. Therefore it is necessary to arrive at a first movent that is not being moved by anything; and this all understand as God.

The example of the hand moving the cane illustrates sharply enough that for a movent to be in act does not mean that the movent actually possesses the form terminating the movement. The hand need not actually have the place to which the cane is being moved. What is meant is that the hand is actually exercising the causality that brings the movement and its term into being. This is efficient causality, the causality that makes things exist. In the present case the things made to exist are accidents. Understood in this light, the cogency of the argument is not hard to see, as in its progress it parallels the reasoning from the existence of finite things to the existence of the uncaused first cause in the *De Ente et Essentia*. Indeed it is the same reasoning, though starting from the restricted sphere of the accidental being that is acquired through movement. If you ask why the immobile movent to which it concludes is recognized at once as God, the answer is to be found in the *Sed Contra* of the article. There God is described in the words of *Exodus* as *I am who am*, understood as meaning that his very nature is to exist. This is the esse *tantum* of the *De Ente et Essentia*. To all who know the God of Scripture, then, his identity with the immobile movent reached by the argument from motion is at once apparent. Both are understood as subsistent being.

The necessity of understanding the argument from motion as a metaphysical argument based upon the reception of being instead of as a physical argument in the Aristotelian sense was strongly emphasized by Suarez.[39] Unless it is interpreted metaphysically, it does not conclude to an uncreated movent. To interpret it metaphysically means to interpret it in terms of being. The movent has to be regarded as the efficient cause that produces movement by imparting existence to the movement and its term. Movement and its formal term are observed to come into being in the sensible world; they have to receive that being from something else, and ultimately from subsistent being. The reasoning is from new existence to subsistent existence. It coincides with the metaphysical journey by which the first cause was reached, as outlined in the first part

[39] *Disp. Metaph.*, XXIX, 1, 8–17; ed. Vivès, XXVI, 23–26. Cf. *ibid.*, no. 20; p. 27.

of the present work.[40] It has the same demonstrative structure and the same conclusion. As starting point it has the acquisition of new being in the fashion most manifest to men, namely in actually observed movement here and now. For this reason it is rightly called by St Thomas the "more manifest" of the "Five Ways."

Argument From Efficient Cause. The second "way" is explicitly based upon efficient causality. Accordingly it has as its middle term the being that a sensible thing has but cannot cause efficiently in itself:

> The second "way" is from the notion of efficient cause. For we find that in those sensible things there is an order of efficient causes. Yet it is not found, nor is it possible, that anything is the efficient cause of itself; for thus it would be prior to itself, which is impossible.

This is clearly enough the reasoning of the *De Ente et Essentia.* It is based upon the priority of being to sensible thing. The being that is meant in the argument is obviously the substantial being that a thing has to have before it can exercise any efficient causality. A thing can give itself accidental being, but not substantial being.[41] Insofar as the second "way" differs from the first, then, it has as its starting point the reception of substantial being through the activity of a secondary efficient cause. That, however, is substantial change. It is not immediately evident in the way accidental change is evident in sensible things. The first "way," in consequence, remains "more manifest" than the second.

The argument then goes on to show the impossibility of infinite regress in a series of causes in which the subordination to a preceding cause is essential:[42]

> But it is not possible to proceed to infinity in efficient causes, for in all seriated efficient causes the first is the cause of the intermediate, and the intermediate is the cause of the last, whether the intermediate causes be many or just one; and if the cause is removed, the effect is removed. Therefore, if there is not a first in the efficient causes, there will not be a last, nor an intermediate.

---

[40] See Chapter 6.

[41] ". . . that something should be the cause of its own being in regard to accidental being, which is being in a certain way. This is not impossible. For some accidental being is found caused by the principles of its subject, prior to which being is understood the substantial being of the subject." *CG*, I, 22, *Amplius Si.*

[42] On essential and accidental dependence in efficient causes, see *ST*, I, 7, 4c; 46, 2, ad 7m. Man may be generated by man *ad infinitum,* for the human race as such would be just one step in the series envisaged for this argument by St Thomas; but these steps as such do not allow an infinite series (*ibid.,* ad 7m).

The argument then concludes to "a first efficient cause, which all people call God." The causes in the series are quite clearly regarded as substances, each of which just would not have being if it were not for the preceding cause. There is no difficulty in recognizing in this argument the metaphysical reasoning that leads from the being of sensible things to their first efficient cause.

Argument From Possible and Necessary Being. The third "way" has explicitly as its starting point the being that is acquired or lost in generation and corruption, that is, in substantial change:

> The third "way" is taken from the possible and the necessary. For we find in things some that have the possibility to be and not to be, since some are found being generated and corrupted, and in consequence with the possibility to be and not to be. But it is impossible that all things that are such always exist, for what is possible not to be, at some time does not exist. But if all things have the possibility not to be, at one time nothing existed in reality. But if this is true, nothing would exist also now, because what does not exist does not begin to exist except through something that does exist. If therefore nothing was existent, it was impossible that anything should begin to exist, and so now there would be nothing. But this is clearly false.

The reasoning is that whatever begins to exist is made to exist by something else, something that already has being. This is the metaphysical reasoning of the *De Ente et Essentia*. The starting point is the contingent aspect of being in sensible things. From contingent beings the present argument goes on to necessary beings:

> Therefore not all beings are possibles, but there has to be something necessary in things. But every necessary thing either has or has not a cause of its necessity from elsewhere. But it is not possible to proceed to infinity in necessary things that have a cause of their necessity, just as it is not possible in efficient causes, as has been proved.

The result is a cause of necessity to other things, without having any cause of its own necessity, a cause that "all people call God." The reason why there cannot be an infinite series of caused necessary beings[43] is the same as in regard to efficient causes. In contingent beings, the essence does not guarantee permanence in existence. In necessary beings, the essence does guarantee that permanence, provided their being is actually caused by an agent that will continue to impart being to them according to the exigencies of their essence. The whole argument, accordingly,

[43] On St Thomas' understanding of "necessary being," see Chapter 10, n. 10. On the Aristotelian background for the third way, cf. L. Chambat, "La 'Tertia Via' dans Saint Thomas et Aristote," *Revue Thomiste*, X (1927), 334–338.

starts from the contingent being of sensible things and leads to the first efficient cause of all finite beings. It is the fundamental metaphysical way to subsistent being, only clothed in a garb that fitted in with a particular historical background.

Argument From Grades. The fourth "way" is taken from the different grades or degrees in which perfections are found participated in things. Being, for instance, is shared in different degrees. Therefore there is something that is being in the highest degree, and the cause of being and of every other perfection to all things that have being, "and this we call God." This is an easily recognizable version, in a Platonic and Aristotelian framework,[44] of the reasoning in the *De Ente et Essentia*. What merely has being, and so is not of its nature being, has that being, ultimately, from something that is being. All other perfections can be imparted only insofar as they are made to exist.

Argument From the Guiding of Things. The fifth "way" has as its middle term the direction of activities in sensible bodies toward a determined goal:

> The fifth "way" is taken from the governing of things. For we see that some things that lack cognition, that is, natural bodies, operate on account of an end. This is apparent from the fact that they always, or more frequently, operate in the same way, in order that they may achieve what is best. Hence it is clear that they arrive at the goal not by chance but by intention. But things that do not have cognition tend toward a goal only if directed by someone with cognition and intelligence, as an arrow is directed by the archer. Therefore there is something intelligent by which all natural things are directed to their goal, and this we call God.

The argument is concerned with a guiding that is actually taking place in the world. This guiding is carried out through efficient causality, as appears in the example of the archer shooting the arrow on the target. The jump to God at the close of the argument is abrupt. Why? The second of the introductory *argumenta* in the article had supposed that

[44] See Plato, *Phd.*, 74D–77A; Aristotle, *Metaph.*, α 1, 993b24–31. Cf.: "For universally in things in which there is a better, there is also a best. Therefore, since among beings one is better than another, there will also be a best, and this will be the divine." Aristotle, *Fr.* 15, 1476b22–24. In *CG*, I, 13, Potest, St Thomas finds a source for the argument in Aristotle's teaching, sketched against a Platonic background of opinion and truth, that the various degrees of truth show the existence of a truth that serves as the norm. See Aristotle, *Metaph.*, Γ 4, 1008b25–1009a5. Cf. St Augustine, *De Libero Arbitrio*, II, 6–12 (*PL*, XXXII, 1248–1260); St Anselm, *Monologion*, cc. 1–4. The structure of the argument is the same as in the *De Ente* and in the three preceding ways of the *Summa*. The series of grades is included in the opening statement of this fourth way, and its conclusion is to "the cause of being."

if God does not exist all natural things can be accounted for by nature. The reply to this *argumentum* states that since nature operates by the direction of a superior agent, whatever is done by nature has ultimately to be referred back also to God as to the first cause. The direction of natural things, accordingly, is envisaged by St Thomas as the work of an agent, an efficient cause, and so as ultimately the work of the first cause. The argument again is that of the *De Ente et Essentia*, starting now from the orderly participation of new being through the activities of sensible things.[45]

This argument is clearly not the argument from design, made notorious by Paley (1743–1805). Paley's argument is only an analogy, a probable argument. It is not a metaphysical demonstration. It merely surmises that just as a watch requires a watchmaker, so the world requires an intelligent artificer.[46]

Identity With God of Abraham. Each of the "Five Ways," then, is but the one metaphysical demonstration dressed in different clothes. Each starts from some being that is known in sensible things, shows that this being has an efficient cause, and ultimately the first efficient cause. Since the first efficient cause is subsistent being, that is, something whose essence is being, it is seen at once as identical with the God who proclaimed to Moses that his name and nature is being. With that understanding of the text from *Exodus* St Thomas approached the "Five Ways." They were forms of reasoning that were familiar and accepted in the theological circles of his day. He could adapt them and understand them in his own way, as he did in the case of many an argument of Aristotle, and in so doing give them a profoundly new meaning. The fivefold arrangement had no metaphysical importance. One of the "ways" could be divided into two, as the argument from movement was in the *Contra Gentiles*, and others could be left out in

[45] ". . . since nature operates for a determined end by the direction of a higher agent, things that happen by nature have to be referred back to God as to their first cause. Similarly also, those that happen through choice have to be referred back to a higher cause. This is not human reason and will, for these are mutable and can be defective; therefore all things mobile and subject to defect have to be referred back to a first principle necessary in itself and immobile, as has been shown." *ST*, I, 2, 3, ad 2m. The probative force of the fifth way, therefore, is that of the second and third ways.

[46] William Paley, *Natural Theology*, in *Works* (London, 1825), V, 1–12. Paley merely multiplies instances upon instances of design in nature in order to drive home the *impression* (V, 374) that a designer is required. The starting point of St Thomas' fifth way, on the other hand, is not that things show design, but rather that something is being done to them, namely, that they are being directed to an end by an efficient cause; cf. *De Ver.*, V, 2c; *CG*, I, 13, Adhuc; *ST*, I, 103, 8c.

groupings on other occasions. The one point that mattered was to start with being as found in sensible things, whether the being of motion and its term, or substantial being, or contingent substantial being, or being whose participated character was shown by grades, or the being that was brought about in orderly fashion in the activities of nature. Such being could then be traced to an efficient cause, and finally to subsistent being as its first cause. The dressing could be altered at will to suit the theologian's apologetic purposes of the moment, as long as the existential starting point and the same demonstrative substructure were preserved. But the temptation remains, here as elsewhere in regard to St Thomas, to confuse dress with demonstration.[47] One of the most regrettable features of Neo-Thomistic metaphysics is the stubbornness with which some contemporaries insist that each "way" be regarded as a new demonstration, and thereby destroy the cogency of any they do not base directly upon existence.[48]

A survey of St Thomas' metaphysical ways for demonstrating the existence of God shows accordingly that regardless of their external form they all proceed from sensible being to its first efficient cause, subsistent being. Being is the proper effect[49] of God in the natural order, and consequently is the only aspect in sensible things that can serve as a middle term or means of demonstration for the proof. Every sensible thing, motion[50] included, can be regarded in its essence and in its existence. From the starting point of its essence, which is a limited nature, it can show the way only to a being or beings among other beings.[51]

---

[47] Maritain warns against confusing "the philosopher's faculty of invention with the ingenuity that inspires the art of the dress designer." *Existence and the Existent* (New York, 1948), p. 1. The problem of the "Five Ways" seems an outstanding instance in which this advice may be applied.

[48] For unaided human reason, being "is the sole direct path leading our mind to the throne of God." Louis-Marie Régis, *Epistemology* (New York, 1959), p. 300.

[49] "But the cause in the first grade is absolutely universal; for its proper effect is being. Hence whatever is, and in whatever way it is, is properly contained under the causality and direction of that cause." *In VI Metaph.*, lect. 3 (ed. Cathala-Spiazzi), no. 1209.

[50] "But in every action, being in act is principally intended and is ultimate in generation; for once it is had, the action of the agent ceases, and the motion of the patient. Being is therefore the proper effect of the first agent, that is, of God." CG, III, 66, Item In. Cf.: "Generation, speaking absolutely, is a way to being, and corruption is a way to non-being. For the form is not the term of generation, nor privation the term of corruption, except because the form causes being, and privation non-being." CG, I, 26, Item Generatio. "For being is the term of making." *De Pot.*, III, 8c.

[51] ". . . a being besides others and as such a part of the whole of reality." Paul Tillich, *The Courage to Be* (New Haven, 1952), p. 184. "But by these means we do not find God. If we could prove a first and conscious cause, still we could prove

Its being, grasped originally in judgment as an act that is other than any finite nature, alone can spark and characterize the demonstration of something outside the whole order of limiting opposites. The formal character of each of the "ways" in which the proof may be clothed, therefore, will be derived from the existence and not from the essence of its starting point. In each case something is brought into being and is found upon investigation to receive that being from subsistent being. For thirteenth-century theological students, with the pertinent texts of Aristotle, Augustine, Damascene, and Avicenna engraved upon their memories, there could be a distinct advantage in developing the proof in the dress of these respective backgrounds. With regard to the present-day undergraduate, whose academic background does not include those loyalties, the frankly Thomistic presentation of the argument in the *De Ente et Essentia* is entirely sufficient and is much less open to confusion.

Résumé. No reasoning in the order of essence can reach anything that of itself is necessarily identical with the God of Christian worship. Demonstration that starts from the being of any sensible thing and finds its first cause in subsistent being does, however, attain this result. To say that one cannot love *ipsum esse* is as wrong as to say one cannot love infinite beauty or infinite good, provided one's notion of subsistent being is derived from being that is judged and not from an abstract concept. God cannot be reached from abstractions, but only, as far as metaphysics is concerned, from being that is actually exercised here and now.[52] While the immediate purpose of metaphysics is merely to help one understand, and not to stimulate devotion in any further way,

---

only such cause as is equivalent to his effect. . . . A very limited Being this would be . . ." William Ernest Hocking, *The Meaning of God in Human Experience* (New Haven, 1928), p. 305.

[52] Kant's critique is directed against a "cosmological" proof that tries to find out from mere concepts the properties of an absolutely necessary being, and so is nothing but the ontological argument. See *Critique of Pure Reason*, B 606–607. The argument from design, called the "physico-theological" proof, is reduced to the cosmological proof and so to the ontological (B 657). The critique is not geared to deal with a demonstration based on what is originally attained by judgment and not by conceptualization, and in consequence it does not even touch the ways of proof used by St Thomas. For Kant, of course, causality is but a conceptual category meant to synthesize a sensible manifold and so cannot be used to reach anything outside the sensible order. For St Thomas, on the other hand, efficient causality terminates outside the whole conceptual or essential realm, namely in being. The critique by contemporary linguistic analysis, similarly to the Kantian, bears upon the deducing of existence in necessary sequence from a nature; e.g., J. J. C. Smart, "The Existence of God," in *New Essays in Philosophical Theology*, ed. Antony Flew (London, 1955), pp. 28–46. This critique likewise does not come to grips with the procedure of St Thomas, which never attempts to deduce existence from essence.

the first efficient cause, as reached by its demonstration, is readily seen to be the supreme Lord revealed in Sacred Scripture and worshiped in Christian cult.

SUGGESTED READINGS AND REFERENCES

Etienne Gilson, *God and Philosophy* (New Haven: Yale University Press, 1941), p. 38 ff.

Gerard Smith, "Before You Start Talking about God . . ." *The Modern Schoolman,* XXIII (1945), 24–43.

Jacques Maritain, *Approaches to God,* tr. Peter O'Reilly (New York: Harpers, 1955). Paperback ed. New York, Collier Books, 1962.

George P. Klubertanz, "Being and God according to Contemporary Scholastics," *The Modern Schoolman,* XXXII (1954), 1–17.

Robert G. Miller, "The Ontological Argument in St. Anselm and Descartes," *The Modern Schoolman,* XXXII–XXXIII (1955), pp. 341–349, 31–38.

L'Existence de Dieu, ed. Collège Dominicain à La Sarte-Huy (Tournai: Casterman, 1961). In *Cahiers de l'Actualité Religieuse, XVI.*

Studies in Philosophy and the History of Philosophy, ed. John K. Ryan (Washington, D. C.: Catholic University of America Press, 1961), I, 1–95.

CHAPTER 25

Divine Essence and Attributes

Divine Essence. The preceding chapter has shown that in terms of existence God is knowable to unaided human reason. That God exists, however, is *what* God is. To know that he exists is thereby to know his essence. But this knowledge is reached strictly from the existence of sensible things, existence that has been grasped not as a nature but only as an act other than any nature. The human mind, accordingly, has no quidditative concept upon which to base its notion of the divine essence. It cannot know the divine essence in terms of *what* God is or of *what* anything else is. From the standpoint of what is originally conceived through simple apprehension, the human intellect cannot form any notion at all of the divine essence. In this respect one can state categorically that men do not know what God is. By the same token men do not know the divine existence. The two are identical. To know the one would be to know the other.[1] In the way in which the one is known, the other is known. In the way in which the one remains inaccessible, the other transcends the capacities of the human mind.

Accordingly the divine *existence*, though a quiddity, remains utterly unknown to the human intellect in quidditative terms. Solely in terms of existential act, as a conclusion from the existential act attained in sensible things through judgment, is it reached by the human intellect. Correspondingly, the divine essence is utterly unknown in its own manner, that is, in the manner of essence. Yet it is an existing, and is

[1] Cf. St Thomas, *CG*, I, 12, Nec hoc; *ST*, I, 3, 4, ad 2m. This situation quite readily gives rise to the difficulties encountered by linguistic analysis in theological language, e.g., in *New Essays in Philosophical Theology*, ed. Antony Flew and Alasdair MacIntyre (London, 1955). For discussions of these problems, see W. Norris Clarke, "Linguistic Analysis and Natural Theology," *Proceedings of the American Catholic Philosophical Association*, XXXIV (1960), 110–126; M. J. Charlesworth, "Linguistic Analysis and Language about God," *International Philosophical Quarterly*, I (1961), 139–167.

knowable in terms of the existential acts found in the sensible world. It can be conceptualized, as any existing can be conceptualized, though only with the loss of what is proper to it. It can be conceptualized as act, as perfection, as something. But in such concepts it is emptied of its proper nature. Just as the human mind has no original concept of being, when "concept" is taken as resulting from an act of simple apprehension, so the mind has no original concept that can express anything proper to God. But being is conceptualized under notions taken from other acts like forms or operations, though originally it is grasped solely through judgment.[2] However, no proper concept of being is attained in this way. Consequently the divine essence, which is the nature of being, cannot be made the object of any simple human concept. Only through the elaboration of other quidditative notions can the being that is demonstrated as subsistent be expressed conceptually. These combinations of concepts, for instance supreme being or first cause, do not express quidditatively what is proper to the divine nature. No proper notion of the divine essence as an essence, then, is attainable by the human intellect.

Attributes. Does this unknowability of the divine essence mean that no positive perfection except being can be predicated of it? It is true that "whatever is in God is his proper being."[3] Any perfection whatsoever that is found in him is his very existing. Since what his existing is remains inaccessible, so what any perfection in God is will remain beyond the pale of human thought.

Can the human mind, then, know that perfections exist in God, without knowing what they are in God? As has already been seen,[4] the transcendent properties of being follow upon subsistent being. God accordingly is one, is good, is true. But what unity means in God remains unknown to men. It is the divine existence, and what the divine existence is cannot be reached by the human intellect. The mind, accordingly, knows that God is one, but does not know what unity means when realized on the divine level.[5] Similarly the mind knows that God is good, in the proper sense of goodness,[6] without knowing what goodness means

[2] See Chapter 4.

[3] "Quidquid autem est in Deo, hoc est suum proprium esse." St Thomas, *De Ver.*, II, 11c. Cf. *De Pot.*, VII, 5c.

[4] See Chapter 8.

[5] The human mind, accordingly, cannot know by reason alone that the unity of the divine essence is triune in person, as believed through revelation.

[6] ". . . that which we call goodness in creatures pre-exists in God, and indeed in a higher way. Hence from this it does not follow that God should be good insofar as he causes goodness, but rather the opposite . . ." St Thomas, *ST*, I, 13, 2c.

when found in God. The same situation holds in regard to truth and beauty. The concepts in these cases are taken from creatures and are applied to God in the full formal sense in which the perfections they express follow upon being. But when the perfections are thereby identified with subsistent being, their meaning while remaining formally the same[7] is raised to a height that completely transcends the conceptualizing power of the intellect.

Further, as has also been seen,[8] all perfections of creatures are found in subsistent being. In God, accordingly, these perfections will be the divine existing. The human mind can know that they exist in God, therefore, without knowing what they are in God. In their predication of God, however, a difference will arise. If the perfection contains no alloy of imperfection in its own notion, it can be predicated of God in its proper concept, just as the transcendentals are predicated. In this way God is said to be wise and just and powerful. If on the other hand the perfection involves any passive potency in its notion, like matter in sensible things, it can be predicated only metaphorically.[9] Through a figure of speech God is called a lion, a tower, a light. But in neither case does the human mind know *what* the perfection is as it is found in God, for in every instance the perfection as applied to God is the divine existing. Though it is the same perfection in God as in creatures, its mode in God is that of subsistent being. Each perfection when attributed to God signifies the divine substance, which is the divine being. But it signifies the divine substance as known to the human intellect, that is, in terms of being and not of quidditative concepts.

Similarity With God. Does this mean that there is no similarity between God and creatures? There can, of course, be no question of a real relation of similarity in God. God is not really

---

Cf.: ". . . insofar as life pre-exists in him, although in a more eminent way than is understood or signified." *Ibid.*, ad 2m. Cf. *CG*, IV, 7, Adhuc Nulla; and expressions of St Thomas like "nobis ignotus" (*ST*, I–II, 112, 5c) and "omnino ignotum" (*In Epist. ad Rom.*, I, 6; ed. Vivès, XX, 398b). The "penitus . . . ignotum" of *CG*, III, 49, Cognoscit, is translated by the English Dominican Fathers as "utterly unknown." On the pertinence of this Thomistic doctrine, see E. Gilson, "La Possibilité de l'Athéisme," in *Atti del XVI Convegno del Centro di Studi Filosofici tra Professori Universitari* (Brescia, 1962), pp. 41–42.

[7] "With regard therefore to what these names signify, they belong properly to God, and more properly than to the creatures themselves, and they are predicated in a prior manner of him. But with regard to the way of signifying, they are not properly predicated of God; for they have the way of signifying that belongs to creatures." St Thomas, *ST*, I, 13, 3c. Cf. *ibid.*, 5c; *De Ver.*, I, 7c.

[8] See Chapter 6, nn. 4 and 10.

[9] See St Thomas, *ST*, I, 13, 3, ad 1m. Cf. Chapter 6, n. 15.

similar to anything else. He cannot be the subject of a real relation to anything outside himself.[10] But may a created perfection have a real relation of similarity to God? Such a relation would provide a basis for an overall assertion of similarity between God and creatures, even though the relation so placed in God is merely conceptual.

All the perfections of creatures pre-exist in God. This means that the same perfection is found on the one hand in God and on the other hand in creatures. The sameness of course can be neither specific nor generic. It is merely the sameness between a perfection as it exists supereminently in subsistent being, and the perfection as it exists in the limited way of a creature. Sameness of this kind is established by the requirement that any perfection in a creature has to be precontained in the first cause.[11] The sameness in the one perfection is enough to make the finite perfection similar to its prototype,[12] for similarity is a relation founded upon a quality or characteristic present in different things. In this respect the similarity of added perfections in creatures with God will also be one of proportionality.[13] What the perfections themselves are in God is subsistent being. What they are in creatures differs radically from subsistent being. Yet the human mind, in knowing that the perfections are precontained in subsistent being, knows that they characterize subsistent being proportionally as they characterize a creature. As a prudent man looks after his dependents, so, proportionally, does God provide for creatures. Both therefore are provident. The human mind knows this not through any understanding of what divine providence is in itself, but merely through the similarity of proportions established in the respective ways of acting. The infinity in God and in his providence is therefore no hindrance to this similarity.[14]

In spite of the similitude, however, the utter ignorance of what the perfections are in God is never to be overlooked. The correct process every time is to show positively that the perfection is in God, and then to complement this positive knowledge with its negative counterpart. Though the human mind knows that the perfection is in God, it is totally ignorant of what the perfection is in God. St Thomas expresses the complementary process as follows: ". . . and again he is known through our ignorance, that is, insofar as to know God is to know that

[10] See Chapter 13, n. 21.

[11] St Thomas, *ST*, I, 13, 2c.

[12] ". . . if there were not some agreement in reality of creature with God, his essence would not be the likeness of creatures; and so in knowing his essence he would not know creatures." St Thomas, *De Ver.*, II, 11c.

[13] *De Ver.*, II, 11, ad 1m, 2m, and 4m.

[14] Cf. *ibid.*, ad 4m, and *ST*, I, 2, 2, ad 3m.

we are ignorant of what God is."[15] The "way of removal" in knowledge of God consists in knowing that God is none of the things he has caused, and he is none of them not because of any lack of what they are, but because the perfections in them are proper to God in a way that ineffably exceeds any way in which the perfections can be represented in creatures.[16] This again goes back to the fundamental consideration that nothing in God can be properly expressed through concepts based upon the natures of finite things as these are known through simple apprehension. Whatever is in God is his existing, and can be understood by the human mind only in terms of the being that is known in sensible things through judgment.[17]

Spirituality. Perhaps the most striking perfection of God in immediate contrast to the material cosmos, which is the source of human knowledge concerning him, is that he has to be a spirit.[18] His nature is existence, the act of all acts and the perfection of all perfections. Since God is existence, then, he is at the summit of actuality. He is entirely free from all potentiality, and so free from all materiality in the sense in which immateriality is the ground of cognition.[19] Accordingly God possesses himself immaterially in the highest way. Thereby he is supremely cognitive and knows himself perfectly.[20] Upon this knowledge, as upon every intellective act, there follows an act of will.[21] Since the knowledge is of the divine essence and so of the infinite good, the act of the will is complete love of and satisfaction in the supreme good. This act of will is not in any way forced or confined by a limiting nature. It is therefore free in the highest manner, even though saturation in the infinite good leaves nothing else able to function as its proper

---

[15] *In De Div. Nom.*, c. VII, lect. 4 (ed. Pera), no. 731.

[16] *Ibid.*; *ST*, I, 12, 12c. The "removal" is on account of supereminent excess.

[17] The statements of St Thomas in this regard, accordingly, are to be interpreted "not in the order of the quidditative concept, but in that of judgment." Etienne Gilson, *The Christian Philosophy of St. Thomas Aquinas*, tr. L. K. Shook (New York, 1956), p. 106. While the God believed in through faith does not change, Gilson emphasizes, the God attained by rational knowledge can be known on this basis with progressively deepened penetration, even though the object in every way transcends conceptual knowledge; see "L'Etre et Dieu," *Revue Thomiste*, LXII (1962), 196.

[18] *N.T.*, Jn., IV, 24; *II Cor.*, III, 17. Cf.: "The person seems to be the supreme value on the human level, and therefore it must needs exist in God." Jean Daniélou, *God and the Ways of Knowing*, tr. Walter Roberts (New York, 1957), p. 69.

[19] On this meaning of immateriality, see Chapter 15, n. 2.

[20] See St Thomas, *ST*, I, 14, 1c and 3c.

[21] *ST*, I, 19, 1c. Cf. Chapter 23, nn. 3–6.

object.[22] Since intellective act and voluntary act imply the powers to perform the acts, intellect and will are accordingly found in God. Power is active potency. In contrast to passive potency, it contains no imperfection in its notion. It is therefore properly a perfection of God. In him it follows upon infinite being, and so it is proportional to infinite being. It is consequently infinite, and is called omnipotence.[23] On account of God's supreme immateriality it consists in intellect and will. As an intelligent and free agent, then, God is most notably a spirit.[24]

Knowledge of Other Things. Since God is the nature of being, and knows himself perfectly, he knows all the ways in which being can be participated. Perfect cognition of the nature of being has to include cognition of the modes of being.[25] But all finite natures are modes of being. God accordingly in knowing his essence perfectly knows all finite essences. He knows them not primarily in themselves but properly in his own essence. Insofar as he knows his essence as imitable by some creature, he knows it as the idea or prototype of that creature. In this way the divine ideas are many though the essence is one. The ideas serve as the exemplars according to which all things in the created universe are produced.

Further, since all effects are precontained in the first cause, they accordingly are in the divine being. But the divine being is the divine intelligence, as has been seen in the consideration of the divine spirituality. All effects, therefore, are in God in the immaterial way that gives rise to cognition. They are all known to God.[26] This holds equally for individual differences and for contingent things, for these are likewise precontained in their first cause. Since God's being is eternal in the full sense of the notion, his knowledge is correspondingly eternal. Everything that happens in time, whether past, present, or future, is coin-

[22] In regard to its proper and principal object, which is the divine goodness, the will of God, like a faculty in general, is said to have a necessary relation. See St Thomas, *ST*, I, 19, 3c and 10c.

[23] *ST*, I, 25, 1c.

[24] Etymologically "spirit" signifies breath, giving the notion of something contrasted with the heaviness and solidity of material things. Philosophically, however, it is applied to God not in any sense of a "ghost-above-the cosmos," but on the basis of the immateriality that is established through a study of cognition. A spirit, known philosophically, is already known to be immaterial.

[25] "God, insofar as he knows himself as the source of being (*principium essendi*), knows the nature of being (*entis*), and all other things insofar as they are beings. . . . God would not perfectly know himself, unless he knew every way in which his perfection can be participated by others; nor would he even know perfectly the nature of being, unless he knew all the modes of being." St Thomas, *ST*, I, 14, 6c.

[26] *ST*, I, 14, 5c.

cident with the eternal now of the divine being and knowledge.[27] God's cognition of things that actually do happen in time is called his "knowledge by vision,"[28] in the sense that God is seeing them as present to him from all eternity. About the fact of God's knowledge from all eternity of free acts of man that actually will take place in time, there is consequently no special problem.

But what about free acts that will never take place, yet would have been performed had circumstances been otherwise? Technically they are called *futuribilia*. Does God know these, and how does he know them? The God believed in through Christian faith does know that Tyre and Sidon would have repented had they seen the miracles worked in Corozain and Bethsaida.[29] The *futuribilia*, however, are not seen in God's eternity, since they are never actually to exist in reality. They are not at all present to his eternity. Is a third or intermediate[30] type of divine cognition required for knowledge of them? This problem raises the question of the means by which God knows the free decisions of creatures, even in his knowledge by vision. Does he know them through the causality he exercises upon them as first cause, or does he know them antecedently to his decision to impart being to them? Effects that take place in necessary sequence from the natures of things are of course known by God in his decisions to create the things. But does this means of knowing extend to God's cognition of the free decisions of men?

---

[27] *ST*, I, 14, 13c. On the notion of eternity, see supra, Chapter 6, n. 11. Because of its complete and absolutely immutable actuality, the divine being is coexistent with every instant of time, in which sensible things attain actuality. The present is the only instant in which a sensible thing is actual. Cf. section on category "when," supra, Chapter 14, p. 206.

[28] ". . . knowledge by vision, which is only of things that are or will be or were . . ." St Thomas, *ST*, I, 14, 12c. In contrast, God's knowledge of things that are possible but "neither are nor will be nor have been" is called "knowledge by simple intelligence." *ST*, I, 14, 9c. The Latin terms are *scientia visionis* and *scientia simplicis intelligentiae*.

[29] *N.T.*, *Mt.*, XI, 21; *Lk.*, X, 13.

[30] The *scientia media* was proposed by Luis de Molina (1535–1600) and occasioned bitter and long-drawn-out controversy. On the bearing of these disputes, see "Appendix" in Gerard Smith, *Natural Theology* (New York, 1951), pp. 273–277. The doctrine was directed against Dominic Bañez (1528–1604), but through Bañez at St Thomas. On this historical location of the discussions, see A. Pegis, "Molina and Human Liberty," in *Jesuit Thinkers of the Renaissance*, ed. Gerard Smith, (Milwaukee, 1939), pp. 75–131. The *scientia media* would allow God to know what a creature would do, before any act of will decides the course of action. The difficulty in this is that the creature's way of acting is settled objectively from all eternity, before any free will, either divine or human, has had a chance to decide. It is hard to see how any room is left for a genuinely free decision and the introduction of an entirely new determination of being. The same applies to Suarez' (1548–1617) explanation that *futuribilia* have objective truth antecedently to their determination by an act of free will.

Providence. St Thomas' fifth way of presenting the demonstration of God's existence has shown that all things are directed efficiently to their goal by the first cause.[31] The plan according to which the universal governance of things takes place is called divine providence.[32] Since all created things depend on the action of the first cause for their production in being, their conservation in being, and their operation, they will without exception come under divine providence even to the smallest detail. From the standpoint of universal providence there is consequently no room for chance or for fate.

By their very natures, inanimate things are meant for the animate, the irrational are meant for the rational, and all spiritual creatures, endowed as they are with intellect that can know God and with will by which they can direct themselves to him, are somehow meant immediately for God. According to divine providence, therefore, inanimate things will give up their being for vegetative life, and individual plants and animals will be expendable in the interests of men. A human life, on the contrary, is not subordinated in its nature to any creature, since it is immediately meant for God. To further the individual's welfare, however, civil government and society are required. These sometimes demand that the individual risk or sacrifice his life in the interests of the equal good of his fellows. Governing things according to their natures, then, it pertains to divine providence to will physical evils incidentally (*per accidens*), that is, not on account of themselves but for the sake of the greater good. Moral evil, on the contrary, cannot be willed even incidentally by divine providence, because it is directly contrary to the divine goodness. It can be merely *permitted* for the sake of greater good, somewhat as a large city in authorizing motor traffic knows that this will result in a couple of hundred deaths on its streets each year. The deaths are not wished or wanted, even though they are foreseen statistically and permitted by allowing the traffic. Accordingly it pertains to the infinite goodness of God to permit evils and draw good from them.

In practice it is easy enough to list the frightful sufferings from accidents and from paralysis and cancer and other diseases, from hurricanes and earthquakes and famine, from wars and inhumanities of men. Often it is quite difficult or even impossible to see clearly the good occasioned by them. Sometimes the good does become apparent when these sufferings bring to life the unexplored potentialities and draw out the unsuspected riches of a human personality. At other times there may appear only frustration. However, enough is known to furnish at least a lead

---

[31] See Chapter 24, nn. 45–46.

[32] St Thomas, *ST*, I, 22, 1c.

in seeing how the physical side of creation is meant for the spiritual, even at agonizing cost. But the particular requirements of the ultimate goal for which man lives are beyond metaphysical scrutiny. The goal is none other than the infinite good to which intellect and will are directed by their nature, but of which no quidditative knowledge is possible to unaided human reason. Here as in all else concerning infinite being, reason can establish that the fact is so without understanding what it is. What divine providence requires for the realization of man's ultimate goal is accordingly beyond the power of the philosopher to fathom. The metaphysician can merely show that divine providence is all-embracing and unfailing, that it guides even the smallest or most repulsive detail in life, and that it is carried out in view of a goal the unaided human intellect cannot grasp. In point of fact the human person is known to be engaged in a *Lebenswelt* replete with suffering, temptation, nausea, anxiety, and dread, but at the same time open to love, joy, and triumph. It is through a path of vibrant tensions in this many-sided world that divine providence guides men to whatever goal it has established for them, a goal that only revelation can make known.

Cause of Freedom. Since divine providence is all-embracing, it extends to free actions as well as to actions determined by a nature. For the activities God wishes to be performed freely, he prepares free agents. For those he wishes to be done as determined by natures, he has made natural things.[33] Each of the agents he moves into operation according to the characteristic proper to it, free agents to act freely, natural things to act in the way already determined by their natures. The nature of a free created agent is of course in itself something limited and determined. Its operative potencies are correspondingly determined accidents. So far everything is in the order of first actuality (*actus primus*). But free decisions are operations (*actus secundi*). Insofar as they are free, they are not determined at all by any nature antecedent to them. There is a completely new determination of being, originated by a creature. It is inexplicable in terms of essence. Accordingly deterministic philosophies are obliged to deny it and explain away as a delusion a primordial fact of consciousness.

No limited essence, then, and so no creature, can fully account for the freedom of a decision as an actual operation, even though the creature is the one that makes the decision. The actual deciding, if it is truly free, requires in some way a higher cause that is entirely unlimited. In a word, every free decision, because it is free, has to be caused

[33] *ST*, I, 19, 8c. Cf. *CG*, I, 85; *In I Periherm.*, lect. 14 (ed. Leonine), no. 22.

efficiently by God. No finite agent is of itself sufficient to rise above the limits of its essence and operate in a way for which it alone, and not its causes, is responsible. It can make a truly free decision only in virtue of a causality that comes to it from infinite existence, that is, from an agent that is not determined in its operation by any limiting essence. Down to the minutest detail of the free decision, therefore, God moves the free created agent to act freely, and in doing so makes the creature's action free.[34]

Not only on account of the new being that is produced by the creature in a free operation, consequently, but also on account of the very freedom of the action, is the divine motion required for a creature's free decision. The divine motion is infallible and efficacious in regard to every detail of the creature's decision, for it is the efficient cause of everything in the creature's operation. Yet it takes place entirely on the plane of freedom. It exercises no violence, no coercion, no compulsion.[35] It is an efficient causality under which the creature infallibly but freely makes the decision to which the creature is moved. It does not determine or predetermine the creature to decide this rather than that, but leaves all determining to the creature's own decision.[36] The human mind, able

[34] ". . . in moving voluntary causes, he does not do away with the voluntary character of their actions, but rather effects it in them; for he operates in each thing according to the thing's proper character." *ST*, I, 83, 1, ad 3m. Cf. ad 2m. See also *In II Sent.*, d. 25, q. 1, a. 2, ad 1m; ed. Mandonnet, II, 650.

[35] "Thus, therefore, God in moving the will does not compel it, because he gives it its proper inclination." *ST*, I, 105, 4, ad 1m. Cf. *CG*, III, 88, Adhuc violentum; *De Pot.*, III, 7, ad 14m. In its very notion freedom of will excludes both determination of the faculty and violence; see *CG*, I, 68, Dominium.

[36] What is known traditionally as the "Thomist School" in this matter explains the divine motion as predetermining the created will to decide this rather than that. St Thomas (e.g., *ST*, I, 23, 1, ad 1m) does use on occasion the term *praedeterminatio*, taken from Damascene, with whom it implied a necessitating determination as in natural agents. Cf. *De Ver.*, V, 5, ad 1m. In *Quodl.*, XII, 4, one of the traditional views on fate is listed as teaching that "all things are predetermined" by providence. *De Ver.*, VIII, 12c, states that effects dependent on free will are "all determined in the first cause." But that is very different from maintaining that God predetermines or determines the decision of the created free will. Under the divine motion, rather, "the determination of the act is left in the power of the reason and will" (*De Pot.*, III, 7, ad 13m) upon which the divine causality is acting. Cf. *CG*, I, 68, Dominium. The divine causality "transcends the order of necessity and contingence" (*In I Periherm.*, lect. 14, ed. Leonine, no. 22) and so is beyond any determining and any fallibility in moving the creature's free will. It moves the created free will infallibly to make whatever decision divine providence wishes, and causes that decision down to its last detail as first cause. In this sense only may what the decision itself is as an object of cognition be regarded as already determined in the first cause, and knowable as such to God. But the deciding or the determining is done by the created free will, under a divine causality that infallibly attains its goal without determining the creature's will in any necessitating way to decide this rather

to understand only the determined and determining motion that proceeds from finite natures, cannot form any proper concept of the unlimited motion that causes a will to make freely but infallibly the decision to which it moves it. Like everything else in God, the human intellect can know that this way of moving creatures exists in God without knowing at all *what* it is.

So understood, the divine motion leaves no crucial problem regarding God's knowledge of the *futuribilia.* If God knows with definite certainty how the free agent would have acted in other circumstances, it is because he knows how he would have infallibly moved the agent to decide freely this rather than that course of action. Antecedent to the divine will there can be no fixed determination in which God could see how the free creature would act, and so no prior determination that would militate against the creature's entire freedom to make its own choice. The medium through which free decisions of creatures are eternally present to God is found accordingly in the decrees of his will. United as it is with the infinite good, the divine will is always good in exercising its causality, even when, permissively, it moves the created agent to make, freely, an evil decision. The creature's free act in this case is sinful, however, because it is specified not by the infinite good but by a limited physical good that happens to be morally evil.

Résumé. The attributes established by metaphysical reasoning in the first cause coincide with characteristics found only in the God of Christian worship. Subsistent being is unique, omnipotent, living, all-knowing, eternal in the full sense, creator, all-perfect, and provident down to the ultimate details of all things, even of human free choice. The metaphysician shows that these perfections, and all perfections seen in creatures, exist in God. But what they are in God he cannot understand. In God they are identified with subsistent existing. The human mind, however, has no original quidditative concept of existing. Accordingly it can have no proper quidditative concept of anything in God.

Knowledge that these attributes are present in subsistent being, however, rounds out the recognition that subsistent being is identical with the God of revelation. It furthers intellectual penetration into something that transcends human conceptualization. Metaphysics, of course, cannot make known to anyone things that are properly supernatural. But on the presupposition that the God of Scripture and the Church Councils is already known by faith, or even known historically by someone

than that. The divine causality is accordingly neither determining nor fallible as it moves the creature to make a free decision.

who has no faith,[37] it is crystal clear that the existence and attributes established through metaphysical demonstration belong to no one else than the God of Christian belief.

SUGGESTED READINGS AND REFERENCES

St Anselm, *Proslogium; Monologium* . . . , tr. Sydney Norton Deane (Chicago: Open Court Publishing Co., 1903).

St Thomas Aquinas, *Summa Theologiae*, I, 3–22; tr. English Dominican Fathers (London: Burns, Oates & Washbourne Ltd., 1911–1925), I, 28–313.

Reginald Garrigou-Lagrange, *God His Existence and His Nature*, tr. Bede Rose, Vol. II (St Louis and London: B. Herder, 1936).

James Daniel Collins, *God in Modern Philosophy* (Chicago: Henry Regnery, 1959).

——— "Analytic Theism and Demonstrative Inference," *International Philosophical Quarterly*, I (1961), 235–263.

Readings in Religious Philosophy, ed. Geddes MacGregor and J. Wesley Robb (New York: Houghton Mifflin Co., 1962).

[37] A. Finili, "Is There a Philosophical Approach to God?" *Dominican Studies*, IV (1951), 101, suggests that only a believer can know a philosophical approach to God for what it is. There can be no question, of course, of a metaphysician who is utterly ignorant of revelation recognizing that the first cause is identical with the triune God. But in the very hypothetical case of a philosopher who has demonstrated subsistent being and who knows and rejects Christian teaching, the God of Scripture could hardly appear as a being other than that first cause of all things. In actual fact, however, it has required centuries of effort to bring about this conjunction, as Gilson points out, "De la Connaissance du Principe," *Revue de Métaphysique et de Morale*, LXVI (1961), 393.

Epilogue

Metaphysics. Has this laborious investigation of things from the viewpoint of their being lived up to its promises? Being, as known in sensible things through judgment, has in point of fact served as a means for reaching the supersensible order, for understanding the universe as a whole, and for establishing the gradation of the sciences. Known first as an act other than any experienced nature, being has, as a result of difficult but cogent demonstration, been shown to subsist as a nature in one instance only. It is shared by other things, not through a necessary formal causality, but through a free efficient causality[1] by which these things are brought into existence or made to be. Unique as a nature, existence when caused must give rise to its own self-specification, which is a nature other than itself. In this way the two entitative principles of finite things are established, being and essence. In their light a metaphysical explanation of things may be given. The diversity of beings, with integration into a single universe throughout the categories, is accounted for by them. Cognition, by which things that exist in themselves are given new existence in a knower, can be understood by their means. Finally, the supersensible world familiar to Christian belief, consisting of spiritual souls, angels, and God, is able to be investigated through these principles, even though in regard to God the very nature of the approach is in terms of being only,[2] and rules out quidditative knowledge.

[1] See Chapter 7, nn. 16–17. The two types of causality remain radically distinct. When both are conceived as participation, care is required not to blur the distinction. This happens in Descartes, where to the type of causality exercised by essence (i.e., formal causality) "the concept of efficient cause can be extended in the same way we are accustomed in the geometrical order to extend the concept of the greatest possible circular line to the concept of a straight line, or the concept of a rectilinear polygon having an unlimited number of sides to the concept of a circle." *Quartae Resp.*; A–T, VII, 239.18–23 (IX, 185). In Spinoza the distinction has vanished; see *Ethics*, I, Prop. XVI, Cor. 1.

[2] See Chapter 25, nn. 1, 3, 5–7, and 17.

Christian Metaphysics. Heidegger[3] and others have claimed that the notion of a Christian metaphysics is a contradiction in terms, like a square circle. Anything Christian is based on faith, metaphysics is not based on faith. The one is subjectivity, the other is objectivity.[4] Does the study just completed allow this dichotomy? Christian topics, like soul, angels, and God, have been examined metaphysically. They have been examined not through principles accepted on faith, but through principles known by reason, namely being and essence. The fact that these topics are basic in Christian life has not infringed upon the strictly metaphysical character of the foregoing investigation, any more than an anthropological inquiry about witch doctors renders itself a superstition. There could not very well be a Christian physics or a Christian chemistry, because these sciences investigate subjects that do not interest a Christian at all differently from other men. The parallel here would be something like industrial chemistry. Chemistry is a science, industry is not. Yet industry has problems that give rise to a special kind of chemical pursuit. Correspondingly, God and the human soul are major topics of Christian concern, and provide a Christian with a special interest in undertaking metaphysical study and in emphasizing aspects in it that are of importance to his life. There is no contradiction whatsoever in this attitude.

A Christian metaphysics, accordingly, stays a metaphysics. It does not become sacred theology, for it never demonstrates through revealed principles. It demonstrates only through principles known by reason, even when it is interested in certain notions because of their connection with topics revealed supernaturally and accepted through faith.

Status as a Science. According to its traditional meaning, science is knowledge of things through their causes. In this sense metaphysics is supremely a science. Metaphysics arrives at the first efficient cause and the ultimate final cause of all caused things, a cause that has no cause. From the viewpoint of causal explanation, accordingly, metaphysics is the highest type of science. Its starting points, namely that sensible things exist both in themselves and in cognition, are immediately known. No emotive factor, like the shock of an encounter with nothingness or the ever present possibility of suicide, is required.

[3] *An Introduction to Metaphysics*, tr. Ralph Manheim (New Haven, 1959), p. 7. Nor can metaphysics be a science for Heidegger, *ibid.*, pp. 26, 43.

[4] "But if Christianity is essentially subjectivity, it is a mistake for the observer to be objective." Søren Kierkegaard, *Concluding Unscientific Postscript*, tr. David F. Swenson (Princeton, 1944), p. 51.

From its immediately known starting points the procedure of metaphysics is demonstrative in the strict Aristotelian sense. The being of sensible things has both necessary and contingent characteristics. The reasoning of metaphysics has been based only upon the necessary features. Any sensible thing, like a stone or a tree, is necessarily a being just as it is necessarily a body. Its being is necessarily dependent on a prior efficient cause, and ultimately on subsistent being. Being necessarily possesses its transcendent properties, is necessarily limited by an essence when it is participated, and so on. The reasoning is never based upon the accidental character of a sensible thing's being. No attempt, for instance, is made to show that sensible things have to follow upon subsistent being, for from that viewpoint being is accidental, not essential, to sensible things. The accidental character of being in sensible things, accordingly, does not hinder it from functioning as a scientific viewpoint, because metaphysical demonstrations are never based upon it insofar as it is accidental, but only insofar as it is necessary through formal requirements.

Metaphysics, of course, lacks the incomparable advantage, enjoyed by the experimental sciences, of verification through further sensible experience. Molecules, for instance, were reasoned to from transference of odors and diffusion of gases and Brownian movements, their activity was verified in numerous experiments, and in recent years very large molecules became visible through the electron microscope. Metaphysics has no such automatically convincing double check for its conclusions. It has only the much harder and less striking way of checking each link in the demonstration through reflection, and of making sure that the starting points were in fact evident. Accordingly there is enviable agreement among astronomers or chemists or physicists in each of the different stages of development in their sciences, while agreement among metaphysicians at any historical period is notoriously lacking. Metaphysical doctrines are not "theories" in any modern acceptation of the term. They are not conjectured hypotheses proposed for experimental verification. They are demonstrated conclusions resting solely but satisfactorily upon the immediacy of their starting points and the cogency of reasoning processes.

Further, metaphysicians are philosophers and so "are in the strange position that all the evidence which bears upon their problems is already available to them."[5] Their procedure, therefore, considered unlike that of science, has been refused the possibility of reaching anything new and

[5] Alfred Jules Ayer, *The Problem of Knowledge* (London, 1956), p. 1.

has been limited merely to an examination of the old. Yet being as a really distinct act, essence as a real potency, subsistent being, faculties, spiritual soul, are no more immediately evident than protons and electrons. Like protons and electrons they are reached by demonstration. In this way metaphysics discovers, and has its proper detective character. Even though the Christian metaphysician is already convinced through religious faith of the existence and spiritual character of God or of the human soul, he seeks to prove these points on evidence acceptable in a philosophic court. Other conclusions, like being and essence as entitative constituents of things, he does not know at all on religious grounds. As far as limiting natures are concerned, he reaches the end of his competence with those that more immediately determine being and allow it to be participated, that is, with the supreme genera or categories. The differences of a particular finite substance from another, of one quantity from another, of one quality from another, and the relations of things within these categories to one another, do not come under his science. His principles are not sufficient to grapple with such problems.[6] Accordingly the metaphysician has not the means of entering into the field of any particular science. He cannot exercise an imperialism over the activities of the other sciences. His immediate evidences are, it is true, limited to being and its more general modes. But they are amply sufficient to serve as starting points for scientific reasoning that is genuinely fruitful and gives metaphysics its rank as a highest science.[7] In its role of a highest science it may also be called a wisdom.

The strictly demonstrative character of metaphysics likewise makes clear that it is not the construction of a system[8] but rather a scientific explanation of things that are already there. It is not an historical cataloguing of presuppositions, as Collingwood maintained, nor a kind of poetizing, nor an illegitimate process of going from the accidental to the necessary.[9] It is a science that proceeds cogently, step by step, from truths that are immediately known to conclusions that are not immediately known. The activity of the metaphysician, consequently, is "not irre-

[6] "But from the *common* principles of that which is insofar as it is (*entis inquantum est ens*), one does not understand that anything that is in a *particular* way is adequately caused." St Thomas, *In IV Metaph.*, lect 3 (ed. Cathala-Spiazzi), no. 559.

[7] See St Thomas, *In I Post. Anal.*, lect. 17 (ed. Leonine), n. 5.

[8] See Jacques Maritain, *The Degrees of Knowledge*, tr. Gerald B. Phelan (New York, 1959), p. xiii; Etienne Gilson, *The Unity of Philosophical Experience* (New York, 1937), p. 317; G. B. Phelan, "The Existentialism of St. Thomas," *Proceedings of the American Philosophical Association*, XXI (1946), 25–26.

[9] See above, Historical Introduction, nn. 36, 39, 45.

sponsible poetizing, not system building, not the pretensions of a *Weltanschauung*, but the plain hard work of demonstration."[10]

Subject of Metaphysics. This Aristotelian notion of science requires that attributes or proper accidents be demonstrated of a subject genus. What is the subject in the case of metaphysics? Metaphysics treats of any being whatsoever insofar as it is a being.[11] Its subject therefore may be designated as beings insofar as they are beings.[12] It deals with things that exist, in both real and intentional existence,[13] and demonstrates what can be known about them on the ground of their existing. As a science it proceeds universally, and accordingly is treating of things insofar as they share the common aspect of being. From this viewpoint the subject of metaphysics may be named common being.[14] Since subsistent being does not come under common being but is rather the cause of common being,[15] the nature of being is not the subject of metaphysics but as efficient cause and final cause is a principle of this subject. It is par excellence *the* principle of the subject, since it produces in their entirety the two finite principles involved, limited existential act and essence. Accordingly God, though not the subject of metaphysics nor included under this subject, is studied by the science insofar as he is the first cause of beings, and therefore insofar as he exists and precontains caused perfections and imparts them to creatures.

Will this subject of metaphysics fit under the Scholastic framework of material object, formal object *quod*, and formal object *quo*?[16] The material object is made up of all the things with which the science deals.

[10] Mortimer J. Adler, "The Demonstration of God's Existence," *The Thomist*, V (1943), p. 189.

[11] "De quolibet enim ente inquantum est ens . . ." St Thomas, *In VI Metaph.*, lect. 1, no. 1147. Cf. Chapter 4, n. 16.

[12] See Chapter 4, n. 12. On subject genus, see Aristotle, *APo.*, I 7, 75a42–b2.

[13] The well-known Suarezian tradition rejects this view and restricts the object of metaphysics to real being. Basing his notion upon Aristotle, Suarez (*Disp. Metaph.*, I, 1, 5–7; ed. Vivès, XXV, 3a–4b) excludes both beings of reason and being *per accidens* from the adequate object of metaphysics, maintaining that these cannot enter into the objective unity required for it. For him the adequate object of metaphysics is being (*ens*) insofar as it is real being (*ens reale* — *ibid.*, no. 26; p. 11a).

[14] See St Thomas, *In Metaph.*, Proem.

[15] See Chapter 6, n. 3; Chapter 8, nn. 3, 12–14. Cf. J. Owens, "Diversity and Community of Being in St Thomas Aquinas," *Mediaeval Studies*, XXII (1960), 264, n. 13.

[16] For this framework, see Joseph Gredt, *Elementa Philosophiae Aristotelico-Thomisticae*, ed. 7a (Freiburg i. Breisgau, 1937), I, 186–187 (no. 230).

It should include everything that is matter for consideration in the science. In this case it should include subsistent being. It does not seem able, consequently, to express in a correct manner the subject of metaphysics. The formal object *quod* is a static aspect according to which the material object is considered in the science. But being, the aspect under which metaphysics treats of things, is not a still-life form but rather, as immediately known by men in sensible things, is a dynamic synthesizing that is continually changing from past through present to future. It does not correspond to the notion of a formal object.[17] Finally, the formal object *quo* is the light in which the inquiry proceeds, and in metaphysics would consist in the third degree of abstraction.[18] But the subject of metaphysics is not constituted by any abstraction, except the abstraction required for the universality of common being. The aspect that characterizes it as the subject of metaphysics, namely being, is not obtained by the activity of simple apprehension called abstraction, but through judgment that separates being from not being.[19] "Separation" in this context is far from just another word for the same notion designated by "abstraction." It designates the crucial difference between the way natures are known by the human mind, and the way being is known.

The framework of material and formal objects, accordingly, cannot be applied very neatly to the subject of metaphysics. It is a framework that provides no help in understanding this subject, and has given rise to much confusion. It is best left out of consideration altogether. One point that its mention serves to bring out, however, is the way the subject is constituted. The being that places a thing under the subject of metaphysics is the being that is immediately known in sensible things through each ordinary, everyday judgment, and that is everywhere universalized by the ordinary man in a subsequent concept. It is not something abstracted from the species and genera by formal abstraction, and perhaps as yet not known even to the most learned of men.[20] Rather, it is what is first grasped through judgment in the concretion of the sensible thing, as the thing is immediately known in sensible experience. It is not some-

[17] Cf.: "Being for the metaphysician is no inert, static 'object' given in perception for analysis . . ." G. B. Phelan, "Being and the Metaphysicians," in *From an Abundant Spring*, ed. staff of *The Thomist* (New York, 1952), p. 347.

[18] See Gredt, II, 1 (no. 613).

[19] See R. W. Schmidt, "L'Emploi de la Séparation en Métaphysique," *Revue Philosophique de Louvain*, LVIII (1960), 373–393; D. Burrell, "A Note on Analogy," *The New Scholasticism*, XXXVI (1962), 225–231.

[20] For this view of Cajetan's, see *In De Ente et Essentia*, Quaest. I; ed. M.-H. Laurent (Turin, 1934), p. 6 (no. 5).

thing esoteric or farfetched, but is familiar to everyone in every cognitive act. To know it as entitatively distinct from finite natures, of course, requires the demonstration that in its primary instances it subsists as an infinite and all-embracing nature in God. But as it actually constitutes the subject of metaphysical consideration, it is known in every cognition of a sensible thing. Metaphysics is emphatically not a study of abstractions.[21] It is a science of things.

[21] For Suarez metaphysics "treats of the most abstract aspect of being as being, and whatever accords with it in the same abstraction and knowable aspect." *Disp. Metaph.*, I, 2, 23; ed. Vivès, XXV, 19b. On the influence of this conception upon Neoscholastic thinking, see Etienne Gilson, *Being and Some Philosophers*, 2nd ed. (Toronto, 1952), pp. 105–107. Against such a background the object of metaphysics "abstracts from the act of existing." Gredt, II, 8 (no. 619, 2).

Index